"The faith and work movement ... often that conversation has rem... *Our Secular Vocation* ably summarizes the current situation and moves beyond mere words to catalyze actual transformation. This book can change how you live and work in God's world."

——**Jordan J. Ballor**, director of research of the Center for Religion, Culture, and Democracy

"This fine book joins a long line of writers on Luther's revolutionary teaching on vocation. Charles critically engages many theological heavyweights in developing his own argument, creatively based on Luther's writings. He delightfully supplements his argument by drawing on biblical wisdom literature to flesh out the meaning of work. This work carries one of the great teachings of the Reformation into a new era."

——**Robert Benne**, Jordan-Trexler Professor of Religion Emeritus and research associate, Roanoke College, and professor of Christian ethics, Institute of Lutheran Theology

"Why is it such a struggle for Christians to live their whole lives as if they were Christians, and to find both joy and holiness in all they do? With the unique blend of humility, wisdom, clarity, and charm we have come to expect from Daryl Charles, *Our Secular Vocation* draws together biblical, historical, and contemporary insight to call us back to the doctrine of calling, as essential to revival and reform in the church as it is to the Bible's message of hope."

——**Greg Forster**, assistant professor of biblical and systematic theology, Trinity Evangelical Divinity School

"Drawing deeply from Scripture and two millennia of Catholic and Protestant theological reflection, Daryl Charles has penned a true masterpiece—certainly on the 'top ten' list of faith, work, and vocation books published over the past four decades. I fervently hope it will be read by seminary professors, pastors, and laity at all career stages. It's that good."

——**David W. Gill**, author of *Workplace Discipleship 101: A Primer* and former Mockler-Phillips professor of workplace theology and ethics, Gordon-Conwell Theological Seminary

"Daryl Charles's book exemplifies his fine qualities, bringing a refreshingly ecumenical perspective to the much-controverted topic of the role of work and calling in the Christian life. The goal here is the achievement of what Robert Benne has called a 'holy secularity,' a way of engaging the world that involves not only a rethinking of the Christian life but a revitalization of the church's role in the sustenance of that life, and the life of the world."

——**Wilfred McClay**, Victor Davis Hanson Chair in Classical History and Western Civilization, Hillsdale College

"We spend most of our days at work. For many of us, in the marketplace. It is high time for a theology of work and the marketplace, but it takes a rare combination of wisdom, courage, and erudition. J. Daryl Charles is uniquely fitted for this task. Every Christian asking for God's perspective on work should read this book."

—**Gerald McDermott**, Anglican chair, Beeson Divinity School (retired)

"The need for quality and thoughtful material that resources Christians for meaningful work and ministry in the marketplace cannot be overstated. Charles powerfully argues for an 'all things belong to Christ' approach to creation and culture, collapsing any possibility of a sacred-versus-secular view. Charles's work is powerfully written, well researched, thoughtful, personal, and timely. A great gift to the church and to her leaders!"

—**Benjamin Quinn**, associate professor of theology and history of ideas and associate director of the Center for Faith and Culture, Southeastern Baptist Theological Seminary

"In *Our Secular Vocation*, Daryl Charles deftly navigates the worlds of biblical studies, theology, church history, and pastoral ministry in addressing the important subject of work and vocation. The book concludes with well-considered pastoral guidance that comes out of his years of ministering to college students. This is not an introductory work. It is for those who are looking to go on a rigorous journey—for those who do, the abundant insights gained will be well worth the effort."

—**Scott B. Rae**, dean of faculty and professor of Christian ethics, Biola University

"Charles's title immediately grabs the reader's attention with its paradoxical assertion. Christians work in a world filled with secular and religious worldviews that diverge from their faith, so navigating work in a pluralistic context matters for both credible witness and personal peace. But the title is also provocative for another reason: biblical believers no longer have 'secular' vocations or occupations, for all they do is rooted in the creation mandate of Genesis 1–2; the redemptive call of Romans 12:1–2 and Colossians 3:17–23; and our ultimate destiny worshiping and working in the new creation (Revelation 19–22). With this paradoxical vision in mind, Charles is effective in helping thoughtful people navigate the fallenness of much of work."

—**Charles E. Self**, visiting professor of church history, Assemblies of God Theological Seminary

OUR SECULAR VOCATION

OUR SECULAR VOCATION

Rethinking the Church's Calling to the Marketplace

J. Daryl Charles

Our Secular Vocation
Copyright © 2023 by J. Daryl Charles
Published by B&H Academic
Brentwood, Tennessee

All rights reserved.

ISBN: 978-1-0877-6576-1

Dewey Decimal Classification: 261.1
Subject Heading: CHURCH AND VOCATION / WORK / VOCATION

Unless otherwise noted, all Scripture quotations are taken from the Christian Standard Bible®, Copyright © 2017 by Holman Bible Publishers. Used by permission. Christian Standard Bible® and CSB® are federally registered trademarks of Holman Bible Publishers.

Scriptures marked AMP are taken from the AMPLIFIED BIBLE: Scripture taken from the AMPLIFIED® BIBLE, Copyright © 1954, 1958, 1962, 1964, 1965, 1987 by the Lockman Foundation. Used by Permission.

Scriptures marked ESV are taken from THE HOLY BIBLE, ENGLISH STANDARD VERSION ® Copyright© 2001 by Crossway, a publishing ministry of Good News Publishers. Used by permission.

Scriptures marked KJV are taken from the KING JAMES VERSION, public domain.

Scripture quotations marked NASB1995 are taken from the New American Standard Bible®, Copyright © 1960, 1971, 1977, 1995 by The Lockman Foundation. Used by permission. All rights reserved. www.lockman.org.

Scriptures marked NIV are taken from the NEW INTERNATIONAL VERSION ®. Copyright© 1973, 1978, 1984, 2011 by Biblica, Inc.™ Used by permission of Zondervan.

Scripture quotations marked NRSV are from the New Revised Standard Version Bible, copyright © 1989 the Division of Christian Education of the National Council of the Churches of Christ in the United States of America. Used by permission. All rights reserved.

Scripture quotations marked RSV are from the Revised Standard Version Bible, copyright © 1946, 1952 and 1971 the Division of Christian Education of the National Council of the Churches of Christ in the United States of America. Used by permission. All rights reserved.

The Web addresses referenced in this book were live and correct at the time of the book's publication but may be subject to change.

Cover design and illustration by Darren Welch.

Printed in the United States of America

27 26 25 24 23 BTH 1 2 3 4 5 6 7 8 9 10

CONTENTS

Abbreviations   xi

CHAPTER 1

Introduction: The Church in Society   1
Why the Marketplace Matters

    Accounting for This Tragic Neglect   5
    The Challenge Confronting the Church: Her Social Presence   15
    The Church's One Foundation   22
    The Church's Responsibility for the World   24
    A Personal Word   27

CHAPTER 2

The Church's Great Neglect   31
Work, Vocation, and the Marketplace

    Rethinking the Church's "Mission" and Commission   33
    Rethinking Resurrection   38
    Rethinking Works   39
    Rethinking Rewards   46
    Rethinking the Doctrine of Vocation   49

CHAPTER 3

Theological Perspectives on Work, Vocation, and Stewardship   57
Tracing the Implications of Creation and Human Design

    Beginning at the Beginning   60
    The Need for a Theology of Work   69
    Why Work?: The Matter of Meaning   83
    Stewardship and Incarnational Reality   88
    An Anatomy of Stewardship: Looking More Closely   93
    Faith and Work: The State of the Question   100

CHAPTER 4

A Renewal of Work, Vocation, and the Marketplace   105
The Lutheran Breakthrough

    The Recasting of Work and "Vocation" in Luther's Thinking   108
    A Contempt for the World   115
    The Role of the Book of Ecclesiastes in Luther's Recasting of Work and Vocation   122
    Modern (and Postmodern) Challenges to Luther on Work and Vocation   134
    Luther on Social Concern   139
    The Revolution of Reformed Protestant Thinking about Work and Vocation   156

CHAPTER 5

A "Wisdom" Perspective on Work   163
Unexpected Insights from the Book of Ecclesiastes

    Wisdom Literature and the Wisdom Perspective   164
    Interpretive Strategy in Ecclesiastes   169
    Discerning the Purpose of Ecclesiastes   174
    Divine Work in Ecclesiastes   180

Human Labor in Ecclesiastes: A Wisdom Perspective 187
Rethinking Human Endeavor in Ecclesiastes 202
Final Wisdom Reflection: The End of the Matter 205

CHAPTER 6

A "Wisdom" Perspective on Vocation — 211
Uniting God's (Providential) Calling and Our Response

The Disappearance of Vocation 212
An Anatomy of Vocation 217
A Theology of Vocation 226
Further Reflections on the Implications of Vocation 238

CHAPTER 7

The Matter of Guidance — 249

On Listening and Developing a Sense of Discernment 252
On Quiet and Christian Community 262
On the Importance of Timing: Vocation and Personal Detours 264

CHAPTER 8

Conclusion — 271
The Impact of the Ordinary: Taking Seriously Our Calling to the World

Bibliography	279
Subject Index	309
Name Index	319

ABBREVIATIONS

AMP	Amplified Bible
AOTC	Apollos Old Testament Commentary Series
BCOT	Baker Commentary on the Old Testament Series
BHHB	Baylor Handbook on the Hebrew Bible
BW	Bible World Series
BWANT	Beiträge zur Wissenschaft vom Alten und Neuen Testament
BZAW	Beihefte zur Zeitschrift für die alttestamentliche Wissenschaft
CBS	Core Biblical Series
CC	Communicator's Commentary
CCC	Catechism of the Catholic Church
CFNP	Cambridge Fundamentals of Neuroscience in Psychology
ESV	English Standard Version
FCB	Fortress Commentary on the Bible Series
HeyJ	*Heythrop Journal*
HHSS	*Historia Hermeneutical Series Studies*
JPS	Jewish Publication Society
JSOT	*Journal for the Study of the Old Testament*

JSOTSS	Journal for the Study of the Old Testament Supplemental Series
LW	*Luther's Works*
MBPS	Mellen Biblical Press Series
NASB1995	New American Standard Version, published in 1995
NCBC	New Century Bible Commentary
NICOT	New International Commentary on the Old Testament
NIV	New International Version
NIVAC	New International Version Application Commentary
NRSV	New Revised Standard Version
OTG	Old Testament Guides
OTL	Old Testament Library
PTM	Paternoster Theological Monograph
RSV	Revised Standard Version
SGBC	Story of God Bible Commentary
SHBC	Smyth & Helwys Bible Commentary
SJSJ	Supplements to the Journal for the Study of Judaism
TOTC	Tyndale Old Testament Commentary Series
VSWB	Vierteljahrschrift für Sozial- und Wirtschaftsgeschichte Band
VTSup	Supplements to Vetus Testamentum
WBC	Word Biblical Commentary
WJK	Westminster John Knox Press

CHAPTER

1

Introduction:
The Church in Society
Why the Marketplace Matters

"I believe the church has largely failed Christians who struggle daily to live out their faith commitments in their places of employment." So protests one business consultant and educator, who finds the church "oddly indifferent" to marketplace challenges and deplores what he sees as the church doing "little or nothing" to equip believers in the workplace. Most Christians, he observes, perceive the church and its clergy to be "preoccupied with the private sphere of life," seemingly disinterested in the ethical issues associated with the weekday. The church, he worries, is "virtually silent on the subject of work"—a rather sobering concern when in fact, most of us are called by God to the marketplace.[1]

The burden of this consultant is shared by many. In fact, the editor of a recent volume on Christian vocation laments, "Religious education,

---

[1] John C. Knapp, *How the Church Fails Businesspeople (and What Can Be Done about It)* (Grand Rapids: Eerdmans, 2012), xi, xii, 25.

sermons, and sacraments or other celebrations seldom address vocation or foster vocational conversation, especially across the lifespan."[2] My own experience in congregational life, both past and present, would seem to confirm the above claims that the church is largely silent about work, vocation, or the marketplace to which most of us are called. This situation, unfortunately, is not a recent development. A significant study from the mid-1990s found that "religion is largely irrelevant to the work experience," which can have "little or no bearing on the way people view work."[3] And there is little indication that this has changed since then. Yet, this perception stands in stark contrast to wider empirical research over the last forty years, up to the present, which suggests that experiencing purpose or meaningfulness in work due to a sense of calling, regardless of its type or social context, contributes *substantially* to people's psychological health and well-being.[4]

---

[2] Kathleen A. Cahalan, "Introduction: Finding Life's Purposes in God's Purposes," in *Calling All Years Good: Christian Vocation throughout Life's Seasons*, ed. Kathleen A. Cahalan and Bonnie J. Miller-McLemore (Grand Rapids: Eerdmans, 2017), 4. Throughout this volume I use the terms *vocation* and *calling* interchangeably.

[3] James C. Davidson and David P. Caddell, "Religion and the Meaning of Work," *Journal for the Scientific Study of Religion* 33, no. 2 (1994): 135–36.

[4] See, for example, Douglas T. Hall and Dawn E. Chandler, "Psychological Success: When the Career Is a Calling," *Journal of Organizational Behavior* 26 (2005): 155–76; Ryan D. Duffy and William E. Sedlacek, "The Presence of and Search for a Calling: Connections to Career Development," *Journal of Vocational Behavior* 70, no. 3 (2007): 590–601; Bryan J. Dik and Ryan D. Duffy, "Calling and Vocation at Work: Definitions and Prospects for Research and Practice," *The Counseling Psychologist* 37, no. 3 (2009): 424–50; Michael F. Steger et al., "Calling in Work: Secular or Sacred?," *Journal of Career Assessment* 18, no. 1 (2010): 82–96; Bryan J. Dik and Ryan D. Duffy, *Make Your Job Your Calling: How the Psychology of Vocation Can Change Your Life at Work* (West Conshohocken: Templeton Press, 2012); Jacob A. Galles and Janet G. Lenz, "Relationships among Career Thoughts, Vocational Identity, and Calling: Implications for Practice," *Career Development Quarterly* 61, no. 3 (2013): 240–48; Robert B. McKenna et al., "Calling, the Caller, and Being Called: A Qualitative Study of Transcendent Calling," *Journal of Psychology and Christianity* 34, no. 4 (2015): 294–303;

The broad perception that religious faith is "largely irrelevant" to the work experience, regardless of its provenance, should deeply trouble and sadden us. But, again, this is no new development. Consider this testimony from a sales manager in the steel industry:

> In the almost thirty years of my professional career, my church has never once suggested that there might be job-related accountability . . . My church has never once offered to improve those skills which could make me a better minister . . . There has never been an inquiry into the types of ethical decisions I must face . . . I have never been in a congregation where there was any type of public affirmation of a ministry in my career.[5]

Did you catch how many times the word "never" appeared in that lament? And, truly, it is a lament. This sort of confession should drive pastors and priests, Christian educators, seminary professors, and church leaders to their knees. In the earliest church, there were no clergy; all were laity. The disciples of Christ functioned *in* the marketplace rather than being called *away* from it.[6] Even the call of Christ to become "fishers of men" did *not* call people away from their vocations; fishermen still fished in the Sea of Galilee. And we can be sure that none of the earliest disciples were itching to leave their nets for some fantasy called "full-time Christian ministry," even though their lives were radically transformed. How far we have fallen in our professionalizing of the clergy and letting dualism continually invade our understanding of calling.

Jina Ahn et al., "A Cross-Cultural Study of Calling and Life Satisfaction in the United States and South Korea," *Journal of Career Development* 20, no. 10 (2019): 1–15; and Evgenia I. Lysova et al., "Calling and Careers: New Insights and Future Directions," *Journal of Vocational Behavior* 114 (2019): 1–6.

[5] William E. Diehl, *Christianity and Real Life* (Philadelphia: Fortress, 1976), v–vi.

[6] Only in time did a distinction arise between clergy and "laity" (from the Gk. *laikos*, meaning "the people"). The laity consisted of those who were not "consecrated" for the service of God.

Three generations ago novelist Dorothy Sayers, perhaps best known for her detective stories,[7] offered something akin to the above complaints in addressing the subject of work:

> In nothing has the Church so lost Her hold on reality as Her failure to understand and respect the secular vocation. She has allowed work and religion to become separate departments, and is astonished to find that, as a result, the secular work of the world is turned to purely selfish and destructive ends, and that the greater part of the world's intelligent workers have become irreligious or at least uninterested in religion.[8]

Sayers was not sparing about the church's abdication on this point. Consider those initial words: "In nothing has the Church so lost her hold on reality. . . ." Her conclusion was in keeping with her characteristically acerbic wit: "How can anyone remain interested in a religion which seems to have no concern with nine-tenths of his [or her] life?"[9]

Sayers's rebuke, offered in the 1940s, remains every bit—if not more—relevant today as the church navigates into the third decade of the twenty-first century. Indeed, how *can* anyone take Christianity seriously, particularly in a post-Christian era, if the church has little vision for that domain in which all people—not just Christians—spend "nine-tenths" of their time? On a subject of universal and timeless importance, the Christian church should be proclaiming a clear message, insofar as it is responsible for relating biblical belief to all of life.

There are three possible explanations for why Christian belief is not regularly influencing public opinion or equipping its own for service in the marketplace: (1) The church is being suppressed in a totalitarian

---

[7] See, for example, Dorothy L. Sayers, *Lord Peter: The Complete Lord Peter Wimsey Stories* (New York: Harper & Row, 1972).

[8] Dorothy L. Sayers, "Why Work?" in *Creed or Chaos? Why Christians Must Choose Either Dogma or Disaster; or Why It Really Does Matter What You Believe*, repr. (Manchester, NH: Sophia Institute Press, 1974), 106.

[9] Sayers, 106.

society. (2) In her beliefs and practice, the church does not differ greatly from wider society. (3) The church has largely withdrawn from social institutions and wider society. This present volume presumes to speak to the latter two scenarios, both of which imply the absence of any moral authority by which to influence the surrounding culture. A large part of the church's lack of authority and social impotence is the fact that we have not equipped those who are in the marketplace, whereby we have wrongly understood "ministry" to be church work.

Accounting for This Tragic Neglect

Among students of history and theology, much is made of the sacred-versus-secular dichotomy that has often attended the church's thinking over the ages. The ancient roots of this disjunction, as characterized by the purported superiority of a *vita contemplativa* over a *vita activa*,[10] can be found in the early church and extend both to the medieval church and beyond. This divide, however, invalidates the very spirit of New Testament teaching, which declares that there is no cultural, social, or occupational hierarchy from the standpoint of Christian faith. Jew and Gentile, male and female, slave and free, married and unmarried, clergy and laity—and white-collar and blue-collar workers—all have equal standing. As striking evidence thereof, the Creator of the universe was

---

[10] Greco-Roman attitudes toward physical labor (as suited chiefly for servants/slaves) over against the contemplative life are, of course, well known. This dualism, nevertheless, would remain through the centuries, even influencing early Christian and medieval thinking about the physical body and physical labor. A very useful—and accessible—critique of this sort of dualistic thinking can be found in Jay Wesley Richards, "Be Fruitful and Multiply: Work and Anthropology," in *Work: Theological Foundations and Practical Implications*, ed. R. Keith Loftin and Trey Dimsdale (London: SCM, 2018), 110–26. The strength of Richards's argument is to point to the unity of the material and nonmaterial within each person.

incarnated as a woodworker,[11] and the "apostle to the Gentiles" worked as a tradesman.[12]

Significant changes accompanied Protestant reform in the early sixteenth century—among these was the understanding of work as a calling. Such changes were of a theological nature, anchored in the conviction of (1) creation's goodness and (2) the "priesthood of every believer." Nonetheless, Protestants today, in their piety, might be every bit as prone as Catholics to erect precisely that longstanding, though false, dichotomy of sacred versus secular. A very strong and resilient centrifugal force seems to exist that, as Sayers noted, keeps work and religious faith as "separate departments." The sacred-secular divide, at bottom, mirrors a decisive theological deficiency. It reflects not only an inadequate soteriology but a deficient ecclesiology and pneumatology as well. In the words of one thoughtful observer, it "shrivels people's theological imagination for how the creator and redeemer God of all things might work in and through them in all of life."[13] This chasmic—and catastrophic—divide cries out for illumination (and elimination!) via the church's teaching ministry.

The tendency toward split thinking must be addressed in every new generation. The focus of the church's teaching, at least among churches and congregations that are thought to have a high view of scriptural authority and are more evangelically oriented, is inclined toward the spiritual and "vertical" rather than an ethical or "horizontal" approach to faith.[14] That is, it tends to be preoccupied with the spiritual life and per-

---

[11] In the Gospel narratives, Jesus is described as the "carpenter's son" (*tektōn*, Matt 13:55; Mark 6:3). No doubt he learned Joseph's trade, which would make him a builder, a designer, and perhaps even a "civil engineer."

[12] See Acts 18:1–4.

[13] Mark Greene, preface, in *Transforming Vocation: Connecting Theology, Church, and the Workplace for a Flourishing World*, ed. David Benson et al. (Eugene, OR: Wipf & Stock, 2021), xiv.

[14] The focus of my burden concerns that part of the Christian church that is theologically orthodox, committed to the authority of Scripture, the lordship

sonal experience of Christian faith—what God does *in* us—rather than supporting a public faith—what God intends to do *through* us. Christian faith in our day is often made a private matter, with any public expression becoming increasingly offensive. In consequence, lay Christians, constituting virtually the whole of the church, end up having a shriveled view of their daily work and believing that they are second-class Christians. All too often, believers individually and collectively are inclined to view the church as a realm of spiritual escape—a sanatorium or refuge from the world.[15] More often than not, the church's teaching has the effect of calling believers *away from* the world rather than into it, given its inability to present the marketplace as a zone of high and noble calling. One fitting analogy that might help us correct the course is to think of the local church as a spiritual gymnasium or training center rather than a sanitorium,[16] as a place where believers are fortified and equipped for the daily ethical and economic challenges of the marketplace. The marketplace, after all, is where we spend "nine-tenths" of our lives.

The matter of why we are here on earth and our role as God's representatives and stewards is taken up more fully in chapter 3, where we will attempt to develop a theology of work. This theology finds its anchor in the opening pages of Scripture. The Genesis creation narrative, progressive in nature and culminating on the sixth day with human creation, is emphatic: *all* of creation is "good" (Gen 1:10, 12, 18, 21, 25), indeed "very good" (1:31). Since humans are the climax of creation, God commands

---

of Christ, salvific faith, and redemptive witness to the world. Here I do not concern myself with those rather amorphous religious communities that might be identified as "mainline" churches or "cafeteria Catholics" (to use the language of John Paul II). This distinction is intended to be less a judgment than a simple observation.

[15] This is not to deny that believers are "resident aliens," in the language of Ps 119:19 and 1 Pet. 1:17. It is, however, to point out that our emphasis on "aliens" often negates the reality of our "residence."

[16] By the latter, I mean a place in which people who are chronically ill convalesce and receive medical treatment or long-term medical care.

us to be fruitful and to tend to the created order. To be created in God's image or likeness (Gen 1:27) is to be made stewards of what God has created, even in its fallen state. To fail to take up this response is to defy or negate our very purpose.[17] Christ's redemptive work does not eliminate this responsibility; rather, it confirms it.[18]

Above I noted the widespread tendency of the church's teaching to call believers away from the world rather than redemptively into it. One contributing factor to this distorted way of thinking undoubtedly is our response to Jesus's exhortation not to "love the world." Many parallel warnings also appear in the New Testament. Consider, by way of illustration, those well-known statements to the disciples on the eve of our Lord's crucifixion. Jesus said, "As it is, you do not belong to the world, but I have chosen you out of the world. That is why the world hates you"; and "My kingdom is not of this world" (John 15:19 and 18:36 NIV). These admonitions appear to be strengthened elsewhere by Pauline teaching:

- Do not be conformed to the world (Rom 12:2).
- In its present form, "this world . . . is passing away" (1 Cor 7:31).
- If anyone is in Christ, old things have "passed away" (2 Cor 5:17).

Critically, "the world" in Scripture carries multiple senses and therefore requires that we differentiate in terms of its meaning where and

---

[17] Paul Marshall and Lela Gilbert, *Heaven Is Not My Home: Living in the Now of God's Creation* (Nashville: Word, 1998), 15–24 and 71–87, have developed the implications of the creation narrative with particular insight.

[18] In virtually every chapter, I argue not only for the importance of theology in the Christian ethic but the central—though supremely neglected—role that a *theology of creation* plays in the church's witness to the world. One source of confusion is in-house in nature. An example illustrates. In *Good Work: Christian Ethics in the Workplace* (Waco: Baylor University Press, 2010), Esther D. Reed argues that "a Christian ethic of work" is rooted in Christ's resurrection. Reed is doubtless representative of many well-meaning Christian writers. But this belief is fundamentally flawed, as chapters 2 and 3 will make clear. Christ does not set in place a *new* ethic that is unrelated to the created order; rather, he confirms and restores what was ordered in creation, *at the beginning*.

when it is used. At least three different uses in the New Testament can be distinguished: (1) the world system, tainted by sin and its surrounding effects and hostile to God's purposes;[19] (2) the world in a geographical or earthly sense; and (3) the entire created order. The above admonitions by Jesus and Paul accord with the first definition: the fallen world system that opposes God's purposes.

Another contributing factor—perhaps the chief factor—behind the perennial sacred-versus-secular mindset is a wrong understanding within the Christian community of the notion of "vocation" or "calling" (the focus of chapters 4 and 6). Vocations outside the church are typically viewed as inferior, and thus less holy than those inside it. Not only does this flaw in our thinking betray who we are as the redeemed community, but it also betrays the world to which we are called, and which needs our preserving influence.[20] Moreover, the relative absence of the church's preserving social presence in the world dishonors the Creator and Redeemer of all things, who seeks "to reconcile everything to himself" (see Col 1:15–20). Although it is never explicitly stated, many (if not most) Christians believe that the workplace represents a secondary or inferior calling when compared to church work, evangelizing, Bible study participation, going on mission trips, and the like. We really don't believe, at the deepest level, that our work *is* our witness, that the church's vocation *is* secular, and that the marketplace *is* the context of our greatest service to God and others. We really don't believe, deep down, that our

---

[19] As the first three chapters of this volume emphasize, human labor is a part of creation's mandate and our design based on the image of God, not *the fall*. Theologically, it is essential to distinguish what the curse is *not*. The curse does not alter (even when it distorts) creation; and where work *is* a curse, it is one of our own making. This claim, I grant, will need some unpacking.

[20] Knapp, *How the Church Fails Businesspeople*, has graphically and persuasively argued this. He goes so far as to argue that the "out-of-the-salt-shaker" imagery, popularized by evangelical writers in recent decades, mirrors part of the problem in our thinking. See, for example, Rebecca Manley Pippert and Mark Mittelberg, *Out of the Saltshaker and into the World: Evangelism as a Way of Life* (Downers Grove, IL: InterVarsity, 1999).

good works in the home and greater community and our work done on Monday through Friday are sufficiently pleasing to God.[21] But the truth is that millions of believers serving God and working for the common good through their various professions constitute proof of life-change that the world simply cannot refute. The marketplace, then, is the chief setting in which Christians impact society. It is there that, day in and day out and generation after generation, Christian influence will produce its greatest effect.[22] But tragically, most pastors and Christian leaders remain ill-equipped to offer counsel on matters of work.[23]

Perhaps, in response to my argument thus far, you the reader have mentally cited the precedent of Acts 6, where the apostles complain that they should not leave their duty to "the ministry of the word" and prayer to "wait on tables" (Acts 6:1–4); after all, at this point in Scripture's narrative, their vocation was evangelization and providing spiritual leadership. This I grant. But those whose vocation is to prepare meals and wait on tables "might with equal justice" protest, "It is not meet for us to leave the

---

[21] As one educator rightly observes, there exists in many evangelical circles a sort of "evangelistic reductionism," by which it is thought that "personal evangelism" is the highest work; see Kenneth A. Cherney, Jr., "Hidden in Plain Sight: Luther's Doctrine of Vocation," *Wisconsin Lutheran Quarterly* 98, no. 4 (2001): 287–88. If, however, we truly saw the nobility of vocation and our service in the Monday-through-Friday, truly extraordinary opportunities for "evangelism" would result.

[22] The theological matter of work, vocation, and the marketplace is not merely a "Western" issue. In many parts of the world, it plays out in significant socioeconomic and political ways, particularly as it concerns the question of poverty. A sturdy theology of work and vocation can lift people to a level whereby not mere poverty alleviation but poverty *prevention* is redemptive and normative; see Greene, *Transforming Vocation*, xv.

[23] One writer has described most clergy as "amateurs" in terms of their relation to many of the important issues facing people in the workforce; see Gordon Preece, "A Job and a Life: Reintegrating Faith, Home, and Work," *St. Mark's Review* (Spring 1998): 25. We need greater emphasis on the church *scattered* than the church *gathered*, argues Preece (30). It is difficult to disagree.

service of our tables to preach the word."[24] To call our congregants away from the marketplace, the realm to which virtually all believers are called, is to violate scriptural revelation, negate our stewardship of the created order, and work against God's purposes.

Our approach to theological education and the way we train emergent Christian leaders tend to confirm a basic distortion in our thinking about work and vocation.[25] A serious examination of the curricula of our seminaries and divinity schools, with few exceptions, shows that little in the way of coursework and degree requirements addresses "vocation" and "calling," properly understood—much less the sacred character of our work in the marketplace.[26] In surveying 154 seminary students

---

[24] Sayers, "Why Work?," 107–8.

[25] In the U.S., the Association of Theological Schools has about 275 member institutions. This does not even include Bible schools and para-church organizations.

[26] An encouraging development has been the recent formation of the Oikonomia Network (ON). The ON advertises itself as "a learning community of theological educators and evangelical seminaries dedicated to raising up church leaders who help people develop whole-life discipleship, fruitful work and economic wisdom for God's people and God's world." "Who We Are," Oikonmia Network, accessed March 10, 2022, https://oikonomianetwork.org/about-us/.

In the context of Christian liberal arts education at the undergraduate level, an initiative administered by the Council of Independent Colleges and funded by Lilly Endowment Inc., the Network for Vocation in Undergraduate Education (NetVUE) was launched in 2009 as a network of colleges and universities "committed to fostering the theological exploration of vocation in their campus communities."

NetVUE advertises itself as "a nationwide network of colleges and universities formed to enrich the intellectual and theological exploration of vocation among undergraduate students." NetVUE grew out of another project launched in 1999, Programs for the Theological Exploration of Vocation (PTEV), which originally supported eighty-eight independent colleges and universities around the country in "establishing or strengthening programs that would (a) help students examine the relationship between their faith and vocational choices; (b) provide opportunities for young people to explore Christian ministry leadership; and (c) enhance the capacity of an institution's faculty and staff to teach and mentor students in this regard." However, the extent to which these programs

at fourteen institutions to find out how future pastors were being prepared to minister to members of the business community, the authors of *Church on Sunday, Work on Monday: The Challenge of Fusing Christian Values with Business Life* found little encouraging evidence.[27] Reflecting on these results, they write, "A church that baptizes (and later marries) your children, helps you worship God weekly, and buries your friends and family members at the end of their lives can also be a church that leaves you unsupported when it comes to who you are as a businessperson."[28]

The results of the above survey squared with a 2009 survey of courses at eighteen leading seminaries and divinity schools,[29] which was able to identify only a few elective courses that addressed work-related issues at all.[30] A perusal of current course offerings in these institutions that might most closely approximate marketplace concerns indicates that not business or commerce or industry per se but urban ministry, social justice or economic justice, ministry to the poor, racial inclusion, and sexual inclusion are viewed as the primary means of addressing the marketplace. And this trend is sure to continue, given the fevered pitch of current

---

have assisted the Christian community and Christian leadership in particular in helping change perceptions of work, vocation, and the marketplace remains difficult to assess. See "About NetVUE," The Council of Independent Colleges, accessed March 10, 2022, https://www.cic.edu/programs/NetVUE.

[27] Laura Nash and Scotty McLennan, *Church on Sunday, Work on Monday: The Challenge of Fusing Christian Values with Business Life* (San Francisco: Jossey-Bass, 2001).

[28] Nash and McLennan, xviii.

[29] These institutions included Asbury Seminary, Boston University School of Theology, Chicago Theological Seminary, Columbia Theological Seminary, Dallas Theological Seminary, Denver Seminary, Fuller Theological Seminary, Harvard Divinity School, Howard University School of Divinity, McCormack Theological Seminary, Pittsburgh Theological Seminary, Princeton Theological Seminary, the University of Chicago Divinity School, the University of Notre Dame Department of Theology, Vanderbilt Divinity School, and Yale Divinity School.

[30] The 2009 survey was undertaken by John Knapp; both the Knapp survey and the Nash-McLennan survey are reported in Knapp, *How the Church Fails Businesspeople*, 37–39.

discourse on race, diversity, and inclusion.[31] In any case, any emphasis on the "priesthood of all believers"—*omnes sacerdotes* ("all are priests")—that calls Protestants back to their roots and to the sacredness of work in the marketplace is scarcely to be found in seminary and divinity school coursework.[32] Substantial curricular change would require institutional reform on a wide scale—reform requiring a different academic model. What is needed in theological education is nothing less than a transformation of its core components. Every course and every theological topic at the seminary/divinity school level needs rethinking, to eliminate the perpetual "sacred-versus-secular" residue and to foster the integration of faith, work, and vocation in a holistic way.[33] At the most basic level, among those things needing serious examination in terms of course content are the following: a theology of creation, a theology of work, human flourishing, a theology of vocation, a history of the "sacred versus secular" divide, the Lutheran breakthrough of the sixteenth century, the importance of engaging competing worldviews, ethical and economic challenges of the workplace, a theology of stewardship, service toward the common social good and community flourishing, and redefinition of "mission."

Relatedly, most seminarians tend to arrive at seminary or divinity school with a generally negative perception of work, business, commerce

---

[31] The current cultural climate and not a commitment to Scripture and historic Christian theology is likely to bring about significant changes in seminary/divinity school course offerings. We should not be surprised when even traditional course offerings in theology, hermeneutics, and biblical studies are eclipsed in the service of so-called social justice.

[32] Theological training today—whether in hermeneutics, systematic theology, historical theology, homiletics, or hymnology—joins denominational life and the wider arena of Christian publishing to indicate that no holistic vision focusing on work and the marketplace exists for the purpose of equipping the layperson for the workweek.

[33] In addition, parachurch groups and organizations such as Cru, InterVarsity Christian Fellowship, Reformed University Fellowship, Baptist Collegiate Network, and other campus ministries need a reorientation as well, where college graduates are being prepared expressly for the workplace.

and wealth, and the marketplace. Rather than rejoicing in their past work and careers, most seem glad to have left them. Virtually all of these individuals seem to be seeking a "higher calling" and a more satisfying career. Even among the most pious, standard responses tend to confirm this unhealthy dualism: "God called me to the pastorate/full-time Christian work"; "God called me out of business"; or "God called me [thankfully] out of my job." Normally implied in such comments is that God did *not* call that person into business, the workplace, or economic life. How refreshing it would be to hear someone say, "God called me into business"; "God called me to corporate work"; or "God called me to be a lawyer/banker/medical professional/farmer/woodworker/social worker/IT specialist/home builder."[34]

True, the last three decades have been witness to something of a faith and work movement within wider Christian circles. And such is encouraging.[35] But as it stands, this movement, ably chronicled by David W. Miller in *God at Work*, has been a largely lay-led and lay-confined phenomenon.[36] Relatively few participants are pastors, priests, and church leaders—Protestant, Catholic, or Orthodox—who have assumed leadership roles.[37] In large part, expressions of a so-called faith and work vision remain lay-led.

But there is a reason for this chiefly lay-led phenomenon, as a cursory survey of standard teaching and preaching from our pulpits reveals. Though 99 percent of our congregants are called to the marketplace to serve others (and thus God) through their creative abilities, few receive nurturing and equipping for the daily ethical and economic challenges they encounter. They are basically left to figure things out for themselves.

---

[34] Any theological orientation that elevates "pastoral ministry" and mission-as-evangelism over the church's calling to the marketplace is a distortion.

[35] Because of my association with the Acton Institute, I have witnessed encouraging signs emanating from the faith and work movement.

[36] See David W. Miller, *God at Work: The History and Promise of the Faith at Work Movement* (Oxford, UK: Oxford University Press, 2007).

[37] A notable exception to this is the organization Made to Flourish, founded by pastor Tom Nelson in Kansas City.

Frankly, the great majority of pastors, priests, and Christian leaders have never spent a significant season of their lives working *in* the marketplace. They therefore lack the vision for the marketplace that is required to equip and nurture most of their congregants—men and women who are butchers and bakers and candlestick-makers, nurses and lawyers and drivers of hearses, psychologists and businessmen, and information technologists.[38]

Sadly, as Douglas Schuurman has correctly pointed out in his important work *Vocation: Discerning Our Callings in Life*, the church-centeredness that dominates most of our congregations and activities mirrors a deficient vision of why the church exists.[39] Surely, pastors and priests would benefit significantly from spending a portion of their lives working in the marketplace. Such would sensitize them in critical ways to the challenges and true needs of their congregants. More important, it would help collapse any sacred-versus-secular dichotomy that might be part of the clerical mindset.

The Challenge Confronting the Church: Her Social Presence

Given the above factors contributing to the church's vision (or lack thereof), there is a vastly compelling need for resources that will enable pastors, priests, educators, Christian leaders, and indeed laypersons themselves to cultivate a vision for (1) the design and dignity of work, (2) the importance of the doctrine of vocation, and (3) the high calling of the workplace. After all, this is where we believers spend much of our lives and can best influence society. Nowhere will our presence be felt as it will in the marketplace. Nowhere else will the fruits of our faith be more on display. This, after all, is a primary context of our service to God and to

---

[38] Whether this lack of vision is due to disinterest or intimidation is difficult to say. Perhaps it is a mixture of both.

[39] See Douglas J. Schuurman, *Vocation: Discerning Our Callings in Life* (Grand Rapids: Eerdmans, 2004), esp. chapter 1.

others. Our work, embedded in the context of our individual callings, is nothing less than worship.[40]

The starting place for any reexamination of work and vocation is necessarily theological.[41] Thus, theological questions arise: What is the uniqueness of the human person in all of creation? What are the implications of being created in the *imago Dei*? Are human beings designed to flourish? What are the implications of the fall, and how are we to understand human depravity? Do the effects of sin's curse nullify the creation mandate? How do the doctrines of creation and redemption intersect? In what ways do the "city of God" and the "city of man" interact? What is the extent to which Christ's ownership and redemption of all things touch and permeate the entire width and breadth, the material and nonmaterial aspects, of creation? And how does the church's eschatological outlook, with its emphasis on a new earth, bear upon her perception of—and daily involvement in—this world?

In the last three decades important writings on work, vocation, and the marketplace have been published. But much of the significant literature was released during the late 1990s and early 2000s, with several volumes having appeared in 2011 and 2012.[42] That means many of

---

[40] Chapter 3 attempts to strengthen the case for this unity. See also John Bergsma, "The Creation Narratives and the Original Unity of Work and Worship in the Human Vocation," in *Work: Theological Foundations and Practical Implications*, ed. R. Keith Loftin and Trey Dimsdale (London: SCM, 2018), 11–29.

[41] This is why seminaries, divinity schools, and church-related colleges should be leading the way in terms of recovering a proper vision of work, vocation, and the marketplace. See also notes 29–33 of this chapter.

[42] Consider, for example, the following list of volumes, comprising the most significant works on the topic(s) to date: Lester DeKoster, *Work: The Meaning of Your Life* (1982); Judith Allen Shelly, *Not Just a Job: Serving Christ in Your Work* (1985); Doug Sherman and William Hendricks, *Your Work Matters to God* (1987); Lee Hardy, *The Fabric of This World: Inquiries into Calling, Career Choice, and the Design of Human Work* (1990); Michael Novak, *Business as a Calling: Work and the Examined Life* (1996); John Paul II, *The Meaning of Vocation* (1998); R. Paul Stevens, *The Other Six Days: Vocation, Work, and Ministry in*

these works are almost two decades old. Thus, fresh perspectives are in order. This is the case not only because of (1) the ongoing neglect in the church's teaching and preaching, and (2) the need for every successive generation of believers to confront its stewardship of creation and human culture, but also because of (3) an evolving, shifting, and highly technological workplace, and (4) the current social unrest as demonstrated, mostly recently, since the spring–summer of 2020. Lately, all facets of our society—particularly the marketplace—have experienced disorientation and dislocation.

At this point, a few specific comments about the aforementioned literature are necessary. The content and character of the existing texts on work and vocation are wide-ranging. Some are more practical and

---

Biblical Perspective (1999); Gordon T. Smith, *Courage and Calling: Embracing Your God-Given Potential* (1999); Parker J. Palmer, *Let Your Life Speak: Listening to the Voice of Vocation* (2000); Gilbert Meilaender, ed., *Working: Its Meaning and Its Limits* (2000); Miroslav Volf, *Work in the Spirit: Toward a Theology of Work* (2001); Laura Nash and Scotty McLennan, *Church on Sunday, Work on Monday: The Challenge of Fusing Christian Values with Business Life* (2001); Gene Edward Veith, Jr., *God at Work: Your Christian Vocation in All of Life* (2002); Douglas J. Schuurman, *Vocation: Discerning Our Callings in Life* (2004); Darrell Cosden, *A Theology of Work: Work and the New Creation* (2004); William C. Placher, ed., *Callings: Twenty Centuries of Christian Wisdom on Vocation* (2005); Os Hillman, *The 9 to 5 Window: How Faith Can Transform the Workplace* (2005); David H. Jensen, *Responsive Labor: A Theology of Work* (2006); Gilbert Meilaender, *The Freedom of a Christian: Grace, Vocation, and the Meaning of Our Humanity* (2006); R. Paul Stevens, *Doing God's Business: Meaning and Motivation for the Workplace* (2006); John D. Beckett, *Mastering Monday: A Guide to Integrating Faith and Work* (2006); Darrell Cosden, *The Heavenly Good of Earthly Work* (2006); David W. Miller, *God at Work: The History and Promise of the Faith at Work Movement* (2007); Amy L. Sherman, *Kingdom Calling: Vocational Stewardship for the Common Good* (2011); Tom Nelson, *Work Matters: Connecting Sunday Worship to Monday Work* (2011); Timothy Keller and Katherine Leary Alsdorf, *Every Good Endeavor: Connecting Your Work to God's Work* (2012); R. Keith Loftin and Trey Dimsdale, ed., *Work: Theological Foundations and Practical Implications* (2018); Daniel M. Doriani, *Work: Its Purpose, Dignity, and Transformation* (2019); and J. Daryl Charles, *Wisdom and Work: Theological Reflections on Human Labor from Ecclesiastes* (2021).

pastoral, some even bordering on the genre of self-help. Some are more serious theologies of work or vocation. Some take the reader on a brief stroll through history to observe diverse perspectives on such topics. And some of the important contributions to the literature are anthologies, pulling together writings on work or vocation from both ancient and modern writers, though usually without practical content or application.

The best and most theologically serious of those works published over the last three decades are useful in probing the design of work or the importance of vocation. Usually this grounding is located in the book of Genesis or in great models of faith. So, for example, in Israel's history we see Moses as the leader extraordinaire, Abraham as the risk-taker, Joseph as the political savior, Deborah as the wise judge, David as the bold warrior, Daniel as the political advisor, and Esther as the politically wise steward of providence. Few volumes, however, combine (1) a serious theology of work or vocation with (2) a historical overview of the church's understanding of work, vocation, and the marketplace, (3) biblical perspectives on stewardship that encompass both Old and New Testament teaching, and (4) a pastorally sensitive vision for educating congregants that is rooted in the conviction that the church's main witness to the world occurs in the marketplace. Of those volumes that do attempt this sort of synthesis and are well written,[43] their publication dates generally range from 1990 to 2004.[44]

This present volume represents an attempt at synthesizing the theological and the hermeneutical, the historical and the contemporary, the ethical and the pastoral. After all, work and vocation are by no means the domain of mere academic study or historical reflection; at the same time, they cannot and must not be reduced to mere self-help or pop theology

---

[43] Several of the more substantive and integrated are those by Hardy, Smith, Jensen, and Schuurman (see n. 42).

[44] Two notable exceptions are the Loftin-Dimsdale and Keller-Alsdorf volumes (see n. 42), the former of which was published in the UK.

topics.⁴⁵ Rather than mirroring the priorities and values of the wider culture, the church must be faithful to the historical Christian tradition while also "translating" transcendent values in meaningful ways. Every generation, as I have noted, is faced with this task; and in every generation the challenges are unique, requiring new perspectives. Therefore, faithfully and meaningfully coming to terms with the cultural climate is the task set before us, although it is not easy. As will become clear in the following chapters, neither isolation, nor capitulation, nor triumphalism represents faithfulness.

In the early twenty-first century, we live in a post-Christian and post-consensus social climate; that much is indisputable, at least for those in Western, largely democratic societies.⁴⁶ This climate is one in which moral principle, traditional values, and historic Christian faith are derided; to affirm such principles in our day is to be branded "hate-filled," "bigoted," and "intolerant." Nevertheless, we are to take our stewardship of the culture seriously. As Christians, there exist three possible responses. First, we could resign ourselves to the impossibility of the task and withdraw, or at least develop a theological rationale for withdrawing as we seek to preserve our Christian identity. This, of course, can be done in multiple ways. One is to adopt the fatalistic mindset, "There's no point in rearranging the chairs on a sinking ship." Such is the stereotypical response of fundamentalism, which in the American context has been characterized by a bloated eschatology wherein otherworldly priorities cancel out or at least diminish the church's attempts at taking

---

⁴⁵ One thinks, in this regard, of more blatant (and best-selling) examples of "self-help," "pop theology," and "motivational psychology" as found, say, in Stephen R. Covey's *The 7 Habits of Highly Effective People* (1989), *The 8th Habit: From Effectiveness to Greatness* (2004), and *The Leader in Me* (2008) or Joel Osteen's *Become a Better You* (2007), *Every Day a Friday* (2011), and *The Power of I Am* (2015).

⁴⁶ See J. Daryl Charles, "Post-Consensus Culture, Natural Law, and Moral Persuasion: Translating Moral Conviction in a Disbelieving Age," in *Wisdom's Work: Essays on Ethics, Vocation, and Culture* (Grand Rapids: Acton Institute Press, 2019), 1–26.

human culture and national citizenship seriously. Another rationale might be that of the Anabaptists, who were part of a minority movement in sixteenth-century Protestantism that confessed a separation from "the world" (and from vocations that were perceived as representing it).[47] To this day, many adherents of this tradition are separatistic.[48] Regardless of its varied justifications, we may call this alternative isolation.

A second response to the cultural situation is the opposite of separation or isolation. In essence, it is insufficiently critical and discerning of the social and philosophical assumptions that drive the culture, so that Christians end up capitulating and being absorbed into the surrounding cultural climate. This posture is typical of the Protestant mainline, so-called cafeteria Catholicism, and of an increasing number of self-professing evangelicals who desperately wish to be perceived by the world as relevant but who, in the end, often sacrifice their theological integrity.[49] In any case, if the first tendency is isolation, the second represents capitulation.

An alternative response is the proper way to live out the profession of faith, with integrity and in faithfulness.[50] This posture mirrors a willing-

---

[47] See the Schleitheim Confession of Faith (1527), which serves as the chief early Anabaptist confession of faith and practice deemed central to Anabaptist conviction.

[48] This tendency remains true even when contemporary Anabaptists, who have taken extraordinary measures to demonstrate social concern (in disaster relief or conflict resolution, for example), chafe under the perception that they are "separatistic." Nevertheless, separatism has been at the center of their theological identity from the very beginning, as historic affirmations such as the Schleitheim Confession (1527) indicate. It is for this reason that today's Anabaptist will not be found working in various sectors of the culture deemed to be "worldly"—for example, in law, economics, philosophy, political science, public policy, banking, government service and public office, diplomacy, the military, police and law enforcement, and security, to name but a few.

[49] What the term "evangelical" means in our day is beyond the scope of the present volume, even when it needs probing.

[50] See Robert Benne, *Good and Bad Ways to Think about Religion and Politics* (Grand Rapids: Eerdmans, 2010).

ness to count the cost of Christian discipleship while remaining engaged citizens of our current communities.[51] It is neither about retreating nor withdrawing in character, nor is it about being spiritually dull, undiscerning, and indiscriminately accommodating; rather, it is about wrestling in serious and committed ways with stewardship of the surrounding culture and the entire created order, and doing so based on an awareness of faithfulness. This posture motivates us to be humble, thoughtful, and confident. We Christ-followers are called to use our gifts and callings to build up the common good and to serve others, not merely ourselves.[52] This response may be described as faithful stewardship, about which I will have more to say.[53]

Being a steward entails a certain vision for bridge building. That is, stewards look for creative, resourceful, and strategic ways to penetrate the social fabric of which we are a part and to contribute to the common good of others. In the ordinary, in the daily nine to five, we find points of commonality with others in the workplace through each task; it is there that we serve God and our fellow image bearers most fully and tangibly. Hence, it is in the marketplace that we demonstrate the greatest level and degree of service both to God and to others. Yet some soul-searching is in order on the part of the church: Wouldn't society, in truth, be better off if the church stopped elevating "full-time Christian ministry" and began encouraging and equipping its own to see the nobility of

---

[51] Two caveats are in order. One is that separatists—here again I have in mind Anabaptists, in whose tradition I grew up—are quick to describe their lifestyle commitments as "radical discipleship." Second, the sort of social engagement I am advancing is not to be confused with the idol of "social justice" that grips contemporary American culture and much of the church, particularly those segments of the church in which theology takes a back seat to social relevance.

[52] While "the common good" occupies an important place in Catholic social teaching, it tends not to be part of Protestants' vocabulary. It is not an exaggeration to connect the dots, as it were, between Protestant—and frequently nondenominational—megachurches and teaching/preaching that appeals almost exclusively to individualism, over against a common good.

[53] See chapters 3, 4, and 6.

the Monday–Friday calling to the marketplace? Without help from the church (and from Bible teachers within it), many believers remain confused, unfulfilled, and/or disillusioned concerning their jobs.

True, it is far easier to retreat into a dualism of "this world over against the next" or the common dualism of "full-time Christian work" over against regular work. The church's temptation in any age is to withdraw from society, on the one hand (even when we construct a theological rationale for building so-called prophetic communities on the cultural sideline[54]), or simply to blend in with surrounding society, on the other. Nevertheless, faithful stewardship—of *all* creation—is our *calling*. The triteness of this formulation should not obscure its truth: the steward's motivation is faithfulness and not so-called success.

The Church's One Foundation

A vibrant, morally guided social ethic, as chapter 3 will argue, does not descend out of thin air. It issues out of individual doctrinal commitments that Christians hold—commitments we each share with others—Catholic, Orthodox, and Protestant—both present and past. More specifically, those commitments will require, as already noted, that we rethink the doctrine of creation, the manner in which creation and redemption are interlocking, and the implications of that unity for the Christian community's social witness (a witness that is chiefly in the marketplace).

Dorothy Sayers is perhaps best known as the creator of Lord Peter Wimsey, the aristocratic amateur detective.[55] Less recognized are her

---

[54] A chief example of which is the work of Stanley Hauerwas and many Anabaptist writers in the mold of John Howard Yoder.

[55] From 1949 to 1957, Sayers served as president of the Detective Club, formed in 1930 by a group of British mystery writers. During this golden age of murder-mystery writing, those belonging to this esteemed fellowship included Agatha Christie, Ronald Knox, Hugh Walpole, Baroness Emma Orczy, R. Austin Freeman, G. D. H. and Margaret Cole, and Henry Wade. The club's first president was none other than G. K. Chesterton.

forays into the realm of theology, which, one discovers, turn out to be exceedingly rich. In such writing, Sayers is impatient with those who in her day viewed doctrine as "hopelessly irrelevant" to the life of the ordinary Christian.[56] *Creed or Chaos?* constitutes Sayers's witty, imaginative, and at times acerbic call to take dogma seriously.[57] She writes, "The word *dogma* is unpopular, and that is why I have used it. It is our own distrust of dogma that is handicapping us."[58] In truth, "the dogma *is* the drama," she insists.[59] But sadly, in her view, our failure to appreciate the role of theology has rendered Christian cultural witness impotent, cutting us off at the knees. Thereby, she laments, we have "efficiently pared the claws of the Lion of Judah" and "certified him [to be] meek and mild."[60] These are strong—and very fitting—words: by our depreciation of—or disinterest in—theology, we render Christian cultural witness impotent, effectively "paring the claws of the Lion of Judah."

For Sayers, doctrine possesses two inviolable functions in the life of the Christian. First, it defines what is distinctive about our world- and life-views. To lose sight of the importance of doctrine is to lose the backbone of the faith we profess and to invite spurious alternatives. Second, doctrine alone furnishes the basis for a uniquely Christian social ethic. Christian theology, after all, is an attempt to describe the nature of the world in which we live, which includes human nature, moral reality, and our place in the cosmos. Without a theological foundation, the church is utterly incapable of explaining, let alone embodying, the contours of a Christian social ethic. Theology

---

[56] Dorothy L. Sayers, "The Dogma Is the Drama," in *Creed or Chaos? Why Christ Must Choose Either Dogma or Disaster (Or, Why It Really Does Matter What You Believe,* repr. (Manchester: Sophia Institute Press, 1974), 50.

[57] In addition to *Creed or Chaos?*, Sayers's best known work in the realm of theology is *The Mind of the Maker*, published in 1941.

[58] Sayers, "The Dogma Is the Drama," 40.

[59] Sayers, "The Greatest Drama Ever Staged," in *Creed or Chaos?*, 5, emphasis added.

[60] Sayers, 9.

alone allows us to contend for a baseline morality in the public square; doing that depends on our awareness of an objective moral order as displayed through creation and the cosmos.[61] But as Sayers well knew, what is needed in the church is not academic theology but a theology of the everyday.

The Church's Responsibility for the World

Undergirding my thinking about work, vocation, and the marketplace is a basic assumption about the relationship between faith and culture. This leads me to ask, What responsibility does the church have for the world? Is the church, in fact, responsible for it? And if so, to what extent? Chapter 3 sets forth a theological premise that is foundational to my argument—a premise established by New Testament texts such as John 1:3; Eph 1:10; Col 1:15–20; and Heb 1:2:

- John 1:3: All things were created through Christ.
- Eph 1:10: All things will be brought together in Christ.
- Col 1:15–20: All things were created by and for Christ.
- Heb 1:2: Christ has been appointed heir of all things.

The guiding premise, then, is that "all things"—visible and invisible, material and nonmaterial—belong to Christ. There is *nothing* that does not belong to him, based both on creation and redemption. As someone has said, everything is "twice his." The Colossians text above is particularly adamant in its proclaiming Christ's supremacy in both creation and redemption. Its language—"all creation," "all things," "everything," "all his fullness"—bears witness to this glorious reality. That Christ reconciles all things "to himself" (v. 20) and that "by him all things hold together" (v. 17) demonstrate that he is both the object and the instrument of all creation. This language, utterly compelling, supports and encourages

---

[61] This will be taken up more fully in chapter 3.

Christians' activity in the culture in the deepest and most profound way, collapsing any possibility of a sacred-versus-secular dichotomizing that religious people might entertain.[62] This language, furthermore, reminds us that our activity in the surrounding culture is intended to *improve* the human condition, not merely to save some from a sinking ship. The combination of common grace, an ongoing expression of God's providence, and Christ's redemptive grace together move human culture in the right direction in accordance with the divine purpose, ennobling and restoring it and allowing people to flourish. Such is true regardless of the particular cultural moment in which we find ourselves. The question is whether Christians, in their basic theological orientation, actually believe this.[63]

This reality, of course, does not relieve us of the tension, complexity, and ambiguity that attend the daily nature of our stewardship over all things. In our work, at the job, in the marketplace, we are confronted with dilemmas and challenges that seem to contradict Christ's ownership of and lordship over all creation. How to mediate that reality as stewards—"coregents," if you will—of the created order requires wisdom, prudence, humility, and hope. But wisdom, humility, and hope are an absurdity—in truth, an impossibility—if (1) work is not that for which we were created, (2) "calling" is reserved only for pastors and priests,

---

[62] On the implications of the Colossians 1 text and how it informs the church's cultural mandate, see the wonderfully rich discussion found in William Edgar, *Created and Creating: A Biblical Theology of Culture* (Downers Grove, IL: IVP Academic, 2017), 148–77 (esp. ch. 8, "The First Vocation"). Edgar's understanding of cultural engagement can be summarized as follows: it is "the human response to the divine call to enjoy and develop the world that God has generously given to his image bearers."

[63] Few have stated the church's role in human culture with greater clarity than Robert W. Jenson, "The Church's Responsibility for the World," in *The Two Cities of God: The Church's Responsibility for the Earthly City*, ed. Carl E. Braaten and Robert W. Jenson (Grand Rapids: Eerdmans, 1997), 1–10. Jenson's argument is essentially this: through the church's instrumentality, we work for and seek to maintain the promise of a *transformation* of all of creation.

the cloistered and the closeted, and (3) the marketplace is simply that ubiquitous sphere of unbearable life which we must somehow tolerate to make ends meet.[64]

Rethinking the ramifications of Christ's lordship over the entire created order, then, is of highest importance. In light of our frequent experience, not only is a proper understanding of the doctrine of creation central to our mission in the world, but as I will argue in the following chapters, a proper understanding of redemption must go hand in hand with it.

Redemption is not merely a rescue operation before impending disaster, or after disaster. It is, rather, the commencement of the "return" or restoring of "all things" to their proper ownership.[65] The Christian church of every generation needs to be confronted with the ramifications of Augustine's two cities metaphor: We believers have two citizenships, one in the city of God and one in the city of man. And while our ultimate allegiance belongs to the heavenly city, this does not mean that we do not take our citizenship in the city of man seriously. Because all things were created by and for Christ, we are therefore stewards of all aspects of human culture (in the city of man). Our two citizenships, therefore, forbid our disengagement from the earthly city. Our stewardship of matters in the earthly city, as it turns out, will be a measurement, on judgment day, of our service to God and to fellow human beings.

---

[64] Chapter 5 probes the book of Ecclesiastes, which confronts the absurdity of finding wisdom, meaning, and hope where such assumptions are based on a false view of ultimate reality.

[65] Theologically, the church confesses that we live in the period of the already-and-not-yet. That is, the kingdom of God has not yet been fully consummated; creation still groans in its expectation as it awaits consummation (see Rom 8:22). Nevertheless, the seeds or "firstfruits" of redemption are now with us. This is the "already" aspect of Christ's transformation of all things. This means, on the one hand, that we eschew any sort of utopian thinking about perfecting society while, on the other, that we work to bring more of Christ's transformative influence into the present.

A Personal Word

I write with motivation that is, broadly speaking, twofold. On one level, I am burdened that within the church we need a rediscovery of the doctrine of vocation and of the design and dignity of work.[66] While we Christians are impeded by both the culture's view of work as well as that of the church, it is the latter that is especially troubling. Having spent most of my professional career teaching at the university level in a Christian liberal arts context,[67] I am struck by how frequently over the years one distinct conversation reoccurs. That conversation almost invariably revolves around what a student should pursue following commencement. It usually starts with one or more of these questions: What am I to do after graduation? How should I use my gifts and abilities? To what am I personally called? Is there a "call" to the marketplace? If so, is a calling to the marketplace as noble as "Christian ministry"? Can the efforts and energy I expend in the workforce be considered sacred? Often, though this question is not usually vocalized, students want an answer to this as well: Is there really any dignity and meaning in work, regardless of what I end up doing?[68]

Importantly, it is not just people entering the workforce that wrestle with the meaning of work and the question of vocation. Middle-aged workers wrestle with this as well, as do retirees, though they are seldom encouraged to vocalize such concerns.[69] What's more, most people—and especially students—are surprised and shocked to find out that such

---

[66] I use the term "rediscovery" for the simple reason that in every successive generation the church must come to grips with these doctrines, which are central to biblical revelation and to the church's cultural witness. Every era is in need of cultural apologists like Martin Luther and Abraham Kuyper and Dorothy Sayers and John Paul II.

[67] Before entering the university classroom, I did public-policy work in criminal justice in Washington, DC.

[68] In no university context in which I have taught has any course been offered that addressed these questions.

[69] The matter of retirement is taken up in chapter 3.

matters are not just relevant in the college years, when career or career choices are often confronted seriously for the first time.[70] My view is that children can be shaped and molded by their parents (and other teachers) toward a sense of purpose and vocational direction. In fact, the contexts of family and community facilitate this learning process quite naturally (at least in theory)—where faith is taken seriously. Every human being has the glorious privilege and frightening responsibility to wrestle individually with these matters and pursue avenues of work and service that correspond to his or her overall calling.

Dorothy Sayers's brilliant essay "Why Work?" was a succinct and forceful attempt both (1) to decry prevailing "Christian" attitudes toward work, vocation, and the marketplace and (2) to elevate these spheres of life on the basis of biblical revelation. Every generation needs such an apologist for the marketplace, someone who is convinced that this is where Christian service and stewardship are most needed. Sayers was right: one important "business of the Church [is] to recognize that the secular vocation, as such, is sacred."[71]

A second personal motivation behind this current volume's creation needs identifying. Rarely, if ever, are the insights of Wisdom literature applied to the matters of work, vocation, and the marketplace. I am not referring merely to proverbial wisdom in Scripture such as one finds in Psalms or Proverbs but to the little-examined and much-misunderstood book of Ecclesiastes, to which a coming chapter is devoted. To the surprise of many, a serious reading of the Bible's Wisdom books yields simple yet stunning perspectives on work, calling, and stewardship. This is

---

[70] While chapter 6 will address such matters more fully, vocation or calling is not chiefly about making certain career choices or deciding what job to take, even when it informs such decisions. Rather, it concerns how we relate Christian faith to the totality of one's life, of which work and the marketplace are a significant part. Vocation concerns broader life stewardship; it is "a theology for living." See Kathryn Kleinhans, "The Work of a Christian: Vocation in Lutheran Perspective," *Word & World* 25, no. 4 (2005): 402.

[71] Sayers, "Why Work?," 105.

especially true of Ecclesiastes, when it is viewed through the lens of faith and in light of the writer's unique literary-rhetorical strategy. Against the backdrop of divine providence and divine inscrutability, the apologetically minded writer argues that for those who revere God, work takes on an entirely different cast than the "meaninglessness" and "vanity" that a materialistic worldview engenders.[72]

The argument of this volume has four principal parts. Chapters 2 and 3 are of a theological nature. They examine the roots of our social and ecclesiastical predicament with a view to then probe its theological underpinnings. Indeed, we may call these "doctrines" of work, of vocation, and of stewardship. Chapter 4 looks back in history to the early sixteenth century in an attempt to appreciate a significant breakthrough in terms of the church's understanding of work, vocation, and the marketplace. It cannot be overstated how important that breakthrough was, both for the church in Martin Luther's day and for the church of any era. Chapters 5 and 6 go together insofar as they illuminate perspectives on work in the Wisdom literature of Ecclesiastes and establish a link between our work and our callings (i.e., our vocations). The volume concludes in chapters 7 and 8 with reflections on the church's presence in society, forming something of an *inclusio* with the introductory chapter; this includes final thoughts on the knotty and perennial questions of discernment and guidance.

The first order of business is to understand why the church has neglected the marketplace. What accounts for the widespread separation of work and religious faith and the failure to understand and respect the secular vocation, which in turn has rendered the church's witness to the culture insubstantial? What attitudes inform this seemingly perennial split in the church's thinking and its teaching? Preliminary reasons for this dilemma have been suggested. Let us probe more deeply.

---

[72] See Charles, *Wisdom and Work: Theological Reflections on Human Labor from Ecclesiastes* (Eugene, OR: Wipf & Stock, 2021).

CHAPTER
2

The Church's Great Neglect
Work, Vocation, and the Marketplace

Three generations ago a thoughtful Christian writer described human labor as one of the "lost provinces" of Christian faith. The result of the church's failure to address this realm in its teaching, preaching, and educating, he lamented, was the rise of the Marxist gospel.[1] Indeed, recent history provides compelling evidence that when and where the anthropological unity of body and soul, the material and the nonmaterial, is lost or denied, the alternative is catastrophic—and, in the end, totalitarian—as Marxism has proven.

That writer's observation, though decades old, should give us pause. In our day, just as in his, the sheer extent to which Marxist ideology and communism have dominated human affairs, decimated culture, and destroyed lives due to a flawed view of human nature is an ongoing tragedy. But what about the questions that author insinuates? Has the church's failure to address human labor facilitated the rise of the Marxist

---

[1] Elton Trueblood, *Your Other Vocation* (New York: Harper, 1952), 15, 25.

gospel, not to mention every generation's new infatuation with socialism? And should such a tragedy be laid at the feet of the church?

Though we can rightly rejoice over the events of 1989 and the fall of the Berlin Wall that brought political and social release to millions in Eastern Europe,[2] the sobering truth is that hundreds of millions of people still languish under communist tyranny—notably, in North Korea and China, but in other corners of the globe as well.[3] And this is fully aside from the tens—if not hundreds—of millions who perished for ideological reasons in the twentieth century, the century of death. For as Robert Conquest and Stéphane Courtois have variously shown, the number of individuals who were offered up for religious and political reasons in the communist experiment called the Marxist gospel staggers the mind.[4] Whether we assume the estimates of Courtois or Conquest to be most accurate, we are left numb and defenseless, caught in an unimaginable realm of calculating murder that simply boggles the mind.[5]

---

[2] Tragically, many who have been born since 1990 have shown a remarkably uncritical attitude toward Marxist-inspired socialism and its political consequences, as the current political climate makes clear. This trend mirrors the failure of both our educational system as well as the present generation of parents.

[3] Having visited Russia shortly after the collapse of the Soviet Union and witnessed dysphoria and disorientation among its people, I hasten to note that modern Russia approximates the former Soviet Union in terms of its rule. That a former KGB operative rules it with uncontested authority, repressing any and all who protest, proves that little has changed in the last three decades. As this manuscript prepares to go to the printer, Vladimir Putin has declared war on Ukraine, and Russian forces have committed unspeakable crimes against humanity and genocide.

[4] Robert Conquest, *Reflections on a Ravaged Century* (New York: W. W. Norton, 2000) and Stéphane Courtois et al., *The Black Book of Communism: Crimes, Terror, Repression,* trans. J. Murphy and M. Kramer (Cambridge, MA: Harvard University Press, 1999).

[5] Courtois and the coauthors of *The Black Book of Communism* estimate the number of people who were killed due to communist ideology to be in the 100 million range. Conquest, in *Reflections on a Ravaged Century*, estimates that approximately 170 million were sacrificed for political reasons. Such estimates

Based on the tragic evidence of recent history, I suggest, without apology, that a new Reformation is needed—that is, a reformation in the church's understanding of human labor, of vocation, and of the significance of our social presence in the marketplace. This assertion, as suggested in chapter 1, is based on the premise that the church, in tangible ways, *is* responsible for the world. Let us now examine more deeply the church's attitudes toward these crucial, life-giving spheres—spheres constituting the so-called secular realm of living—which, sadly, more often than not, have been neglected in our spiritual formation.

Rethinking the Church's "Mission" and Commission

It is appropriate to begin by rethinking what is meant by "missions."[6] Let us start at the beginning. Missions originates not at the Christian advent but at creation, as the opening chapters of Genesis make clear. Humans were made stewards of creation, tasked not only with multiplying in number but also with subduing and ruling the larger created order (Gen 1:28–29; 2:19–20).[7] This mandate did not apply merely to life in Eden, nor was it retracted in Genesis 3, even when creation experienced the effects brought on by human disobedience. Moreover, it should be noted that not work itself but the ground is "cursed" in the Genesis 3 narrative (see also Gen 5:29). To distinguish between work as an inherent aspect of the *imago Dei* and "the ground" (Gen 3:17) as the external environment of

---

dwarf Nazism's remarkable record within a much shorter span of years. We must not allow our tendency toward historical amnesia to deaden us to the stupefying proportions of social-political evil.

[6] I find the language of being "missional" that is employed by most contemporary Christian writers and speakers to be both voguish and unhelpful; it usually is devoid of content and utterly vacuous.

[7] It is not the divine commission as expressed in Genesis 1 but the fact of human sin that leads to exploitation of nature and abuse of the created order. God calls us neither to carelessness or shameless exploitation of creation nor to detached noninterference.

creation being affected by humans is theologically decisive.[8] God's work did not cease with human creation; neither did it cease with human disobedience. As the following chapter will clarify, this distinction is no mere case of theological gnat-straining; it is crucial to a proper understanding of the life of faith and of obedience to the Creator, both in the old and the new covenants.[9] Where work seems a curse, it is one of humans' own making, not God's, as this volume will continuously argue. Since work is participation or cooperation in God's purposes and activity in the created order, it has an intrinsic ethical value of its own. This cooperation with God informs work's inclusion in the Ten Commandments: "You are to labor six days and do all your work" (Exod 20:9). The rationale—imitation of God the Creator—follows: "For the LORD made the heavens and the earth, the sea, and everything in them in six days" (2:11).

We will repeatedly return to the doctrine of creation throughout this volume and consider its implications. God's work during the first five days of creation week (Gen 1:3–22) reveals a progression as God builds and shapes as a master craftsman. The creation of the human creature on the sixth day (1:26–27) represents the high point—the culmination—of God's creative purpose. That purpose, in the end, was pronounced "very good" (1:31). Not only is the order of God's creative plan significant, but it reveals the rationale behind it. The sixth day of creation, the finale, unveils God's purpose. That purpose is that human beings mirror God's likeness—his express "image" (1:27)—and rule over and care for the created order. Note, in this regard, the language of Ps 8:5–6: "You [God] made [humanity] little less than God / and crowned [them] with glory and honor. You made [them] ruler over the works of your hands; / you

---

[8] Perhaps the most widespread distortions in our thinking about work can be reduced to four basic types: work is (1) meaningless, (2) cursed, (3) passing away (and thus of no lasting benefit), or (4) everything (and thus an idol). Each of these distortions is addressed, in one form or another, in chapters 3–6.

[9] This assertion, I grant, may surprise many a Christian believer.

put everything under [their] feet." To be rulers over "the works of [God's] hands" and to have "everything" placed under the feet of humans speaks of creation realities and is reminiscent of Genesis 1.

Several theologically important questions arise. Did God's work cease when he created human beings? Did removal from the garden mean that work itself is cursed? Are the tasks given to Adam and Eve paradigmatic? What are the implications of tending the garden? Clearly, work predates the fall; it existed in the garden, as part of the *imago Dei*. To work is to reflect God's nature, his very likeness.[10] The implications of this creation reality are clear: we remain responsible for God's world. As Douglas Schuurman observes:

> God created all things; sin affects all things; God redeems all things (through Jesus Christ); Christians, like the Christ whose name they bear, share in God's redemptive and creative purposes in all things... Therefore, Christian vocation includes all aspects of cultural and social life.[11]

Or, as theologian Cornelius Plantinga has expressed it, "Creation is stronger than sin and grace [is] stronger still."[12] So, not work itself, which is anchored in our being created in the image of God, but the environment is affected by sin and stands "under the curse." Vocation has *not* been revoked.

From the standpoint of biblical theology and missions, these theological distinctions are decisive. What is tragic is that many Christians separate the Great Commission of Matt 28:19–20 (i.e., go,

---

[10] It is crucial to Christian belief that sin's entrance into the world did not eliminate the image of God in human beings. The ongoing presence of the *imago Dei* as a part of personhood helps explain how even the ungodliest person can choose to do that which is good and right.

[11] Douglas J. Schuurman, *Vocation: Discerning Our Callings in Life* (Grand Rapids: Eerdmans, 2004), 51.

[12] Cornelius Plantinga, Jr., *Not the Way It's Supposed to Be: A Breviary of Sin* (Grand Rapids: Eerdmans, 1995), 199.

disciple, baptize, and teach) from what might be designated the Cultural Commission,[13] which is based on the Genesis 1 narrative. This deficient reading of the New Testament proceeds on certain assumptions that are both imported from a particular reading of the Old Testament and further enforced by a reading of the Gospel narratives that is divorced from the doctrine of creation—a doctrine which should anchor our understanding of both Testaments. The texts cited in chapter 1—for example, John 1:3; Eph 1:10; Col 1:15–20; and Heb 1:2—offer collaborative and incontrovertible evidence that nothing in the created universe is outside of Christ's control and reign. Redemption, then, is not the negation of creation but its renewal and advancement. Mission, properly understood, announces the fact of Christ's utter and uncontested lordship over all of the created order, as the apostle Paul declares in Colossians 1.

In Lutheran language, believers are "priests" of all creation. This reality, however, will require rethinking the relationship between the "already" and the "not yet" of the kingdom of God, between the city of God and the city of man, between the eschaton and the temporal order. So, why *are* we here on earth? And why are we not raptured away from earthly responsibility immediately after conversion?[14]

One plausible reason for our disdain for "the world," as suggested in chapter 1, has to do with how we parse Jesus's words in John 17:16 about how we are "not of the world." Not infrequently, we fail to contextualize Jesus's statements in the Last Supper discourse. He said, "I am not praying *that you take them out of the world* but that you protect them from the

---

[13] R. Paul Stevens, *Doing God's Business: Meaning and Motivation for the Marketplace* (Grand Rapids: Eerdmans, 2006), 82, uses this terminology.

[14] The answer to this question needs to extend beyond Protestant evangelicals' thinking that believers are left on earth merely to save souls with the gospel message. That rationale mirrors an unscriptural dualism between the spiritual and nonspiritual realms, between nonmaterial and material creation. It fails to take the entire created order seriously.

evil one . . . As you sent me into the world, *I also have sent them into the world*" (John 17:15–18, emphasis added). Note Jesus's burden here: "not that [God] take [his followers] out of the world," but rather "that [he] protect them" as they are in the world (17:15). This contradicts any view suggesting that the saints should be excused from earthly stewardship. It speaks, rather, to their sustenance and protection while serving God *in the world* with the Holy Spirit's help.

Further, Jesus addresses those who will embrace the faith in the future. He says, "I pray also for those who will believe in me through [the disciples'] message" (John 17:20 NIV). This, of course, is a multigenerational burden, the consummation of which no one can predict or know; it is continuing. Our theology, in every generation, might be doing us the disservice of distorting a proper understanding of the church's commission—a commission that is predicated on our being in rather than apart from the world.

I propose a change in the way we think about missions—or in contemporary parlance, how we construe being missional. For starters and as a sign of what we should believe, why not have commissioning services not for those who are headed abroad to foreign missions or to seminary but for those in our congregations—the 99 percent—who are butchers and bakers and candlestick makers and such? Why not commission carpenters, lawyers, businesspeople, accountants, social workers, educators, medical professionals, and IT personnel? After all, they comprise the majority in our local congregations as well as much of the body of Christ.

Such an approach would reflect to all within the church family a proper understanding of work, vocation, and the marketplace. It might even revolutionize our social witness. Participating in "Bible studies for businesspeople," doing "street evangelism," or going on weeklong missions trips alone fail to equip congregants for the marketplace, the very place where the transforming influence of Christ in our lives can be most powerfully observed. Our mission *is* the marketplace.

Rethinking Resurrection

Another factor in our possible disdain for "the world" is the widespread belief among Christians that the created order and our bodies will permanently pass away. We tend to think that after death, we will forever exist in some disembodied state, with no association to earthly realities. But this contradicts the church's historic confession of a resurrection of the body—a confession that squares with the teaching in Rev 21:1 concerning "a new heaven and a new earth." In the words of one writer, "[The believer's] destiny is an earthly one: a new earth, an earth redeemed and transfigured. An earth reunited with heaven, but an earth nevertheless."[15] The Bible's language of new bodies—for example, 1 Cor 15:47–57—and a new earth indicates some form of continuity that will be discernible to us all. Without continuity between the present world and the eschaton, work has no significance. This theological reality is crucial in terms of how we should view our mission in the present life. Yet, one seldom hears this emphasis in standard teaching and preaching.

If we are convinced that everything in this temporal world is doomed to go up in smoke, why should we—indeed, why *would* we—take the present, the ordinary, and the daily seriously, since it has no real value anyway? Were this belief anchored in reality, the more accurate explanation of our earthly existence might be this: we are trapped in a physical prison, waiting for release into a heavenly reality that will deliver us from this purgatory. But such represents a gross, heretical distortion of the doctrines of creation and redemption.[16] As I will argue in the following chapter, we are placed here on earth—and left here—for the redemption of human life, in all of its proportions. After all, our Lord himself prayed, "Our Father, . . . Your kingdom *come.* / Your will *be done / on earth* as it is in heaven" (Matt 6:9–10,

---

[15] Paul Marshall and Lela Gilbert, *Heaven Is Not My Home: Living in the Now of God's Creation* (Nashville: Word, 1998), 11.

[16] The conversations and debates of the early church with Gnostic proponents, who denigrated the physical, material realm in favor of the spiritual, are instructive here.

emphasis added). This prayer expresses nothing less than the divine intention, namely, that Christians influence the world around them, in the present age, for the glory of God.[17] To the surprise of many, at the center of this redemptive project is the restoration of human labor.[18]

What has been called a "lifeboat theology" is present in the thinking of every generation of Christian believers. It is a framework of belief that assumes that because of sin, the goodness of creation and God's original purposes for human beings in stewarding the created order have been eliminated. It thus treats creation as a sort of *Titanic*. What remains important now is simply rescuing people from the wreckage, since the ship is rapidly sinking and its disappearance is imminent.[19]

Author Paul Marshall has suggested the antidote to this skewed way of viewing human history, human endeavor, and Christian social ethics. He argues that not a "lifeboat theology" but an "ark theology" expresses more accurately God's intention. In Noah's day, following the flood that God sent due to sin, God's creational purposes were covenantally renewed in an eternal manner (Gen 9:12, 15–17). God keeps faith with all of creation—past, present, and future—and guides the ongoing process of human history by means of common grace. Sin, though part of earth's story, is not *the* story, insofar as it parasitically feeds off of the goodness of God's creation. Hence, no realm of the created order remains outside of God's good purposes and human stewardship.

Rethinking Works

A related theological deficiency in assessing a negative view of this world needs our attention. I refer to our understanding of work and human

---

[17] The extent to which we seem successful in this endeavor is irrelevant; what matters is the church's faithfulness.

[18] As chapter 1 suggests, human labor has dignity based on creation, not on Christ's work since then. The new covenant restores or confirms creation's reality.

[19] Marshall, *Heaven Is Not My Home*, 30–32, has graphically captured the essence of a lifeboat theology.

works, which is partially anchored in the legacy of the Reformation heritage. And because many sincere Christians suffer from an inferior view of their work, many need liberation and transformation in terms of their perception of the Monday-through-Friday. The Reformation breakthrough, and particularly Martin Luther's role therein (to be taken up in chapter 4), can help us here.

Luther's immensely important revolt in the sixteenth century needs to be appreciated against the backdrop of a prevailing view of human works as meritorious for salvation and a means of earning favor with God. When we probe more deeply, we find that there exists a strange irony in Luther's theological response and rationale. On the one hand, Luther broke with medieval and late-medieval tradition, insisting that a person is not justified by works but by faith. This, as he discovered to his everlasting credit, was the undergirding of Pauline theology as developed in the Letters to the Romans, the Galatians, and the Ephesians. At the same time, Luther's reaction—one that we can well understand in light of the religious climate of his day—caused him to bias Paul's writing over against other parts of the New Testament, such as the book of James. James, Luther concluded, did not deserve a place at the heart of the New Testament canon, when compared to Romans, Ephesians, 1 Peter, and the Fourth Gospel in their "evangelical purity."[20] The specific theological reasons for this conclusion were essentially twofold: the letter's lack of Christ-centeredness and the writer's statements concerning the value of works—for example, faith

---

[20] Nor did Jude, Hebrews, and Revelation, in Luther's view. While Luther does not attempt to excise James from the canon of the New Testament, he does place it at its periphery, having a two-tiered understanding of the New Testament writings. In fairness to Luther, James does appear in all of the editions of Luther's German New Testament. He also acknowledges that James contains moral truth, which allows him to preach from James in accord with the church's calendar year (unlike later generations of Lutherans). Importantly, at the 1530 Augsburg convocation the entire canonical tradition was reaffirmed in the interest of church unity.

without works "is dead" (Jas 2:17), and a person "is justified by works" and "not by faith alone" (Jas 2:24).[21]

Yet a further factor in Luther's thinking, rooted in his training at the University of Erfurt, was the importance of studying Aristotle. Required of every university student were eight months of studying Aristotle's *Nicomachean Ethics*, six of his *Metaphysics*, and six of his *Politics*.[22] Having read Aristotle early in his career, Luther did not reject everything the philosopher espoused. However, concurrent with his growth in understanding of divine grace, Luther came to hold Aristotle in broader contempt, as is mirrored in his declaration, "[Aristotle] is to theology as darkness is to light."[23]

If we attempt to sympathize and agonize over finding favor—*meritorious* favor—with a righteous God in an ecclesio-cultural climate in which human works are deemed salvific, Luther's reaction seems justified. Such statements, then, as Luther finds in James would be, quite simply, an anathema. Based on his personal experience and the contemporary ecclesiastical climate that shaped that experience, statements found in James and Paul give the appearance of being fundamentally at odds. After all, Luther had been utterly liberated by Paul, who underscores that the Christian believer is justified by faith, and faith alone.[24]

Despite the need for reform in light of the church's practices and teachings in Luther's day, not all of his fellow Reformers read James in the same way. Another Reformer and colleague of Luther's at the University of Wittenberg read James quite differently—as did Zwingli

---

[21] Cf. Gal 2:16.

[22] Michael Massing, *Fatal Discord: Erasmus, Luther, and the Fight for the Western Mind* (New York: Harper, 2018), 81.

[23] Martin Luther, Theses 50 of *Disputation against Scholastic Theology* (1517), in *Luther's Works*, ed. Harold J. Grimm (Philadelphia: Muhlenberg Press, 1957), 31:12.

[24] Shedding helpful light on Luther's relationship to James, as well as on later Lutheran interpreters, is Jason D. Lane's *Luther's Epistle of Straw: The Voice of St. James in Reformation Preaching*, HHSS 16 (Berlin: Walter de Gruyter, 2018).

and Calvin. Philip Melanchthon, who was fourteen years Luther's junior, was the one chiefly responsible, by Luther's own confession, for teaching him the Greek of the New Testament and the words of the apostle Paul, whose theology would revolutionize Luther's own life as well as much of the church to come.[25] For Melanchthon's role in his life Luther was enormously thankful, as his public statements regarding Melanchthon throughout his career indicate. It is interesting that Luther never criticized Melanchthon publicly. And for a Reformer who was excommunicated from the church by a papal bull in 1521 and who tended toward schism, denouncing along the way those with whom he disagreed, this is remarkable.[26] As it turns out, not Luther (the "confessor") but Melanchthon (the "professor") would be the chief representative of the Lutheran and Reformation cause in the years to come.

Yet Melanchthon differed from his senior colleague on the matter of works as taught by James. Without question, Luther acknowledged the necessity of good works in terms of obedience, as his 1520 *Treatise on Good Works* indicates.[27] And, indeed, the much-neglected aspect of Luther's

---

[25] It is remarkable that in his own lifetime and not posthumously, Melanchthon would earn the title *Praeceptor Germaniae*, the "Teacher of Germany," such was his influence as a teacher both on Luther (fourteen years his elder) and others. Elsewhere I have examined Melanchthon's personal life, teaching career, and influence on Luther; see J. Daryl Charles, "Natural Law and Protestant Reform: Lessons from a Forgotten Reformer," in *Wisdom's Work: Essays in Ethics, Vocation, and Culture* (Grand Rapids: Acton Institute, 2019), 61–87.

[26] *Exsurge Domine* was issued by Pope Leo X in June 1520 as a warning to Luther; it listed forty-one charges of heresy. In January 1521 formal excommunication occurred via *Decet Romanum Pontificem*.

[27] Martin Luther, *Treatise on Good Works*, in *Luther's Works*, ed. James Atkinson (Philadelphia: Fortress, 1955), 44: 21–114. The essence of Luther's view of good works as described in the *Treatise* can be summarized thus: There are no good works apart from those which God has commanded (no. 1). Faith in Christ is the highest of all good works (no. 2). A sinner can do works, but only a Christian can please God (no. 4). Through faith all works become equal, wherein all distinctions fall away (no. 5). Faith will lead us to fulfill the first of the Ten Commandments (no. 9). There are four kinds of people: the righteous, libertines,

social concern, particularly his commitment to "poor relief," attests to his view of good works. Nevertheless, it is significant that on his personal reading of James he questioned the apostolic authority of the letter on the basis of some of its contents, while Melanchthon affirmed it. James, in Luther's estimation, was a "right strawy epistle" when compared to Romans, Galatians, and Ephesians and thus warranted a place at the periphery of the canon.[28] Why? Two basic deficiencies, for Luther, were decisive: its lack of Christ-centeredness and, for our present purposes, its opposition to the Pauline teaching of justification by faith alone. Concerning the second criticism, Luther comments in his *Lectures on Genesis*:

> Abraham was righteous by faith before God acknowledged him as such. Therefore James concludes falsely that now at last he was justified after that obedience; for faith and righteousness are known by works as by their fruits. But it does not follow, as James raves: "Hence the fruits justify," just as it does not follow: "I know a tree by its fruit; therefore the tree becomes good as a result of its fruit."[29]

It needs emphasizing, however, that Luther is less tendentious elsewhere—for example, in *The Babylonian Captivity of the Church*—in his assessment of James. There he notes that "many assert with much

---

the wicked, and the childish (no. 14). And the Ten Commandments are central to true faith (no. 18).

[28] This claim is found in Luther's introduction to the New Testament, written in 1522; see *Luther's Works*, ed. E. Theodore Bachmann (Philadelphia: Fortress, 1960), 35:362.

[29] Martin Luther, *Lectures on Genesis, Chapters 21–25*, of *Luther's* Works, ed. Jaroslav Pelikan (St. Louis: Concordia, 1964), 4:133–34. This commentary on Abraham concludes with two rather contentious statements: "Therefore let our opponents be done away with their James, whom they throw up to us so often. They babble much but understand nothing about the righteousness of works." Luther's criticism of James also appears in his preface to the book of James; see Martin Luther, "Preface to the Epistles of St. James and St. Jude," in *Luther's Works*, ed. E. Theodore Bachmann (Philadelphia: Fortress, 1960), 35: 396–97.

probability that this epistle is not by James the apostle, and that it is not worthy of any apostolic spirit; although, whoever was its author, it has come to be regarded as authoritative."[30] And in the preface to his commentary on James, Luther writes, "I praise it and consider it a good book, because it sets up no doctrines of men but vigorously promulgates the law of God . . . I would not thereby prevent anyone from including or extolling him as he pleases, for there are otherwise many good sayings in him."[31] In the end, however, Luther perceives James deficient in terms of its apostolic pedigree and expresses his wish as late as 1542 (four years before his death) that James not be taught at Wittenberg.[32]

Melanchthon, by contrast, resisted the temptation to pit James against Paul, thereby bringing the necessary corrective to Luther's understanding. For Melanchthon, good works verify authentic faith, over against a distorted view of merit. Commenting on James's declaration, "You see [then] that a man is justified by works and not by faith alone" (2:24 NASB1995), Melanchthon responds that James 2:19 indicates the possibility of having knowledge yet standing under condemnation; demons, after all, know yet tremble. James, according to Melanchthon, "is not in conflict with Paul"; rather, the writer is refuting the error of those "who imagine that they are righteous on account of their profession . . . of dogmas."[33]

---

[30] Martin Luther, *The Babylonian Captivity of the Church* (1520), *Luther's Works*, ed. Abdel Ross Wentz (Philadelphia: Fortress, 1959), 36:118.

[31] Luther, "Preface," 35:395–97.

[32] This sentiment appears, for example, in a 1542 "Table Talk," in *Luther's Works*, ed. Theodore G. Tappert (Philadelphia: Fortress, 1967), 54:424–25. Luther insists, "We should throw the epistle of James out of this school [Wittenberg], for it doesn't amount to much. It contains not a syllable of Christ. Not once does it mention Christ, except at the beginning. I maintain that some Jew wrote it who probably heard about Christian people but never encountered any. Since he heard that Christians place great weight on faith in Christ, he thought, 'Wait a moment! I'll oppose them and urge works alone.' This he did."

[33] Philip Melanchthon. *Loci Communes* (1543), Locus 9: "Good Works." I am relying here on the translation provided by J.A.O. Preus (St. Louis: Concordia, 1992), 111.

We may side, then, with Melanchthon—as well as other magisterial Reformers, for that matter[34]—and not Luther on the topic of justifying works: James was not opposing the Pauline emphasis on justification. He was, rather, clarifying and accentuating the role that works play in terms of the Christian's verification of true faith. According to Melanchthon, the "classic text" on grace and "faith alone" is expressed in Eph 2:8–9: "For you are saved by grace through faith, and this is not from yourselves; it is God's gift—not from works, so that no one can boast." Additionally, Melanchthon grasped the ramifications of the apostle's statement in Eph 2:10: "For we are God's *handiwork*, created in Christ Jesus to do *good works*, which God prepared in advance for us *to do*" (NIV, emphasis mine). It would appear, then, that we have here Paul's answer to the nagging question, Why were we created? After insisting that works are not salvific, the apostle declares that we are created for work and for good works.[35] Not only that, but God has "prepared" this mandate in his providential purposes.

James's teaching, as it turns out, squares with that of Jesus, who fuses faith and works with the double commandment of loving God and loving one's neighbor (Matt 22:34–40 and Mark 12:28–34). In fact, one cannot love God without loving one's neighbor, and this is foremost a matter of works. The teaching of James does not suggest that works in some manner contribute or lead to our salvation, only that they are the fruit or the evidence of it. True faith, after all, will show itself concretely by helping

---

[34] Calvin, for example, writes, "I am fully content to accept this epistle, when I find it contains nothing unworthy of an apostle of Christ." John Calvin, *A Harmony of the Gospels: Matthew, Mark and Luke; and James and Jude*, ed. Thomas F. Torrance and David W. Torrance and trans. A. W. Morrison and T. H. L. Parker (Grand Rapids: Eerdmans, 1995), 259.

[35] In the words of Darrell Cosden, *The Heavenly Good of Earthly Work* (Peabody: Paternoster and Hendrickson, 2006), 105, we affirm "salvation *with* works," not "salvation *by* works"; stated differently, "our justification becomes work's justification" (107).

those who are in need or in distress (see Jas 1:27; 2:14–16). Paul could not have agreed more.[36]

Fully aside from Luther's view of James, the New Testament reader encounters incontrovertible evidence that Old Testament saints were in fact "justified" through their faith and hence through their works. The "hall of fame" listing that appears in Hebrews 11 could not be clearer: works "justify" from Abel, Enoch, and Noah to Abraham, Sarah, Isaac, and Jacob to Moses and even Rahab, as well as countless others ("What more can [we] say?" concludes the writer in v. 32). Counter to Luther, then, James and Hebrews are central to the New Testament canon, not peripheral.[37]

Rethinking Rewards

Related to the broader question of works is the biblical teaching on rewards and judgment according to works, a matter that comes up in Eccl 12:14; Acts 10:42; 1 Cor 3:13; 2 Cor 5:10; Heb 10:30; 1 Pet 1:17; and Rev 20:12–13, among others. At the most basic level, we might ask why our works would be the measurement of our lives at the final judgment. Judgment and accountability only make sense if human beings are moral agents, possessing a basic moral sense and the freedom to realize their full, God-given potential.[38] Judgment, hence, throws light on human motivation.

---

[36] In fairness to Luther, standard accounts of the Reformation typically bypass or minimize Luther's social concern and work in poor relief. In this regard, Luther deserves high praise. I address this deficiency in chapter 4 (see the section "Luther on Social Concern").

[37] Much Old Testament interpretation proceeds on the assumption that only through Christ—and therefore in the new covenant—does one find meaning and satisfaction in work. But this view is mistaken, creating a false split between creation and redemption.

[38] This basic moral sense within every human accords with the natural law, which is affirmed by Paul in Rom 1:18–20 and 2:14–15.

The apostle Paul observed that "each one's work will become obvious. For the day [of judgment] will disclose it, because it will be revealed by fire; the fire will test the quality of each one's work" (1 Cor 3:13). This testing is further clarified: "If anyone's work that he has built survives, he will receive a reward" (3:14). In considering the various biblical texts cited above, the reader discerns a particular context undergirding and informing those statements. That context and theological rationale assume the possibility—indeed, the frequency, given human nature— that human beings will *not* make wise decisions, that they will *not* obey, that they are often wrongly motivated.³⁹ In this regard, the teaching on works found in James serves as a perennial reminder of an important spiritual truth: our works, our deeds, our behavior all *verify or deny* the faith profession that we make.⁴⁰ One example employed by James should give us pause: even the demons "believe" (Jas 2:19). In what sense, we might ask, do demonic powers do so? The accurate sense in which works justify is further clarified by James in the next two examples, Abraham and Rahab (2:21–25). Both individuals are justified based on what they *did*—that is, based on what they believed to be ultimate reality, which in the end ordered their actions.

This perspective on judgment according to works and rewards assists us in making sense of Jesus's teaching on stewardship, notably in the parable of the talents (Matt 25:14–30), and in the Pauline teaching that judgment "test[s] the quality of each one's work" (1 Cor 3:13). The teaching of rewards in the New Testament is predicated on the assumption of the value of work done with right motivation. Human works and deeds are to be judged according to their motivation and intention. So, why do people act? What reasons inform a person's behavior? If those

---

³⁹ That is to say, human beings "fall short," which approximates the more literal definition of sin in Rom 3:23.

⁴⁰ This is the sense in which we may understand Jesus's declarations "You'll recognize them by their fruit" (Matt 7:16, 20) and "Each tree is known by its own fruit" (Luke 6:44).

reasons and motivations are fundamentally self-serving rather than God-centered, then it is accurate to conclude that those who do them serve the god of self rather than the God of all creation. Moreover, the desire to please the Lord of creation will ultimately result, as the parable of the talents suggests, in the investment of one's life, one's abilities, one's gifts, and one's works or deeds in the marketplace. The teaching of the parable is that this investment is in fact service to the Master himself, granting him exceeding joy; lasting rewards will accompany such service.[41]

Similarly, the Pauline imagery employed in 1 Cor 3:12 serves to underscore the significance of the fruits of one's personal investment: fire only makes more valuable "gold, silver, [and] costly stones," while it utterly destroys and consumes "wood, hay, or straw." Its negative application notwithstanding, the positive implication of this important doctrine should not be lost on us: our work and our works matter. Our deeds have lasting—indeed, eternal—consequences and merit. Despite our tendency to overestimate the extraordinary and underestimate the ordinary, this realization should exhilarate us,[42] infusing the ordinary, the everyday, and our service in the marketplace with meaning, purpose, and a sense of contentment.[43] This, of course, is the implication of Eccl 9:10: "Whatever your hand finds to do, do it with all your strength." The passage underscores both our marvelous freedom and the fact that we cannot understand the scope of the fruit of our labors undertaken in faith. And the positive implication of the final statement in Ecclesiastes—"For God will bring

---

[41] For further commentary on this parable, see chapter 3.

[42] I am not suggesting that every day is filled with great joy, excitement, and exhilaration. Part of the reality of Christian discipleship, in fact, is that we must suffer and endure hardship. But what I am arguing is that we can expect a normative measure of joy, peace, and satisfaction both in and through our work. Such thinking will be developed more fully in chapters 3, 5, and 6.

[43] Remarkably, in my own forty-five-year journey as a Christian, I've never heard a sermon, as best I remember, devoted to the lasting fruits of our earthly work and endeavors, especially as it applies to our professions and the workplace. From the standpoint of Christian theology and pastoral care, this is tragic.

every act to judgment, including every hidden thing, whether good or evil" (12:14)—should not be lost on us either: God will reward every believer for every good deed that is done to honor him and serve others. Judgment and accountability not only purge and eliminate but affirm and validate.

Our works are not transitory or passing; the good we do will not be forgotten. Rather, it will "adorn the world to come."[44] This aspect of theological truth should be taught to every believing individual.

Rethinking the Doctrine of Vocation

A further, related reason for the church's inattention to work (or works) and the marketplace is her loss—indeed, her seeming abandonment—of the central doctrine of vocation, a subject to be taken up more fully in chapters 4 and 6. The notion of vocation speaks to human beings' deepest longings and the believer's deepest sensibilities about God's nature, divine grace, human flourishing, and our response to divine initiative. It relates to both our basic identity as Christian disciples and our "itinerary," as writer Edward Hahnenberg points out.[45] But while it recognizes and incorporates the importance of discernment and decision-making, the notion of vocation does not prostitute human freedom through that contemporary idol of choice or therapeutic self-actualization;[46] nor does it reduce it to

---

[44] Marshall, *Heaven Is Not My Home*, 243.

[45] Edward P. Hahnenberg, *Awakening Vocation: A Theology of Christian Call* (Collegeville: Liturgical, 2010), xiii. It is perhaps significant for our time that Hahnenberg writes as a Roman Catholic, and thus as a product of post-Vatican II thinking. Hahnenberg is forthright: "Luther introduced into Christianity a wholly new way of talking about vocation—one that celebrates the ordinary and everyday occupations of Christians as true 'callings' coming from God. In response, Catholics reasserted a narrower identification of vocation with certain official states of life. While Vatican II opened up a broader view, in postconciliar church documents and in much of the popular Catholic imagination, a narrow and deductive conception carries on" (xv).

[46] Hahnenberg, *Awakening Vocation*, 12–13, expresses the balance of human freedom and divine initiative in a most thoughtful manner.

the so-called purpose-driven life, as many would understand it. Rather, it acknowledges that the discernment we exercise and the decisions we make are all guided by and in response to that which is transcendent. It wrestles with the fundamental issue of how, over a lifetime, we each respond to God's gracious initiative in ways that are specific to us as individuals.

Tragically, evidence of the centrality of the doctrine of vocation is almost nowhere to be found in the teaching offered by the Christian church. In my experience, one largely strives in vain to find in the church *any* serious discourse or instruction related to this crucial doctrine. The topic tends to be handled chiefly by self-help gurus, business-motivational speakers or authors, and those who occasionally publish work-related essays in journals of psychology and career counseling.[47] And in this context, vocation is not infrequently presented as conforming to a person's own wishes and sense of self-actualization. To the extent that God does enter these presentations, he is depicted as the guarantor of "the authenticity of the self."[48]

The consequence of the church's failure to address the doctrine of vocation has been twofold, leading first to the creation of a false and persistent sacred-versus-secular dichotomy that stretches over the better part of two millennia in the Western cultural tradition. Closer to our own time, it has led to the wholesale secularizing of the notion of vocation. Even Merriam-Webster's definition of "vocation" emphasizes "a divine call to the religious life" and includes "an entry into the priesthood or a religious order.[49] Note how such language is skewed in the direction of ecclesiastical work.

One Christian writer has observed correctly that of the three major teachings characterizing the Protestant Reformation, two remain in

---

[47] Aside from occasional essays in journals of psychology, vocational behavior, and career counseling, the exceptions to this unfortunate situation, in my own experience, come from the organization Made to Flourish, which is dedicated to helping pastoral vision; the Acton Institute, an educational think tank; and the Institute for Faith, Work, and Economics.

[48] So says Jeffrey Scholes "Vocation," *Religion Compass* 4, no. 4 (2010): 217.

[49] Merriam-Webster, s.v. "vocation," defs. 1a, b, accessed July 20, 2022, https://www.merriam-webster.com/dictionary/vocation.

part—justification and scriptural authority—while the third, vocation, has been lost.[50] In this transmutation, vocation has come to mean anything from a work ethic, to a job, to a formal job skill, to vo-tech or career training. Restoring a proper understanding of the concept will require the church's recognition that vocation has an inherently religious character—though it is for *all* of the saints, not merely the clergy.[51] Luther's revolt against monasticism, based on a priesthood of all believers, was lodged in the conviction that monastic life, with its removal of Christ's followers from "the world," had ceased to serve the church's real mission. After all, the church, not the monastery, constitutes the community of the saints.[52] The thrust of Christian community—indeed, the Holy Spirit's work—will

---

[50] Gene Edward Veith, "Vocation: The Theology of the Christian Life," *Journal of Markets and Morality* 14, no. 1 (Spring 2011): 119. Whether the first two Reformation teachings have been retained by Protestants in general, however, is a matter worth questioning. Already a century ago liberal Protestantism began eschewing the interaction between the supernatural and natural orders. And though it wishes to retain a moral façade, in its rejection of confessionalism (and attendant wholesale embrace of secular modernity), mainline Protestantism has essentially sold its birthright.

To his credit, D. H. Williams has pressed the argument that theology and vocation together are legitimate objects of study in a Christian liberal arts context, as education in prior centuries indicates. D. H. Williams, "Protestantism and the Vocation of Higher Education," in *Revisiting the Idea of Vocation: Theological Explorations*, ed. John C. Haughey (Washington, DC: The Catholic University of America Press, 2012), 141–62.

[51] Even the language of clergy and laity contributes subtly to this distortion.

[52] The needed response in our post-Christian era is not to withdraw from the world to monastic communities, though of course these can bear witness to nonbelievers too. While the book *The Benedict Option* (2017) has, understandably, garnered considerable attention, my own inclination is to call for an "Augustinian option" or even a "Kuyperian option" instead. While Benedict calls the saints to monastic community, Augustine and Abraham Kuyper—fourteen centuries removed—call us to vigilant yet responsible engagement *in* the culture. As argued above, the thrust of the Holy Spirit's work will always be *toward* the world, not *away* from it. See, in this regard, J. Daryl Charles, "The Kuyperian Option: Cultural Engagement and Natural Law Ecumenism," *Touchstone* (May–June 2018): 22–28.

always be *toward* the world, not away from it. Properly viewed, then, vocation will require changes in the way that the church thinks about its mission and missions, about people's professions and everyday work, and about the nature of the marketplace.

Let us consider the ramifications of Jesus's words. The emphasis here is my own:

> Matthew 5:14: "You are the light of the world. A city situated on a hill *cannot be hidden*."

> Matthew 5:16: "In the same way, let your light shine before others, so that they may see *your good works* and give glory to your Father in heaven."

To the author and agent of creation (cf. John 1:3 and Col 1:16), work and works are critically important. Jesus's words stand in full agreement with those of the book of James: works matter and validate the authenticity of faith. What is more, the fruits of our work and our works endure, bringing great joy to the Lord of creation. We see this principle in Matt 25:21, 23: "Well done, good and faithful servant! You were faithful over a few things; I will put you in charge of many things. Share your master's joy." Pauline teaching, moreover, will confirm the burden of Jesus and James: "For we are God's *handiwork*, created in Christ Jesus to do *good works*, which God prepared in advance for us to do" (Eph 2:10 NIV, emphasis added).

Basic to the argument developed in this volume is the fundamental conviction that the Christian church's rediscovery of the doctrine of vocation will help equip individual Christians to discover and embrace their own particular vocational callings. While I grant it is possible to be in a career that is not one's calling, it is optimal to find and labor in it; after all, the clear teaching of the New Testament is that as various members of the body of Christ, we have different functions and different gifts (see Rom 12:4–8; 1 Cor 12:4–6). These various equippings do not apply to us only when the Christian community is assembled.

Why is it that people often feel trapped in terms of their present situations, their professions, or their work? What factors contribute to the present season of life in which believers as individuals find themselves? Without a sense of vocation, of calling, our lives are adrift. Not only does a proper and personal sense of vocation go hand in hand with a rediscovery of the worth and dignity of work, but it also helps us make sense of the different seasons and stages of life.

One "business of the church," Dorothy Sayers writes, is "to recognize that the secular vocation as such is sacred."[53] The fact is that most of us are called, in some form, to the marketplace. That calling is a holy enterprise. And it is not only important for work and the Monday-through-Friday, but it guides us throughout our lives—in terms of our relationships, our education, our spiritual formation, our leisure, and our overall trajectories.

Calling (*vocatio* in Lat.) is not merely an inner impulse but a rational, willful response to perceived ultimate reality and divine direction. It can be doubted, ignored, or resisted. And it is not static but evolving, which means that it likely will entail hardship, self-denial, and even suffering. Nevertheless, vocation is anchored in the *imago Dei* (see Gen 1:27). That image is not yet perfected, nor will it be until the eschaton. We believers can, however, become increasingly conformed to its perfected state as represented in Christ (Rom 8:29).

Thirty years ago Calvin College philosopher Lee Hardy published his important work *The Fabric of This World*,[54] which thoughtfully undertook a theological and historical examination of the Christian view of work

---

[53] Dorothy L. Sayers, "Why Work?" in *Creed or Chaos? Why Christians Must Choose Either Dogma or Disaster; or, Why It Really Does Matter What You Believe*, repr. (Manchester: Sophia Institute Press, 1974), 105.

[54] Lee Hardy, *The Fabric of This World: Inquiries into Calling, Career Choice, and the Design of Human Work* (Grand Rapids: Eerdmans, 1990).

and vocation. His volume remains one of the most helpful resources for Christians who wish to rethink the value of work based on our creation in the image of God and the nature of vocation as it applies to the believer. In addition to his firm grasp of Christian theology and history, Hardy offers sage advice in helping Christ's followers with practical application to their own contexts.

Hardy begins the volume, published in 1990, by noting the observations made five years earlier by Cal Berkeley sociologist Robert Bellah and his coauthors in their landmark volume *Habits of the Heart*.[55] They had examined what they observed to be the primacy of private advancement over public contribution in American social life—a trend which they lamented to be corrosive of society and broader democratic institutions. Bellah identified two sorts of individualism at work: the utilitarian, which tends to be hardworking and success-oriented, and the expressivist, which tends to be leisure-oriented and escapist in character. Both forms, it was argued, are individualistic, and neither serves the common good. Historically, however, American society's roots are very different, mirroring republican and biblical traditions. An important key, according to Bellah, in improving our "social ecology" and common life is "a change in the meaning of work." Work in the sense of vocation, Bellah argued, can never be an entirely private or personal matter, since vocation, properly understood, links us with the public world, existing for the common good and not the self alone.[56] As it turned out, Hardy's book, which took Bellah's social critique seriously, represented an attempt to flesh out these neglected traditions, consider their histories and their religious meaning, and probe contemporary application.[57] Both the social

---

[55] Robert Bellah et al., *Habits of the Heart: Individualism and Commitment in American Life* (Berkeley: University of California Press, 1985).

[56] Bellah, *Habits of the Heart*, 65–71, 287–89.

[57] Two examples of the thoroughness of Hardy's critique are noteworthy. One is his overview of contrasting views of work throughout history (e.g., among the ancient Greeks, during the medieval era, in the Renaissance and Reformation, in the context of Marxist thought, and in Catholic social teaching).

critique offered thirty-five years ago by an eminent sociologist and the ecclesial critique by a Christian philosopher shortly thereafter are all the more true today—and all the more necessary.[58]

As we enter the third decade of the twenty-first century, the extent to which the Christian community rediscovers the inherently religious and biblical sense of work and *vocatio* is largely a question of vision, which grows out of the church's theological moorings and commitments. Any response to God and thus to the culture around us must be first and foremost a theological one, but thinking theologically is not some luxury reserved for theologians; nor is theology a mere academic exercise. Hence, none of us can properly think about calling or vocation apart from a deep appreciation of the meaning and dignity of work. It is to this theme we now turn.

Another is the book's attempt to engage the reader, who encounters questions about calling and career choice, at the personal level.

[58] See as well Timothy Keller and Katherine Leary Alsdorf, *Every Good Endeavor: Connecting Your Work to God's Work* (New York: Riverhead Books, 2012), 1–2, for insight into the importance of Bellah's findings for our day.

CHAPTER
3

Theological Perspectives on Work, Vocation, and Stewardship

Tracing the Implications of Creation and Human Design

At the dawn of each semester, I fire an opening shot at the university students I teach. "Ladies and gentlemen," I declare, "the study of theology in which you are presently engaged is literally a matter of life and death." Most students, of course, roll their eyes at this, their expressions basically communicating, "Dr. Charles, give us a break. Don't be so ridiculously melodramatic!" Yet repeatedly, usually before the end of the semester, those same students thank me for the seriousness with which the case for theology's importance is made in the classroom. In fact, not infrequently, I receive letters or emails from former students who communicate their gratitude in strong terms. Why this post-graduation correspondence? They've been planted in the marketplace and the public square, working in a near all-consuming environment that requires—indeed, *demands*—from them a reason for the hope within and a reason for being in the marketplace.

None of us can think seriously and responsibly about work, vocation, or the marketplace without siding with Dorothy Sayers, as I attempt to argue in chapter 1. A deeper appreciation of this realm of human existence (the secular), begins with a deeper appreciation of the meaning, value, and dignity of work itself. Such appreciation, alas, cannot proceed apart from a sturdy theology of work, as Sayers well intuited. In our present cultural context, however, serious obstacles confront us as we attempt to discover any meaning or value in our jobs. Compounding the cultural dilemma is that the church tends to view the marketplace and the world of industry and commerce in the following stereotypical ways:

- as a realm in which we can witness to others purely by telling them about Christ;
- as a realm that keeps us from doing the *real* work of the ministry;
- as a realm in which we pray for the salvation of our colleagues and clients;
- as a realm of activity that each must endure in order to obtain a paycheck and make a living;
- as a realm that we would gratefully quit and leave behind in order to go into the ministry or to seminary, even though such an opportunity will be offered to very few of us;
- as an unstable realm of shifting duties and allegiances and no permanence; or
- as a realm that, at best, is a necessary evil and, at worst, a curse.

And, of course, the church can adopt the world's values, viewing work and the marketplace in these ways as well:

- as a realm under the sun that is meaningless, pointless, and in the end futile;
- as a realm that facilitates the idolatrous pursuit of self-glorifying or self-actualizing goals;

- as a realm whose sheer boredom, without engagement or challenges, drives people, like Sherlock Holmes, to various addictions;[1]
- as a realm of alienation and dehumanizing tendencies; or
- as a realm which, at best, creates and eventually facilitates the greater good and goal of personal leisure.

Many Christians, if not most, have struggled with a view of both work and leisure that expresses itself in ways ranging from frustration, discontentment, alienation, and boredom to being workaholics, finding our personal identities in our professions, and/or pursuing material or self-constructed idols. Compounding these distortions is the typical and persistent sacred-versus-secular dichotomy lodged in the thinking of many believers, as has been noted. If any or several of the above stereotypes and tendencies represent the actual experience of most people, where does that leave the great majority of us who are in the marketplace—those of us who, by the end of our lives, will have spent roughly 100,000 hours in non-church-related work?[2] The tragic reality is that few people see

---

[1] "My mind," says Holmes, "rebels at stagnation. Give me problems, give me work, give me the most abstruse cryptogram or the most intricate analysis, and I am in my own proper atmosphere. I can dispense then with artificial stimulants. But I abhor the dull routine of existence." See Arthur Conan Doyle, *The Sign of the Four* (London 1890), ch. 1, https://www.gutenberg.org/files/2097/2097-h/2097-h.htm. Holmes's sentiment is reproduced in Gilbert C. Meilaender, *Working: Its Meaning and Its Limits* (Notre Dame, IN: University of Notre Dame Press, 2000), 48.

[2] This estimate comes from Chris R. Armstrong, "Refocused Vocation," *Leadership Journal* (Winter 2013): 44–48. A similar estimate comes from a 2017 survey by researchers in London who concluded that the average person in the West, based on a seventy-six-year lifespan and assuming fifty years of paid employment, spends 92,210 hours working. The source of this data is the "Annual Survey of Hours and Earnings," supplied by the Office for National Statistics (UK). Inasmuch as these figures represent European work standards rather than North American, where longer workweeks are the norm, we North Americans might extrapolate further. While a 1994 report issued by the World Health Organization indicated that most of the world's population—58 percent—spends *one-third of adult life* at work, this figure probably has not

their daily work as connected to the purposes of God and as a means by which to flourish. And despite the relatively high percentage of people in the United States who profess religious faith, contemporary society and culture are being molded with very little Christian social presence. This state of affairs simply should not be.

Beginning at the Beginning

Three workers stood with tools in hand, breaking massive rocks into pieces. Each was asked what he was doing. One worker responded, "I'm making little rocks out of big rocks." Another replied, "I'm just making a living." The third, however, said, "I am building a cathedral."[3] That third worker is the one who understood that there exists a design and meaning in the human endeavor.[4] Precisely this, in fact, is the ethical component that distinguishes the Judeo-Christian tradition. No other interpretive framework for ultimate reality, past or present, understands human labor in this manner.

---

changed significantly in the last twenty-five years; in fact, for many those figures are probably low. Of course, these surveys do not even begin to evaluate how much of a given workday or workweek is devoted to productive work, over against, say, entertainment, news, and social media.

[3] See J. J. Ryan, "Humanistic Work: Its Philosophy and Cultural Implications," in William J. Heister and J. W. Houck, eds., *A Matter of Dignity: Inquiries into the Humanization of Work* (Notre Dame, IN: University of Notre Dame Press, 1977), 11; the illustration is reproduced in Gilbert C. Meilaender, *Working: Its Meaning and Its Limits* (Notre Dame, IN: University of Notre Dame Press, 2000), 1.

[4] One commentator notes, "There are three types of people at [the] workplace." Some, he says, see their work as a job, some as a career, and some as a calling. That third type often continue working even after their shifts are over because they love what they do. Their labors are expressive of their very character and priorities, and their work ethic is palpable. Their aptitudes and giftings are in full use, so to them, work is a joy, not a drudgery. They derive satisfaction from their workplace endeavors. See Brett Steenbarger, "Why Your Career Is Not Your Calling," *Forbes*, December 6, 2015, https://www.forbes.com/sites/brettsteenbarger/2015/12/06/why-your-career-is-not-your-calling/?sh=62a7235262cf.

In the beginning, "there was work," as Timothy Keller and Katherine Leary Alsdorf emphatically declare in their important volume, *Every Good Endeavor*.[5] In fact, according to the Genesis account, God's initial creative activity was performed in what would become humanity's own workweek of seven days—six days creating and one day resting. Human beings, upon their creation, were tasked with working in the garden (see Gen 2:15). This opening revelation and pattern—namely, the creation of the universe by the Master craftsman followed by human creatures acting in his image, his very likeness—already suggest the importance of work to human flourishing. Surely it is not insignificant that with relative frequency the Old Testament describes God's activity as "the work/works of his hands" (see, for example, Pss 8:3, 6; 19:1; 92:4; 102:25; 138:8; 143:5; Isa 60:21; and 64:8).

Working is one thing that distinguishes the human being from other creatures. Animals' ability to perform basic functions needed for them to survive, after all, cannot be viewed as true work. That is because animals lack rationality, self-consciousness, reflective ability, moral intuition, freedom, and the creativity to meet their needs—much less the needs of other created things—through diverse means. Those qualities mirror the divine nature.

The Wisdom perspective, as we have seen, honors and extols work, which—viewed properly—bestows freedom and blessing:

Do you see a person skilled in his work?
  He will stand in the presence of kings. (Prov 22:29)

The diligent hand will rule,
  but laziness will lead to forced labor. (Prov 12:24)

The sleep of the worker is sweet, whether he eats little or much,
  but the abundance of the rich permits him no sleep. (Eccl 5:12)

---

[5] Timothy Keller and Katherine Leary Alsdorf, *Every Good Endeavor: Connecting Your Work to God's Work* (New York: Riverhead Books, 2012), 19.

We work because God works, and therein is lodged work's intrinsic dignity. That dignity, moreover, attends all human labor, irrespective of its remuneration, status, or estimation.[6] All legitimate work is an extension and expression of God's work. If our purpose in this world is to glorify God, then work has intrinsic meaning, and stewarding God's creation in one way or another becomes everyone's primary task. That stewarding, as we shall observe, honors and pleases God; hence, it is nothing less than worship.[7]

The very idea that presenting our material bodies as "living sacrifice[s]"—sacrifices that are "holy and pleasing to God"—constitutes "true worship" (Rom 12:1), as well as the anthropology behind this remarkable statement, would have been revolutionary to most in a first-century audience. The prevailing Gentile view of that time likely would have been that the body is evil or at best an obstacle and unimportant to human flourishing.[8] Hereby Paul, the apostle to the Gentiles, collapses the sacred-versus-secular (i.e., the holy-versus-unholy) distinction in a simple statement.

The Genesis creation narrative distinguishes itself from other ancient Near Eastern accounts of creation by the gods in important ways.

---

[6] I do not deny that some forms of work are morally wrong. Helping us evaluate that are questions like these: Does the job violate any moral laws? Does it contribute to human dignity, to worthwhile goals, and to the common good? Is it a legitimate form of service to others, i.e., does it help meet legitimate human need?

[7] Nowhere in Scripture do we find particular priorities assigned in terms of *how to steward* or *what kinds of work* do the stewarding. All types of work are noble and sacred, provided they do not violate moral law.

Interestingly, Scripture does not advance either a Franciscan lifestyle or a system of capitalism. Rather, the believer is called to exercise discernment in such matters, so as not to fall into the trap of misplaced values (whether covetousness and greed, on the one hand, or withdrawal and isolation, on the other) that perhaps are encouraged by the surrounding culture or reactions to the culture. This remains the case even when some individuals might indeed be called to live like a Franciscan or work in business and corporate finance.

[8] Ascetic and Gnostic or Manichean notions of the *sōma*, the body, were common in the first century. Most denied the goodness of material creation.

The Israelites were the only people group in ancient Near Eastern culture whose God was a worker who also rested.[9] This uniqueness displays itself in terms of the Creator's identity—he has no equal—and how he operates—he creates, cultivates, and extends in his likeness. Moreover, in contrast to the paganistic thinking of surrounding ancient cultures, wherein work would have been generally despised, this Creator-God not only works but portrays work as having exceeding worth and dignity; he even declares its results to be "good" (Gen 1:10, 12, 18, 21, 25, 31).[10] Remarkably, Wisdom literature paints a portrait of God in his creating that suggests sheer delight in that activity. In Prov 8:27–31, "Lady Wisdom" informs the reader:

> I was there when [God] established the heavens,
> when he laid out the horizon on the surface of the ocean,
> when he placed the skies above,
> when the fountains of the ocean gushed out,
> when he set a limit for the sea
> so that the waters would not violate his command,
> when he laid out the foundations of the earth.
> I was a skilled craftsman beside him.
> I was his delight every day,
> always rejoicing before him.
> I was rejoicing in his inhabited world,
> delighting in [humankind.]

---

[9] The amount of literature devoted to ancient Near Eastern creation narratives is massive. See, for example, James B. Pritchard, ed., *The Ancient Near East Volume I: An Anthology of Texts and Pictures* (Princeton, NJ: Princeton University Press, 1958); James B. Pritchard, ed., *The Ancient Near East Volume II: A New Anthology of Texts and Pictures* (Princeton, NJ: Princeton University Press, 1975); and James B. Pritchard, ed., *Ancient Near Eastern Texts Relating to the Old Testament*, 3rd ed. (Princeton, NJ: Princeton University Press, 1969).

[10] Keller and Alsdorf, *Every Good Endeavor*, 21, wonderfully summarize this act of divine fiat: "God worked for the sheer joy of it. Work could not have a more exalted inauguration."

No other religious tradition, past or present, exists in which such a joyful depiction of creation occurs. And none other views the material and nonmaterial realms—matter and spirit—as conjoined and existing in an integrated metaphysical unity.

The Judeo-Christian tradition, moreover, distinguishes itself in that the ordinary—that is, the sphere of work, wherein the material and nonmaterial meet—is holy, which bestows upon it meaning, purpose, and direction (see 1 Pet 1:15–16). The so-called secular, we discover, is sanctified.

Work is a gift, instituted at creation. As a gift, it conveys a sense of dignity, value, and fulfillment. Proof of this reality is the way people respond to the experience of unemployment. Consider common responses when people lose their jobs: some develop anxiety; many struggle with self-worth and even seem to shrivel emotionally; others commit suicide.[11] Why these negative responses to unemployment? Because it leaves people suspecting that life is devoid of meaning and purpose. It suggests we need to labor.

The Christian is responsive to God by living out of gratitude and thus with a keen awareness of stewardship; we respond, as David Jensen has correctly observed, "through our various vocations."[12] It is, then, not incidental that the primary doctrines of historic Christian faith depict God in terms of his work and activity: he creates, he cultivates, he makes covenant, he incarnates, he delivers, he redeems, he justifies and sanctifies, and he promises to bring about consummation. From Genesis to Revelation, from creation to the new Jerusalem, "the biblical narratives overflow with work."[13] The language of calling (that is, vocation) per-

---

[11] See, for example, Garen Staglen, "Job Loss, Suicide and Substance Abuse: A Watershed Moment," *Forbes*, June 9, 2020, https://www.forbes.com/sites/onemind/2020/06/09/job-loss-suicide-and-substance-abuse-a-watershed-moment/?sh=645af40664bc.

[12] David H. Jensen, *Responsive Labor: A Theology of Work* (Louisville: WJK, 2006), ix.

[13] Jensen, 22.

vades Scripture.¹⁴ When we view work through the lens of calling, work is creative, redemptive, and providentially guided.

When we make the effort to observe the New Testament's notable accent on our works, we find confirmation of this. Consider the most poignant example from the Gospel narratives: God-Incarnate, the eternal Logos, Jesus Christ, spends the better part of three decades of his earthly life not preparing as a warrior-King or deliverer but apprenticing and working as a tradesman. Indeed, there is no evidence that before his unveiling to the world Jesus was itching for the chance to do "real ministry." And surely no one would suggest that the Son of God did shoddy woodwork or designed mediocre structures or made second-rate furniture as he waited for the messianic part of his life to begin.¹⁵

Significantly, throughout his messianic activity Jesus frequently uses worker themes and imagery, as his parabolic teaching attests. Moreover, after his ascension, career fishermen/disciples still fished in the sea of Galilee, even though they had been made "fishers of men." And the "apostle to the Gentiles" did not abandon his tentmaking, even though that particular trade is not the focus of his New Testament letters. Only

---

¹⁴ This is true even when the nature of "calling" changes in the New Testament, given the function in the Old Testament of God's "calling" as it relates to theocratic Israel and covenant.

¹⁵ Dorothy L. Sayers, "Why Work?" in *Creed or Chaos? Why Christians Must Choose Either Dogma or Disaster; or, Why It Really Does Matter What You Believe*, repr. (Manchester: Sophia Institute Press, 1974), 106–7, puts it this way: "No crooked table legs or ill-fitting drawers ever, I dare swear, came out of the carpenter's shop at Nazareth. Nor, if they did, could anyone believe that they were made by the same hand that made Heaven and earth."

In the same vein, C. S. Lewis, in his short but trenchant essay "Good Work and Good Works," in *The World's Last Night* (New York: Harcourt Brace, 1952), 71, 80, depicts the "great masses" of people in heavily industrialized societies as "victims" of a social context that "almost excludes" the very idea of work well done "from the outset" (71). But this problem is "not solely the result of original or actual sin," nor are we "victims" in the passive sense, he cautions his Christian reader (71). If our work is not *well done* and *worth doing*, he concludes, then religious faith becomes "marginal" and "amateurish" (80).

when we reflect seriously on the New Testament's accent on work and works are we in a position to consider contemporary attitudes toward work, most of which are deficient. The New Testament's ethic can be summed up memorably in statements such as these:

- "Let your light shine before others, so that they may see your *good works* and glorify your Father in heaven" (Matt 5:16);
- "Faith, *if it does not have works*, is dead" (Jas 2:17);
- "A person is justified *by works* and not faith alone" (Jas 2:24);
- "Present *your bodies* as a living sacrifice . . . which is your true worship" (Rom 12:1); and
- "Whatever you do, *work at it with all your heart*, as working for the Lord, not for human masters, since you know that you will receive an inheritance from the Lord as a reward" (Col 3:23–24 NIV).[16]

As we cultivate, tend, and manage all that God has created through the various gifts and abilities given to each of us, human labor achieves an exalted and noble place in the economy of God and thus in life itself.

Scripture prevents us from assuming—or even entertaining the thought—that work is merely to be tolerated as a necessary evil or some form of demeaning necessity.[17] Such an understanding of work—

---

[16] Emphasis has been added to these five passages.

[17] This position is contrary to that of Jacques Ellul, *The Ethics of Freedom* (Grand Rapids: Eerdmans, 1976), 495–505; *Reason for Being: A Meditation on Ecclesiastes* (Grand Rapids: Eerdmans, 1990), 93–106; and John H. Sailhamer, *The Pentateuch as Narrative: A Biblical-Theological Commentary* (Grand Rapids: Zondervan, 1992), 101, 110.

For Ellul, the fall is so radical that nothing good remains from creation. Utterly absent in his theological framework is the Christian doctrine of common grace, whereby the Lord of creation sustains "all things by his powerful word" (Heb. 1:3) by means of general grace (which did not begin with the new covenant). "There are no normative ethics of the good," Ellul maintains, only grace and salvation. Ellul, *The Ethics of Freedom*, 43. Hence, there exists in his thinking a radical and *oppositional* relationship between creation and redemption, rather than a completion or restoration. Work, therefore, for

at least, of physical labor (consonant with the *vita activa*) over against the reflective life (the *vita contemplativa*)—can be seen not only in antiquity but also in medieval life and thought, with vestiges surfacing even in the modern era. Most writers trace the roots of this attitude to classical Greek culture—in which human dignity was best preserved and expressed by withdrawing from the material world, in Aristotelian fashion, to a more contemplative existence.[18] Lee Hardy's *The Fabric of This World*, noted in the previous chapter, and William Placher's fine anthology titled *Callings* both employ a fourfold division in their respective historical overviews of cultural attitudes toward work. Hardy's examination traces those attitudes (1) among the ancient Greeks, (2) during the medieval era, (3) in the context of the Renaissance and Reformation; and (4) in Marxist thought.[19] Placher's schema concerns itself with attitudes representative of (1) the early church (c. AD 100–500), (2) the medieval era (c. 500–1500), (3) the Protestant Reformation (c. 1500–1800), and (4) the modern and post-Christian era (c. 1800–the present).[20]

What should strike us as remarkable is the utter resilience of the view, which spans more than two millennia, that physical labor is inferior to reflection, contemplation, and mental work.[21] For example, even Thomas

---

Ellul, cannot bring any measure of satisfaction whatsoever; it is a product of the fall rather than a reality anchored in the divine nature and hence part of the fabric of creation.

[18] See, for example, Aristotle, *Nicomachean Ethics* I.5 (1095b–1096a), and *Politics* VII.8–9 (1328b–1329b). In the former, Aristotle identifies those active in political life (i.e., the "cultivated" people) and those who study (especially philosophers) as those who are the "most favored." The modern idea that we work to have leisure, on which happiness depends, traces back to Aristotelian thinking.

[19] Lee Hardy, *The Fabric of This World: Inquiries into Calling, Career Choice, and the Design of Human Work* (Grand Rapids: Eerdmans, 1990), 6–43.

[20] William C. Placher, ed., *Callings: Twenty Centuries of Christian Wisdom on Vocation* (Grand Rapids: Eerdmans, 2005), 1–12.

[21] It is difficult to deny that the early Christian and medieval emphasis on "imitating Christ," valuing the secluded and mystical life, and self-denial had the

Aquinas, well into the thirteenth century, holds to this idea, noting in the *Summa Theologica* that the contemplative life is "more excellent" than the active life. Here he sides with Aristotle, citing eight reasons for this alignment. Such convictions are rooted in a perceived superiority of the inner life.[22]

The Protestant Reformers, by contrast, hold a different view of the matter. Luther considers it "pure invention" that the pope, bishops, priests, and monks are the "spiritual estate" while magistrates, princes, farmers, and craftsmen are called the "temporal estate." Indeed, for Luther, this distinction amounts to a bit of "hypocrisy," for the simple reason that all Christians constitute the "spiritual estate"; all are "priests" before God.[23] To help illustrate this equality, Luther uses an analogy: if a king has ten sons, all ten have equal status as heirs, regardless of how rule of that kingdom would continue.[24] For Luther, serving God and serving our neighbors has the effect of leveling the ground between individual believers without regard to a person's social role. Calvin stands in fundamental agreement, holding the view that "no task" can be viewed as "base" or below human dignity, provided that the believer obey his or her "calling therein"; rather, that task will "shine" and be reckoned "very precious" in the sight of God.[25]

Again, in Scripture, work is the expression of the image of God and part of human design, not the result of sin's curse.[26] The *imago Dei* expresses itself in human creation through moral agency, reason and reflection, working with purpose, stewarding our abilities, service to

---

effect of urging people *away* from ordinary life and to the altar, as it were. This inclination, of course, fueled the monastic movement.

[22] Thomas Aquinas, *Summa Theologica* (Westminster: Christian Classics, 1981), II-II q. 182., a. 1.

[23] This language appears in Martin Luther's open letter *To the Christian Nobility of the German Nation Concerning the Reform of the Christian Estate* in *Luther's Works*, ed. James Atkinson (Philadelphia: Fortress Press, 1966), 44.

[24] Luther, *To the Christian Nobility*, 44:128.

[25] John Calvin, *Institutes of the Christian Religion*, ed. John T. McNeill, trans. Ford Lewis Battles (Louisville: WJK, 2006), III.10.6.

[26] See, for example, Gen 5:29.

others, and worship to our God. God works, creates, sustains, cultivates, and restores, and humans mirror his likeness. In the creation narrative, the divine mandate for humankind to "rule" over various aspects of the created order is recurring (Gen 1:26–28). As evidence of human beings sharing God's likeness, they are still described as "in the image of God" *after* the fall (Gen 9:6; cf. Col 3:10). In this vein, the language of the psalmist is instructive; he declares that God has "crowned" human beings with "glory and honor" (Ps 8:5). He even proclaims to God, "You made [humankind] ruler over the works of your hands; / you put everything under [their authority]" (8:6).

How we understand human labor depends on our reading of the creation narrative as well as how we interpret the curse described in Genesis 3. The meaning of work is anchored in work's inherent dignity, which in turn is anchored in the *imago Dei*. Neither the dignity of work nor our stewardship and cultivation of the created order has been eliminated by sin's curse; in the same way, childbirth and parenthood have neither been eliminated nor rendered unfulfilling as a result of the effects of the fall. Despite the pain of labor contractions in the childbearing process, children are perceived—almost universally—as good gifts of divine design, and as one of life's greatest and most satisfying delights.

The Need for a Theology of Work

In light of work's exalted place in Scripture, on the one hand, and the utterly despairing view of work displayed not only in society but in segments of the Christian church on the other, we stand before a dilemma—one that is massive in scope, perennial in nature, and tragic in its implications. For this reason, I cite—and forcefully reject—the position of Christian social thinker Jacques Ellul, laid out in his fascinating volume *Reason for Being*. Ellul claims:

> In the long run, work is not worth it: what a person achieves is immediately dissipated like smoke. Consequently, we are warned

[through Ecclesiastes] that work has no meaning or value in itself. It provides no justification for living . . . Work has meaning only through what it produces in the final analysis . . . [W]e have seen with [the writer of Ecclesiastes] that the things we can obtain through work (money and power) amount to just that: vanity. Through work we can neither enable humanity to progress nor change anything basic or decisive . . . Work is a necessity. It is no virtue, good, remedy, human expression, or revealer. It holds no value . . . [T]here is no relation of cause and effect between work, related to a person's qualities and effort, on the one hand, and the result, on the other . . . Thus all our work becomes utterly futile, and if we are successful, we have not deserved our reward.[27]

Lest one assume these statements appear out of context or are only in reference to the negative view of human labor that appears in qualified fashion in Ecclesiastes, Ellul's "Christian" perspective comes to expression elsewhere, and just as forcibly. In *The Ethics of Freedom*, Ellul writes that, based on his "cursory study of the Bible," work "is not presented as service to God." "It *has* to be done" as a pure necessity, and "the Bible is realistic enough not to overlay this necessity with superfluous spiritual ornamentation." To him, work is "the *painful lot* of all men but it is *not particularly important*." Moreover, work "has *no specific value*," and the Bible "never speaks of it as vocation"; rather, "work is *a result of the fall*." Alas, work constitutes "part of the divided, separate, and *alienated condition* of man"; and it is "an alienating factor, irrespective of social or economic conditions or of ideology." Finally, according to Ellul, "Jesus *never* calls upon anyone to work. On the contrary, he constantly takes the

---

[27] Jacques Ellul, *Reason for Being: A Meditation on Ecclesiastes*, trans. Joyce M. Hanks (Grand Rapids: Eerdmans, 1990), 93–96. Later Ellul is caught in a contradiction when he describes work as "a gift from God" (101). The contradiction and resultant confusion are strengthened by his qualification of this gift: "So we must work, not because work is *useful*, but because it is a gift!" (101, emphasis his).

men he calls *away* from their work." Therefore, Ellul concludes, we must accept work's "absurdity"; it has "no ultimate or transcendent value" and is only "that which makes our survival possible."[28]

These are serious claims, and they come from a serious thinker.[29] What's more, many people will affirm these claims, given their own experience in the workforce or in private life. Yet these claims stand counter to what Scripture teaches and are a loud reminder that many Christians' thinking about work is in need of a death and resurrection.

Ellul is by no means the only significant Christian voice advancing the mistaken view that work is a necessary evil. Those critical of the Protestant reformational attempt to anchor a theology of work in creation include Karl Barth,[30] Stanley Hauerwas,[31] Miroslav Volf,[32] and Gerrit de Kruijf.[33] While their various critiques contain partial truths, they both overlook or seriously misconstrue aspects of the traditional Protestant view of vocation and misunderstand the "kingdom of God," which is not

---

[28] Jacques Ellul, *The Ethics of Freedom* (Grand Rapids: Eerdmans, 1976), 495–506, emphasis mine. See also Jacques Ellul and David Lovekin, "From the Bible to a History of Non-Work," *Cross Currents* 35, no. 1 (1985): 43–48.

[29] In other contexts, Ellul has demonstrated remarkable perception and insight as a Christian thinker. See, for example, his *The Technological Society*, *The Humiliation of the Word*, and *The Subversion of Christianity*. All are brilliant and penetrating in their critique of modern society.

[30] See Karl Barth, *Church Dogmatics, Volumes 3 and 4*, ed. G. W. Bromiley, T. F. Torrance, and T. Forsyth and trans. A. T. Mackay et al. (Edinburgh: T&T Clark, 1961).

[31] See Stanley Hauerwas, "Work as Co-Creation: A Critique of a Remarkably Bad Idea," in *Co-Creation and Capitalism: John Paul II's Laborem Exercens*, ed. John Houck and Oliver Williams (Washington, DC: University Press of America, 1983), 42–58, reproduced in Stanley Hauerwas, *In Good Company: The Church as Polis* (Notre Dame, IN: University of Notre Dame Press, 1995), 109–24.

[32] See Miroslav Volf, *Work in the Spirit: Toward a Theology of Work* (Oxford: Oxford University Press, 1991).

[33] See Gerrit de Kruijf, *Ethiek onderweg: Acht Adviezen* (Zoetermeer, NL: Meinema, 2008). The title of this work translates to "Ethics along the Way: Eight Recommendations."

simply future but eternal (and thus applicable to the present). Several of these critiques warrant some response.

First, Hauerwas's criticisms take the form of a reaction to Pope John Paul II's 1981 encyclical on work, *Laborem Exercens*, which was delivered on the ninetieth anniversary of Leo XIII's encyclical *Rerum Novarum*. The theme of both encyclicals is human labor. Following John Paul's introduction, the encyclical contains four principal parts: (1) the subordination of work to the human person; (2) the primacy of the worker over the elements that condition the work environment; (3) the rights of the human person in light of socioeconomic and technological developments; and (4) human beings' union with Christ through their work.

Of all this Hauerwas writes, "A great chorus of praise has greeted Pope John Paul's encyclical, *Laborem Exercens*, but I cannot join it. *Laborem Exercens* is a disaster both in the general perspective it takes toward work as well as its specific arguments. I wish I could find a way to interpret the encyclical in a positive manner, but I find I cannot."[34] Hauerwas worries that attributing to work more significance than is warranted renders our efforts in the marketplace "idolatrous."[35]

The inaccuracy—which borders on recklessness—of the above judgment aside, Hauerwas's opposition to working as an expression of the *imago Dei* is anchored in at least three flawed assumptions: (1) the view that "co-creating" denies the fallenness of the work environment; (2) the view that Luther's rediscovered understanding of *vocatio* wrongly confers religious meaning on secular life, and (3) the view that economics is a "violent" (and hence often unjust) sphere of public activity, scarcely redeemable by Christian faith.[36] It is unfortunate that nowhere in this response to John Paul does one find Hauerwas engaging in theology proper, much less in a theology of work that mirrors some association to the creation

---

[34] Hauerwas, "Work as Co-Creation," 42.
[35] Hauerwas, 48.
[36] Economic "violence" is the pacifist Hauerwas's terminology.

narrative and the *imago Dei*. The thrust of Hauerwas's argument—work as "co-creation" is a "bad idea"—is itself rebutted by Pauline theology: "For we are God's coworkers" (1 Cor 3:9).[37]

The criticisms of Miroslav Volf, by contrast, are more substantive. Volf's "pneumatological theory of work" is rooted in his opposition to and rejection of a creation-oriented, vocation-centered understanding of work as the Reformers affirmed it.[38] Historic Christian theology affirms that the model of creation-fall-redemption-consummation must inform our theological perspective. Volf, however, insists that eschatology—and thus the consummated state—must be at the center of our theology of work.[39] Correlatively, Volf worries that Luther's understanding of work and vocation helps to preserve a static and unjust status quo in the workforce.[40] Hence, the reader readily senses Volf's seeming affinity with Marxist thinking and his strong accent on the "alienation" of the modern

---

[37] For a more scriptural perspective on co-creation, see Michael Novak, "The Lay Task of Co-Creation," in *On Moral Business: Classical and Contemporary Resources for Ethics in Economic Life*, ed. Max L. Stackhouse, et al. (Grand Rapids: Eerdmans, 1995), 903–8.

[38] Volf, *Work in the Spirit*.

[39] Strangely, Volf expressly argues that it is a "mistake" to attempt to formulate a "theology of work" by starting with biblical data (*Work in the Spirit*, 77, 159). Where one should then begin to construct a "pneumatological" understanding of work, as Volf does, is alas a mystery. Perhaps Volf himself does not need Scripture to develop his eschatological framework; perhaps "the Spirit" simply reveals it to him apart from biblical revelation. We can acknowledge, of course, that no full-blown systematic theology of work presents itself in Scripture. But the same can be said of ecclesiology or the sacraments or marriage or civil authority, and yet these are *central* to Christian theology.

[40] Volf identifies several "serious limitations" (107) of what he understands to be Luther's view. Among these are (1) its "indifference" toward "alienation" in work, (2) its ambiguity in adjudicating between spiritual and external callings, (3) its ideological misuse, (4) its inapplicability to a mobile, modern, technological society, and (5) its contributing to an almost "religious" view of work. Most of these are the result of Volf's anachronistic reading; he imports modern questions back into the early sixteenth century.

workplace.⁴¹ The Achilles' heel of Volf's position is twofold: (1) its failure to ground vocation in creation, and hence in design, and (2) the fact that it limits—if it does not reject—the possibility of redemption operating on this side of the eschaton, thus creating an unnecessary divide between creation and restoration. After all, properly viewed, redemption is not the abrogation or negation of creation but its renewal. Negating creation ends up depriving resurrection and redemption of their force and dynamic in this current world.⁴² The very doctrine of redemption in Christian theology informs us that what introduced pain, sorrow, and despair—mankind—becomes transformed—we might even say *transmuted*—by trust in the Second Adam (see 1 Cor 15:20–28). Volf's position, moreover, fails to recognize that redemption is continual and perpetual, as is creation. Correlatively, Volf's position negates the reality of common grace and providence. After all, providence and vocation go hand in hand.

As several thoughtful Christian writers have noted in their critiques of Volf's argument, to place eschatology rather than creation and redemption at the center of our theological framework is theologically and ethically deficient.⁴³ In truth, against Volf, a pneumatological under-

---

⁴¹ Some cultural historians—as well as theologians like Volf—have sought to lay blame for the problems of the modern work environment (for example, "alienation," isolation, fragmentation) at the feet of the Protestant Reformers, and chiefly Luther. However, there are two problems with this critique: (1) it overlooks developments in the early-modern and modern era and hence is anachronistic, and (2) the language of "alienation" in work is Marxist and not Christian. While I acknowledge the fact of technological development, changes in the workplace, and economic developments, human inclinations remain constant; they do not change, based on the *imago Dei*. Work is a perennial matter, even when it is variously conditioned, and thus needs to be addressed as such.

⁴² Oliver O'Donovan, *Resurrection and the Moral Order: An Outline for Evangelical Ethics* (Grand Rapids: Eerdmans, 1986), 15–19, has pressed this argument persuasively.

⁴³ See, for example, Lee Hardy's review of *Work in the Spirit* (Miroslav Volf), *Calvin Theological Journal* 28, no. 1 (1993): 191–96; Douglas J. Schuurman, "Creation, Eschaton, and Social Ethics: A Response to Volf," *Calvin Theological Journal* 30, no. 1 (1995): 144–58, whose interaction with Volf's basic argument

standing of work—that is, work in "the Spirit"—is far more susceptible to ideological error (which "spirit"?) than the vocational understanding of the Protestant Reformational tradition to which he reacts. The Reformational tradition has thorough scriptural support, being anchored in the doctrine of creation. At a practical level, one critic of Volf's position sagely points out the "already-but-not-yet" tension.[44] Reinhold Niebuhr would insist that "love and the Spirit"—so central to Volf's argument—may triumph over evil in the eschaton, but within unfolding history, where humans remain sinners, the political problem remains; only a foolish idealism would deny this. As illustration hereof, take, for example, the eschatological promises concerning peace and war found in Isaiah and Micah:

> [Nations] will beat their swords into plows
> and their spears into pruning knives.
> Nation will not take up the sword against nation,
> and they will never again train for war. (Isa 2:4; Mic 4:3)

> The wolf will dwell with the lamb,
> and the leopard will lie down with the goat.
> The calf, the young lion, and the fattened calf will be together;
> and a child will lead them.
> The cow and the bear will graze,
> their young ones will lie down together, . . .
> An infant will play beside the cobra's pit,
> and a toddler will put his hand into a snake's den. (Isa 11:6–8)

---

and critique are extensive; and John W. Taylor, "Labor of Love: The Theology of Work in First and Second Thessalonians," *Southwestern Journal of Theology* 59, no. 2 (Spring 2017): 201–18.

[44] Schuurman, "Creation, Eschaton, and Social Ethics," 155–58, points to Niebuhr's essay "The Ethic of Jesus and the Social Problem," in D. B. Robertson, ed., *Love and Justice: Selections from the Shorter Writings of Reinhold Niebuhr* (Louisville: WJK, 1957), 29–39, esp. 34–35.

These biblical images point to future, not present, realities. Purely eschatological, otherworldly thinking can be utopian and not realistic for this time in which we await Christ's return and the blessings it brings. Yes, there will indeed be triumph over evil in the eschaton; but in the meantime, the political problem remains. The Christian may not dispense with the difficult task of working for the common good in the face of evil and injustice.

We can agree with Volf that a future transformation will occur; however, an emphasis on continuity and restoration is not a denial of newness or transformation.[45] The eschatological perspective tends to deny or ignore the incarnational reality of God's work in the present.[46] The truth is that Christians cannot dispense with working for—and preserving—the common good. Christian ethics, after all, concerns the present life and the broken way the universe is, not the eschaton.[47] The most important element in promoting the common good is our individual and collective work.

In the end, Volf fails to interact with the totality of Scripture; hence, his "theology of work" is really no theology properly understood. He cuts off the Judeo-Christian understanding of human labor at its knees.[48]

---

[45] As O'Donovan, *Resurrection and the Moral Order*, 56, has judiciously framed it, "The eschatological transformation of the world is neither the mere repetition of the created world nor its negation."

[46] To illustrate, "The Word became flesh and dwelt among us. We observed his glory" (John 1:14). Christ continues his incarnational reality in the world through his people (see Col 1:27).

[47] To be rooted in the present does not mean we are reduced to Stoicism or fatalism or the bondage of the world system.

[48] Lutheran theologian Marc Kolden, who has written extensively about vocation, describes Volf's *Work in the Spirit* as "flawed" in its understanding of work and vocation. According to Kolden, "Volf misunderstands Luther's view by reading him through the eyes of reactionary nineteenth-century German Lutheranism," with the result that Volf fails to observe "the dynamic possibilities" in Luther's notion of vocation that are anchored in the created order. Marc Kolden, "Work and Meaning: Some Theological Reflections," *Interpretation* 48, no. 3 (1994): 271.

Against Volf, it is not work that is transformed; it is people.[49] Moreover, our world is *God's* world, the world of God's creation—in all of its dimensions and parts.[50]

A final noteworthy critique that underscores human labor's "regretful necessity" comes from Dutch ethicist Gerrit G. de Kruijf. Work, he argues, is necessary for survival and at best a relative good, a means of sustaining life; but it is not a joy, and this conclusion is based on his reading of Genesis 3. Work should therefore not be associated with idealistic notions of vocation, he says, which are rooted in a "romantic ideal of self-realization."[51] Social institutions, moreover, remain structures of power and hence possess and promote no intrinsic value, he believes; they may benefit some people but will disadvantage others, even to the point of being oppressive. What is more, work's value will be viewed differently around the world, based on social and economic realities.

While de Kruijf's is not a household name in North America and remains unknown outside of narrower Reformed theological circles, his position deserves mention because of that against which he writes. Particularly troublesome to de Kruijf is what he believes to be a tendency in recent Dutch history toward the theocratic temptation, that is, a Christianizing of the government and the people for the purposes of directing social life according to Christian conformity.[52] In response, we may simultaneously agree with de Kruijf in his concern regarding the

---

[49] In the end, Volf's sympathetic critique of Marxism (*Work in the Spirit*, 35–45, 55–68) ends up making a mockery of his emphasis on the "new creation" (88–97).

[50] Hardy, in his review of Volf (see n. 43 above), correctly points out that to use eschatology rather than creation as a starting point is "parasitic" (195), since eschatology is predicated on creation.

[51] de Kruijf, *Ethiek onderweg*, 41.

[52] Gerrit G. de Kruijf links this tendency with the interplay between historic Reformed theology and Dutch culture. See, for example, his essay "Is Prophetic Witness the Appropriate Mode of Christian Participation in Public Discourse in the Netherlands?" *Teologiese Studies* 66, no. 1 (2010), https://hts.org.za/index.php/hts/article/view/781/1151, and de Kruijf, "The Christian in the Crowded

theocratic temptation and take issue with his deficient view of work—a view that severs work from the anchor of human vocation. Criticism of de Kruijf is rooted in the theological reality that creation and not the fall, as I have established, is constitutive of work's inherent worth and dignity. Right understanding is essential in helping people confidently discern what specific path each should follow in response to God. That is, vocation concerns not only the fact or the event of one's calling but the object and trajectory of that particular calling as well.[53]

Interestingly, it is from a fellow Dutchman that a more constructive—and biblically-grounded—perspective on work is offered. We find this century-old perspective in the writings of Abraham Kuyper, whose remarkable public career spanned working as a Parliamentarian, founding two newspapers, founding a political party, founding a university, and serving as the Dutch prime minister (1901–1905)—all of this in addition to his work as a serious theologian.[54]

Theologically, Kuyper's Calvinism presumed the existence of three autonomous spheres of sovereignty: society, state, and church. The autonomy of these spheres is relative and not absolute; that is to say, there is interaction back and forth between them, which in the end permits the redemptive influence of Christian faith outside of the church. For Kuyper, it is divine providence which impels and guides us toward all spheres of life. Given God's providential care, Kuyper believed that Christians are called to preserve, cultivate, and improve the created order.[55] Kuyper's

---

Public Square: The Hidden Tension between Prophecy and Democracy," *Annual of the Society of Christian Ethics* 11 (1991): 21–42.

[53] See Pieter Vos, "The Relative Good of Work: Reconsidering Vocation Eschatologically," *Christian Higher Education* 16, nos. 1–2 (2017): 19.

[54] Kuyper's theological work retains remarkable influence in some Reformed theological circles.

[55] While Kuyper's emphasis on sphere sovereignty and cultural involvement permeates virtually all of his writings, they are particularly concentrated in *Het sociale vraagstuk en de chrustelijke religiee* (Amsterdam: J. A. Wormser, 1891). An English translation of this work, "The Social Question and the Christian Religion," can be found in Jordan J. Ballor, ed., *Makers of Modern Christian Social*

convictions, it should be emphasized in light of de Kruijf's concerns about the theocratic temptation, did not arise from theocratic vision; they issued, rather, out of a vision of principled pluralism. Kuyper, then, and not de Kruijf, furnishes a more accurate perspective on work and on a social environment in which the laborer might flourish.[56]

The problem, as this chapter argues, is not work itself; rather, it is work without meaning and purpose, as observed in the book of Ecclesiastes: "What does a person get with all his work and all his efforts that he labors at under the sun? For all his days are filled with grief, and his occupation is sorrowful; even at night, his mind does not rest" (Eccl 2:22–23).[57] Finding satisfaction in one's work is the opposite—the very antithesis—of pursuing the wind, to follow the language of the writer of Ecclesiastes further. In fact, where human beings experience meaning and purpose, they can bear drudgery, when and where it occurs.

In surveying the literary landscape, one might notice a booming industry that has emerged in the last several decades to address workplace spirituality, broadly construed, so that people might find some degree of meaning and/or spiritual satisfaction in their work. Many of these titles are familiar; after all, we see them regularly in airports and bookstores:

- *A Passion for Success*
- *The 7 Habits of Highly Effective People*
- *The Corporate Mystic*

Thought: Leo XIII and Abraham Kuyper on the Social Question (Grand Rapids: Acton Institute Press, 2016), 47–117.

[56] See Kuyper's writings on common grace, which have been translated and incorporated into the "Abraham Kuyper Collected Works in Public Theology" series, produced by the Acton Institute: Abraham Kuyper, *Common Grace: God's Gifts for a Fallen World*, 3 vols., ed. Jordan J. Ballor, Stephen J. Grabill, and J. Daryl Charles and trans. Nelson D. Kloostermann and Ed van der Maas (Grand Rapids: Acton Institute and Lexham Press, 2015, 2019, 2020).

[57] See Chapter 5, "A 'Wisdom' Perspective on Work," which examines Ecclesiastes and the apparent meaninglessness or futility of human labor in further detail.

- *The Power of I Am*
- *Awakening the Buddha Within*
- *Jesus, CEO: Ancient Wisdom for Visionary Leadership*
- *Primary Greatness: The 12 Levers of Success*
- *The Monday Connection: A Spirituality of Competence, Affirmation, and Support in the Workplace*
- *The Management Methods of Jesus*
- *Next Level Thinking: 10 Powerful Thoughts for a Successful and Abundant Life*
- *The Path: Creating Your Mission Statement for Work and for Life*[58]
- *The Seven Spiritual Laws of Success*
- *Every Day a Friday: How to Be Happier 7 Days a Week*[59]

From a distinctly Christian standpoint, though, what we need is not another self-help or pop-psychology approach to finding meaning and fulfillment in the workplace but a serious and sustained theology of work—which should come from our seminaries, divinity schools, training institutions, and local church teachers. After all, as sure as the Word of

---

[58] See especially chapter 8 of *The Path*: "The Eight Action Steps for Success."

[59] While many of the titles in this wider self-help or pop-psychology genre seem to be a mix of the religious and the secular, some are conspicuous in their borrowing from religious principles yet bleaching of the transcendent. Two examples of note are Richard J. Leider and David A. Shapiro, *Work Reimagined: Uncover Your Calling* (San Francisco: Berrett-Koehler, 2015), and Sasha and David Chanoff, *From Crisis to Calling: Finding Your Moral Center in the Toughest Decisions* (San Francisco: Berrett-Koehler, 2016).

In both volumes, the reader is admonished to explore the inner self in order to discover true meaning and purpose. Discovery, however, occurs wholly apart from any reference to the divine. On Leider's website, his biographical section reads, "Everything that exists has a purpose. We were born for a reason and we live in a purposeful world. Every one of us has unique gifts and a purpose to use those gifts to contribute value to that world. My purpose is to help you to UNLOCK YOUR PURPOSE." (See https://richardleider.com/). How Leider knows these things—for example, that there *is* purpose to everything—we are not told. Nevertheless, here we see representative parasitic use of theological (i.e., revealed) truth.

the Creator took on flesh and dwelt among us (see John 1:14), the church is the incarnation of that reality to the surrounding world. Jerusalem and Athens *do* have to do with one another, contrary to the very public argument set forth by the increasingly sectarian early church father Tertullian, for whom the answer to his famous rhetorical question—"What does Jerusalem have to do with Athens?"—was "little or nothing."[60]

In terms of Christians' social witness, the two realms have everything to do with one another. In fairness, Tertullian was objecting primarily to what he perceived as intellectual currents of his day. "Athens," of course, represented intellectual culture and the life of the mind, while "Jerusalem" was emblematic of our heritage in Christ. The divide, he argued, was clear; after all, he reasoned, we will not be judged on the last day on the basis of how much worldly wisdom or cultural refinement we have assimilated or how much we have accomplished. He was questioning the relative worth of those things that typically comprise the present life.[61]

---

[60] Tertullian's rhetorical question appears in the late-first-century work *Prescription against Heretics*. An English translation thereof can be found in volume 3 of *The Ante-Nicene Fathers*, ed. A. Roberts and J. Donaldson (New York: Charles Scribner's Sons, 1903), as well as online: https://www.newadvent.org/fathers/0311.htm.

Much is made by some of the "social distance" between the early Christians and the surrounding world, but Tertullian is not necessarily representative. To illustrate, by the late second century, Christians were already present in the Roman Legions. Even the pacifist Tertullian, in his *Apology* (which predates *Prescription*), acknowledges, "We are sailors along with yourselves; we serve in the army; we engage in farming and trading; in addition, we share with you our arts; we place the products of our labor at your service. How we can appear worthless for your business, when we live with you and depend on you, I do not know." Again, Tertullian's views on Christian involvement in the public sphere, which changed markedly over his lifetime, should not be taken as representative or normative, even when they are instructive.

[61] Few have critiqued Tertullian's stance with greater insight and clarity than John F. Crosby, "Education and the Mind Redeemed," *First Things* 18 (December 1991): 23–28.

Still, the difficulty with the Tertullian mindset—at least that of the later, increasingly sectarian Tertullian—is that it is fundamentally escapist in character. Like Volf's, its focus is eschatological to the extent that it severs any meaningful allegiance to the temporal order in the interest of remaining "faithful" to the heavenly. An unbalanced eschatology places an unhealthy focus on our removal from creation, as we focus on the heavenly to the point that we neglect the idea of a restoration of creation.[62] But believers' dual citizenship, even when our ultimate allegiance is to the city of God, nevertheless requires that we take our responsibilities to the city of man in earnest. A proper eschatological perspective holds the temporal and the eternal in a proper tension. This posture, in turn, allows the Christian community to avoid succumbing to the entrapments of its cultural surroundings or fleeing the world altogether and thus eschewing responsible participation. The sovereign Lord Almighty places each of us in particular cultural contexts for a purpose (see Eph 2:10), so we must take our stewardship of those callings seriously.

Yes, in terms of the church's social witness—and the marketplace is by far the widest realm in which our witness will be felt—the two spheres, Athens and Jerusalem, have everything to do with one another, provided we confess an ultimate allegiance to the city of God.[63]

---

[62] The church needs a comprehensive vision. See, in this regard, Brian J. Walsh and J. Richard Middleton, *The Transforming Vision: Shaping a Christian World View* (Downers Grove, IL: InterVarsity, 1984); Albert M. Wolters, *Creation Regained: Biblical Basics for a Reformational Worldview* (Grand Rapids: Eerdmans, 2005), and Paul Marshall and Lela Gilbert, *Heaven Is Not My Home: Living in the Now of God's Creation* (Nashville: Word, 1998).

[63] If this were not the case, then Christians, following their conversion, would simply be removed from the face of the earth and taken immediately into the direct presence of God. Elsewhere I have attempted to press this basic, though frequently contested, theological reality. See the preface of J. Daryl Charles, *Wisdom's Work: Essays on Ethics, Vocation, and Culture* (Grand Rapids: Acton Institute, 2019), vii-xv. See also Marshall and Gilbert, *Heaven Is Not My Home*, which counters the Tertullian error in practical ways.

Why Work?: The Matter of Meaning

Only recently and by accident did I stumble upon Viktor Frankl's brief, significant work titled *Man's Search for Meaning*.[64] Frankl (1905–1997) survived stays in two of the Nazis' most notorious death camps, Auschwitz-Birkenau and Dachau. His closest family members—father, mother, brother, and wife—were sent to the gas ovens; only a sister avoided that fate. Having been stripped naked, left cold and hungry, and forced to exist in bestial conditions, Frankl nevertheless survived and went on to practice psychotherapy in Vienna after the war. He was a student of Freud.[65]

Frankl writes that in his practice he would sometimes ask his patients who were suffering from various forms of torment why they did not commit suicide. From their answers, he would derive therapeutic strategies to suit them. Frankl observed three general types of reasoning among all these patients. For some, love of their family members prevented them from ending their lives. For others, lingering memories of the past served as an obstacle. But for yet others, there was a sense of responsibility to use, and not waste, their lives and talents. Frankl was especially intrigued by this third type of reasoning. For those who held it, life seemed worthwhile, even while they were facing dreadful conditions. In light of this, which accorded with his own observations and experience as a former prisoner, Frankl came to believe that survival is made possible not only by relationships but by finding meaning in present suffering.[66] Bearing

---

[64] The edition I am using is Viktor E. Frankl, *Man's Search for Meaning* (Boston: Beacon, 1959). The title of the German original, which appeared in 1946, is *Ein Psychologe erlebt das Konzentrationslager* ("A Psychologist's Experience in a Concentration Camp").

[65] Interestingly, whereas Freud believed that anxiety is rooted in the sphere of the sexual and/or the pleasurable, Frankl found meaning through suffering.

[66] For Frankl, survival in the camp was made tolerable by several other factors too, including religious conviction, a "grim sense of humor," and "healing" glimpses of nature. Frankl, *Man's Search for Meaning*, xi.

suffering, he concluded, is "a genuine inner achievement," anchored in life's intrinsic meaning and purpose.[67]

A major revelation for Frankl was to learn that even in a concentration camp the human person can preserve a vestige of spiritual freedom. Conversely, a prisoner who saw no meaning, purpose, or hope was doomed.[68] But meaning, Frankl observed, had to be discovered personally by each prisoner. An important aspect of Frankl's experience and his later therapeutic work can be summarized this way: suffering is not mere suffering where meaning and purpose can be identified.[69]

As one who has spent most of his career teaching in a Christian liberal arts environment, I confess my concern that the Christian community generally fails to help adults who struggle with the depression and despair that lead toward suicidal tendencies. Though most people's despair cannot compare to that experienced by Frankl and his peers, suicide rates in our day are rising in extraordinary fashion. Perhaps even readers of this volume have wondered, *Why not end it all, since I see no way out of my present darkness?*

This chapter's argument is not an attempt to offer counseling or therapy, nor is it about suffering per se. Rather, it takes with utmost seriousness Frankl's discovery that daily life is rendered more valuable where meaning and purpose are identified. Specifically, it addresses the common temptation almost all of us have had to throw a particular job or occupation in the toilet, given its utterly dissatisfying and unfulfilling character. Foundationally, this chapter concerns our attempts as Christian believers to find clarity regarding our vocational callings in a way that ennobles and inspires the daily and redeems the ordinary. That clarity begins by

---

[67] Frankl, 66.

[68] The phases of prisoners' reaction to their treatment, according to Frankl, were shock, followed by delusions of reprieve, occasional suicidal thoughts, emotional apathy or embracing death as self-defense, self-preservation, and, finally, either giving up or clinging to meaning.

[69] Frankl writes, "Man's main concern is not to gain pleasure or to avoid pain but rather to see a meaning in his life" in *Man's Search for Meaning*, 115. Frankl describes his therapeutic method as logotherapy.

coming to terms with—and embracing—the dignity and value of work and our places in the created order based on divine providence. Should we fail to do that, the "nine-tenths" of our lives spent in the marketplace—*at work*—may well be spent in futility.[70]

Previously, I cited Dorothy Sayers's provocative essay "Why Work?" Underlying her position as a Christian apologist was the fundamental conviction that people do not really have a problem with work per se; rather, people struggle with the perception that work—and particularly, the work in which they personally engage—has no meaning or purpose. The greater question which Sayers addresses, as her response to the question "Why Work?," then, is essentially, "Well, why do we live?"

In very practical though quite different ways, both Frankl and Sayers aid us as we struggle to answer the *why* question of human existence. My own experience and observations from thirty years of teaching at both the undergraduate and graduate levels (aside from my experience in the local church and in doing public-policy research) convince me that finding meaning behind it all needs recovery in our day. Such can apply not only to college students, who become increasingly anxious about major life decisions as they move toward graduation, but to those of us who are at mid-career stages of life and agonize over changing jobs, major moves, and reconciling the demands of our careers with family, church involvement, and personal interests. Even those of us who are at or nearing retirement age struggle with meaning and purpose questions, wondering how or whether we should invest ourselves since the bulk of a day's activity will not always come with a paycheck.

"Retirement," in fact, is a particularly relevant case in point as we contemplate the meaning of our days. Why? Because in our cultural context it is almost universally viewed as a *release* from work. However, this

---

[70] In chapter 5, I probe this realm of "futility" and meaninglessness in connection with the sphere of work as it is mirrored in the book of Ecclesiastes. To the surprise of many, however, "meaninglessness" is not the message of Ecclesiastes; it is, rather, the fruit of a false view of ultimate reality.

perspective lacks any biblical warrant. Scripture nowhere releases human beings from their labors and service to others as long as they can breathe. Our lives, though finite, are part of something transcendent, that is, the purposes of God. That means we do not retire from our true callings; we do not retire from public service and from contributing to the common good. Our gifts and abilities are to be used until we are either called from this life or can no longer employ them due to declining health.

Though we hear little on the matter, retirement as conceived in Western societies should not bring an end to work or serving others; in fact, it should simply open a new phase of one's calling. If this sounds idealistic, consider what often happens when people retire from their decades-long careers. Many just choose a new form of busyness, working part-time and even full-time long after they've stepped down from long-held positions. Why? Because that nagging sense a retiree gets of "I really must find something productive to do with my time" is itself a reminder that human beings are *created* for work. There really is meaning and purpose to productivity, regardless of its nature and irrespective of whether there is a financial incentive accompanying it.

Interestingly, numerous studies point to the fact that most people do find at least a measure of meaning in work, and for this reason continue to work after retirement age.[71] These studies share widespread agreement in their findings. Here are some examples:

- Research generally indicates that incentive, psychological motivation, and creativity do not decline with age.

---

[71] Until the early twentieth century, retirement was uncommon. One significant factor in its growth was a shift from a largely agrarian, family-oriented economy to a more industrial one. In addition, the creation of Social Security in 1935 had the effect of institutionalizing retirement, during which time the retirement age dropped officially from seventy-three to sixty-three. On the broader effects of this development in the US, see Gary Burtless and Joseph F. Quinn, "Retirements Trends and Policies to Encourage Work among Older Americans," in *Ensuring Health and Income Security for an Aging Workforce*, ed. Peter P. Budetti et al. (Kalamazoo: Upjohn Institute, 2001), 375–415.

- Even when a mix of reasons contributes to people working beyond retirement age, nonfinancial benefits—being useful and productive, finding fulfillment, being socially engaged, and contributing to the needs of others—are far more important.
- Four out of five (80 percent) of workers aged fifty or older have never retired, while 75 percent expect to work after retirement. Roughly half of today's retirees continue to work.
- Those working beyond retirement age tend to work for almost another decade.
- Those working in retirement are highly satisfied and engaged in their work, with 50 percent saying that they are very satisfied and 40 percent saying they are moderately satisfied.
- Those working in retirement remain healthier longer.
- The majority of working retirees report working full-time and wanting to work the same (or more) hours in the future.
- The negative effects of retirement begin to appear after the first few years of ceasing to work.
- The impact of work and employment on the richness of social networks and social connectedness is considerable. Early retirement appears to have negative effects on the breadth and intensity of social relationships.
- Many working retirees work for a nonprofit (40 percent) or do volunteer work (25 percent), indicating that this phase increases opportunities for service.
- A surprising percentage of working retirees (39 percent) are entrepreneurial, owning their own businesses or being self-employed.[72]

---

[72] My sources for this data analysis are Melissa Brown et al., "Working in Retirement: A 21st Century Phenomenon," study published by the Families and Work Institute (2010), https://www.familiesandwork.org/research/2010/working-in-retirement-a-21st-century-phenomenon; Axel Börsch-Supan and Morten Schuth, "Early Retirement, Mental Health, and Social Networks," in David A. Wise, ed., *Discoveries in the Economics of Aging* (Chicago: University of Chicago Press, 2014), 225–50; "Work In Retirement: Myths and Motivations,"

Scripture promises that our endeavors, however long we live and regardless of whether we are paid, have enduring value. For one, our service to our neighbors in a career or volunteer context is service to God—and thus worship. Second, a Christian's loving, obedient work and service will be rewarded. Paul promised our "labor in the Lord is not in vain" (1 Cor 15:58), a statement that is typically "spiritualized" by most Christian readers. The very context of these words—rewards for earthly endeavors—excludes this kind of interpretation. Our efforts on earth count.

According to the *Catechism of the Catholic Church*, human work "honors the Creator's gifts and the talents received from him." In work, the person "exercises and fulfills in part the potential inscribed in his nature." "Work," therefore, "is for man, not man for work."[73] The implications of this statement—"Work is for man," and not the reverse—are important. The *imago Dei* is what grants dignity, sanctity, and meaning to human beings. An awareness of these gifts guards us against adopting various forms of materialist reductionism, like metaphysical naturalism, Marxist atheism, or postmodern nihilism. Therefore, the value of a proper understanding of both material and nonmaterial reality which inhere in creation and redemption cannot be overstated. It guides our engagement with and participation in the world.

Stewardship and Incarnational Reality

At the heart of Christian presence in the world lies the cultural mandate that is based on our design. Humankind is to express the Creator's likeness—creating and producing, tending and nurturing, cultivating and

---

a study published by Merrill Lynch and Age Wave, https://www.shrm.org/ResourcesAndTools/hr-topics/benefits/Documents/MLWM_Work-in-Retirement_2014.pdf; and Gabriel Heller-Sahlgren, "Retirement Blues" (2017), https://ssrn.com/abstract=2741815.

[73] *Catechism of the Catholic Church* (Washington, DC: United States Catholic Conference, 1994), nos. 2427–2428.

developing, extending and working toward the redemption of the created order. Based on the doctrines of creation, providence, redemption, and incarnation, we humans are still to steward all of creation, utilizing all the resources God has given to us. Our work, which expresses itself in and through our individual callings, serves as a vehicle through which we can bring redemption to the world in ways social, cultural, and spiritual.

For this reason, and against the Tertullian mindset previously discussed, we must take human culture seriously. Therefore, any theological framework or rationale that calls us *away* from the world, society, or the marketplace is aberrant and a denial of historic Christian faith.[74] The realities of providence, incarnation, and redemption lead us neither to pronounce a wholesale judgment on the world and curse it, nor to flee from it, nor to isolate ourselves within it. At the same time, the Christian community must not succumb to the temptation to idolize culture or become absorbed into the world around us so that we are scarcely distinct from it. Nevertheless, based on the fact of creation, the development and extension of human culture is, quite simply, part of humanity's DNA; it is part of bearing the image of God. This mandate is confirmed throughout Scripture, which reiterates that *all things* belong to Christ through both creation and redemption.[75] We believers must not simply wait until the eschaton has arrived in order to invest ourselves in God's redemptive purposes.

We are to offer ourselves in service to God and to others, investing the gifts and talents he gives us in strategic ways. We trust—and wholly expect—that doors of opportunity for service will continually present themselves throughout our lives so that through our ownership of those chances, redemptive light might shine into the created order. Indeed, when my own efforts join those of millions of other believers—yes, in the context of our families and in our relationships but also in the marketplace, where so much of life unfolds—there is manifest a "wonderful,

---

[74] See Christ's prayer for his followers in John 17:15.
[75] See, for example, John 1:1–3; Eph 1:10; Col 1:15–20; and Heb 1:2.

grand interconnectedness of the Holy Spirit" that puts the biblical metaphors of salt and light into action.[76]

Thus far I have placed considerable emphasis on the doctrines of creation and redemption. Rarely, however, is the doctrine of incarnation developed in their light.[77] And yet creation and redemption are magnified by the doctrine of incarnation. If Christians truly believe that because of the ongoing presence of the *imago Dei* we are still under the commission to develop, expand, shape, and mold the world for his glory, then it follows that just as the eternal Logos put on flesh, his people can carry on his redemptive work in part by incarnating the life of Christ in all corners of society. What needs redeeming and restoring is not merely the soulish dimension of human nature, after all, but the totality of human existence in its composite unity. Reverencing the Creator, then, entails not only nonmaterial reality but material reality as well.[78]

There is value in that which is natural, human, and earthly. I say that because the heavens and the earth, representative of the whole created order, "are not destined for an eternal ash-heap, but for a transformation."[79] When the apostle Paul speaks in Romans 8 of the transformation of the

---

[76] So Harry Blamires, *The Will and the Way: A Study of Divine Providence and Vocation* (New York: Macmillan, 1957), 62.

[77] Here I am distinguishing between the doctrine of the incarnation—Christ's taking on human flesh—and the use of the word "incarnation" to refer to the way the life of God is to be continually revealed and fleshed out through God's people. The present discussion focuses on this latter use.

[78] Marshall, *Heaven Is Not My Home*, 11–12, minces no words in this regard. He says that to believe that the body and the material realm will eventually pass away never to rise again is, quite simply, "heresy" and wholly unbiblical. Indeed, the very Christian creeds which we confess speak of "the resurrection of the body," just as Scripture teaches that there will be "a new heaven and a new earth." The material realm matters.

[79] John Courtney Murray, *We Hold These Truths: Catholic Reflections on the American Proposition* (New York: Sheed and Ward, 1960), 190. Murray stands against the popularity of what he calls an "eschatological humanism," the essential character of which is to diminish the importance of the created order because of hyper-focus on the arrival of the eschaton.

created order, he observes that "creation itself will also be set free" and brought into a "glorious freedom" at Christ's return. This is the language of renewal and transformation, not destruction (see Rom 8:18–25). Yes, all of creation will become "new"; but at the same time, we will still recognize it as God's good creation. Wonderfully familiar, yet minus all the effects of sin. Thanks to the already-but-not-yet tension Christ's resurrection has set in place, restoration of the created order and incarnational reality are occurring in the present (in the already) through providence and common grace based on Christ's mediating work, even as they will be completed in the future (in the not yet).

The doctrine of incarnation lies at the center of the cultural mandate as each successive generation of Christian believers wrestles afresh with how to translate their convictions in meaningful ways.[80] And as we engage in this struggle and live within the already-but-not-yet tension, wisdom and creativity are needed. While there is continuity from generation to generation with the historic Christian tradition[81] in terms of our message and the nature of truth, there will always necessarily be discontinuity in terms of our methods and strategies. For example, the strategies of evangelism that worked in a previous generation may be ineffectual today, and therefore, inapplicable. Given this, we should continually expect the Holy Spirit to inspire new methods in every successive generation. In fact, it is incumbent on us to adapt creativity to the surrounding culture in ways that are meaningful to that context. Creativity is a wonderful thing when it is divinely inspired, for it has a divine precedent: God the Creator took on flesh (see John 1:1–5, 14). As sure as God chooses to communicate to us through human language, the challenge before us is to connect with fellow human beings in ways that are both relevant and faithful to the gospel.

---

[80] The language of "cultural mandate" is not intended to mirror a sense of triumphalism. Even where the Christian community is persecuted, the reality of creation and redemption still applies. How the church is to express itself under such conditions, however, is a different question.

[81] The Latin word *traditio* means "that which is to be delivered or passed on." Thus, every generation of Christians is responsible for what we have inherited.

One example of the sort I have in mind comes from the life of Paul, the "apostle to the Gentiles" (Rom 11:13). In 1 Corinthians 9 we find him stating his philosophy of ministry. Consider the manner in which he chooses to engage his contemporaries. He observes:

> Even though I am free before all people, I've made myself a servant to all, in order to persuade some. To the Jews I've become as a Jew, in order to persuade Jews . . . And to those who are outside the [Jewish] law, I've become the same, in order to persuade those outside the law. To the weak I've become weak, in order to persuade the weak. I have become all things to all people, in order that by all means I might persuade some. (1 Cor 9:19–22, my translation)

"I have become all things to all people." That means Paul adapted or accommodated himself to his surroundings in order to be persuasive, in order to be effective.[82]

Anyone who has lived in a foreign culture for an extended period knows precisely why accommodation is so important. As a stranger in a strange land, either one must find touchpoints to the host culture or one will be largely ignored. In fact, no one who lives in a foreign culture will be effective or successful in any endeavor—or taken seriously—if he or she fails to learn how to speak the language. Mastering it demonstrates to those in the host culture that they and their culture are valuable. This principle of seeking meaningful connectivity, quite simply, is nonnegotiable from the standpoint of sharing the Christian faith, since human culture is the vehicle through which truth is expressed. Incarnation, as it turns out, is at the heart of stewardship.[83]

---

[82] Accommodation, of course, can be positive or negative. It is only a virtue when and where it is motivated by faithfulness to Christ.

[83] In virtually all my classes at the college and university level through the years, I have challenged students who sensed that they might be living or working abroad to engage in a *minimum of two years* of language study before heading abroad.

Connecting with the culture of which we are a part, in order that we might bear influence on that cultural context, is our regular task in the marketplace. No daily routine there, in fact, lacks the dignity of being patterned after God's work, as Keller and Alsdorf remind us:

> No business megadeal or public policy initiative is so lofty that it can transcend God's patterns . . . for work. What's more, God has not left us alone to discover how and why we are to cultivate his creation; instead, he gives us a clear purpose for our work and faithfully calls us into it.[84]

But do we understand the daily routine as part of our stewarding of the created order?

An Anatomy of Stewardship: Looking More Closely

Not surprisingly, the notion of stewardship surfaces conspicuously in our Lord's teaching and specifically in his use of the wisdom tradition and parables. One such parable, that of the talents in Matt 25:14–30, is particularly worthy of our attention. A few comments on the rules of parabolic teaching and storytelling in the ancient wisdom tradition, however, are in order.

First, parables arise from daily, real-life situations, unlike allegories.[85] They represent personal encounters with people in typical situations, challenging the hearer in ways that abstract talk simply cannot. Second, they always involve contrast, pitting the wise against the foolish, the just against the unjust, or virtue against vice. Third, they frequently employ the rule of three. For example, there are three travelers in the parable

---

[84] Keller and Alsdorf, *Every Good Endeavor*, 52.

[85] In an allegory like Bunyan's *Pilgrim's Progress*, every detail has a particular figurative or spiritual meaning. The parable, by comparison, has one essential point; its details simply contribute to that teaching. There was a tendency among some in the early church to approach parables as allegories. This tendency persisted into the medieval era.

of the good Samaritan, three excuse-makers in the parable of the great supper, and three stewards who are given various talents and investment responsibility in the parable of the talents.[86] Fourth, they typically follow the rule of climax, whereby the spotlight falls on the last person or action; this is especially the case in the parable of the talents. And finally, parables always seek to evoke a response—for example, "What do *you* think?" or "He who has ears to hear, *let him hear*" or "See, judge for *yourselves*."[87]

In reference to the Matthew 25 text, it should be noted that in the New Testament era, a talent was a unit of coinage that possessed considerable value. In present-day terms, a talent would be worth much. The five-talent person might possess, say, anywhere between $25,000 and $250,000, the two-talent between $10,000 and $100,000, and the one-talent between $5,000 and $50,000, depending on how the stock market, local economies, or other factors might affect it.[88] The precise amounts, however, are not the focus since the parable is about faithfulness as a steward, not simply finance.[89]

Though Matthew has contextualized this parable in material intended to speak first to Israel's leaders on the eve of Christ's crucifixion, its implications apply in general terms to the timeless economics of faith

---

[86] A parallel adaptation is found in Luke 19:11–27. There ten stewards are called by the nobleman although three, as in Matthew's account, are highlighted.

[87] Emphasis mine. In the words of George A. Buttrick, *The Parables of Jesus* (New York: Harper & Bros., 1928), xxi, parables "arouse the imagination," "smite the conscience," and "move the will."

[88] I derive these various amounts from assorted New Testament commentaries, most of which differ on the details but are united on the wider meaning.

[89] This parable must not be used to argue for economic prosperity or a prosperity gospel as is done in some modern circles of the Christian church. It does not concern itself with success as most North Americans understand it either. While its original context situates it between the parable of the ten virgins and Jesus's promise of the coming of the Son of Man, and hence constitutes a warning to Israel's leaders that the Son of Man will come back to judge, it does nevertheless underscore how the true disciple of the kingdom—the steward—is to live. Hence, it has both a near and an extended application.

and stewardship. It touches on demonstrating faithfulness in small things leading to faithfulness in larger things; use and misuse (or even nonuse!) of what has been given to us; and use, abuse, or nonuse of authority entrusted to us. Consider these points:

1. The master gives differing gifts. By extension, human beings as stewards have differing talents, all of which ultimately belong not to them but to the master. Nevertheless, service is not compulsory. Yet, note the language: the master *calls* them and *entrusts* to them—that is, he puts them in charge in such a way as to exhibit trust toward his servants.

2. The master goes away for an extended, unspecified period ("a long time," v. 19). The servants do not know when he will return, but it is assumed that his return is not imminent. Perhaps the third, unwise steward assumed that the master's return would be thus, contributing to his being inactive. In any case, his inactivity incurs the master's wrath.

3. What matters in the parable is not the gift per se or its quantity. The master gives differing talents to different stewards, in accordance with the parable's interesting language: "depending on each one's ability" (v. 15). What matters is *how* each steward uses whatever has been given.

4. The master does not require from a steward what that particular steward does not possess; what he requires, rather, is that each person use to the fullest whatever was entrusted.

5. Serving (v. 14) is the guiding motivation for use of the various gifts; serving, in fact, is the essence of being a steward.

6. Two of the three stewards put their talents right to work, trading on their talents and doubling their investments (vv. 16–17). The third essentially did nothing with his (v. 18).

7. Two of the three stewards receive commendation (vv. 21 and 23) and rewards for their work and service, which is said to be "well done." They are commended as "good and faithful." This

indicates that the master experiences great pleasure and joy when investments are made, as his stewards face the unknown and an uncertain future in enterprising ways.[90]

8. Part of the reward the servants receive is being given more work or greater responsibility (vv. 21, 23).
9. No investing or multiplying of the talents displeases the master; what does displease him is an unwillingness to take risk and try.
10. When the master informs the lazy steward that he should have invested the talent with bankers so it would at least have accrued some interest along the way (v. 27), the master is clearly infuriated that no profit came of the investment given to him.
11. The third steward's actions and words reveal that he is worried about risk, change, and liability; significantly, he has a distorted view of the master (he calls him a "harsh" master, v. 24) and consequently does nothing. Though the failure is the steward's own, he blames the master.
12. In the end, not using or investing what was given means losing it (v. 28).

Far from being a harmless or entertaining story, this parable can come across as more of a punch in the face because of the truth it bears.[91] It asks of the listener not, *How much do you have?* but *What are you doing with what you have been given?* While it is true that human beings are created equal in terms of their worth and dignity, not all are given the same gifts and opportunities. And not all are equal in terms of their motivation, resolve, willingness to take risk by faith, and desire to serve.

The stewardship applications we might glean from this parable are many, and doubtless readers will detect things in it that I failed to

---

[90] This point contributes to the wider biblical doctrine of accountability and rewards.

[91] See Buttrick, *The Parables of Jesus*, 241. Archibald M. Hunter, *The Parables Then and Now* (Philadelphia: Westminster, 1971), 10, describes this parable as "an ambush by the unexpected."

observe.[92] But definitely at work here are expressions of a central law in the universe—one as true and constant as the law of gravity. It is the law of sowing and reaping; and simply stated, it means that we reap what we sow.[93] This is true in both material and spiritual terms, in economics and in morality, in private and in public life. There is simply no avoiding this law. And given the common ground between material and nonmaterial reality, one would suppose that theologians and economists might have many common interests.[94]

If faithfulness in the small leads to faithfulness in the greater, it is also true that unfaithfulness in the small will result in unfaithfulness in the greater. In fact, this is the lesson drawn from another pertinent parable of Jesus, one which is perhaps the most puzzling of all the parables employed by our Lord. Here I refer to the parable of the dishonest

---

[92] One attempted application, which must be rejected, is that of Justin Ukpong, "The Parable of the Talents (Matt 25:14–30): Commendation or Critique of Exploitation? A Social-Historical and Theological Reading," *Neotestamentica* 46, no. 1 (2012) 190–207. It proceeds on the assumption that the exploitation of the poor by the rich going on in Jesus's day was the historical context of the parable. The essay thus concludes that the parable is a critique of this system, and by extension, a critique of modern exploitation.

While the realities of exploitation imported by the Nigerian author of this essay cannot be denied, he, nevertheless, has engaged in fanciful eisegesis (i.e., importing meaning *to* the text from the outside) rather than faithful exegesis (i.e., drawing the intended meaning *from* the text itself). He ends up making the parable say almost the opposite of what was intended by Jesus. Any interpretation or application that does that must be avoided.

[93] See, in this regard, Job 4:8; Prov 11:18; 22:8; 2 Cor 9:6; and Gal 6:7.

[94] In another context, our friend Dorothy Sayers makes this observation about moral reality: "Defy the commandments of the natural law, and the race will perish in a few generations; co-operate with them, and the race will flourish for ages to come. That is the fact; whether we like it or not, the universe is made that way. This commandment is interesting because it specifically puts forward the moral law as the basis of the moral code: because God has made the world like this and will not alter it, therefore you must not worship your own fantasies, but pay allegiance to the truth." Dorothy L. Sayers, "The 'Laws' of Nature and Opinion," in *The Mind of the Maker* (New York: Harcourt Brace, 1941), 12.

manager found in Luke 16:1–13. Therein Jesus appears to be praising a scoundrel accused of squandering the master's resources. Indeed, this manager ends up being commended because "he had acted shrewdly" (16:8). So, why does Jesus commend this man?

Critically, our Lord is not praising him for his dishonesty, his deceit, and his defrauding per se. He praises him, rather, because of his resourcefulness and creativity, that is, because he acted shrewdly. The people of this world, observes Jesus, are often wiser in dealing with their own kind than the people of the light are (v. 8). Indeed, some pagan unbelievers, whose character or whose causes believers might even loathe, are perhaps more devoted to their causes, with greater commitment, than we as Christians are devoted to working to honor our Lord. A comparison is being made. And notice the closing lesson; it is a corollary of the law of sowing and reaping: "If you have not been trustworthy in handling worldly wealth, who will trust you with true riches?" (16:11–12 NIV).

Indeed, if someone cannot be entrusted with small entities in the sphere of daily living, how can that person be trusted with greater functions, greater responsibilities, or greater wealth—not just here, but in the world to come? Returning to the parable of the talents, we should keep in mind that the loss confronting the unwilling steward is not merely a threat; it reflects a material and spiritual law. That is, if I neglect using my gift, it will vanish; it will disappear. The implication is that in not investing our talents in God's service, we must live with the torment of knowing that we wasted or depreciated the gifts God has given and that we will face attendant consequences. At minimum, then, the parable urges us to courageously invest what God has entrusted to us.

In this vein, we might consider a parallel admonition from Wisdom literature: "Whatever your hands find to do, do with all your strength" (Eccl 9:10). This imperative is one of six recurring refrains throughout Ecclesiastes (see chapter 5) that implore the reader to receive enjoyment and satisfaction in life as a gift from the hand of God.[95] What makes this particular exhortation noteworthy is its suggestion that the sky is the limit when it comes to how we can honor God within the glorious realm of freedom entrusted to each of us personally. The question left unanswered is, What will we do with it?[96]

A final thought on stewardship, though not overt in the parable of the talents, is its collective or corporate character. Stewardship is both individual and communal, personal yet collective in nature. It is impossible, in fact, to overstate the importance of the common good in a "me-first" cultural climate such as ours. But the nature of vocation, properly understood, is that we serve others (our "neighbors") and thereby work for the common good.

It is impossible to miss this collective emphasis in Paul's teaching on spiritual gifts as it relates to the body of Christ, of which every believer is a part. We all have different gifts and abilities, "according to the grace given to us" (Rom 12:6). Stewarding these well affects both the personal and the public. Yes, we are endowed with talents that can be fulfilling and bring us enjoyment. But their use is designed to bear results not just for us but in the public sphere, benefitting others and bringing honor to God. One might even say that stewardship involves identifying and matching opportunities to serve the needs of others with one's own gifts and abilities.[97] If we fail to have this very public and service-oriented vision in terms of our work, if we fail to see our jobs and professions

---

[95] That work and the enjoyment of it are gifts from God is also suggested by Ps 127:1: "Unless the Lord builds a house, / its builders labor over it in vain." In work, humans experience an utter and enriching dependence upon God.

[96] While I have more to say in chapter 6 about the question of personal vision, burden, and passion, part of stewardship has to do with paying attention to enduring burdens and passions in our lives that do not lessen with the passing of time.

[97] As illustrated by the parable of the talents in Matthew 25, stewardship entails recognition of the gifts one has been given, taking investment risk amidst uncertainty, serving so as to please the master, and accountability.

contributing to the common social good, then we fail to see the design of work based on God's intention.

What matters most is not one's occupation but one's vocation, as chapter 6 will argue. Jobs may (and usually will) change, but one's underlying calling does not, since it is given by God and transcends a job, an occupation, or a particular season of life.[98] We cannot simply discharge our vocations as we might jobs, duties, or even career paths. Calling gives authority and meaning to our occupations, whatever they may be and however they might evolve. Knowing our vocational callings frees us from worrying about what will happen to our jobs. It grants us a measure of contentedness.

Faith and Work: The State of the Question

In a wonderfully incisive PhD dissertation published just over a decade ago, David W. Miller chronicles the development of a "faith in the workplace" thought mode that has been surfacing since the 1980s.[99] Miller surveys what over several decades has been labeled as a "faith and work" (hereafter FAW) movement, understood by him as a complex and largely lay-led phenomenon, whose essence is rather ecumenical and eclectic in nature. Writings on various aspects of religious faith and the workplace associated with this trend can be found in a wide variety of publications, ranging from *Fortune* and *Business Week* to *Christianity Today* and *Theology Today* and to more academically focused studies found, for example, in the *Journal of Vocational Behavior* and the *Journal of Organizational Psychology*. The basic burden of those comprising the FAW movement is the disconnect between Sunday and Monday, a bifurcation that is typically felt

---

[98] For a thoughtful treatment of the relationship between vocation and occupation, see Judith Allen Shelly, *Not Just a Job: Serving Christ in Your Work* (Downers Grove, IL: InterVarsity, 1985).

[99] David W. Miller, *God at Work: The History and Promise of the Faith at Work Movement* (Oxford: Oxford University Press, 2007). Please note that my attempt to represent Miller's work here is in summary form and will not cite specific pages.

by those in the marketplace. Hence, the pressing need for integration of a committed faith and the workplace.

While much of the FAW movement is owing to theologically Reformed Protestantism, its composition is broadly evangelical, ranging from Pentecostal, Wesleyan, and Reformed thinking to mainline/liberal Protestantism.[100] The focus of Miller's research, however, remains chiefly historical rather than theological, and this focus reveals the emergence of several waves of FAW thinking. Three such waves come under Miller's consideration.

The first wave concerned "the social question," the beginnings of which are mirrored in the encyclical writing of Pope Leo XIII, *Rerum novarum* (1891) and the previously mentioned Protestant response by the Dutch Calvinist Abraham Kuyper in sundry writings. The social question was central to the social gospel era of roughly 1890 to 1945. While Kuyper was impatient with liberal Protestant forays into the sphere of public policy, he was far more open-minded—and principled—than his liberal Protestant brethren when it came to ecumenical unity and cultural confrontation. In his opening address at the first Christian Social Congress, delivered on November 9, 1891, Kuyper conceded, "We must admit, to our shame, that the Roman Catholics are far ahead of us in their study of the social problem. Indeed, very far ahead. The action of the Roman Catholics should spur us to show more dynamism."[101]

What contemporary readers might fail to appreciate about Kuyper's position at the turn of the last century, despite his strong disagreements with Rome, is his concession that two specific realms—creedal confessions and morals—are "not subject to controversy between Rome and

---

[100] Given this denominational breadth, the FAW movement might be found under a variety of descriptors, including spirituality and work, spirituality and the workplace, soul at work, or faith at work.

[101] A recent English translation of Kuyper's opening address can be found in Jordan J. Ballor ed., *Makers of Modern Christian Social Thought: Leo XIII and Abraham Kuyper on the Social Question* (Grand Rapids: Acton Institute, 2016), 47–117.

[Protestants]."[102] For, in his words, "what we have in common with Rome, such concerns that are precisely those fundamentals of our Christian creed, [are] now most fiercely assaulted by the modern spirit." What is more, "We should not lose sight of the fact that in Christian *works* and devotion Rome still outstrips us."[103]

The second FAW wave, as Miller understands it, stretches from roughly 1945 to 1980 and is highlighted by the ministry of the laity. The third wave, extending from the 1980s onward, has been characterized by several features: (1) economic changes, reflected in the fact of economic corporate/industrial mergers and acquisitions; (2) the general perception that the 1980s constituted a decade of greed; (3) an increasingly visible role of public discourse on social and economic issues; (4) technological change and innovation in the workplace; and (5) spiritual and theological shifts toward seeker-friendliness and postmillennial theology.

Given Miller's assessment of the church's recent history, we are justified in asking what the church's response, in terms of its teaching and preaching, has been in light of current sociocultural developments in Western nations. Miller finds that FAW developments in recent decades, though having a notable ecumenical quality, have been (and remain) fundamentally lay-led. Evidence indicates that the church—or at least the church's leadership—has been largely uninterested in, unaware of, or uncertain about how to respond to these developments. What's more, this evidence, according to Miller, comes from both the local and the wider denominational level. But corroborating evidence comes from our seminaries and divinity schools as well. The disconnect, as Miller sees it, is fundamentally theological in nature. That is, theological institutions, tragically, are not addressing concerns of the marketplace—concerns that the FAW movement, at the lay level, arose to address. Moreover, a

---

[102] Abraham Kuyper, *Lectures on Calvinism,* repr. (Grand Rapids: Eerdmans, 1987), 183.

[103] Kuyper, *Lectures on Calvinism*, 188.

strongly antibusiness, anti-capitalist mindset characterizes these institutions, as it does throughout the wider academy.[104]

The question that confronts us as we head into the third decade of the twenty-first century is where the Christian church should turn to redirect her path. What sources of wisdom and direction might guide her? As it turns out, an appreciation of history—a history that broke upon the Western world 500 years ago—offers important signs that might help redirect our theological and ethical orientation.

---

[104] Many young adults today have no memory, or even general awareness, of the evils of socialism/communism, nor do they empathize with the millions who still languish under communist tyranny in China, North Korea, and Islamist cultures where religious freedom is nonexistent. This generational ignorance helps to foster in young adults attitudes that are often critical of the free market and democracy—an ignorance that should deeply concern us, given the importance of basic freedoms that we take for granted.

CHAPTER
4

A Renewal of Work, Vocation, and the Marketplace
The Lutheran Breakthrough

While from our twenty-first-century vantage point a secularist-materialist perspective strips life and vocation of their inherently religious meaning, vocation properly understood infuses mundane secular life—the ordinary—with meaning and significance. Such renewed understanding of the ordinary occurred in significant ways 500 years ago in Western history. One of the breakthroughs of early sixteenth-century Protestant reform was to recover a deeper understanding of the notion of vocation, which—for the first time in over a millennium—granted to ordinary work in the marketplace a sacred (and thus important) status. It is scarcely possible today to fully appreciate the radical nature of this development, given our distance from the Reformers, whose conviction that more than a millennium of the church's devaluing of human work aside from a calling to the priesthood or the monastery needed both indictment and redemption.

The clergy-laity distinction is what gave birth to a hierarchy of holiness in the patristic church. This persisted throughout the medieval era and would be exacerbated by yet another factor, monastic life.[1] Whether disillusioned with the church's accommodation to the authorities or driven by external meritorious attempts to achieve holiness, monks devoted themselves to an ascetic lifestyle through their flight to the desert (both literal and figurative) or their retreat into monasteries, where through various forms of rigorous discipline and abstinence they strove to embody lives "set apart" to God. Catholic theologian Edward Hahnenberg summarizes the ensuing dilemma:

> If the laity were seen in contrast to the clergy on the level of leadership and activity, now they were seen in contrast to the monk on the level of holiness. The result was a significant strain on any positive evaluation of the Christian life in the world, which was increasingly presented as a compromise to the monastic ideal . . . This monastic model of sanctity was shaped in no small way by the influence of Greek philosophy and its persistent dualism.[2]

The dualism assumed here is the Platonic opposition between body and soul, with its disparaging of the material world and the "active" (or physical) life that is associated with it. Here the contrast is between *praxis*—which concerns those activities associated with life's sustenance—and *theoria*[3]—that is, the activity associated with the life of the mind and "the philosopher's special prerogative."[4] Such a distinction has the effect

---

[1] For thoughtful (albeit very different) discussions of and challenges to the clergy/laity distinction, see Jay Wesley Richards, "Be Fruitful and Multiply: Work and Anthropology," in *Work: Theological Foundations and Practical Implications*, ed. R. Keith Loftin and Trey Dimsdale (London: SCM, 2018), 110–26; R. Paul Stevens, *The Abolition of the Laity: Vocation, Work and Ministry in Biblical Perspective* (Carlisle, UK: Paternoster, 1999); and Gordon Preece, "A Job and a Life: Reintegrating Faith, Home, and Work," *St. Mark's Review* (Spring 1998): 24–32.

[2] Edward P. Hahnenberg, *Awakening Vocation: A Theology of Christian Call* (Collegeville: Liturgical, 2010), 7.

[3] Literally, a beholding or observing; in Latin, the *contemplativus*.

[4] Thus Hahnenberg, *Awakening Vocation*, 7.

of creating a certain understanding of behavioral and social hierarchy. When added to ideals of physical renunciation and self-denial, the result lends credence to the notion that monastic callings are superior to and holier than any work done outside monastery walls. Remarkably, not only Augustine but even Thomas Aquinas, almost nine centuries later, would still hold to this dualism.[5]

In the case of Augustine, the contemplative-versus-active dualism is helpfully illustrated in his discourse on Mary and Martha.[6] Augustine comments, "What Mary hath chosen; there shall we be fed, and shall not feed others. Therefore there will that be that in fulness and perfection which Mary hath chosen here; from that rich table, from the word of the Lord did she gather up some crumbs."[7] Even when Augustine does not create as strong a dichotomy between the two characters as other patristic and later medieval writers, Mary nevertheless represents the higher model toward which the Christian should strive. It is not surprising that during the medieval period Mary and Martha would serve as an abiding illustration of the priority of the contemplative over the active life.

In the same way that Mary was representative of a perfected or mature understanding of the faith, a monk was so perceived. Monastic departure from the world and devotion to ascetic practice, mixed with contemplation and prayer, would result in the perception of greater

---

[5] In *City of God* XIX.2 and 19, Augustine identifies three kinds of lives: the leisurely or contemplative, the active or busy, and that which is a mixture. Aquinas's comparison of the contemplative and the active life is found in *Summa Theologica* II-II q. 182. Aquinas reproduces Aristotle's argument for the superiority of the contemplative life, citing eight specific reasons (cf. *Nicomachean Ethics* X. 7–8 [1177a–1178b]) and the exchange in Luke 10:41–42 between Jesus and Martha. In addition, according to Aquinas, the state of spiritual "perfection" requires that vows of poverty, continence, and obedience be part of the Christian life (*Summa Theologica* II-II, q. 186).

[6] See Luke 10:38–42. Mary and Martha are the subject of Sermons 103 and 104 by Augustine, found in Philip Schaff, ed., *The Nicene and Post-Nicene Fathers*, Series I, vol. VI (Buffalo: Christian Literature, 1888), 427–30.

[7] Augustine, Sermon 103, no. 6, in *The Nicene and Post-Nicene Fathers*, 428.

holiness both inside and outside the monastery—whether the monk's devotion to God was more than surface-deep or not. Life in the world, thus, came to be viewed as a concession, set in contradistinction to the realm of the sacred. Hahnenberg comments, "By the high Middle Ages a two-tiered hierarchy of holiness had become firmly established, built around states of life and their relation to the temporal world. The counsels of poverty, chastity, and obedience are for those striving for perfection. The commandments are for the rest who are just muddling along."[8]

Holiness in the medieval era would be widely characterized by imitating the monks. People would largely assume that "if holiness [was] to be attained by lay folks, it [was] achieved *despite* their life in the world, not because of it."[9] As described by one church historian, the term "vocation" thus came to be "seized" by monasticism, creating a false hierarchy by which the biblical notion of a person's individual calling (*vocatio*) was utterly negated.[10] It would take a disgruntled ex-monk to spark a revolution that would challenge this understanding and bring about change.

The Recasting of Work and "Vocation" in Luther's Thinking

In his work as a Reformer, Martin Luther is located at the beginning of early modern theological reflection on the dignity of work and the

---

[8] Hahnenberg, *Awakening Vocation*, 9. Hahnenberg, who writes as a Catholic theologian, describes the monastic ideal as "the flip side" of "the denigration of lay life in the world." But vows of "poverty, chastity, and obedience," as Luther came to see them, negated true faith, since they encouraged a distorted understanding of good works. See, for example, *The Judgment of Martin Luther on Monastic Vows*, in *Luther's Works*, ed. James Atkinson (Philadelphia: Fortress, 1966), 44:251–400.

[9] Hahnenberg, *Awakening Vocation*, 10 (emphasis added).

[10] Karl Holl, "The History of the Word Vocation (*Beruf*)," *Review and Expositor* 55 (1958): 136.

centrality of vocation.[11] Luther's reaction to more than a millennium of the church's devaluation of work and a two-tiered understanding of *vocatio* was nothing short of revolutionary. But the reason for this was his theological orientation, which for its day was nothing short of revolutionary. Not mystical contemplation or meritorious works, not almsgiving or sacramentally infused grace, but *faith*—justification by grace through faith—renders the believer, *every* believer, a priest before God. For Luther, a redefinition and proper understanding of vocation was the immediate need in light of the doctrine of justification and universal priesthood.[12]

To challenge the ecclesio-social system dominating medieval life in Europe would have been viewed as rebellious, and to affirm that every sphere (or "estate") of life and nearly every type of work can stem from a calling coming from God would have been "heretical" in Luther's era.[13] His revolt, however, needs qualification. The Reformer was not alone in his wrestling with the ecclesio-social system that pervaded late-medieval European life. In the late 1400s, church and society were in transition. Similar stirrings were to be found, for example, in Spain, albeit for different reasons. Thus, innovation in Germany at about 1500 was not a strange occurrence.[14]

---

[11] Where Luther is directly cited in this chapter, I draw from primary rather than secondary sources, being dependent on Luther's own writings, as mediated through the fifty-five-volume English translation of *Luther's Works* that was published in the 1950s through the 1970s. Because so much has been written about Luther, it is not uncommon to find in secondary sources an interpretation of Luther that lacks accuracy.

[12] German theologian Oswald Bayer, in *Martin Luther's Theology: A Contemporary Interpretation*, trans. Thomas H. Trapp (Grand Rapids: Eerdmans, 2008), argues that while Luther was no "systematic theologian" in the conventional sense, four doctrines inform most of his work: Christian freedom, justification by faith, the law-gospel distinction, and the width and breadth of creation.

[13] I say "nearly" here because a profession such as prostitution or drug dealing, for instance, cannot reflect a "calling" from God, given its inherently immoral, sinful nature.

[14] For a helpful assessment of social-cultural developments in Germany by the end of the fifteenth century, see Heinz Schilling, *Martin Luther: Rebel in*

Luther, in his reaction to the system of which he was once a part, rejected the distinction between "spiritual" and "temporal" vocations. All believers have vocations, and all vocations come from God, since there is no status in the kingdom of God or the church. By way of illustration, Luther would say there is no such thing as Christian cabinetmaking, but the Christian has the opportunity to build a better cabinet, thereby glorifying God and serving his or her neighbor. By insisting that the layperson has equal spiritual status with the clergy—that monk and miller and miner and mother-at-home have equal standing before God—Luther stood the accepted medieval social hierarchy on its head.[15] Both work and works were being redefined.

For Luther, the secular is indeed sacred. That is, butchers and bakers and candlestick makers, as well as parents and farmers and cobblers and miners (like those in Luther's family)—yes, even princes—are "called" to their respective work. What's more, these vocations are every bit as noble and pleasing to God as those of monks, nuns, and priests were considered. Luther writes, "A cobbler, a smith, a peasant—each has the work and office of his trade, and yet they are all alike consecrated priests and bishops . . . [I]n this way many kinds of work may be done for the bodily and spiritual welfare of the community, just as the members of the body serve one another.[16]

Hereby Luther, the Augustinian monk, intended to affirm the spirituality and religious significance of everyday life. He encouraged life lived *in* the world rather than *apart* from it. Life done in the world—at

---

an Age of Upheaval, trans. Rona Johnston Gordon (Oxford: Oxford University Press, 2017).

[15] In his attempt to level the clergy-laity distinction, Luther was not negating a call to those few whose job is to preach the Word and administer the sacraments. Rather, the doctrine of universal priesthood implies that *all* believers participate in the mission and ministry of the church based on their individual gifts and abilities. God works redemptively in the world through all roles, regardless of how menial or unnoticed they might be.

[16] Martin Luther, *To the Christian Nobility of the German Nation Concerning the Reform of the Christian Estate* (1520), in *Luther's Works*, ed. James Atkinson (Philadelphia: Fortress, 1966), 44:130.

work, in the home, and in the marketplace—should not be seen as that of second-class citizens of heaven. Moreover, it should not be viewed as a form of distraction from our pursuit of holiness. Rather, it is in these very places and in these very contexts that the Christian lives out his or her God-given vocation. Through our daily work, we can cooperate with God.[17] In the famous words of the Reformer, God "will be working all things through [us]; He will milk the cow through [us] and perform the most servile duties through [us]"; indeed, "all the greatest and least duties alike will be pleasing to Him."[18] In the domain of work and vocation, Luther's influence was indeed revolutionary.

In our attempts to come to grips with Luther's burden, multiple factors could be identified as contributing to his prophetic revolt.[19] Two require particular focus. First, as already indicated, was his concern with the longstanding monastic system and the many perceived abuses thereby entailed. These included the two-tiered hierarchical understanding of work and vocation that the system promulgated, with an attendant distortion of the church's understanding of poverty. The second was the tendency of the monastic movement to isolate Christian community, thereby preventing the church from its mandate of neighbor-love.[20] In

---

[17] Like *vocatio*, *cooperatio* is a key term for Luther; both appear frequently in his writings. See the discussion on God's "masks" below.

[18] Martin Luther, *Lectures on Genesis Chapters 31–37*, in *Luther's Works*, ed. Jaroslav Pelikan (St. Louis: Concordia, 1970), 6:10.

[19] The extent of background literature devoted to the historical, ecclesial, socioeconomic, and political factors informing the late fifteenth and early sixteenth centuries and the two-tiered social hierarchy being described in the present chapter is massive. More recent literature tends to speak in terms of "reformations" (i.e., a plural phenomenon) rather than one Reformation (as traditionally viewed through the prism of Luther, Calvin, Zwingli, et al.). These various reform movements are thought to extend from the fifteenth to the seventeenth centuries. See, for example, Carter Lindberg, *The European Reformations*, 2nd ed. (London: Wiley-Blackwell, 2010).

[20] In the frequently cited words of Gustaf Wingren, *Luther on Vocation*, trans. Carl C. Rasmussen (Philadelphia: Muhlenberg Press, 1957), 10, which are

The Babylonian Captivity of the Church, published in 1520, Luther's burden is obvious:

> I advise no one to enter any religious order or the priesthood, indeed, I advise everyone against it—unless he is forearmed with this knowledge and understands that the works of monks and priests, however holy and arduous they may be, do not differ one whit in the sight of God from the works of the rustic laborer in the field or the woman going about her household tasks, but that all works are measured before God by faith alone.[21]

A year later, in his 1521 treatise *De votis monasticis* ("On Monastic Vows"), Luther took full aim at the monastic system.[22] Christian freedom over against legalistic bondage, after all, is an important theme in Luther's writings. "Monkery," as Luther called it, or works-righteousness, mirrors the mistaken belief that we can somehow merit favor or grace from God. It suggests that external imitation (presumably of other saints) and salvation by works aim to achieve what only the internal work of grace produces. The monastic line of thinking is erroneous on several levels. In addition to its dependence on works-righteousness, it wrongly assumes (1) that a person can never be sure of salvation; (2) that vocation is self-chosen; and (3) that monastic works are of a superior or "holier" quality than those of the average laborer.[23]

---

often attributed to Luther himself, "God does not need our good works, but our neighbor does."

[21] Martin Luther, *The Babylonian Captivity of the Church*, in *Luther's Works*, ed. Abdel Ross Wentz and Helmut T. Lehmann (Philadelphia: Fortress, 1959), 36:78.

[22] See Luther, *The Judgment of Martin Luther on Monastic Vows* (see n. 8 of this chapter).

[23] According to one biographer, publication of Luther's *On Monastic Vows* would virtually empty the monasteries of north Germany in a relatively short period. See Martin Brecht, *Martin Luther: Shaping and Defining the Reformation, 1521–32* (Minneapolis: Fortress, 1994), 23–25.

Moreover, Luther worried that the monastic mindset removes people from their neighbors, who need the expression of our love. While work is not an end in itself, it is a means—indeed, the primary means—by which we serve God by serving others. Relatedly, and even worse, making monastic vows to "poverty, chastity, and obedience" easily causes those who make them to view the neighbor as spiritually inferior. Such vows, therefore, should be forsaken.[24] Thus, early on in Luther's work, this former monk who had entered the Order of Hermits of St. Augustine in July 1505 made concerted attacks on the monastic system.[25] But lest we forget how much the spirit of monasticism had influenced Luther, there are frequent allusions to his past throughout his sermons and writings.[26] The spirit of monasticism, he is clearly aware, remains an ever present danger, always

---

[24] At some points in *On Monastic Vows*, Luther vehemently insists the very foundation of vow-making is "godlessness," "blasphemy," and "sacrilege," insofar as through their so-called works monks are rejecting Christ's offering. In the same year (1521), Luther would apologize to his father in a letter for having "disobeyed" him in taking those vows sixteen years earlier. (Part of what had enraged his father was that only two months into his legal studies Luther quit in order to enter the monastery. Relatedly, part of his father's exasperation resulted from the fact that his son had not told him in person that he was becoming a monk; he was simply informed through a letter.) Luther acknowledges that the vows themselves were "worthless" and that his father's sense was correct. Interestingly, Luther's father would die three months after the letter was written. See Martin Luther, "Letter to Hans Luther" (November 21, 1521), in *Luther's Works*, ed. Gottfried G. Krodel (Philadelphia: Fortress, 1963), 48:329–36.

[25] Interestingly, Luther was still wearing his monk's habit as late as 1524. Only after October of that year did he wear normal clothing in public, having officially cut ties with his monastic identity. He would marry in June of 1525, at the age of forty-one.

[26] Luther's work mirrors a mixture of torment due to soul-searching and boldness due to his personal liberation; he vacillates between self-assurance and self-doubt. Over time, the former would give way increasingly to the latter, as evidenced by his use of a new pen name, Eleutherios, a Greek form of "the liberated/free one."

threatening to undermine faith and Christian liberty.[27] For this reason, Luther gives the impression, both in his preaching and in his writings, that marriage is a better "school" for Christian character than the cloister.[28]

An additional factor that contributed to Luther's overall burden deserves our consideration as well. Unlike the phenomenon of monasticism, however, it rarely, if ever, sees the light of day—whether among theologians or historians. In Luther's reaction to the church's historic devaluation of work outside the church, it is utterly fascinating to find that the book of Ecclesiastes played no small role in helping shape his thinking on human labor and *vocatio*.[29] While Luther's interaction with that book is discussed in more detail in the following section, it is necessary to mention the connection here in order to establish a proper context for Luther's overall thinking. In *Notes on Ecclesiastes*, Luther offers the following pronouncement: "No less noxious for a proper understanding of [Ecclesiastes] has been the influence of many of the saintly and illustrious theologians in the church, who thought that in this book Solomon was teaching what they call "the contempt for the world" [*contemptus mundi*].[30] Here Luther is citing Jerome, who encourages fourth-century monastic life in the preface of his *Commentarius in Ecclesiastia*[31] and

---

[27] It is unfortunate that what is perhaps the best resource for understanding Luther's dispute with—and rejection of—monasticism remains untranslated from the German. It is Bernhard Lohse's *Mönchtum und Reformation* (Göttingen: Vandenhoeck & Ruprecht, 1963).

[28] For an appreciation of medieval attitudes toward the monastic lifestyle, see Beryl Smalley, "Some Thirteenth-Century Commentaries on the Sapiential Books," *Dominican Studies* 2–3 (1949/1950): 41–77, 236–74.

[29] Luther lectured on Ecclesiastes at the University of Wittenberg from July until November of 1526. In time, his lecture notes would be turned into a commentary. In 1972, it was translated into English by Jaroslav Pelikan. See Martin Luther, *Notes on Ecclesiastes; Lectures on the Song of Solomon; Treatise on the Last Words of David* in *Luther's Works* (St. Louis: Concordia), 15:3–187.

[30] Martin Luther, *Notes on Ecclesiastes*, in *LW* 15:4.

[31] For an English translation, see St. Jerome, *Commentary on Ecclesiastes*, ed. and trans. Richard J. Goodrich and David J. D. Miller (New York: Newman, 2012).

whose "contempt for the world" interpretation would be embraced by most of the church for over a millennium.[32]

The first teaching to observe in Ecclesiastes's message, according to Luther, is that the book condemns not the realm of the created but "depraved affection and human striving." The second noteworthy point he makes is that the book's writer is "clearly himself within the limits of human nature," that is, within "the efforts, the endeavors, and the desires" that are acceptable based on creation.[33] At the heart of the book's message is a human tendency: "the vanity of the human heart . . . is never content with the gifts of God that are present."[34]

A Contempt for the World

More needs to be said about patristic interpretation, which will go unchallenged, for the most part, throughout the medieval era. First, Jerome's interpretation of Ecclesiastes, against which Luther was reacting, has been described as less an exegesis of the text than it was a *reinterpretation* in his own likeness.[35] Second, while Jewish and other Christian

---

[32] For Jerome, the creation order is not "good" in an ontological sense or in the sense that Reformed theologians would understand creation; rather, it is "vanity," based on Eccl 1:2 and 12:8 (KJV). Endel Kallas, author of "Ecclesiastes: *Traditum et fides evangelica:* The Ecclesiastes Commentaries of Martin Luther, Philip Melanchthon, and Johannes Brenz Considered within the History of the Interpretation" (PhD diss., Graduate Theological Union, 1979), whose definitive study explores Ecclesiastes interpretations from Jerome down to the sixteenth-century Protestant Reformers, argues that no medieval exegete challenged Jerome's interpretation of Ecclesiastes. The evidence would seem to support Kallas's argument.

[33] Luther, *Notes on Ecclesiastes, LW* 15:9.

[34] Luther, 15:10.

[35] Iain Provan, *Ecclesiastes, Song of Songs,* NIVAC (Grand Rapids: Zondervan, 2001), 25. Luther was reacting to Jerome on several levels and not merely his interpretation of Ecclesiastes. For example, according to Luther, Jerome glories in celibacy, not Christ (see Gal 3:28 and 1 Cor 7:1–40), which would seem to verify Jerome's interpretation of Ecclesiastes, namely, that everything in this

interpreters had also developed a spiritual/allegorical interpretation of Ecclesiastes, Jerome's particular interpretation would be lasting, being normative from the fourth until the sixteenth century.[36] Given the opening message of the book—that everything is vanity—there were good reasons, in Jerome's view, for being detached from this temporal world. If everything that God made really is still "good," then how can everything be not only *vanitas* but *vanitas vanitatorum*? he reasons.[37] Offering commentary on Eccl 1:3, Jerome observes that men sweat "in vain in the labor of this world"; "they carry nothing from all their labor with them" out of this life.[38] "All things pass away," he bemoans, and "the universe declines toward its own end."[39] Significantly, Jerome's interpretation of 1:2 is figurative: "If a living person is vanity, it follows that a dead person is the vanity of vanities."[40] And with an allusion to 1 Cor 13:10, Jerome concludes that "all is vanity until the perfect comes."[41]

Contemptus mundi ("contempt for the world"), then, was to be understood as a *necessary* good for the Christian believer.[42] The fallen world, as Jerome sees it, is *pro nihilo* and not "good." "Goodness" and "vanity," he

---

present life is "*vanitas*"; see Martin Luther, "The Judgment of Martin Luther on Monastic Vows," *Luther's Works*, ed. James Atkinson (Philadelphia: Fortress, 1966), 44:306–7.

[36] Kallas, "Ecclesiastes: *Traditum et fides evangelica*," 172, describes the influence of Jerome's allegorical interpretation of Ecclesiastes, until the Lutheran breakthrough, as a "stranglehold." In one of the few studies that examines medieval exegesis of Ecclesiastes, Eric J. Eliason, "*Vanitas Vanitatum*: 'Piers Plowman,' Ecclesiastes, and Contempt of the World" (unpublished PhD diss., University of Virginia, 1989), 18–19, observes that interest in the book of Ecclesiastes peaked in the early fourteenth century.

[37] St. Jerome, *Commentary on Ecclesiastes*, 1.2, 35.
[38] St. Jerome, 1.2, 36.
[39] St. Jerome, 1.2, 36.
[40] St. Jerome, 1.2, 35.
[41] St. Jerome, 1.2, 36.
[42] See Eliason, "*Vanitas Vanitatum*," 57. Eliason is one of the few to underscore this important, though unfortunate, interpretive tendency in the church's history—both in the patristic and medieval era.

reasons, can be neither equated nor reconciled. The implication, therefore, is clear: since *everything* in this world is *vanitas,* passing away and subject to mutation, we are to live in a detached manner. Understandably, something of an apocalyptic tone informs and colors much of Jerome's commentary on Ecclesiastes, which, of course, is to be anticipated if the writer assumes the standpoint of *contemptus mundi.*

Importantly, Jerome's *contemptus mundi* did not simply appear out of nowhere. It is an interpretive outlook that is traceable to earlier church fathers, not to mention ancient rabbinical commentary that shares similar assumptions. In the late second century, as I have previously noted, Tertullian posed the famously provocative question, "What does Jerusalem have to do with Athens?" in his *Prescription against Heretics* in a way that would help define the thinking of many believers not only in the early church but for centuries to come in terms of their involvement in temporal affairs.[43] Tertullian's question, of course, was rhetorical. His answer, spelled out not only in *Prescription* but also in his well-known *On Idolatry* (written several years later), was essentially "little to nothing."[44] Such was a response rooted in a presumption of *contemptus mundi.*[45]

We should recall that by "Athens" Tertullian was referring primarily to intellectual culture and the life of the mind—whether the study of philosophy, language, history, literature, the arts, or the sciences. And, of course, by "Jerusalem" he meant the life of faith and redemption through Christ. Offering further context to his rhetorical question, Tertullian observes, "We want no curious disputation after possessing Christ Jesus, no inquisition after enjoying the gospel! With our faith, we

---

[43] Tertullian, *The Prescription against Heretics* 7, in *The Ante-Nicene Fathers,* ed. Alexander Roberts and James Donaldson, repr. (Grand Rapids: Eerdmans, 1968), 3:246.

[44] Tertullian follows this with a second rhetorical question: "What concord is there between the Academy and the Church . . . between heretics and Christians?" Tertullian, 3:246.

[45] The earlier Tertullian, for example, as mirrored in his *Apology,* was far less isolationist than the later, sectarian version.

desire no further belief. . . . [T]here is nothing which we ought to believe besides."⁴⁶ Since we have Christ, who is the end of all things, he reasons, why do we need Athens at all?

The Tertullians of any age tend to remind us that although we are in the world, we are not *of* it. They prefer, with not only Tertullian himself but a host of fathers, including Jerome in some respects, to emphasize the "not of it" part of the in-but-not-of formula. Hence, not the goodness of creation and the related creation mandate of Genesis but *contemptus creatio* is to be accentuated. The ever-present Tertullian error, alas, fails to take seriously all of creation, which was declared intrinsically "good" (Gen 1:10, 12, 18, 21, 25, 31). Thus, *contemptus mundi* downplays or ignores human culture and the temporal world in which we live and of which we are a part. Consequently, it fails to appreciate the width and breadth of redemption—a doctrine which, as noted in the previous chapter, is properly understood as creation restored.

The early monastic tradition, as one historian points out, appears to have inherited the attitude that those who chose to work for a living were second-rate Christians, with the consequence that

> work often came to be seen as a debasing and demeaning activity, best left to one's social—and spiritual—inferiors. If the social patricians of ancient Rome regarded work as below their status, it has to be said that a spiritual aristocracy appears to have developed within early Christianity with equally negative and dismissive attitudes towards manual labor. Such attitudes probably reached their height during the Middle Ages.⁴⁷

Thus, in the early centuries, there was "very little disagreement" over what the Teacher taught in Ecclesiastes:

---

⁴⁶ Tertullian, *Prescription against Heretics* 7, n.p.

⁴⁷ Alister McGrath, "Calvin and the Christian Calling," *First Things* (June 1999): 33.

His subject was contempt for the world. The . . . descriptions of the world in constant but unproductive change suggested to medieval readers very good reasons for withholding one's trust in the *temporalia* which make up the world. As a result, the major enterprise in commenting on Ecclesiastes in the Middle Ages was the effort to distinguish between those things which last and those things which don't.[48]

The remarkably dominant influence of Jerome's interpretation can be seen even 800 years later. One very popular and influential *contemptus mundi* reading in the Middle Ages was Pope Innocent III's *De miseria condicionis humane* ("On the Misery of the Humane Condition"), published in 1195. Written by Innocent while he was still Cardinal Losario, the work survives in almost 700 manuscripts and, remarkably, had undergone nearly fifty printed editions by Luther's day. The three principal sources of human moral failings identified by Losario in *De miseria* are riches, pleasures, and honors. The following extract illustrates contemporary medieval thinking about the world:

> There is nothing without labor under the sun, there is nothing without defect under the moon, there is nothing without vanity in time. For time is the period of motion of mutable things. "Vanity of vanities," says Ecclesiastes, and "all is vanity." O how various are the endeavors of men, how diverse are their efforts! Yet there is one end and the same consequence for all: labor and vexation of spirit.[49]

Consider that statement carefully: "There is one end and the same consequence for all: *labor and vexation of spirit*" (emphasis mine). Surely, these words resonate with every human being, whether ancient or modern. But

---

[48] Kallas, "Ecclesiastes: *Traditum et fides evangelica*," 51.

[49] Losarío dei Segni (Pope Innocent III), *De miseria condicionis humane*. I am dependent here on the translation of *De miseria* provided by Robert E. Lewis (Athens: University of Georgia Press, 1978), 108.

does this mean that the statement is true, that all but the most "spiritual" things we do are pointless?

Far more familiar to the average reader is another medieval tract, Thomas à Kempis's *The Imitation of Christ*, which mirrors a similar attitude toward the temporal realm.[50] Thomas writes, "Strive to withdraw your heart from the love of visible things, and direct your affections to things invisible. For those who follow only their natural inclinations defile their conscience, and lose the grace of God."[51] Tellingly, the introductory section of *Imitation* is titled "Of the Imitation or Following of Christ, and of the despising of all vanities of the world." Among those things it condemns as "vanity" are seeking after "riches that shall perish," coveting "honors," pride and "to lift [oneself] on high," and "to desire a long life." The introduction to *Imitation* concludes with a citation of Ecclesiastes: "The eye is not satisfied with seeing, nor the ear with hearing. Strive, therefore, to turn away thy heart from the love of things that are seen, and to set it upon the things that are not seen."[52] Neither Luther nor his Renaissance contemporary Erasmus would be counted among those who esteemed *Imitation*; after all, Thomas à Kempis advocated the inner life and a distancing from the temporal world, while the two Reformers affirmed the opposite.

---

[50] Although it first appeared in manuscript form in the early 1470s, over 100 editions of *Imitation* had been published by 1500. Having been translated into nearly 100 languages and appearing in more than 5,000 editions, the work remains the best-selling book after the Bible; see Michael Massing, *Fatal Discord: Erasmus, Luther, and the Fight for the Western Mind* (New York: Harper, 2018), 18.

[51] Thomas à Kempis, *The Imitation of Christ* 1.1; I am dependent here on the translation of *Imitation* provided by L. Sherley-Price (London: Penguin, 1976), 28.

[52] Thomas à Kempis; cf. Eccl 1:8b. For a helpful summary of readings and interpretations of Ecclesiastes before Luther, see Eric S. Christianson, "Ecclesiastes in Premodern Reading," in Mark J. Boda et al., eds., *The Words of the Wise Are Like Goads: Engaging Qohelet in the 21st Century* (Winona Lake, IN: Eisenbrauns, 2013), 3–36.

During the medieval era there existed a remarkable fascination with the figure of King Solomon and his persona.[53] Jerome, in his writing, assumed not only Solomonic authorship of Ecclesiastes but also that Solomon had repented of his sins. Thus, the virtues of repentance would figure ever more prominently in the medieval era. By the late-medieval period in the Protestant Reformers' day, new forms of penitential piety were growing, whereby satisfaction or atonement for sins was understood to be achieved through elaborate, painstaking steps and *labor*—labor that often entailed physical discomfort and pain. By Luther's day it was commonly believed that to take monastic vows and therewith be subject to the external rigors of monastic life allowed one to accrue merit and divine favor. (Luther, of course, as an Augustinian monk, had partaken of such ordeals before his conversion.) If Solomon truly repented, a confession of the *vanitas* of all one's deeds would not only be expected but multiplied, so that the inevitable result is what was taken to be his post-repentance contempt for the world. Ecclesiastes would have been read and understood by Luther's day as teaching a flight from this world, as a sign of true repentance.

But for Luther, a "contempt for the world" meant that Christians inter alia would have to "forsake the household, the political order . . . [and more] to flee to the desert, to isolate oneself from human society, to live in stillness and silence; for it was [deemed] impossible to serve God in the world."[54] Luther was thus at pains to counter the longstanding tradition of ascetic monasticism and isolation that had accrued over the centuries.[55] In his view, that outlook on "the world" was counter

---

[53] See Eliason, "*Vanitas Vanitatum*," 40–56.

[54] Luther, *Notes on Ecclesiastes, LW* 15:4.

[55] While it is true that the monastic communities following the Benedictine Rule worked as well as prayed, as Lee Hardy, *The Fabric of This World: Inquiries into Calling, Career Choice, and the Design of Human Work* (Grand Rapids: Eerdmans, 1990), 50, points out, they worked with the goal of maintaining their own communities. Furthermore, by the late-medieval period, "The liturgical practices within the major orders had grown to the point that the monks no

to a proper understanding—and acknowledgement—of creation's *essential* and not merely relative "goodness" (see Gen 1:12, 18, 21, 25, 31). Monks, however, were disengaged, which caused Luther to polemicize against the world-fleeing monastic tendency.[56] "Some foolish men," he observed,

> have not understood [what Ecclesiastes condemns] and have therefore taught absurd ideas about contempt for the world and flight from it, and they themselves have also done many absurd things . . . The proper contempt of the world is not that of the man who lives in solitude away from human society, nor is the proper contempt of gold that of the man who throws it away and who abstains from money, as the Franciscans do, but that of the man who lives his life *in the midst* of these things and yet is not carried away by his affection for them. This is the first thing that should be considered [by those reading Ecclesiastes].[57]

The Role of the Book of Ecclesiastes in Luther's Recasting of Work and Vocation

Luther's break with standard medieval interpretation of Ecclesiastes was philological, theological, and ethical.[58] Luther turned the medieval read-

---

longer had time to work to support themselves at all. Instead they lived off of the gifts and endowments given by the aristocracy in exchange for a share of the spiritual benefits of the monastery." What is more, wandering monks (the friars) also did not work for a living but were dependent on the charity of those whom they encountered.

[56] In this light, Luther was led to rail against the "monkish" lifestyle: "Indeed, the menial housework of a manservant or maidservant is often more acceptable than all the fastings and other works of a monk or priest, because the monk or priest lacks faith" (Luther, *Babylonian Captivity*, *LW* 36:78).

[57] Luther, 15:9 (emphasis added).

[58] This is argued with considerable precision by Al Wolters, "Ecclesiastes and the Reformers," in Boda et al., *The Words of the Wise Are Like Goads*, 55–68.

ing on its head by affirming, rather than denying, the ordinary affairs of this life. The only problem with work of any kind, as Luther saw it, is sin's presence in the world, *not* any lack of goodness in creation. His *Annotationes in Ecclesiastea* ("Notes on Ecclesiastes"), published in 1532, contains one comment that perhaps best summarizes his overall burden: "For all things that God has made are very good and have been made for the use of man, as Paul says in very clear words in 1 Tim 4:4–5."[59] Indeed, work is part of the created order, not a by-product of sin.[60] Adam was to plant, cultivate, and tend before the fall. For the believer, as Luther understood it, the implications of this are staggering: "Through [the believer's] faith, he has been restored to Paradise and created anew."[61]

Luther believed that two priorities are to govern our biblical interpretation: the author's purpose and the author's unique style. The aim of the writer of Ecclesiastes, in this light, is thereby clarified for Luther; it is "to put us at peace and to give us a quiet mind in the everyday affairs and business of this life, so that we live contentedly in the present without care or yearning about the future."[62] What Ecclesiastes condemns, Luther asserts, is not creation or the created order but rather "depraved affections," human striving, and a lack of contentment.[63] The natural order remains good." *Misuse* of the good, not its *use*, is what leads to *vanitas*.[64] In this light, then, the expression "under the sun," Luther insists, should be understood not in cosmological or physical sense but

---

[59] Luther, *Notes on Ecclesiastes*, *LW* 15:8.

[60] In Luther's writings, the topic of work is generally not treated comprehensively or systematically as, for example, justification, marriage, secular authority, war, or Christian freedom. It usually arises when Luther is discussing particular scriptural passages. The one exception is his *Notes on Ecclesiastes*.

[61] Martin Luther, *The Freedom of a Christian* (1520), in *Luther's Works*, ed. Harold J. Grimm (Philadelphia: Fortress, 1957), 31:360.

[62] Luther, *Notes on Ecclesiastes*, *LW* 15:7.

[63] Luther, 15:8. Discontentment, according to Luther, is "always looking for something that is lacking" (11).

[64] Luther, 15:8–9, 12–14.

religiously and philosophically, so that we do not exclude the good works of God the Creator.[65]

In addition to the tendency of medieval exegesis to be anchored in a contempt for the world, a second notable—albeit related—feature was inherited from the early Christian fathers since the days of Origen. It extended through Jerome, Ambrose, Augustine, and down to Luther's day.[66] As suggested above (recall Jerome's rendering of Eccl 1:2), interpretation of Ecclesiastes was characterized by a conspicuous spiritualizing of the text. Jerome's opening in his commentary on Ecclesiastes was essentially to afflict the comfortable; he assumed that any person expecting or hoping to be at home in the temporal world is living under an illusion. Jerome seems to have had Epicurean thinking—or a reasonable facsimile thereof—in the back of his mind. For this reason, then, food and drink needed to be allegorized. Hence, the allusions in Ecclesiastes to eating and drinking, which along with work are the practical expressions of God's gifts, are understood allegorically by him. He took them as references to the Lord's Table and not to be interpreted in a literal manner.[67] In Jerome's treatment of Eccl 2:24–26, for example, he observes, "What is good is to take the true food and the true drink, which we find in the divine books concerning the body and blood of the

---

[65] Luther, 15:13–15.

[66] The earliest surviving Christian comments on Ecclesiastes are found in Origen's prologue to his commentary on the Song of Solomon, and it is not surprising that Origen allegorizes. Origen elsewhere—*On First Principles* 1.7.5, cited in J. Robert Wright, ed., *Ancient Christian Commentary on Scripture Vol. IX: Proverbs, Ecclesiastes, Song of Songs* (Downers Grove, IL: InterVarsity, 2005), 194—calls vanity "the possession of material bodies." For his part, Ambrose cites the circus, horse-racing, and the theater as examples of vanity; therefore, we are to seek the word of God and "flee from this world" (Ambrose, *Flight from the World* 1.4, cited in Wright, *Ancient Christian Commentary on Scripture*, 194).

[67] St. Augustine, in *City of God* 17.20, employs the same line of interpretation. The general sentiment among Christian historians and Old Testament scholars is that allegorizing ended up rescuing Ecclesiastes among the early fathers, insofar as it dulled perceived contradictions and heterodox statements.

Lamb."⁶⁸ Jerome would apply this sacramental, "bread and wine"/"body and blood" interpretation in Ecclesiastes again to eating and drinking in 3:12–13; 5:19; and 8:15. Similarly, in his understanding, "enjoyment" in these verses means holiness. Jerome could not accept the conclusion of Eccl 2:24–26 and the subsequent enjoyment refrains that *God sanctions material joy*; but those ideas aroused discomfort among medieval Jewish commentators as well.⁶⁹ Finally, behind the entire book's interpretation stands Christ, whom Jerome will make the Preacher (that is, the book's speaker), who then is directing the words of Ecclesiastes to the church.⁷⁰

But Luther rejected this allegorizing and spiritualizing of Scripture, foremost because of its disregard for the doctrine of creation and attendant world-fleeing, isolating tendency. Ecclesiastes 2:24–26, for example, was for Luther a most "remarkable passage."⁷¹ One reason for this, in his mind, was that the writer used few words in making a positive statement, in contrast to the many words before and after that he employs to make a negative one. The rationale for this, according to Luther, is "to prove and show us our foolishness" and to demonstrate "that we accomplish nothing by our [own] counsels and toils."⁷² Luther read Eccl 3:22 in a similar fashion: the ungodly get nothing out of their labors, in stark contrast to the righteous, whose "lot" or "portion" is to receive joy.⁷³

As a good Augustinian, the Reformer affirmed the reality of the two cities. And while it is uncontested that our ultimate allegiance is to the heavenly city of God, this does not mean that we take our earthly citizenship lightly. Rather, we are stewards of various callings that have been

---

⁶⁸ St. Jerome, *Commentary on Ecclesiastes,* 2.24, 54.

⁶⁹ See Nava Neriya-Cohen, "Rashbam's Understanding of the Carpe Diem Passages in Qoheleth," *Revue des études juives* 175, nos. 1–2 (2016): 30–37.

⁷⁰ St. Jerome, *Commentary on Ecclesiastes* 1.1; for a broader understanding of this spiritualized interpretation by Jerome, see the commentary's "Introduction," 1–31.

⁷¹ Luther, *Notes on Ecclesiastes, LW* 15:46.

⁷² Luther, 15:46–47.

⁷³ Luther, 15:61.

given by the Lord of creation. We occupy various stations in life, which have been assigned to us by the Lord, using those outposts and the attendant gifts and abilities that go with them to serve God and serve others. Ecclesiastes agrees with this outlook in its statements that our "portion" or "lot" (*ḥeleq*) has been assigned by God (see, for example, 3:22; 5:18; 5:19; 9:6; and 9:9). If we flee to the desert or to the monastery, we are fleeing the created order, and it is *to* the created order that Christian believers—indeed *all*—are called. Luther was convinced that Ecclesiastes is not escapist, that it does not call the reader out of the world.[74] Properly read and understood, it does not breed a *contemptus mundi*.

This perspective is not only implicit in Ecclesiastes; it is strengthened, as Luther understood it, by the notion of *vocatio* ("calling"), as we noted above. And while vocation is a wholly biblical concept, it was perhaps most thoroughly—and practically—developed by Luther. Recall that in the medieval mindset, to have a calling (*vocatio*) was to become a monk or nun or enter the priesthood in the service of the church. Over against those ordinary occupations of the marketplace—for example, farming, toolmaking, leatherworking, housekeeping, soldiering, or even a ruling as a prince—monastic or a priestly life of celibacy and retreat from public life was understood to be *the* only means by which to serve God fully.

Among Luther's most important innovations, as previously noted, was his theological accent on the "priesthood of every believer," according to which every Christian is made holy, sanctified, and set apart unto God for service through Christ. Rather than point laypeople back toward vocation through various monastic or priestly orders of the church, Luther reversed the process, emphasizing that *every type of work* is a *sacred* calling—and a calling every bit as noble as the priest's.[75]

---

[74] Philip Melanchthon, Luther's colleague at the University of Wittenberg, will also publish a commentary on Ecclesiastes in 1550 (*Enarratio brevis concionum libri Salomoniscuius, cuius titulus est Ecclesiastes*). Like Luther, he emphasizes the goodness of creation—a goodness that is providentially preserved.

[75] This is a particular point of emphasis by Luther in his open letter *To the Christian Nobility of the German Nation*; see *Luther's Works*, 44:115–217.

Luther (as would Calvin) recast "calling" to the everyday life of living in the world. McGrath comments on the impact of that switch:

> Work was thus [newly] seen as an activity by which Christians could deepen their faith, leading it on to new qualities of commitment to God. Activity within the world, motivated, informed, and sanctioned by Christian faith, was the supreme means by which the believer could demonstrate his or her commitment and thankfulness to God. To do anything for God, and to do it well, was the fundamental hallmark of authentic Christian faith.[76]

Work, therefore, because of the Reformed emphasis on the believer's priesthood, had the effect of transforming the daily, the ordinary, the mundane, and the necessary.[77] It collapsed the longstanding distinction between sacred and secular, demonstrating that *all of life*, based on the underlying goodness of creation, is sacred and therefore is a means by which both to serve God and neighbor.[78]

One memorable way in which Luther describes vocation is to call it a "mask of God" (*larva Dei*). This is to say, God both reveals and conceals himself in his dealings with human creation. In the Old Testament,

---

[76] McGrath, "Calvin and the Christian Calling," 34.

[77] To illustrate in a very practical way, Luther wrote to a professional soldier who also served as a counselor to a duke who was sympathetic to the Reformation cause. Thereby Luther reminds the soldier, a man of Christian faith, "In the first place, we must distinguish between an occupation and the man who holds it, between a work and the man who does it. An occupation or a work can be good and right in itself and yet be bad and wrong if the man who does the work is evil or wrong or does not do his work properly"; see Martin Luther, *Whether Soldiers Too, Can Be Saved* (1526), in *Luther's Works*, ed. Robert C. Schultz (Philadelphia: Fortress, 1967), 46:94.

[78] It is no overstatement to argue that the doctrine of the priesthood of every believer, though in some circles a forgotten legacy of sixteenth-century reform, is central to the church's continual reform. See Wim A. Dreyer, "The Priesthood of Believers: The Forgotten Legacy of the Reformation," *Teologiese* Studies 76, no. 4 (2020), https://hts.org.za/index.php/hts/article/view/6021/16223.

in fact, we find that God must veil himself in his dealings with human beings.[79] Luther applies this concept to our everyday lives as we await Christ's return. He says God "hides" himself in the ordinary, in the family, and in the daily, which includes the marketplace and the secular realm. Nevertheless, human beings' work performed in the context of their various stations in life and vocations is quite simply their cooperation with God. Here Luther wishes to instruct us: God is present and providing, even when he is "hidden." Importantly, Luther's hidden God (*Deus absconditus*) hides in order to be found; he is concealed in order that he might be revealed. Luther, of course, is keenly aware that God, in his pure majesty and naked splendor, is inaccessible to human beings.[80] And such, he recognizes, is the unmistakable teaching of Ecclesiastes 3, which concurs with wider biblical theology: if God is immanent, then he *must* mask (which is to say, veil) himself. Wisdom, however, allows us to discern what is behind the mask, and thus, the purpose of the mask. God's transcendence, and hence his inscrutability, does not mean his absence.

---

[79] Here we might recall texts such as Exod 33:20—"You cannot see [God's] face, for humans cannot see [God] and live"—and Isa 45:15—"[Y]ou are a God who hides, / God of Israel, Savior." The concept of God's hiddenness, of course, is counterbalanced in Scripture by God's omnipresence, as in Ps 139:7 and 23— and by the fact that God the Son put on flesh so that he *could* physically dwell among men (John 1:10-14 and 14:8–10).

[80] From both a theological and pastoral perspective, it is not always easy to distinguish between God's presence and his absence. In truth, we readily conflate the two. Because our perception of either has to do with our existential experience, we agonize over God's silences. Both God's "revealing" and "concealing" are complex and, so to speak, multilayered. Demonstrating an inordinate sensitivity to this theological conundrum, as well as to Luther's wrestling therewith, is J. Cilliers, "The Absence of Presence: Homiletical Reflections on Luther's Notion of the Masks of God (*Larvae Dei*)," *Acta Theologica* 30, no. 2 (2010): 36–49. In considering Luther's teaching on the masks of God, Cilliers suggests that Christians should (1) speak about both God's so-called absence and his presence; (2) learn more from silence; (3) acknowledge that doubt is very real and not sin; and (4) allow for mystery—a perennial sign of which, he says, is the Eucharist. Therein God is veiled behind the sacraments.

At the same time, part of God's hiddenness—his veiling or masking—is his presence and provision in human affairs. God's purpose in hiding is benevolent; that is, his hiddenness is a "condescension with purpose."[81] To say that God provides and reveals himself through masks is simply another way of saying that he sustains creation through common grace. Whether our work is in the field or in the shop or in government or at home, whether it concerns supplying food, clothing, shelter, or protection, that work becomes God's means of providing for human beings; our work becomes a mask of God.[82] Luther believed that in daily life and in all spheres God is at work—in "everything that pertains to the regulation of our domestic and our civil or political affairs."[83]

The manner in which God masks himself, as Luther understood it, is varied. Yes, it occurs in the daily, the ordinary, through work, but God also masks himself through creation, through suffering, through the preaching of the Word and the sacraments, and—ultimately, of course—through the incarnation. The latter, of course, is the mask of God par excellence, by which God hides through the manger and then again through the cross.[84]

---

[81] So says Steven D. Paulson, "Luther on the Hidden God," *Word & World* 19, no. 4 (1999): 363. Paulson illustrates this helpfully with the game of hide-and-seek. The game always ends in discovery; it never continues indefinitely with someone remaining in hiding (364).

[82] Luther's use of the language of God masking himself through our daily work is notable in his treatment of various Psalms. See, for example, his exposition of Psalm 127 and of Psalm 147. In the latter, Luther writes, "We have the saying: 'God gives every good gift, but not just by waving a wand.' God gives all good gifts, but . . . you must work and thus give God good cause and a mask." Martin Luther, *Psalm 147*, in *Luther's Works*, ed. Jaroslav Pelikan (St. Louis: Concordia, 1958), 14:115.

[83] See Martin Luther, *The Large Catechism* (1529), in *The Book of Concord*, ed. and trans. Theodore G. Tappert (Philadelphia: Fortress, 1959), 430.

[84] See Martin Luther, *Lectures on Genesis Chapters 15–20*, *LW* 3:107–8, 274–75. Preaching and teaching, when led by the Spirit, can aid us in helping interpret God's revealing as well as his concealing. Any attempt to find God through

Doubtless in Luther's day, as in ours, people sought God in the mystical and the miraculous. But for many, to come to the realization that God is actually *present* in the ordinary, foremost in the workplace, is revolutionary, even when it may be difficult to embrace. It is an understanding that can be life-changing, infusing all types of labor with dignity and value. And to grasp the implications of the enjoyment refrains in Ecclesiastes with their implications for work, as Luther began to do, is no less transformative. Hence, vocation entailed for Luther a call to love one's neighbor through the tasks and duties that are a part of one's "station" or social context in life.[85]

But *who is my neighbor?* Precisely this was the rhetorical question posed to Jesus by "an expert in the law" (Luke 10:25). Every vocation and station of life, of course, will present us with "neighbors"; and based on the parable of the good Samaritan which follows in Luke 10:30–37, we will surely encounter unexpected ones. In any case, the purpose of Christian faith is not to abandon the world but to live in its midst, for people around us are in need of the Christian's good works.[86]

The implications of Luther's teaching were realized not only in terms of viewing work as vocation but also as it concerned a proper view of wealth and the material realm. In his commentary on Eccl 5:18–20, Luther notes the contrast between the miser and the God-fearer. Luther is struck by the previous description of the plight of the miser. In vv. 12–14 the miserly individual is depicted as poor amid his riches; in fact, the more he has, the more he wants, which confirms the power of greed.

"unveiled" or "unmasked" means, according to Luther, is a satanic temptation and heresy (*Lectures in Genesis Chapters 6–14*, 2:48).

[85] That context may or may not be paid employment or one's formal occupation. Moreover, a station is not to be confused with modern conceptions of social standing, status, class, or rank.

[86] On the importance of serving our neighbors, an important theme in Luther's writings, see Gene Edward Veith, "Martin Luther on Vocation and Serving Our Neighbors," March 30, 2016, https://www.acton.org/pub/commentary/2016/03/30/martin-luther-vocation-and-serving-our-neighbors.

Alas, in his misery this man cannot sleep (v. 12).[87] The admonition to enjoyment which follows the critique of the miser is decisive (see Eccl 5:18–20); it constituted for Luther, as did Eccl 2:24–26, "the conclusion of [the] entire book."[88] The gifts of God, reiterated in these verses as coming from the hand of God (see Eccl 2:24), were reassuring to Luther. That "God keeps [a worker] occupied with the joy of his heart" (5:20) is the opposite of anxiety, as Luther was careful to point out.[89]

The topic of anxiety is very important to the Reformer, as his comments regarding Eccl 3:13 indicate.[90] Given the emphasis on providence and divine hiddenness/inscrutability that is developed throughout Ecclesiastes 3, Luther was moved to admonish believers to commit their anxiety about the future to God. The language of verse 13 is especially comforting: our basic needs are met and come to us as "the gift of God."

Luther was particularly struck by the contrast between the language of Eccl 2:24 and 3:13—"this is from God's hand"; this "is also the gift of God"—and the description of the miser (Eccl 5:13–17), already noted. He concluded that the Teacher is not condemning riches, nor is he forbidding that we acquire food and drink and material things. Rather, he is urging us to understand these things as gifts from our loving Creator.

---

[87] Luther's commentary in *Notes on Ecclesiastes*, LW 15:87–90 is fascinating, almost entertaining.

[88] Luther, 15:93.

[89] Luther, 15:93.

[90] The average reader, some 500 years removed from Luther, is perhaps prone to forget—or be inattentive to—the pangs of conscience that characterized the Reformer's life. We do well to remember that Luther had been part of the monastic system, with its vows, its isolation, and its emphasis on merited holiness. Anxiety for him, then, would have been a constant companion; hence, the extraordinary liberation that comes to him when he discovers that God's grace is not merited but freely received by faith. The earlier Luther wrestled with issues of conscience, while the later Luther would wrestle with the responsibilities of his vocation. In any event, the language of Ecclesiastes in these "joy" refrains—developed in more detail in chapter 5—surely came to Luther as a source of great relief.

For Luther, such expressions of grace come to us not for the purpose of rejecting or abstaining from them; gifts are to be received. What is more, the statement "Because God keeps him occupied with the joy of the heart" (5:20) indicates that the human being does have "joy in his toil here," and even amid evils one can therefore acknowledge that one is entering momentarily "into Paradise."[91] In fact, Luther's reading of Eccl 7:13–14 caused him to insist that we endure adversity differently when we find our contentment in God.[92] Moreover, his reading of the statements in Eccl 8:15 prompted him to regard adversities as a "necessary repetition"—necessary because of our "forgetfulness."[93] In the Reformer's thinking, joy given to the human heart suggests not mere toleration but delight.

When Luther approached the joy refrain found in Eccl 9:7–10, two elements stood out. First, he rendered the last part of verse 7 ("God has already approved your works," NASB1995) as "God accepts your works and actions." This is in keeping with Luther's concern to validate—and redefine—good works in his day. Second, in a fascinating way he tied the concluding admonition of verse 10—"Whatever your hand finds to do, do it with all your might"—to the admonition found in 1 Sam 10:7—"do whatever your hand finds to do, for God is with you." As Luther viewed it, the wisdom of the Teacher here is of the very same type commanded by Samuel of the newly appointed King Saul. What the two texts have in common, according to Luther's understanding, is the aspect of "the now" that is part of every believer's vocation. God is in the present, as the language of "whatever your hand finds to do" suggests. Luther was interested in the tension of each present moment; we recognize both God's providence and our freedom, and we are free—*gloriously* free—to act. Therefore, the Christian need not be paralyzed by the fear of making the wrong decision or doing the wrong thing. The biblical writer's statement

---

[91] Luther, *Notes on Ecclesiastes, LW* 15:93.
[92] Luther, 15:120.
[93] Luther, 15:142.

"God has already approved what you do" (Eccl 9:7) was, for Luther, a huge source of confidence to the godly.[94]

How often have we heard or perhaps even offered to others the well-intended statement "God loves you and has a wonderful plan for your life"? Since its implication is that we must search for that one unique plan, which is thought to be shrouded in mystery, much like a maze, this is advice that may well need to be put to rest. For many of us, the images associated with that search are often anxiety-producing—two in particular. One we might call a personal "will-of-God" train that is leaving the station at five minutes before midnight on a certain date, and if I am not on that train, I have forever missed God's will for me. A second common notion of "God's will" is analogous to wandering my way through a completely unmarked labyrinth without directions. I surely hope that I can find my way out of this maze, given my assumption that it has only one exit.[95] As Luther intuited, grace—and its correlative doctrine of vocation—releases us from this sort of supremely paralyzing "hit-or-miss" mentality.[96]

Let us return to Luther's Ecclesiastes "Notes." The last of the joy refrains, found in Eccl 11:7–12:1, reminds Luther of the basic need to be cheerful yet sober. For "When the heart has been correctly instructed,"

---

[94] Luther, 15:148.

[95] As one who has spent most of his professional career as a college professor in a Christian liberal arts context, I can vouch that these images are very real—and paralyzing—to many. College students today will be told to expect multiple "career changes." Thus, they will need grounding that transcends "occupation," the "market," the "workplace," and "the state of the economy." A sense of "vocation," which transcends all these, even when it encompasses these, is imperative, for vocation helps shape our sense of responsibilities to the world around us (the "common good"), and hence our responsibilities to the "neighbor."

[96] Kathryn Kleinhans, "The Work of a Christian: Vocation in Lutheran Perspective," *Word and World* 24, no. 4 (2005): 400, is helpful here: "Justification by faith" does not mean always "getting it right." Rather, "[T]he Christian is free to act, accepting the possibility of failure while trusting in Christ's victory over sin and death."

he notes, "no joy or happiness will harm it, so long as it is a genuine joy and not a happiness that brings corruption." What is more, as Luther sees it, these verses counter the attitude of the monks, who are legalistic, ascetic, and self-denying.[97] Again, we observe in Luther's interpretation a contrast between the religious system which he left, as a former monk, and the glorious liberty into which he entered as a result of his conversion through the discovery of divine grace.

In summarizing the message of Ecclesiastes, Luther notes that "the vanity of the human heart . . . is never content with the gifts of God that are present." Nevertheless, "with thanksgiving we may use the things that are present and . . . generously given to us and conferred upon us by the blessing of God." What is more, we should do so "without anxiety" about the future, each seeking to have "a tranquil and quiet heart and mind filled with joy." Such will allow us to "be content with the Word and work of God."[98] Contentment, tranquility, and grateful acknowledgement of God's good gifts—these represent the teaching of Ecclesiastes, confirming for Luther the importance of work and *vocatio*. Therefore, he concludes, we should take stock of the good things we have.[99]

Modern (and Postmodern) Challenges to Luther on Work and Vocation

In recent years it has become customary—perhaps even fashionable—to criticize the Reformed breakthrough of the early sixteenth century concerning vocation. Often this critique proceeds on a misunderstanding of Luther's emphasis on "vocation" and "stations" in life, based on the supposition that Luther wished to buttress the status quo and not encourage

---

[97] Luther, *Notes on Ecclesiastes, LW* 15:177.
[98] Luther, 15:10–11.
[99] Luther, 15:11.

social mobility.[100] But part of this critique can also be attributed to an ignoring of the strong accent, in the writings of both Luther and Calvin, on neighbor-love, mutual service, and the common good.

Regarding the first criticism, part of the backlash against Luther is his use of the language of "stations" or "states" (*Stände*, in German) and his reliance on the texts of 1 Cor 7:17 ("Let each one live his life in the situation the Lord assigned when God called him"), 7:20 ("Let each of you remain in the situation in which he was called"), and 7:24 ("Brothers and sisters, each person is to remain with God in the situation in which he was called"). These various "stations" in life, as Luther saw them, are actually themselves callings that come from—or, are assigned by—God. Luther's understanding of the 1 Corinthians 7 texts is not that one *may* not change, only that one *need* not change, in order to serve God.[101] Whether or not we agree with Luther's particular interpretation and application of these Pauline admonitions, the accent on contentment in one's particular "calling" (Gk.: *klēsis*; German: *Beruf* or *Stand*, i.e., "station" or "location," and by extension, "calling") is peculiarly Lutheran, speaking to the believer's everyday work and responsibilities. For Martin Luther,

---

[100] While part of the criticism of Luther as "buttressing the status quo" is based on his "high" view of political authority, this concern brings us too far afield of the present discussion. Suffice it say that his social concern, addressed below, did not mean merely acquiescing to political authority, as his many treatises and correspondence to various public authorities bear out, even when Luther was acutely aware of the importance of political protection for the Reformation cause. And even when the peasant revolts of the mid-1520s claimed, at least in part, their inspiration from Luther's teaching, they went far beyond his understanding of political authority properly construed. Thus, for example, we may understand the importance of Luther's treatises *On Temporal Authority* (1523), *Against the Robbing, Murdering Hordes* (1525), *An Open Letter on the Harsh Book against the Peasant* (1525), and *An Admonition to Peace. A Reply to the Twelve Articles of the Swabian Peasants* (1525), and the spirit in which they are written.

[101] Properly interpreting Luther here is Kleinhans, "The Work of a Christian," 399–400.

one's "station" was that specific arena in which one serves God and serves the common good—this under the umbrella of God's providential care.

In chapter 3 we noted perhaps the most vigorous opposition to Luther's accent on vocation, marshaled by Yale theologian Miroslav Volf.[102] Volf's attempt to build an eschatological theology of work proceeds on a fundamental assumption: we must resist any attempts to understand work in terms of vocation as Luther understood it. Volf worries that vocation rooted in the creation order, to which Luther tied it, is insensitive to the status quo in which worker "alienation" and unjust economic systems of the modern world predominate.[103] This view of Luther, however, misconstrues his view of creation, which is not static or fixed but rather an ongoing, daily project, based on an awareness of divine providence.[104] It also ignores a theme prominent in Luther's sermons and writings, namely, his concern for the poor and his decrying of injustice. What is often overlooked in the literature on Luther—and Volf is only illustrative—is the degree to which theological reform of the sixteenth century led to social reform. Thus, viewed with a wider and more culturally discerning lens, Luther's approach to vocation mediates the tension between stability and mobility, between the status quo and positive change.[105] Finally, Volf's position ignores the value that Luther placed on rest, which prevents us from believing

---

[102] See Miroslav Volf, *Work in the Spirit: Toward a Theology of Work* (Oxford: Oxford University Press, 1991).

[103] To examine the idolization of work or the alienating, fragmenting, and dehumanizing effects of work in the modern era—a conspicuously Marxist theme—takes us too far afield of the Lutheran breakthrough of the sixteenth century. Against Volf and those who share his view, it is inaccurate and anachronistic to lay these problems at the feet of Luther, who lived "between the times" and is responding to distortions in a conception of vocation and work whose roots extend back well over a millennium.

[104] See, for example, Luther's *Larger Catechism* (1529), in *The Book of Concord*, ed. and trans. Theodore G. Tappert (Philadelphia: Fortress, 1959), esp. 430.

[105] So, correctly in my view, Wingren, *Luther on Vocation*, xii.

that his accent on work and vocation mirrors an idolizing and hence unhealthy view of work.[106]

It needs reiterating that Volf inter alia is anachronistic in his criticisms of the early sixteenth century. In truth, Luther was very much concerned about addressing social needs in his day and not merely intent on blessing the status quo. And as a university professor he encouraged education for the youth of his day—both boys *and* girls—as he considered the future.[107] This, as he intuited, was the chief means by which social mobility—where it was possible—might occur. So, for example, in his 1524 address "To the Councilmen of All Cities in Germany That They Establish and Maintain Christian Schools," Luther pointed to education as part of that which is essential to serving the needs of a changing society.[108] Luther well recognized that a proper understanding of vocation helps shape our sense of responsibilities, and hence, how we view education and training.

Moreover, Luther's emphasis on the individuality of calling and Christian freedom needs accentuating. In his *Lectures on Genesis* (1535), Luther wrote, "Just as individuals are different, so their duties are different; and in accordance with the diversity of their callings, God demands diverse works of them."[109] In fact, not the nature of any individual work but the call to serve others guided Luther's understanding. We should consider "nothing except the need and the advantage of . . . [the] neighbor."[110] The accent on neighbor-love in Luther's writings and sermons answers any criticism that he was mainly intent on affirming the status quo.

Before we turn to Luther's concern for the poor and underprivileged, the focus of which is broadly lacking in many contemporary assessments

---

[106] In many respects, Volf devotes more attention to Marx than to Luther.

[107] Luther's advocacy of education for girls would have been trendsetting.

[108] The address can be found in *Luther's Works*, ed. Walther I. Brandt (Philadelphia: Fortress, 1962), 45:341–378.

[109] Luther, *Lectures on Genesis Chapters 6–14*, *LW*, 2:113.

[110] Luther, *The Freedom of the Christian*, *LW* 31:365.

of the Reformer, two further examples of criticism as it concerns Luther's understanding of vocation are worth noting. In his essay "Rethinking Work as Vocation: From Protestant Advice to Gospel Corrective," Scott Waalkes looks at Luther's emphasis on vocation and demonstrates a sensitivity to the danger of transforming vocation into egoistic "self-discovery" and denying the cross.[111] This concern, particularly in our day, to avoid distorted, self-centered conceptions of vocation is surely commendable. At the same time, Waalkes's gospel corrective seems to misread Luther on the topics of the cross and Christian discipleship and has the feel of a Quaker or Anabaptist reaction to Reformed thought. Luther himself, it turns out, offered the needed corrective to the purported corrective. He noted that it is "highly necessary that we suffer," not only "that God may prove his honor, power, and strength against the devil," but also "in order that when we are not in trouble and suffering this excellent treasure which we have may not merely make us sleepy and secure."[112] Moreover, he observes, "Christian suffering is nobler and precious above all other human suffering because, since Christ himself suffered, he also hallowed the suffering of all his Christians."[113]

In a second essay, "Vocation in Theology and Psychology: Conflicting Approaches?," Marco Rotman explores what he believes to be the inadequacies of the Protestant Reformation's emphasis of work as vocation, arguing that "practicing the love command" and a restoration of "God's intentions for creation" best define vocation in biblical theology.[114] Here it needs stating that the church stands in fundamental agreement with Rotman insofar as charity and creation indeed are at the heart of

---

[111] Scott Waalkes, "Rethinking Work as Vocation: From Protestant Advice to Gospel Corrective," *Christian Scholar's Review* 44, no. 2 (Winter 2015): 135–54.

[112] Martin Luther, *Sermon on Cross and Suffering*, in *Luther's Works*, ed. John W. Doberstein (Philadelphia: Fortress, 1959), 51:207.

[113] Luther, 207.

[114] Marco Rotman, "Vocation in Theology and Psychology: Conflicting Approaches?," *Christian Higher Education* 16, nos. 1–2 (2017): 23–32.

God's intentions. And in actuality, lodged at the very heart of Luther's own understanding of vocation were precisely these two components, which are amply demonstrated in his writings. Rotman's seeming inability to detect in Luther's writings the "practice of the love command"—a remarkable omission—serves as an invitation to reexamine Luther's commitment to social reform. It is to this topic I now turn.

Luther on Social Concern

Before summarizing the overall effects of the early sixteenth-century Lutheran breakthrough, we turn briefly to Luther's concern for the disadvantaged. It is remarkable that this particular focus is generally lacking in many contemporary assessments of the Reformer.[115] Sadly, Luther's work in social reform and concern for the common good are generally neglected.[116] It is this very lack that leads church historian Mark Noll to

---

[115] Notable exceptions to this include Jaroslav Pelikan, "After the Monks—What?," *The Springfielder* 31, no. 3 (1967): 3–21; Samuel Torvend, *Luther and the Hungry Poor: Gathered Fragments* (Minneapolis: Fortress, 2008); Carter Lindberg, *Beyond Charity: Reformation Initiatives for the Poor* (Minneapolis: Fortress, 1993); Lindberg, *The European Reformations*, 108–29, esp. chapter 5; and Carter Lindberg and Paul Wee, ed., *The Forgotten Luther: Reclaiming the Social-Economic Dimension of the Reformation* (Minneapolis: Lutheran University Press, 2016).

[116] The frequent criticism is that Luther's world was relatively static, with little social mobility. This criticism, however, needs severe qualification. It is anachronistic to make comparisons between late-medieval and modern or contemporary society, whether they pertain to ecclesial affairs, political developments, or social-economic realities. To claim that Luther was beholden to the status quo assumes that late-medieval society was fluid and that Luther did not use his platform to encourage ecclesial, political, or socioeconomic change. Both assumptions, of course, are false. That Luther did in fact utilize his platform to encourage change, in virtually every aspect of late-medieval life, is clear. His own life tells us much. He came from a miner's family to the study of theology and a university professorate, by which he helped create various faculties of learning (including law and medicine). Moreover, a serious and honest reading of his writings and sermons confirms this assessment. An examination of Luther's

point out, "Where Protestant evangelicalism tends to be weak, Lutheran theology is strong, integrating in a holistic manner a responsible social-political model into the public sphere without confusing ultimate spiritual values and secondary social or political ends."[117] In light of that comment, we surely do well to revisit Luther's social concerns.

Let us begin with Luther's context. The years of 1470 to 1530 are generally considered transitional in economic, social, and religious terms. Throughout his career as a Reformer, many of his opponents were accusing Luther of abandoning good works, some of which resulted from his emphasis on justification by faith and some of which issued out of his assessment of the letter of James—a matter I addressed in chapter 2.[118] In addition, lest we forget, Luther, the son of a miner, studied law and theology, and—as a university professor—was living proof that education could help facilitate a measure of social mobility.[119] And lest we also forget, in Luther's lifetime the bubonic plague swept into Wittenberg

---

correspondence, in fact, estimated by historian Lewis W. Spitz ("Luther's Social Concern for Students," in Lawrence P. Buck and Jonathan W. Zophy, eds., *The Social History of the Reformation* [Columbus: Ohio State University Press, 1972), 249) makes clear that Luther wrote *thousands* of letters during his career. Many of them reveal "an astonishing preoccupation with the physical and social well-being of his students." Examples of Luther's council to various students have been reproduced in Spitz, pp. 263–65.

[117] Mark Noll, "What Lutherans Have to Offer Public Theology," *Lutheran Quarterly* 22 (2008): 125–36.

[118] Luther's heirs, it is true, have not always held faith and works together well.

[119] Moreover, Luther's son Paul would become a noted physician. A second son, Martin, studied theology but died at a fairly young age (in 1565). A third son, Hans, became a jurist. In addition, Luther together with his theologically minded colleague Philip Melanchthon would be instrumental in the development of a medical faculty at the University of Wittenberg.

three times—in 1521, in 1527, and again in 1535.[120] By the end of the second plague, Luther had lost two brothers and a sister. On the first occasion, the Reformer had been exiled in the Wartburg castle, following his excommunication from the church via a papal bull in 1521. On the second and third occasions, Luther chose—against the stream and convictions of his chief patron—to remain in Wittenberg and serve the sick and dying.

In both of these dreadful periods, Luther's pastoral side was abundantly on display. In his treatise *Whether One May Flee from a Deadly Plague* (1527), Luther offers his rationale for remaining in Wittenberg at a time when virtually all students and fellow faculty were fleeing the city.[121] While fleeing per se is not a bad thing, according to Luther, it can be done for the right or the wrong reasons. One must not leave a neighbor in need, particularly if one is a shepherd of God's flock. For Luther, fear and faith are very different responses.

While standard biographical accounts of Luther's life are attentive to Luther's fear of death—which he never totally overcame even as he labored according to these convictions—the reality of the Black Death clearly fueled his torment. Described by one Luther biographer as a "three-year crucible of terror," this three-year period was witness to "parents abandoning their children, streets filled with corpses, and towns becoming morgues."[122] During the 1527 plague, some eighteen deaths had occurred in Wittenberg only two weeks into the ordeal, causing one

---

[120] In 1542, four years before his death, Luther wrote about this: "I have now lived through three pestilences and have visited several persons who suffered from [the] sickness." Martin Luther, *Table Talk* (October 1542): "Should Minsters Flee in Time of Pestilence?" in *Luther's Works,* ed. Theodore G. Tappert (Philadelphia: Fortress, 1967), 54:434. By most estimates, roughly one-third of Europe's population died between 1348 and 1350.

[121] See Martin Luther, "Whether One May Flee from a Deadly Plague," *LW* 43:119–38.

[122] Massing, *Fatal Discord,* 25.

observer to note, "For a small village, an average of at least one [plague] death a day must have been frightening."[123] Worse, several of those deaths involved Luther's family members—two brothers and a sister—as well as friends.[124] It is generally thought that the sheer despair and challenges of this season induced Luther to write the magnificent hymn, "A Mighty Fortress Is Our God."[125]

Relatedly, yet to the surprise of some, Luther maintained "a passionate and nearly lifelong commitment to addressing the systemic causes of hunger and poverty."[126] There existed for the Reformer no single, scripturally mandated model of economics or market activity to which the Christian might look.[127] What undergirded Luther's social conscience, rather, were inherently theological realities—chief among these were Christian freedom (mediated by grace) and faith acting through love. Moreover, what usually receives even less attention is Luther's domestic situation. In addition to their own six children, Luther and his wife, Katie, adopted four children born to his sister, who died in 1529.[128] What is more, an aunt on Katie's side, Magdalene von Bora, also lived with them until her death in 1537. This is fully aside from the fact that university students rented rooms from the Luthers and guests frequently stayed in their home.

---

[123] See Nathan Runham, "Why Did Luther *Not* Flee from the Deadly Plague?" *The Presbyterian Banner* (May 2020), May 17, 2020, https://hail.to/laidlaw-college/publication/z0YvCh2/article/otABdxy.

[124] Luther, "Whether One May Flee," *LW* 43:115–16.

[125] See Andreas Loewe and Katharine R. Firth, "Martin Luther's 'Mighty Fortress,'" *Lutheran Quarterly* 32, no. 2 (2018): 128–29. Luther viewed "A Mighty Fortress" as a *Tröstpsalm*, a psalm of comfort. Although the hymn's exact occasion is undocumented, it first appeared in the late 1520s and was widely sung throughout Protestant Europe by 1546, the year of Luther's death.

[126] See Paul Wee and Conrad Braaten, "Introduction," in Lindberg and Wee, *The Forgotten Luther*.

[127] We do well, 500 years removed, to remember and apply this general rule.

[128] On Luther's family life, see Martin Brecht, *Martin Luther: The Preservation of the Church, 1532–1546* (Minneapolis: Fortress, 1993), esp. chap. 9.

If we limit our assessment only to socioeconomic concerns and exclude the *Ninety-Five Theses* (which addresses ecclesio-social issues[129]), the treatise *To the Christian Nobility of the German Nation* (in which Luther addresses political, ecclesial, and economic realities as they together affect the German lands[130]), as well as his many sermons (in which Luther the pastor speaks to the true needs of his congregants), we find no less than seven of Luther's published works dealing specifically with social and economic issues. In fact, given the strong accent in Luther's writings on neighbor-love and the common good, coupled with his frequent criticism of the social vices of greed and extortion, it becomes impossible to miss Luther's genuine concern for the disadvantaged. As supremely practical evidence thereof, we discover that he was instrumental in helping establish in Wittenberg a primitive social welfare system through the creation of a community chest—a development that would spread to other towns and cities in Germany. Widows and orphans and the truly disadvantaged, he believed, simply must not be forgotten.

To further evidence Luther's social concern and refute the common criticism that Luther was only "buttressing the status quo" and not

---

[129] Luther's *Ninety-Five Theses* was both theological and economic in trajectory. Therein, he addresses charity and poor relief in at least four places—in theses 41, 45, 50, and 51. In thesis 41 Luther writes that people may "erroneously think that [indulgences] are preferable to other good works of love"; however, these do not "promote charity." In thesis 45 Luther notes that giving indulgences while seeing "a needy man" and "passing by" has the effect of "buying God's wrath." In thesis 50 Luther observes that, if the pope knew of the strategies of indulgence preachers, "he would rather that the basilica of St. Peter [be] burned to ashes"; sadly, the indulgence sellers are "skinning" the sheep, while the common people have little or nothing left. And in thesis 51 Luther insists that the pope should help the truly poor, "even though he had to sell the basilica of St. Peter," since so many people are barely scraping by. Here I am dependent on Martin Luther, *Explanations of the Ninety-Five Theses*, in *Luther's Works*, ed. Harold J. Grimm (Philadelphia: Fortress, 1957), 31:79–252.

[130] From a purely economic standpoint, this treatise includes Luther's condemnation of pilgrimages, indulgences, and hoarding—all of which, he felt, mirrored a misuse of wealth and earthly goods.

encouraging social mobility, let me summarize four of the seven aforementioned works: *An Ordinance of a Common Chest* (1523), *On Trading and Usury* (1524), *To the Councilmen of All Cities in Germany (That They Establish and Maintain Christian Schools)* (1524), and *Sermon on Keeping Children in School* (1530).[131]

In *On Trading and Usury*, Luther exhorts his readers toward a golden rule ethic in business and economic activity. In his view of money, wealth, and property, he worries that avarice leads to an unscrupulous use of interest (that is, usury). However, there are important economic—and ecclesial— reasons why he was worried about this matter, with one being particularly galling. St. Peter's Basilica in Rome was being built as a result of banking practices aided by the payment of annual plenary indulgences.[132] In fact, the specific reasons standing behind Luther's publication of the *Ninety-Five Theses*, the creation of which was done in the conventional mode of an academic disputation, were the purchase of ecclesiastical offices and the selling of indulgences—in short, the increasingly commercial nature of dispensing spiritual merit.[133] In Thesis 66, for example, Luther complains

---

[131] The other three publications concern Luther's reaction to the peasant revolts of the mid-1520s.

[132] Illustrating Luther's dilemma is the fact that Albrecht of Brandenburg had sought the Archbishopric of Mainz (which position he would hold from 1514 until 1545), knowing that funding coming from the Fugger banking house would assist him. Given the preaching of indulgences by Johann Tetzel in the wider region beginning in 1516, a commission that received Albrecht's blessing, Luther would vehemently object, resulting in a letter of protest to Albrecht. Soon thereafter a copy of Luther's *Ninety-Five Theses* would be sent both to Albrecht and to Pope Leo X. One Reformation historian, observing that the medieval church had become very adept at "wedding the market economy with the economy of salvation," cites a 1530 broadsheet—"The Minter's Reply"— which complained that the pope sold not only indulgences, dispensations, and offices but, ultimately, salvation itself; see Carter Lindberg, "Luther on a Market Economy," *Lutheran Quarterly* 30 (2016): 375.

[133] We are thus justified in arguing that Luther's heretical status, from the standpoint of Rome, was both theological and economic in nature. The latter element causes economic historian Philipp R. Rössner, "Burying Money?

that "the treasures of indulgences are nets with which one now fishes for the wealth of men."[134] In the words of one German historian, indulgences had become "an unholy alliance" between "early modern financial wizardry and the pastoral needs of the people."[135] What's more, bribery in Luther's day was perceived as commonplace, as is suggested both by the tone of *On Trading and Usury* as well as Luther's famous words uttered in another context: "The world is one big whorehouse, completely submerged in greed," wherein "big thieves act as judges of [and hang] little thieves."[136]

Luther's own view of wealth, it should be noted, was largely one of indifference. Despite the widespread perception, Luther was not opposed to a market economy, only its worst abuses. He was a proponent of neither poverty nor riches; contentment, as he saw it, was the desired outcome toward which we should strive. *On Trading and Usury* begins by him citing Paul's admonition to Timothy to beware of greed (1 Tim 6:10)—a vice that Luther worried was rampant in "all lands." Its general burden is that people tend to acquire monetary wealth by dishonest means. In the end, Luther admonished his readers to give to others where and when they can, in the same way that Christ our Lord gave himself away.

Any criticism that Luther was an economic "reactionary," given his outspoken position on avarice, greed, and extortion, misses the mark. In fact, one economic historian insists that the common caricature of Luther as a sort of "medieval ignoramus" with little economic insight who is "shooting against the forces of modern capitalism" is false and in need

---

Monetary Origins and Afterlives of Luther's Reformation," *History of Political Economy* 48, no. 2 (2016): 254, to argue that "the Reformation of 1517 had monetary origins."

[134] Luther, *Ninety-Five Theses*, in *LW* 31:31.

[135] Schilling, *Martin Luther*, 128.

[136] Martin Luther, *The Sermon on the Mount*, in *Luther's Works*, ed. Jaroslav Pelikan (St. Louis: Concordia, 1956), 21:180, and idem, *Lectures on Romans*, in *Luther's Works*, ed. Hilton C. Oswald (St. Louis: Concordia, 1972), 25:172, respectively.

of debunking.¹³⁷ In fairness, it needs to be acknowledged that this period represents a transition from a chiefly agricultural to an early industrial economy.¹³⁸ Therefore, one can expect that Reformers would be responding to and reacting against excesses becoming normative in an environment in which a "profit economy" was taking hold. Moreover, we do well to recall that Luther's father was a miner (and an entrepreneur, at that), at a time when various regions of Germany were experiencing something of an economic boom due to the discovery of mining possibilities like copper and silver.¹³⁹ Significantly, one of the leading economic historians of the early-modern period argues that Luther was one of the earliest voices of this transitional economic era in contending for "principled economics."¹⁴⁰

The transition in Germany from a chiefly agricultural to an increasingly industrial economy needs some comment. Cultural innovation in German territories around 1500, as one German historian observes, was no "foreign import"; by the late fifteenth century, church and all

---

¹³⁷ See Philipp R. Rössner, "Martin Luther and the Making of the Modern Economic Mind," *International Review of Economics* 66 (2019): 233.

¹³⁸ Few have captured the character of this socioeconomic transition more effectively than Schilling, *Martin Luther,* 9–115, and Lindberg, "Luther on a Market Economy," 373–92.

¹³⁹ Economic historian Philipp Rössner estimates that even before the 1550s, more than 50 percent of silver available for global trade was being produced in this region of Germany ("Martin Luther and the Making of the Modern Economic Mind," 237). And Luther biographer Lindal Roper estimates that 80–90 percent of European copper came from Mansfield where Luther grew up and south Tyrol. *Martin Luther: Renegade and Prophet* (New York: Random House, 2016), 419–20, n. 5. According to Rössner ("Burying Money?," 225–63), the silver boom in Germany occurred in the 1470s.

¹⁴⁰ See Philipp R. Rössner, *Deflation—Devaluation—Rebellion: Geld im Zeitalter der Reformation,* VSWB 219 (Stuttgart: Franz Steiner Verlag, 2012); Rössner, *Martin Luther: On Commerce and Usury (1524)* (New York: Anthem, 2016); Rössner, "Burying Money?," 225–63; and Rössner, "Martin Luther and the Making of the Modern Economic Mind," 233–48.

of society were in a state of transition.[141] A new dynamism was infusing politics,[142] economic affairs, the arts, and education.[143] The mining expansion noted above, in which Luther's father was embedded as a smelting entrepreneur,[144] was only part of the reason for socioeconomic change. Wittenberg, situated by the Elbe River, was host to growing commerce; and when Luther arrived in 1511 following his studies at the University of Erfurt, the city's transformation was well underway.[145] But

---

[141] Schilling, *Martin Luther*, 32.

[142] At this time Niccolò Machiavelli of Florence (1469–1527) was developing his secular political model.

[143] The University of Wittenberg, through the vision, graces, and financial provision of Frederick the Wise, would be created in 1502, in accordance with his commitment to Renaissance developments throughout Europe. The man's resources were in part due to silver mines in his territory, which would help build the new university. Until this time, the University of Erfurt, founded in the late fourteenth century and at which Luther studied, was one of only two universities in central Germany. By 1513, only eleven years after its founding, Wittenberg has four faculties—theology, the arts, law, and medicine—and forty-four professors. Its enrollment would peak in 1544, two years before Luther's death, at 814 students (Schilling, *Martin Luther*, 100). Based on archival evidence, no fewer than 16,300 students attended the university between 1520 and 1560, coming from all over Europe. See E. G. Schwiebert, *Luther and His Times: The Reformation from a New Perspective* (St. Louis: Concordia, 1950), 2–3.

[144] Luther grew up in a mining boom occurring in the Harz Mountains and Saxony. On occasion in his work, Luther would note, with some delight, that he was the son of a "poor minor" (*Bergheuer*). However, while it is true that Luther's grandfather was a peasant, his own reports of a poor heritage are somewhat exaggerated. The truth is that his father was by no means poor; by most accounts, he did well in business, which may explain his exasperation when his son decided to become an Augustinian monk. Regardless, upon his death, Luther's father reportedly bequeathed a minor fortune (see Rössner, "Burying Money?" 230). Fascinating background information in this regard can be found in Schilling, *Martin Luther*, 39–41, and Martin Brecht, *Martin Luther: His Road to Reformation, 1483–1521*, trans. James L. Schaaf (Minneapolis: Fortress, 1985), esp. chapter 1.

[145] Erfurt, in Luther's day, was one of the four largest cities in Germany and a commercial center, at which major routes intersected. It was also considered "little Rome" inasmuch as it was home to an estimated 800 clergy and monks

what would be perhaps the most important factor for Luther was the patron and creator of the young university, Prince Frederick the Wise himself;[146] for it lay in his "sovereignty" to protect Luther and the early Reformation cause.

In addition to socioeconomic changes that surrounded him even before he arrived at Wittenberg, Luther was himself an educator, and this would have necessitated that he be confronted with financial matters on every side. That was particularly the case at the fledgling University of Wittenberg. One of Luther's great concerns was that his enormously gifted younger colleague, Philip Melanchthon, would be hired away by other universities.[147] It was fortunate, given Luther's awareness of socio-

---

(see Brecht, *Martin Luther: Shaping and Defining the Reformation*, 26) as well as twenty-one parish churches, eleven monastery churches, and four endowed churches (see Massing, *Fatal Discord*, 76).

[146] As a Renaissance man, Frederick was "second only to Emperor Maximilian" in embodying the ideal of "an energetic Renaissance prince," according to Schilling (*Martin Luther*, 94).

[147] Upon listening to Melanchthon, Luther gives the impression of being spellbound, causing him to declare, "While Philip is alive, I desire no other Greek teacher"; see Martin Luther, "To George Spalatin," in *Luther's Works*, ed. Gottfried G. Krodel (Philadelphia: Fortress, 1963), 48:78. A year after Melanchthon's 1518 arrival at the university, Luther writes that the "little Greek scholar outdoes [him] even in theology itself"; see Martin Luther, "To Johannes Lang" (1519), in *LW* 48:136. Indeed, it is Melanchthon who would be "the chief teacher and instructor, the scholarly publicist, and the theological diplomat" of the early Reformation cause; see Robert Stupperich, *Melanchthon: The Enigma of the Reformation*, trans. Robert H. Fischer (Philadelphia: Westminster, 1965), 151. And while, in the eyes of many, the "confessor" (Luther) is greater than the "professor" (Melanchthon), the Protestant Reformation could never have been established or carried through without the latter as argued by Franz Hildebrandt, *Melanchthon: Alien or Ally?* (Cambridge: Cambridge University Press, 1946), xi. Interestingly, in his own lifetime, Melanchthon was accorded the remarkable title *Praeceptor Germaniae*, the "Teacher of Germany." Elsewhere I have examined Melanchthon's extraordinary—though oft forgotten—influence in J. Daryl Charles, "Natural Law and Protestant Reform: Lessons from a Forgotten Reformer," in *Wisdom's Work: Essays on Ethics, Vocation, and Culture* (Grand Rapids: Acton Institute, 2019), 61–87.

economic realities, that Luther's wife, Katie, to his great joy, was remarkably adept at running a large household, and thus attuned to social need. She is known, in addition to having rented out rooms in their home,[148] to have had her hand in various real estate purchases.[149] By the time of his death, Luther was one of the wealthier individuals in Wittenberg, his vehement criticisms of greed and usury notwithstanding. Hence, the very notion that Luther was economically "naïve" or "reactionary" is simply uninformed.

The context for *An Ordinance of a Common Chest* is the late-medieval practice of almsgiving. Therein Luther observed what he insisted was a wrong motivation behind this practice: giving to the poor was often done as an act of self-merit rather than neighbor-love. He decried how the church had gotten "fat," because the "spiritual estate" was filled with greed. Through much of his life Luther would excoriate greed and an "unregulated profit economy" that exploited others, whether that was done inside the church or out.[150] In medieval and late-medieval society, two principal forms of charity existed: the private and the institutional, the latter instrument being the monastery, since monks were perceived as mediating between God and the common folk.

Luther's response to this ecclesial distortion was twofold. He believed that the political authorities should intervene and take the bloated possessions that had accrued in the monasteries and redistribute them accordingly to those who stood in real need. Concomitantly, the community

---

[148] The Luthers' home, the "Black Cloister," was a former monastery well suited for renting rooms to university students.

[149] One Reformation historian writes that Katie dealt with the various responsibilities of a large household "so expertly that the provisioning of the household generated a profit that could then be invested in property" (Schilling, *Martin Luther*, 287). On the rather remarkable wife who stood alongside Luther, see Martin Treu, "Katherina von Bora: The Woman at Luther's Side," *Lutheran Quarterly* 13 (1999): 157–78.

[150] Luther's attacks on greed were the flip side of his promotion of the common good through neighbor-love.

chest ordinances in many German cities helped to create the needed alternative, both by redefining poverty and charity and by calling local communities to be responsible for their own "poor relief." Foundationally, Luther opposed begging (what he called "mendicancy") and almsgiving. Because the latter had come to be viewed as meritorious, even salvific, by the fifteenth century, begging had proliferated, often taking advantage of well-intended but misguided "Christian charity."[151] "Poverty" tended to lose its halo, as it were, due to Luther's emphasis on the universal priesthood. The "common chest" represented a discriminating form of charity, with its rejection of professional begging and its understanding of poor relief as stewardship. Poverty then, Luther insisted, is not to be "recommended, chosen, or taught."[152] At the same time, Luther believed that every town or city had the responsibility of helping its own disadvantaged. Christian love, he argued, should motivate us. Faith working through love expresses for Luther a theology of practice.

In 1522, Luther praised the creation of the Wittenberg *Kastenordnung*—literally, a regulation or ordinance for a common chest—that was established for the truly poor. He called it a model for other communities. The common chest had weekly collection and disbursements and was overseen by four stewards (townspeople). It funded orphans, children of the poor, poor women with no dowries, education for poor children, and work training for the underemployed.[153] A year later, Luther would write the town council of Leisnig, located southeast of Wittenberg, to

---

[151] Indeed, Christian charity has a duty to the poor (Jas 1:27), and that is noncontroversial. The controversy is lodged in how we define poverty and why people are poor. Luther recognized that charity so-called can be misguided and wrongly motivated.

[152] Martin Luther, *Lectures on Deuteronomy* (1525), in *Luther's Works*, ed. Jaroslav Pelikan (St. Louis: Concordia, 1960), 9:148.

[153] Eventually, the Wittenberg "common chest" added a physician who was paid with funds from the chest itself. On the development of social welfare in Wittenberg, see Carter Lindberg, "Luther and the Common Chest," in Lindberg and Wee, eds., *The Forgotten Luther*, 9–29.

encourage the establishment of a common chest there as well. Although attempts to set up this fund in Leisnig would meet considerable ongoing challenges, the concept of a community chest would become, in time, a model of social welfare in Germany that continued into the nineteenth century, appearing in even the major cities of Augsburg, Nuremberg, and Erfurt. Remarkably, the city archives of Wittenberg have accounting records of the community chest stretching from 1524 to 1806.[154] In terms of public welfare, Luther's Wittenberg was trendsetting.

From about the time of Luther's conversion, there appears in his writings the idea that education is important for the poor and the young—both girls and boys. Above all, what one detects in these writings, in addition to Luther's denunciation of the monastic system, is that education has social value. This is the broader burden of his treatise *To the Councilmen of All Cities in Germany*. Luther's appeal is to leaders in the community. And that appeal would have an effect: by about 1600, some 300 schools were established throughout Germany in different regions—a phenomenon admired even by Roman Catholics of the day.[155] Luther was convinced that education will prosper a people.[156]

In this vein, Luther worried that the common people of his time were indifferent to education. What's more, the church did not help matters. A fundamental conviction, which grew out of his conversion and his belief in the universal priesthood, was that failing to develop a child's gifts and abilities is to be unfaithful. After all, Luther reasoned in his published sermon *On Keeping Children in School*, where will tomorrow's leaders

---

[154] Albrecht Steinwachs, "The Common Chest as a Social Achievement of the Reformation," *Lutheran Quarterly* 22, no. 2 (2008): 192.

[155] What surely abetted Luther's efforts in education was the influence of his younger but extraordinarily gifted colleague at the University of Wittenberg, Philip Melanchthon. On Melanchthon's relationship to Luther and wider influence, see Charles, "Natural Law and Protestant Reform, 61–87 (see n. 147).

[156] Based on archival evidence, Luther's reputation at Wittenberg, a relatively young university (founded in 1502), contributed to a sharp increase in enrollment. See Schwiebert, *Luther and His Times*, 3.

come from if young people are not prepared to lead? Given the importance of wisdom in the human experience, as taught in Proverbs, who will govern Germany according to law in the future? Who will become her judges, her secretaries, her notaries, her leaders, and her rulers? Without the study of history and theology and law, Luther reasons, a society—and certainly German society—has no real future. There has never been a better time than the present to study, he admonished his readers.

Examining the late medieval relief of the poor, Reformation historian Carter Lindberg argues that Luther was the "first major Reformer to address the theory and praxis of early modern poor relief and social welfare,"[157] as evidenced in the Wittenberg Church Order of January 22, 1522. The notion of poor relief, however, is here in need of some context, and not a little cleansing.

The late-medieval church received the longstanding notion of poverty as godliness. This understanding can be traced back over a millennium to the patristic era. Closer to Luther's day, monastic orders would have routinely cited from the Sermon on the Mount in support of a "poverty-as-godliness" theological premise. Benedictines tended to cite Matt 5:3—"Blessed are the poor in spirit"—while Franciscans were inclined to cite Luke 6:20—"Blessed are you who are poor." Luther, though, would argue that the words "Blessed are the poor in spirit" mean something entirely different than they assumed. "No one is blessed," Luther observed, "because he is a beggar and owns nothing of his own"; nor are these words intended for "spiritual athletes" in cloisters and full-time ascetics.[158] Rather, "poverty" here in the Gospels is qualified by the word "spiritually," which refers to an inner attitude of faith.[159] Moreover, in Luther's words, "Though a [believing] common laborer, a shoemaker, or a blacksmith may be dirty and sooty and small because he is covered

---

[157] Lindberg, *The European Reformations*, 109.

[158] See Martin Luther, *Sermon on the Mount and the Magnificat*, in *Luther's Works*, ed. Jaroslav Pelikan (St. Louis: Concordia, 1956), 21:12–13.

[159] Luther, 21:12.

with dirt and pitch," and "though he stinks outwardly, inwardly he is pure incense before God."[160] And if "a poor housemaid has done her duty and is a Christian in addition, then before God in heaven she is a lovely and pure beauty, one that all the angels admire and love to look at."[161]

According to the medieval construal, begging had become honorific, with voluntary charity understood as conferring spiritual benefits on the practitioner. The giving of alms came to be viewed as the meriting (and accruing) of holiness—atoning and salvific in its effect. But by the fifteenth century, poverty was no longer merely a theological issue (which it was), based on a mistaken view of merit and virtue, but in fact a genuine social issue as well.[162] Luther was among the first to seriously challenge this system, largely due to his emphasis on justification by grace, over against merit. Attending this theological breakthrough was the reality that neither being poor nor giving alms was salvific or in any way meritorious.[163] True penance, insisted Luther, is nothing less than whole-life repentance, which results in the acceptance of unmerited grace.[164]

Some local context is helpful here. In Wittenberg alone, there existed twenty-one devotional charities (or orders) called brotherhoods, each operating on a system of merit.[165] This raised in the Reformer's mind a question: What really constitutes good works and to what extent has the

---

[160] Luther, 21:34.

[161] Luther, 21:34.

[162] See Lindberg, *The European Reformations*, 108–29.

[163] Significantly, even in his *Ninety-Five Theses* of 1517 Luther rejects the view that the poor are the "treasure" of the church.

[164] The question of meritorious grace, of course, was intricately bound up with the issue of indulgences, which would become the focal point of Luther's initial revolt. Four "chief graces" were believed to comprise the matter of indulgences: (1) remission of all sins; (2) remission of sins at death; (3) remission of sins for dead relatives; and (4) remission of punishment in purgatory. See Brecht, *His Road to Reformation 1483–1521*, 180–82.

[165] Lindberg, *The European Reformations*, 113–14. For a valuable resource in understanding the local realities of the monastic system against which Luther revolted, see Pelikan, "After the Monks—What?," 3–21.

notion of good works been polluted? "If a sow were made a patron saint of such a brotherhood," Luther thus quips, "she would not consent" to standard brotherhood practices, so perverted have "works" become and so corrupt have become the "brotherhood's" system. Luther was confronted with distinguishing between "poverty" as a religious virtue and poverty as a socioeconomic reality, which, in the late-medieval period, was no small task.[166] To his credit, Luther wished to de-spiritualize poverty.[167]

Rather than looking to the monastic brotherhoods, Luther argued that community leaders, *in every region*, should help establish a common treasury for the truly poor.[168] And because he saw the church as unwilling to make necessary changes, Luther admonished rulers toward "the abolition of all begging [being done by mendicant orders] throughout Christendom."[169] Why this insistence?[170] As it happened, on their rounds, various mendicant orders would itinerate in a given region, visiting the same town as many as six or seven times a year apiece. If in any

---

[166] Perhaps in our own century we have come full-circle, though for different reasons. We are forced to qualify "poverty"—that is, to identify those who are truly disadvantaged and in need—and along the way learn to practice a discriminating mindset that discourages an unwise Christian charity.

[167] See Carter Lindberg, "Luther and the Common Chest," 18–19.

[168] See Martin Luther, *The Blessed Sacrament of the Holy and True Body of Christ, and the Brotherhoods* (1519), in *Luther's Works*, ed. E. Theodore Bachmann (Philadelphia: Fortress, 1960), 35:45–73, esp. 68. This conviction is communicated elsewhere by Luther to rulers on various occasions.

[169] Luther, *To the Christian Nobility of the German Nation, LW* 189.

[170] Assisting us in contextualizing Luther's thinking is German historian Renate Blickle, "From Subsistence to Property: Traces of a Fundamental Change in Early Modern Bavaria," *Central European History* 25, no. 4 (1992): 377–82. He describes the legal and social norm of Luther's day as "domestic necessity." Accordingly, economic resources were to be distributed (or redistributed) according to the need of the household. This mindset is on display in Luther's thinking about a common chest. Its basic assumptions are (1) the corruption of the church's system regarding charity; (2) the distortion of how poverty and the poor were understood; (3) the importance of redefining true need; and (4) communal responsibility for an area's own, based on neighbor-love.

given region this was multiplied by five or six brotherhoods,[171] the result, according to Luther, would be perhaps that a town was "laid under tribute" about sixty times annually.[172]

Luther's argument, then, consists of two basic parts: (1) providing for the truly poor based on need and (2) prohibiting itinerant mendicancy. Begging and almsgiving, in any case, should be forbidden, he was convinced, not merely in Wittenberg but throughout all of Germany.[173] Luther views begging, so-called poverty, and mendicancy together as negating the gospel as well as being a burden to society. In his *Lectures on Genesis*, he even criticizes St. Francis as "naïve" and "foolish" in equating the gospel with the mandate to "sell everything and give it to the poor." The fault, he insisted, lies not in the things that we possess but, rather, in the one who possesses them.[174] Thus, if we step back and attempt to understand Luther's burden, his attacks on the late-medieval system are simultaneously against works-righteousness and abuses stemming from an early profit economy wed to a corrupt church. Social need and the

---

[171] These most likely would have been Franciscans, Benedictines, Dominicans, Augustinians, Cistercians, Carmelites, or Servites. Although Wittenberg in 1517 had a single parish church, three monasteries of mendicant orders lived there (Schilling, *Martin Luther*, 92).

[172] Luther, *To the Christian Nobility of the German Nation*, in *LW* 44:190.

[173] Luther's colleague Philip Melanchthon is only slightly less critical of the monasteries in this regard. He comments, "Though once upon a time [monasteries] were schools of Christian instruction, they have degenerated as from a golden age to an iron age . . . Some of the richest monasteries just feed a lazy crowd that gorges itself on the public alms of the church." See the *Apology of the Augsburg Confession* (1531), Art. 27, in Theodore G. Tappert, ed., *The Book of Concord: The Confessions of the Evangelical Lutheran Church* (Minneapolis: Fortress, 1989), 269.

[174] For Luther's rationale, see Luther, *Lectures on Genesis Chapters 6–14*, *LW* 2:326. The context here in Luther's Genesis commentary concerns Abraham's wealth, which was criticized in Luther's day by the monks. Abraham, according to this view, "should have lived in poverty," especially since "he was an exile" (325). "Beggary," as viewed by the monks, was "an act of worship toward God" (326).

common good, Luther is convinced, outweigh personal gain. Vocation, properly understood, helps address these—regardless of what century it is.

The Revolution of Reformed Protestant Thinking about Work and Vocation

Esteemed German theologian Jürgen Moltmann has described vocation as "the third great insight of the Lutheran Reformation"—after Word and sacrament.[175] Whether one is Protestant, Catholic, or Orthodox, it is difficult to deny the general force of Moltmann's statement. American Lutheran theologian Kenneth Cherney makes an even stronger one. Cherney observes that vocation is "the second most frequent emphasis in [Luther's] writings, after justification by faith."[176] Permit me to add yet a third, though related, assertion: Luther precipitated a revolution in the church's understanding of work that was both essential and eternal.

If Moltmann and Cherney are correct, it is difficult to understand the church's remarkable silence on this momentous topic. Consider the historical context alone. In few (if *any*) areas of Christian doctrine and conviction has there been another example in which the Christian church has largely gotten it wrong for over a millennium as it did work and vocation. Thus, the praise and priority assigned to Luther by both Moltmann and Cherney might even understate the significance of what the Reformer did—for work and the worker, for the marketplace, for the church, and for society as a whole.

---

[175] Jürgen Moltmann, "Reformation and Revolution," in Manfred Hoffman, ed., *Martin Luther and the Modern Mind* Toronto Studies in Theology 22 (Lewiston: Edwin Mellen, 1985), 186.

[176] Kenneth A. Cherney, "Uncovering Our Calling: Luther's Reformation Re-emphasis on Christian Vocation," accessed March 28, 2022, http://www.abidingpeace.org/home/140000215/140000215/files/Uncovering%20Our%20Calling.pdf.

On one hand, we should refrain from simplistically citing Luther without qualification; he is 500 years removed from our current context. On the other, we must not dismiss or ignore his relevance to our day.[177] In fact, the very distance between us can help us see beyond our blind spots and biases. Perhaps against the spirit of the age in which we live, we should acknowledge Luther's contributions to our own cultural tradition. We can do this without idolizing or condemning the magisterial Reformer, acknowledging that we have benefitted from his views of theology, education, and social welfare. Luther's understanding of work and vocation, it needs emphasizing, is theologically grounded and at the same time diverse and integrated, suggesting extended application outside of Luther's own context. For example, he understood human relations and was attuned to the human need around him. He distinguished between two kinds of righteousness—namely, that which is salvific and that which sanctifies and attests to Christian love; he refused to collapse justification into sanctification. At the most fundamental level, he understood

---

[177] Not insignificantly, in the 1980s, during the pontificate of John Paul II, the Roman Catholic Church confessed Martin Luther to be a "witness to the gospel" and "[their] brother"—a confession that would have been impossible previously. Even a century ago, Luther was demonized by Roman Catholics. John Paul's recognition suggests the Catholic Church's wider acceptance, in our day, of Luther's understanding of faith as well as work. The former pontiff's praise of the Reformer, who was excommunicated by the church in 1521 and anathematized in the mid-sixteenth century at the Council of Trent, came in the form of a letter to Johannes Cardinal Willebrands, president of the Pontifical Secretariat for the Union of Christians, on November 5, 1983, to commemorate the 500th birthday of Luther. Further evidence of important movement in the direction of reconciliation comes from the fact of dialogue between Lutherans and Catholics on the matter of justification; see, for example, Karl Lehmann and Wolfhart Pannenberg, eds., *The Condemnations of the Reformation Era: Do They Still Divide?*, trans. Margaret Kohl (Minneapolis: Fortress, 1990); Karl Lehmann, ed., *Justification by Faith: Do Sixteenth-Century Condemnations Still Apply?*, trans. Michael Root and William G. Rusch (New York: Continuum, 1999); and the *Joint Declaration on the Doctrine of Justification*, signed by both the Lutheran World Federation and the Roman Catholic Church in 1999.

the centrality of the doctrine of creation, which itself declares "holy" and "good" all forms of human work and endeavor; correlatively, he understood that God's continual preservation and benevolence are part of creation; hence, God is involved with creation and present.

At the experiential level, this resulted in Luther's recognition of both the central place and the practical ramification of the priesthood of all believers, and thus an awareness that the doctrine is crucial to the church's continual reform. He recognized the importance of the common good, and he perceived the unity of faith and love, without which our works neither glorify God nor serve our neighbors. He insisted that "faith working through love" must affect local structures in various communities to help the truly disadvantaged. This indicates that he refused to pit charity against justice—or, in our day, social justice—thus creating a false dichotomy. Rather, his own view seems to be that if we clarify what is meant by charity, justice *will* be done; or, stated in the reverse, justice clarified—and purified—will be the expression of charity.[178] Luther was convinced that neighbor-love and serving others lend strong support to the common good, which in turn furnishes a robust, ecumenical Christian witness to the world.

Luther further recognized that vocation, properly understood, is not self-chosen but "assigned" by God, having its anchor and proper grounding in creation (and our *design*), not redemption.[179] Relatedly, he recognized that all callings (vocations) are of equal worth, which itself gives

---

[178] Charity and justice are two cardinal virtues inherent in the character of God; therefore, they must not be viewed as oppositional. On their organic unity, see J. Daryl Charles, "Toward Restoring a Good Marriage: Reflections on the Contemporary Divorce of Love and Justice and Its Cultural Implications," *Journal of Church and State* 55, no. 2 (2013): 367–83.

[179] While a discussion of Luther's affirmation of the natural law takes us beyond the scope of the present discussion, Luther believes that the natural law, in accordance with the Ten Commandments, defines our basic moral obligations. He agrees with Paul in Rom 2:14–15: the natural law is "a practical first principle" in the realm of public morality (*LW* 45:120–26).

value and meaning to all work. Foundationally, Luther was motivated, based on his own liberation, by the reality of Christian freedom; grace truly challenged and changed the way he saw all of life.

Luther's view of work and vocation, then, if we might reduce it in summary fashion, had a wondrous double effect. It punctured the false piety of his era, and it awakened believers to the spiritual and universal significance of the daily, the ordinary.[180]

It should be remembered that about the same time this Reformer was preparing his *Notes on Ecclesiastes,* John Calvin was reflecting and writing on work and vocation in his systematic theology: *Institutes of the Christian Religion.*[181] In Book III of *Institutes*, Calvin writes that the Lord bids each of us in all of life's actions to look to his calling. This is especially important, he notes, given the "great restlessness" and "fickleness" of the human heart. Therefore, to prevent confusion within the individual believer, God has "appointed" particular duties for every person in different spheres of life. These appointed duties correspond to each individual's vocational calling. Every person's vocation is a "sentry post" that is "assigned" by the Lord, so that the person "may not heedlessly wander about throughout life."[182] Vocation, as Calvin understood it, imparts steadiness and strength to believers.[183] Calvin shared Luther's redemptive assessment of the daily, the ordinary. No work or task, he insists, is "so sordid and base, provided you obey your calling in it, that

---

[180] Few have summarized this twofold effect of Luther's breakthrough more helpfully than Kenneth A. Cherney, Jr., "Hidden in Plain Sight: Luther's Doctrine of Vocation," *Wisconsin Lutheran Quarterly* 98, no. 4 (2001): 278–90.

[181] Luther's *Notes* were published in 1532, while the first edition of Calvin's *Institutes* was published in 1536.

[182] John Calvin, *Institutes of the Christian Religion* III.10.6. I am relying on the two-volume English translation provided by Ford Lewis Battles, ed. John T. McNeill (Philadelphia: Westminster, 1960), 1:724.

[183] Our awareness of the Lord's calling to particular spheres of living is, for Calvin, the "foundation" of our attempts at "well-doing." Otherwise, he believes, we will not hold true to a "straight path" in terms of our duties, and our lives will lack "harmony" (Calvin, *Institutes of the Christian Religion*, 1:725).

it will not shine and be reckoned very precious in God's sight."[184] For Calvin, as for Luther, the work of believers possesses a significance that goes far beyond the visible results of that work. As noted by theologian Alister McGrath, "There is no distinction between spiritual and temporal, sacred and secular work. All human work, however lowly, is capable of glorifying God. Work is, quite simply, an act of praise—a potentially *productive* act of praise. Work glorifies God, it serves the common good, and it is something through which human creativity can express itself."[185]

Like Luther, Calvin was careful to emphasize the dignity of all kinds of work. Not the nature of any particular occupation but the call to serve others guided Lutheran and Calvinist thinking about vocation. We should

---

[184] Calvin, *Institutes* III.10.6. Tellingly, Calvin offers commentary on our Lord's interaction with Mary and Martha as recorded in the Gospel narrative (Luke 10:38–42). Herein the Reformer takes aim at the longstanding exaltation of Mary—the "contemplative" one—which had dominated medieval spirituality. Because this text, according to Calvin, has been "basely distorted" through an elevation of a "Contemplative life," therefore "we must inquire into its true meaning." We discover, alas, that "nothing was farther from the design of Christ" than to encourage us to indulge in "useless speculations." This understanding of Mary and Martha, Calvin notes, is "an old error," namely, that "those who withdraw from business" and devote themselves entirely to a contemplative existence supposedly lead "an Angelical life"; see John Calvin, *A Harmony of the Gospels Matthew, Mark and Luke; and James and Jude*, ed. Thomas F. Torrance and David W. Torrance, trans. A. W. Morrison and T. H. L. Parker, repr. (Grand Rapids: Eerdmans, 1995), 142. Calvin's corrective is simply this: "On the contrary, we know that men were created for the express purpose of being employed in labour [*sic*] of various kinds, and that no sacrifice is more pleasing to God, than when every man applies diligently to his own calling, and endeavours [*sic*] to live in such a manner as to contribute to the general advantage." In the spirit of Luther, Calvin concludes, "It is, therefore, a foolish attempt of the monks to take hold of this passage, as if Christ were drawing a comparison between a contemplative and an active life, while Christ simply informs us for what end, and in what manner, he wishes to be received" (Calvin, *A Harmony of the Gospels*, 143). Calvin here was quite simply—and properly—pointing out that Jesus's criticism of Martha did not concern her work, but rather the timing—as well as the excess—of her efforts.

[185] McGrath, "Calvin and the Christian Calling," 34.

consider "nothing except the need and the advantage of . . . [the] neighbor," wrote Luther in *The Freedom of a Christian*.[186] To withdraw from civic affairs, as encouraged by both the monastic system and Anabaptists of the Reformers' day, was to abandon, rather than serve, neighbors.

Luther and Calvin together contributed to the abolition of the medieval hierarchy that distinguished those who "lived in contemplation," studying and praying and begging, from those who worked. According to both, Christians find in the notion of vocation (properly understood) a deep affirmation of ordinary life. Monasticism, understood classically, however, ignores real life. Vocation entails the grateful awareness and recognition that the Christian—indeed *every* believer—is equipped with various giftings and placed by providence in a particular sociocultural context. Luther and Calvin insisted that God assigns duties to every individual, and that monasticism, as broadly viewed in their day, undermines God's purpose for the church in terms of its witness by calling people away from the world. The work done in our individual callings, by contrast, becomes the very means by which we can demonstrate worship to God and love to our neighbors, thereby contributing to the common good. Over time, this has the effect of reforming the entire social order.[187]

The Lutheran and Reformed breakthrough of the sixteenth century served to democratize the language of vocation in response to a prevailing elitist understanding and bifurcation of sacred versus secular tasks. No work, no occupation, no endeavor is more or less noble than another. At the same time, neither Luther nor Calvin equated vocation with work, even when one's work is perhaps the most significant expression of his or her vocation. Every person has a vocation, a calling, whether he or she has a job or not. And because vocation is a call to each believer, it requires responses. One need neither sell one's possessions nor head to some foreign mission field; for virtually all individuals, the mission field is simply

---

[186] Luther, *The Freedom of a Christian*, *LW* 31:365.

[187] Calvin's work in Geneva will mirror this wider, corporate vision.

the marketplace. It is there, as Luther reminds us, that the church best demonstrates neighbor-love and serves the world's needs.

The significance of the notion of calling has been well described by Reformed theologian Emil Brunner. He writes that in its effect, "the idea of the Calling"—which is to say, vocation—"makes us free from all feverish haste, from bitterness, and from the—finally inevitable—hopeless resignation of the Reformer; at the same time it keeps the door open for [us] to undertake such reforming work when it is the duty appointed to [us] in the exercise of [our] particular 'office[s].'"[188]

Guided by a sense of vocation, the believer is not consigned to groping blindly, stumbling aimlessly, or being plagued by an uneasiness about the future. An awareness of vocation undergirds the Christian with a sense of confidence—even inspiration and joy—in one's work, as the following chapter will suggest. Luther, reinforced by Calvin, can help us, regardless of our distance from the sixteenth century.[189] Work is a heavenly vocation and divine gift to be received with gratitude. The book of Ecclesiastes—surprisingly, to some—stands in fundamental agreement; and it is to this almost universally misunderstood book that we must now turn.[190]

---

[188] Emil Brunner, *The Divine Imperative*, trans. Olive Wyon (Philadelphia: Westminster, 1947), 200.

[189] For a thorough yet accessible overview of the contributions made by Luther and Calvin to work and vocation against the backdrop of the late-medieval church and society, see Hardy, *The Fabric of This World*, 44–67.

[190] Elsewhere I discuss the recasting of work and vocation resulting from the Lutheran breakthrough in chapter 6 of J. Daryl Charles, *Wisdom and Work: Theological Reflections on Human Labor from Ecclesiastes* (Eugene, OR: Cascade Books, 2021). Elements of that discussion have been used here by permission of Wipf and Stock Publishers, www.wipfandstock.com.

CHAPTER

5

A "Wisdom" Perspective on Work
Unexpected Insights from the Book of Ecclesiastes

Thus far we have examined a great neglect in the church's standard teaching and preaching, in its educating, and in its equipping of Christian congregants. The resulting lack of any biblical understanding of the dignity of work or vocation properly understood among congregants has led to the resultant diminishment of the marketplace and the Monday-through-Friday in their minds.

The previous chapter, however, presented the Lutheran breakthrough. And whereas a secularist-materialist conception of life strips work and vocation of their religious meaning, a theologically Reformed perspective in which work possesses both design and dignity and in which embracing vocation is viewed as an individual response of gratitude to divine sovereignty, infuses life—*all* of life—with wondrous meaning and significance. This vibrant "infusion" applies not only to the relatively few who are employed in a religious context, such as a pastor or seminary professor, but to those who work in every productive setting of society, including the home.

What is peculiar, and hence worth probing, is the role that the book of Ecclesiastes played in the evolution of Luther's thinking in particular. Published in the year 1532, his commentary as found in *Notes on Ecclesiastes* mirrors both the practical ramifications of the doctrine of the "priesthood of every believer" as well as the degree to which Christians for centuries had misread (and thus misunderstood) the message of Ecclesiastes.[1] This misreading, alas, has not withdrawn; it is still with us. But let us focus on Luther's groundbreaking understanding of this remarkable piece of literature.

Wisdom Literature and the Wisdom Perspective

Treated with some suspicion by ancient rabbis and largely misunderstood by the Christian church through much of her history, Ecclesiastes belongs to the literary genre of Wisdom literature. This work contains language and idioms that have bestowed upon it a virtually universal recognition. Who in Western culture, at least, has not heard expressions such as "vanity of vanities," "to everything there is a season," "there is nothing new under the sun," "cast your bread upon the waters," and "the end of the matter"? Yet at the same time, it has been accompanied by a greater diversity of interpretation than perhaps any literary work, regardless of provenance, has ever generated. Despite these many difficulties, some of which are examined below, the question of why the book of Ecclesiastes continues to fascinate—even rivet—the reader's attention, regardless of time, culture, and social location, remains. Part of the reason may have to do with its literary home, namely, the genre of Wisdom literature.

Significantly, the wisdom perspective was by no means confined to ancient Israel; indeed, it was part of the fabric of broader ancient Near

---

[1] See Martin Luther, *Notes on Ecclesiastes*, in *Luther's Works*, ed. Jaroslav Pelikan (St. Louis: Concordia, 1972), 15:3–187.

Eastern culture.² Old Testament texts such as 1 Kgs 4:30–31, Prov 30:1–31:9, and Jer 49:7 provide evidence that ancient Near Eastern sources of so-called wisdom were well established in Israel's day.³ Hence, we are justified in maintaining that Hebrew wisdom did not arise in a social or cultural vacuum; rather, it was a part of human civilization that was both universally knowable and universally accessible.⁴

Part of the universal and enduring nature of the wisdom perspective is its central motif—namely, how to live—and for this reason Wisdom literature is applicable to ancient as well as modern life. Although the question of exactly what identifies Wisdom literature is the subject of lively—even vigorous—debate among Old Testament scholars;⁵ the wisdom genre emits several notable, constant features. These include a peculiar language, vocabulary, and literary form;⁶ a strongly didactic character

---

² The Wisdom literature of the Old Testament includes the books of Job, Proverbs, and Ecclesiastes, with a number of psalms—for example, 1, 37, 49, 73, 78, 91, and 126—also falling into this category. Apart from the Protestant Old Testament canon, the wisdom of Ben Sirach, frequently under the title of Ecclesiasticus, is another well-known exemplar. On the presence of Wisdom literature in ancient Mesopotamian, Greek, and Egyptian cultures, see, Martin Noth and David Winton Thomas, eds., *Wisdom in Israel and the Ancient Near East* VTSup 3 (Leiden: Brill, 1969), and Claus Westermann, *Roots of Wisdom: The Oldest Proverbs of Israel and Other Peoples*, trans. J. Daryl Charles (Louisville: WJK, 1995), esp. 140–64.

³ Egyptian culture bears witness to the earliest known forms of Wisdom literature. Some of these specimens date as early as the third millennium BC.

⁴ Although the sheer volume of literature on ancient Near Eastern wisdom is exhaustive, one of the more concise and helpful summaries of this phenomenon as it relates to Ecclesiastes can be found in Michael A. Eaton, *Ecclesiastes: An Introduction and Commentary*, TOTC (Downers Grove, IL: InterVarsity, 1983), 28–36.

⁵ See, for example, Mark R. Sneed, ed., *Was There a Wisdom Tradition? New Prospects in Israelite Studies* (Atlanta: Society of Biblical Literature, 2015).

⁶ Wisdom literature, in its shape and style, can take multiple forms. These include, for example, parable, allegory, riddle, proverb, didactic poetry, or philosophical reflection. Broadly speaking, Ecclesiastes may be located in this last classification, even when it incorporates several of the former types in its literary

that places accent on practical living; the relationship between observation (of both human and natural phenomena) and human experience; an indirect theological adaptation that is rooted in theistic creation and the surrounding universe; the pedagogical tendency to draw inferences from the physical world which bear upon human nature;[7] and juxtaposition of wisdom and foolishness or right and wrongdoing in a way that mirrors social concern.

A further, and foundational, characteristic of the wisdom genre needs comment—namely, the assumption that wisdom has its origin and existence in the fear of God.[8] This latter feature distinguishes itself insofar that ancient Near Eastern, non-Israelite wisdom does not mirror this correlation between wisdom and revering God.[9] By contrast, from Israel's standpoint, the fear of God is the very source of human wisdom and discernment.[10] The result of this correlation is decisive: one's knowledge of the Creator yields the knowledge of one's self. This knowledge is bounded by limitations as the human person experiences the surrounding world. In this awareness wisdom is to be found. Apart

---

arsenal. In the words of R. Charles Hill, Wisdom literature has "many faces" yet "still a recognizable complexion." See *Wisdom's Many Faces* (Collegeville: Liturgical, 1996), 3–4.

[7] The natural world, in fact, teaches human beings invaluable lessons, as Ecclesiastes 3 illustrates with its accent on the proper time or season for everything (see also Eccl 8:6). Animals gather and store food in particular "seasons," trees produce fruit in "in their time," birds migrate in particular "seasons," and farmers sow seeds and harvest crops in the appropriate "season."

[8] Here, in properly conceiving the fear of God, we must distinguish between panic and terror over against wonder, respect, and inner affirmation. Wisdom, rightly understood, entails the latter.

[9] See Gerhard von Rad, *Wisdom in Israel*, trans. James D. Martin (New York: Abingdon, 1972), 53–73.

[10] See Prov 1:7; 9:10. Moreover, wisdom is said to have framed all of creation (Prov 3:19; 8:22–31; Ps 104:24; cf. as well Job 28:28; Ps 111:10; Prov 1:7, 29; 2:5; 3:7; 9:10; Col 1:17; 2:3; and Heb 1:2;). Its value is supreme, surpassing that of gold or silver and all things deemed precious in the material world (see Prov 3:13–15).

from wisdom, people groups and societies are reduced to instability and foolishness.

Broadly construed, then, wisdom manifests itself both personally and publicly. As it concerns the latter, it manifests itself in the streets and the marketplace: "To you, O men, I call, / And my voice is to the sons of men" (Prov 8:4 NASB1995). Its language "calls out in the street," raising its voice "in the public squares," taking its stand "beside the gates leading into the city," and crying out "from the highest points of the city" (Prov 1:20; 8:2–3; and 9:3).[11] Not only is wisdom accessible to all, but people are able to *increase* in wisdom. It is for this reason that we find statements in Wisdom literature such as these: "Your heart must hold on to my words" (Prov 4:4); "Cherish [wisdom], and she will exalt you" (Prov 4:8 NIV); "If you embrace her, she will honor you" (Prov 8:8); "Get wisdom, get understanding" (Prov 4:5); and "Though it cost all you have, get understanding" (Prov 4:7 NIV).

Wisdom literature suggests itself to the contemporary Christian reader for multiple reasons. Much of Western culture despises any claims in the public sphere that call for virtuous behavior or moral discernment. Alas, wisdom, in our day, is supremely unpopular. In addition, it is the norm in twenty-first-century society to account for wisdom or virtue and its opposite in terms of biology and neuroscience.[12] Science, however,

---

[11] Wisdom is the fruit of creation and providence, accessible to all, and may be understood theologically as a central aspect of common grace. In Calvinist theological terms, "common grace" is distinct from "particular" grace. By the former, all creation is maintained and preserved through God's providential care; by the latter, that is, what we call special revelation, we enter into communion with God through Christ by means of cleansing from sin and walking in newness of spiritual life.

[12] See, for example, Stephen S. Hall, *Wisdom: From Philosophy to Neuroscience* (New York: Alfred A. Knopf, 2010); Paul W. Glimcher, *Foundations of Neuroeconomic Analysis* (Oxford: Oxford University Press, 2011); Richard J. Haier, *The Neuroscience of Intelligence,* CFNP (Cambridge: Cambridge University Press, 2017); Merim Bilalić, *The Neuroscience of Expertise,* CFNP (Cambridge: Cambridge University Press, 2017); Marie T. Banich and Rebecca J. Compton,

cannot replace wisdom, for science is incapable of producing wisdom, nor can it replace moral agency and value judgments. While it is typical of those working in science to overestimate human capabilities, wisdom makes us aware of our limits—as the book of Ecclesiastes abundantly demonstrates.[13]

Yet another reason for wisdom's reprioritization among believers thrusts itself upon us: namely, the way we educate our own. Only to our great peril do we deprive ourselves and our descendants of inestimable insights and practical discernment through our neglect of the wisdom perspective.[14] And because this perspective unites all of humanity, given our creation in the image of God, it is a thread that weaves its way throughout both the Old and New Testaments if we but look for it. Jesus's abundant use of wisdom techniques in his teaching is a forceful reminder of this.[15]

A serious reading of Ecclesiastes suggests that coming to terms with the awareness of human limits over against divine mystery and the reality of divine providence constitutes an important aspect of wisdom. As will be argued in the following section, two approaches to ultimate reality—one that fails to reckon with divine providence and inscrutability, and

---

Cognitive Neuroscience (Cambridge: Cambridge University Press, 2018); Kees van Heeringen, *The Neuroscience of Suicidal Behavior*, CFNP (Cambridge: Cambridge University Press, 2018); Francesca Mapua Filbey, *The Neuroscience of Addiction* CFNP (Cambridge: Cambridge University Press, 2019); Antonio Damasio, *Feeling & Knowing: Making Minds Conscious* (New York: Pantheon Books, 2021); and the mammoth *Principles of Neural Science*, ed. Eric R. Kandel et al. (New York: McGraw Hill, 2021). For Hall, the vocabulary of human virtue reduces to "the eight neural pillars of wisdom" (19, 59).

[13] Few demonstrate greater sensitivity to this distinction than Westermann, *Roots of Wisdom*, 135–37.

[14] Among these insights are an awareness of human limits, the importance of virtue and moral formation, lessons from physical nature that bear upon human nature, the value of suffering and adversity, the reality of divine providence in light of life's mystery, and an anatomy of stewardship.

[15] In addition to Jesus's parabolic teaching, the wisdom perspective on display in James is notable.

thus is "meaningless," and one that humbly embraces them—are in dialogue. The former leads to an outlook that is despairing and marked by resignation; the latter receives life, with its fleeting moments, and everything in it—inclusive of human labor—as a "gift" of God.[16]

Interpretive Strategy in Ecclesiastes

In our day it is supremely rare to hear teaching or preaching from Old Testament wisdom texts. This is particularly true of Ecclesiastes.[17] Contributing to this neglect is the matter of interpretive difficulties surrounding this "strange and disquieting" book that were alluded to in the previous section.[18] Among the chief interpretive difficulties surrounding Ecclesiastes is the reader's ability to come to terms with—and properly understand—the book's apparent internal contradictions. Much professional commentary, it needs stating, has not provided much help in resolving these. In fact, while summarizing the state of modern commentary on Ecclesiastes, one Old Testament scholar observes with sadness that "one is tempted to despair when one realizes the extent to which scholars still disagree about it."[19]

---

[16] Elsewhere I examine more extensively Wisdom literature and the wisdom outlook in "Wisdom and Work: Perspectives on Human Labor from Ecclesiastes," *Journal of Markets and Morality* 22, no. 1 (2019): 7–9, and chapter 2 of *Wisdom and Work: Theological Reflections on Human Labor from Ecclesiastes* (Eugene, OR: Cascade Books, 2021). Parts of that discussion have been used here with permission.

[17] In my own forty-five years of Christian faith, I cannot recall ever hearing from the pulpit (or through adult education, for that matter) an exposition of the book of Ecclesiastes.

[18] See Michael V. Fox, *Ecclesiastes* JPS Bible Commentary (Philadelphia: The Jewish Publication Society, 2004), ix. For a useful overview of modern interpretation of Ecclesiastes, see Craig Bartholomew, "Qoheleth in the Canon?! Current Trends in the Interpretation of Ecclesiastes," *Themelios* 24, no. 3 (May 1999): 4–20.

[19] Bartholomew, "Qoheleth in the Canon?!," 13.

People throughout the ages have not read Ecclesiastes in a detached or dispassionate manner; after all, the book fascinates us and grips us in remarkable ways. Nevertheless, it does remain the case that one simply cannot speak of any clear consensus regarding the book's interpretation—whether its genre, its message, its structure, its portrayal of God, its literary style and strategy, or even its place in the biblical canon. In fact, none other than the authors of the best-selling *How to Read the Bible for All Its Worth* offer a most unflattering assessment of Ecclesiastes—one that would surely prevent any serious layperson from reading the book. For this reason, their appraisal, which is really an indictment, deserves to be taken seriously; after all, significantly, by 2014 *How to Read the Bible* had already appeared in its fourth edition. The authors' conclusion is that the "consistent message" of Ecclesiastes is that "life has no *ultimate* value" and that the advice given in the book "has no eternal value."[20]

But we learn more from the authors of this best-selling volume. They write, "Ecclesiastes seems to deny an afterlife . . . , criticize key aspects of the Old Testament faith . . . , and generally encourage attitudes very different from the rest of Scripture." Anticipating the reader's obvious reaction to the question "Why, then, is it in the Bible at all?," their answer is this: "[Ecclesiastes] is there as a foil, i.e., as a contrast to what the rest of the Bible teaches . . . It is the secular fatalistic wisdom that a practical (not theoretical) atheism produces." The book, readers of *How to Read the Bible* are thus informed, serves as a "reverse apologetic for cynical wisdom"; that is, "it drives its readers to look further because the answers that the 'Teacher' of Ecclesiastes gives are so discouraging." In the end, we learn, "The advice of Eccl. 12:13 (keeping God's commandments) points

---

[20] Fee and Stuart, *How to Read the Bible for All Its Worth* (Grand Rapids: Zondervan, 1992), 192–93; emphasis added.

away from Ecclesiastes to the rest of Scripture," to a place "where those commandments are found."[21]

No wonder, then, that the book of Ecclesiastes is barely opened in the pulpit and that the average reader of the Bible is prevented from receiving its wisdom. When biblical scholars—"the experts"—view the book as theologically deficient, we should not be surprised that Ecclesiastes remains shuttered—and essentially removed—from the church's thinking. If professional students of the Old Testament are inclined to view Ecclesiastes as so difficult and problematic,[22] it is little wonder that the book remains virtually inaccessible to the contemporary reader. As one perceptive observer comments, we seem to stand in need of a genuine "paradigm shift" in the study of Ecclesiastes.[23]

So, given all the difficulties surrounding this book, why does Ecclesiastes continue to occupy—perhaps mesmerizing, perhaps infuriating—generation after generation of readers? Part of the reason, no doubt, is the way its message is couched. Mirroring a standard technique found in Wisdom literature, the wider strategy of the writer of Ecclesiastes[24] is to juxtapose perspectives and then to repeat

---

[21] Fee and Stuart, 193, emphasis added. In the end, one is left to conclude, based on *How to Read the Bible*, that Ecclesiastes appears never really to have fully made it into the biblical canon on its own merits; it was always only a foil.

[22] One term frequently used by Old Testament scholars to depict Ecclesiastes is "heterodox." It is broadly assumed that Ecclesiastes is intended to convey skepticism and thereby challenge conventional—i.e., traditional—notions of wisdom.

[23] Annalie E. Steenkamp-Nel, "Transformative Joy in Qohelet: A Thread That Faintly Glistens," *HTS Teologiese Studies* 75, no. 3 (2019), posted January 23, 2019, hts.org.za/index.php/hts/article/view/5126.

[24] I simply assume the writer to be Qoheleth (lit., "the assembler"), the Hebrew form of the word translated "Preacher" or "Teacher" (1:1); being implied here is one who teaches publicly. In fact, in Aramaic-Syriac the root *qhl* connotes not only "to summon to an assembly" but also "to be argumentative" or litigious; see Edward Ullendorff, "The Meaning of *qhlt*," *Vetus Testamentum* 12,

various insights.²⁵ In fact, this pattern of contrast and repetition recurs throughout the book, perhaps to the consternation of most. When we are attuned to the writer's dialectical method, by which he intentionally keeps despair and "meaninglessness" in the foreground (at times even depressingly so), we can see that this is often followed by strategically placed glimpses of the alternative. Meaninglessness is dislodged by meaning and purpose.²⁶ However, from the writer's standpoint, for people to interpret life properly, they must have their false assumptions

---

no. 2 (1962): 215. It is fitting, then, that the ostensible title of the writer is "the arguer," which hints at my basic assumption in approaching Ecclesiastes that the book is designed to be a sort of apologetic. Moreover, I take into consideration the fact of literary transcription, as found, for example, in Prov 25:1—"These too are proverbs of Solomon, / which *the men of King Hezekiah of Judah copied*" (emphasis added)—a transcription that would have occurred in the late eighth or early seventh century BC. The transcription of Solomon's proverbs noted in Prov 25:1 allows for two possibilities: the "men of King Hezekiah" edited and arranged part of that book, or they took oral tradition and put it in writing. This hint at editorial work agrees with the third-person language emerging in the conclusion of Ecclesiastes. While it can be acknowledged that commentators as far removed as Jerome (fourth century) and Matthew Henry (eighteenth century) believed the author to be a repentant Solomon in old age who was offering a penitential lament of his own folly (a position that lacks scriptural warrant), I do not concern myself here with questions of authorship, dating, canonicity, literary genre, or linguistics—matters that are sufficiently addressed in standard critical commentaries. Rather, I wish to assess the value of wisdom as it informs an important subtheme in the treatise—that is, the meaningfulness or meaninglessness of human labor.

²⁵ Thus, for J. A. Loader, *Polar Structures in the Book of Qohelet* BZAW 152 (Berlin: Walter de Gruyter, 1979), internal coherence of Ecclesiastes entails recognition of polarities or "polar structures." The "wisdom" literary-rhetorical features of juxtaposition and repetition are two trademarks of Ecclesiastes. Moreover, repetition occurs in terms of both the work's vocabulary and phraseology. An important means of discerning the message of any literary work, and thus of Ecclesiastes, is to observe the recurrence of particular statements or phrases that act as a sort of refrain. Indeed, this assists us in interpreting Ecclesiastes.

²⁶ To be rejected, however, is the interpretation advanced by not a few commentators, who interpret the writer's own position as a mixture of despair and

and hopes pulverized.[27] For this reason, meaninglessness appears as the dominant organizing principle.

Apart from a theocentric outlook on all of human existence, the human experience indeed is "profitless"[28] and "meaningless" (*hebel*); and the reason for this, though not expounded by the writer, is the fall and sin's curse (intimated in Eccl 7:29 and 9:3). What Ecclesiastes calls for, then, in its indirect theological method is a radically altered human perspective, anchored in reverence for the Creator (see Eccl 3:14; 5:7; 7:18; 8:12–13; 12:13), whose ways and works are inscrutable.[29] As the periodic refrains highlighted below suggest, joy and contentment follow the

---

rarely occurring joy, of meaninglessness and meaning. A hybrid philosophy of life is not at the heart of Ecclesiastes.

[27] G. S. Hendry, "Ecclesiastes," in *New Bible Commentary*, ed. Donald Guthrie and J. A. Motyer, (Grand Rapids: Eerdmans, 1970), 570–71, and Derek Kidner, *The Wisdom of Proverbs, Job and Ecclesiastes* (Downers Grove, IL: InterVarsity, 1985), 93–94, are among the few commentators to grasp this rhetorical strategy in Ecclesiastes. R. B. Y. Scott's famous remark, that "all this sounds like an argument for suicide," is true if we fail to get the message right. Scott, *Proverbs, Ecclesiastes*. AB (Garden City, NY: Doubleday, 1965), 203.

[28] Recall the original question posed in Eccl 1:3 and then again in 3:9 and 5:16, essentially the very question Jesus posed in Mark 8:36: "What does it profit a man . . . ?" (ESV).

[29] The foundations of the writer's theological framework are divine providence, divine inscrutability, and divine judgment. Consider the reflections gathered in the passage beginning at 3:1—reflections that would appear to reconcile what are incongruities in human experience and underscore the realities of providence, inscrutability, and judgment. There is a "time" and "season" for everything "under heaven." This assertion is followed by the declaration "[God] has made everything appropriate in its time" (3:11). The sense of these verses has to do not with a mechanistic or deterministic predestination but rather with human discernment of various seasons of our lives. Hence, an important lesson of this poetic, didactic material is *discernment*—discernment of (1) the particular season that impacts our lives and (2) what action or actions would be appropriate, given that season. Any measure of discernment presupposes the recognition of divine omnipotence and providence, which requires that we acknowledge and respect our limits as humans. This is the fruit of reverence.

person who pleases and reveres God, receiving everything as a divine gift. This, then, is true wisdom. What is more, wisdom sheds light on all of human experience, especially labor.[30]

Discerning the Purpose of Ecclesiastes

Assisting the reader in the interpretive process is the writer's repeated use of catchwords—"meaningless" (*hebel*),[31] "to rejoice" (*śāmah*) or the noun

---

[30] If the writer were, in fact, a true skeptic himself, then we could assume that (1) he would not have injected periodic refrains of joy and satisfaction throughout the treatise, and (2) he would not have concluded on the strongly theistic note that he did. Rather, death would have been viewed as a release from this absurd and wicked world, wherein no human endeavor is, in the end, meaningful. This is precisely the flaw of secular materialism, given its utter inability to account for both human evil and death. For this reason, we may understand death to constitute an essential—though not obsessive—part of the writer's apologetic strategy, against much commentary.

[31] Most commentators render the Hebrew *hebel*, which appears thirty-eight times in Ecclesiastes, as "smoke," "vapor," or "breath," as "vanity," "meaninglessness," "futility," "pointlessness," or "absurdity." Others translate it "transience," "fleetingness," "enigma," "incomprehensibility," or even "irony." Though the term allows a wide range of inflections, these possibilities are close enough that the reader can discern the writer's general literary-rhetorical strategy and the book's basic message. My own position is to generally translate it figuratively/metaphorically as "vanity," "meaninglessness," or "futility"—as most versions of the Bible do. The reason for this is simply that a literal translation—"vapor" or "breath"—fails to capture the moral sense of disappointment, failure, or even repugnance in which *hebel* often appears, both in Ecclesiastes and throughout the entire Old Testament (see Deut 32:21; Ps 78:33; Prov 21:6; Isa 57:13; Jer 8:19; 10:8; and 51:18). More is going on in Ecclesiastes than mere transience. Divine judgment (Eccl 5:6; 9:1–2; 11:9; and 12:14) is not for that which is merely vaporous or fleeting; it exists for human reckoning, based on moral judgments that humans made in their lifetimes. Added to this is the fact that translating *hebel* as "transient" or "fleeting" makes little sense in its superlative form, as found in 1:2 and 12:8. Finally, parallel echoes of "futility" or "vanity," which affirm the perspective of Ecclesiastes, are found in numerous New Testament texts (see Acts 14:15; Rom 1:21; 8:20–21; 1 Cor 3:20; 15:17; Eph 4:17; and Titus 3:9). Elsewhere I have defended this view in Charles, *Wisdom and Work*, 62–66. See

form "enjoyment"/"satisfaction" (*śimḥâ*),[32] "good" (*tôb*),[33] "labor" (*'āmāl*),[34] "portion"/"lot"/"reward" (*ḥeleq*),[35] "see"/"behold"/"observe" (*raah*),[36] and "profit"/"gain" (*yitrôn*)[37]—as well as catchphrases—"under the sun,"[38] "chasing after the wind,"[39] "revering God,"[40] "what God has done," "the gift of God," and "what God has given"[41]—and recurring themes—"This, too, is meaningless"[42] and "so that men will revere God."

These lexical elements, coupled with the aforementioned features of contrast and repetition, are a key to interpreting the book properly, pointing the reader toward the book's message. At play in Ecclesiastes is

---

also Douglas B. Miller, *Symbol and Rhetoric in Ecclesiastes: The Place of* Hebel *in Qohelet's Work* (Atlanta: Society of Biblical Literature, 2002).

[32] The verb and noun forms together appear seventeen times, demonstrating its centrality in the writer's argument. Agustinus Gianto, "The Theme of Enjoyment in Qohelet," *Biblica* 73 (1992): 529, argues that the writer's use of the root *śmḥ* is every bit as artful as his use of *hebel*; thus, joy or enjoyment in Ecclesiastes stands in deliberate contrast to meaninglessness.

[33] This term appears a remarkable fifty-two times in Ecclesiastes, even more than "meaningless" (*hebel*).

[34] One of three terms translated "work," *'āmāl* appears thirty-five times in Ecclesiastes—thirteen times as a verb and twenty-two as a noun—and is variously rendered in its noun form as "toil," "work," "deed," "labor," or "business." This frequency alone makes work an important theme in the book, showing that human labor is one of the writer's central ideas. It is unfortunate, though, that the English word "toil," which is a frequent translation of *'āmāl* in Ecclesiastes, has an almost universally negative connotation. Sometimes a particular translation will use the word "toil" when the context is, in fact, positive and affirmative.

[35] This term appears eight times in Ecclesiastes.

[36] This term appears a remarkable forty-seven times in Ecclesiastes.

[37] This term appears ten times in Ecclesiastes.

[38] This phrase occurs twenty-nine times in Ecclesiastes.

[39] This phrase occurs seven times in Ecclesiastes.

[40] Fearing or revering God occurs seven times in Ecclesiastes.

[41] Such phrasing occurs eleven times in Ecclesiastes.

[42] Ecclesiastes begins and ends with the refrain "Meaningless, meaningless . . . everything is meaningless!" (1:2 and 12:8 NIV) but has the shorter version—"This, too, is meaningless"—interspersed often throughout (for example, in Eccl 2:15, 21, 26; 4:4, 8, 16; 5:10; 6:9; 7:6; and 8:10, 14).

a contrasting of two perspectives on life: one issues from what we might call "under-the-sun secularism," while the other might be termed "under-heaven theism." Two approaches to interpreting reality, two understandings as to what constitutes meaning or meaninglessness. Importantly, those things that in a fallen world appear meaningless "under the sun" have meaning if they are viewed in the light of the Creator whose providential ways are incomprehensible.[43]

What is the purpose of the book of Ecclesiastes? It is a work of apologetics—that is, a work that defends divine providence by

---

[43] To fail to discern this comparative strategy is to lapse into an interpretation that Ecclesiastes is mirroring "a loss of trust in the goodness of God" who, in the end, is "unknowable" (James L. Crenshaw, *Old Testament Wisdom: An Introduction* [Louisville: Westminster John Knox, 1998], 4); or to believe that the message of Ecclesiastes is "rigorously hopeless" (Francis Watson, *Text, Church, and World: Biblical Interpretation in Theological Perspective* [Edinburgh: T&T Clark, 1994], 283); or to argue that faith as depicted in Ecclesiastes cannot be squared with "the faith of the other biblical writers" (Roland E. Murphy, *The Tree of Life: An Exploration of Biblical Wisdom Literature*, 3rd ed. [Grand Rapids: Eerdmans, 2002], 58); or to proceed on the assumption of the book's "total abandonment of the traditional religious concepts of the Jewish people" and "unvarnished declaration that religious actions, worship, and morality are ultimately irrelevant" (J. A. Loader, *Ecclesiastes: A Practical Commentary*, trans. J. Vriend Text and Interpretation [Grand Rapids: Eerdmans, 1986], 14).

As I argue elsewhere, a failure to discern this strategy forces upon the interpreter a sort of literary and theological schizophrenia, inasmuch as statements that stand in blatant, diametric opposition are forced to stand side by side, only to be resolved by a multiauthor/multi-editor patchwork explanation. One is left, then, with the position that apart from the epilogue the message of Ecclesiastes is despair and resignation, and that in Ecclesiastes we are witnesses to two distinct theologies—that of Qoheleth and that of an editor in the book's conclusion. A version of this position is advanced, for example, by Gerald H. Wilson, "'The Words of the Wise': The Intent and Significance of Qohelet 12:9–14," *Journal of Biblical Literature* 103, no. 2 (1984): 175–92. In my *Wisdom and Work*, 48–80, I have critiqued in a more extensive manner the failure of much Old Testament scholarship to discern juxtaposition in the literary-rhetorical strategy of the writer of Ecclesiastes.

underscoring "the grimness of the alternative."[44] Qoheleth is writing with a view to present—and demolish—the wider social-cultural view of human existence in his day that was "bounded by the horizons of this world"; "he meets [it] on [its] own ground, and proceeds to convict [it] of its inherent vanity."[45] After destroying the materialist's outlook of "*nothing* matters," he responds that "*everything* matters." The latter perspective is founded on certain assumptions about reality that are not shared by the materialist: humans must (1) acknowledge their limitations, (2) receive from the hand of Creator God, and (3) revere this God who is also Judge. The book's message, then, can be understood as a counterargument to a materialist worldview, according to which humans attempt to construct and master their own reality. This illusion, in consequence, leads to endless and futile attempts to acquire power and influence, wealth and possessions, knowledge, reputation, pleasure, and profit. All of these attempts are "meaningless"; they are utterly bound to fail. The world and all it offers cannot satisfy.

As it applies to the theme of work and human endeavor, the writer's message is decisive. What is the "burden" that God has "laid on" humanity" (1:13 and 3:10)? It is the search for meaning—the very question posed at the outset—"What do people gain from all their labors?" (1:3 NIV) that is essentially repeated in 3:9 and 5:16. And it is this very question that was posed by Jesus: "What does it profit a man if he gains the whole world but forfeits his soul?" (Matt 16:26; Mark 8:36; Luke 9:25, my translation). The world that human beings inhabit is one of limitations, and those who can accept these boundaries, with their attendant mysteries, are those who find contentment. The universe is designed to mirror

---

[44] Eaton, *Ecclesiastes*, 44. Eaton's interpretation finds support from Hendry, "Ecclesiastes," 570, who observes—correctly, in my view—that "Qoheleth writes from concealed premises" and that Ecclesiastes is in reality a work of "apologetic theology." This "theology," however, consistent with Wisdom literature, is an *implicit* theology.

[45] Hendry, "Ecclesiastes," 570.

a proper—which is to say, dependent—relationship to its Creator.[46] All of life is to be received as a gift of God. It is in this awareness that joy and contentment are experienced. And although this linkage escapes most commentators, the concepts of "profit" (*yitrôn*) and "good" (*tôb*) are coupled in the message of Ecclesiastes. What this linkage suggests is that true "gain" or "profit" in life is not material or commercial; it is, rather, spiritual in its constitution.

Thus far we have argued that due to the writer's repeated contrasting of opposing outlooks, there are shifts—unannounced shifts—running throughout his treatise. One conspicuous, recurring shift in the book needs explanation. It concerns the value of human "toil" and work. The introductory material in Ecclesiastes well illustrates: 1:2–2:23 delineates the "meaninglessness" of various expressions of human existence and activity, including our labors. This material, in essence a lament, is followed by a shift in perspective in 2:24–3:15. Whereas human labor is described as "meaningless" in the lament ending in 2:23 (NIV), it is presented in a vastly different light in 2:24. Therein the reader is told that the Creator "has made everything beautiful in its time" and has "set eternity in the human heart" (3:11 NIV). The consequence of this is that "it is also the gift of God whenever anyone eats, drinks, and enjoys all his efforts" (3:13). This conclusion is strengthened by the following observation: "So I saw that there is nothing better for a person than to enjoy their work, because that is their lot" (3:22 NIV).

This shifting perspective on human labor is recurring. Consider the following rather remarkable observation: "When God gives someone wealth and possessions, and the ability to enjoy them, to accept their lot and be happy in their toil—this is a gift of God. . . . God keeps them

---

[46] A word of application to the present day is appropriate. In an age of the supremacy of science such as ours, Ecclesiastes performs the valuable service of exposing human pretensions. In short, human existence has boundaries. Accepting limitations dispels the tendency toward despair and skepticism; our acknowledgement of those boundaries is the beginning of contentment. This, then, is the enduring message of Ecclesiastes.

occupied with gladness of heart" (5:19–20 NIV). And consider the rationale given here: satisfaction in one's work is "a gift of God," which repeats and underscores an earlier statement. This fact is reinforced later in the treatise: "joy will accompany [the believer] in [his] toil all the days of the life God has given . . . under the sun" (8:15).[47]

I am arguing, then, for the presence in Ecclesiastes of a double theme. One of those themes, the meaninglessness of all things, is demonstrated repeatedly and with unremitting force, as evidenced by the organizing brackets of Eccl 1:2 and 12:8. This, however, is not the only theme, as evidenced by attention to (1) keywords, (2) refrains in the writer's

---

[47] Interestingly, I have come across only one other volume devoted specifically to the subject of work in Ecclesiastes: Tyler Atkinson's *Singing at the Winepress: Ecclesiastes and the Ethics of Work* (London: T&T Clark, 2015). The subtitle of that volume is somewhat misleading, however, for the book's focus is less on work than it is on the hermeneutic of two fathers of the church—St. Bonaventure and Martin Luther—and their respective understandings of a *contemptus mundi* ("contempt of the world") reading of Ecclesiastes. The next closest examination of the theme is an unpublished master's-level paper, written half a century ago, titled "The Concept of Work in Ecclesiastes," by Albertus L. DeLoach. Further illustrating the utter absence of the theme of work in the wider literature, I can locate *only three* essays written in the last 100 years devoted specifically to the topic of work in Ecclesiastes: H. G. T Mitchell's 1913 essay "'Work' in Ecclesiastes" examines the writer's usage of three terms in the book that are translated "work" or "labor." Mitchell concludes that enjoyment "offsets" the wearisome nature of labor, serving at best as "solace" rather than expressing satisfaction in and through our work. Stephan de Jong's 1992 essay "A Book of Labour" devotes itself to "structuring principles" in Ecclesiastes that are thought to highlight the theme of work. Despite the essay's title, de Jong strangely never gets around to actually examining and interpreting the various refrains in Ecclesiastes that highlight enjoyment and satisfaction in work—that is, refrains that comprise an essential part of the book's argument. Finally, William H. U. Anderson's 1998 essay "The Curse of Work in Qoheleth" bears the character of its title: work itself—rather than the ground, as pronounced in Genesis 3—is "cursed"; therefore, any joy that appears in Ecclesiastes cannot be reasonably or rationally expected as the norm, especially in our labors. Also absent from Anderson's essay is any interaction with the six "enjoyment" refrains in the book that explicitly commend satisfaction in and through our work.

literary-rhetorical arsenal, and (3) the book's conclusion, the "end of the matter." Negative and positive units of materialism, pessimism, and faith are interlaced throughout Ecclesiastes.[48] Not only does this strategy of alternating between pessimism and faith have the effect of engaging—perhaps even shocking—readers, but it also prods them toward a verdict in terms of life-orientation. No dimension of human existence is affected by this verdict as much as is labor.[49]

Divine Work in Ecclesiastes

In light of the varied interpretive issues already noted and the implicit character of theology that typifies Wisdom literature, one finds in the relevant literature comparatively little analysis of the concept of God in Ecclesiastes. A remarkable though little-examined feature of the treatise concerns the frequency with which God is mentioned throughout the work. No fewer than forty texts, in a total of 222 verses,[50] refer to God—a truly significant fact given the brevity of the book. Moreover, in Ecclesiastes the writer always uses the term *Elohim*, which designates God in general and which is used in the Genesis creation narrative, rather than *Yahweh*, the God who reveals himself to his covenant people.[51]

---

[48] This is not to argue that despair and faith coexist, contrary to much commentary.

[49] The matter of interpretive strategy in Ecclesiastes has been examined more extensively in chapter 3 of Charles, *Wisdom and Work*. Parts of that material are used here with permission.

[50] Daniel Lys, *L'Ecclésiaste ou Que vaut la vie? Traduction, Introduction générale Commentaire de 1/1 à 4/3* (Paris: Letouzey et Ané, 1977), 78; and Murphy, *The Tree of Life*, 57.

[51] Elsewhere I compare this usage with the apostle Paul's address to the Areopagus Council of Acts 17:22–34, where any sense of Hebrew particularity is absent and a universal character of the "unknown" God who has revealed himself is being accented. See Charles, "Wisdom and Work," 14, and idem, *Wisdom and Work*, 71 n103.

From a theological standpoint, the divine portrait in Ecclesiastes is worthy of examination because it helps the reader interpret and understand the book. In Ecclesiastes God is essentially portrayed in three roles: he creates, he acts inscrutably and remains so to human creation, and he judges.[52] These three elements can be understood as interlocking themes that undergird the writer's overall argument—one that possesses a universal character.

Although the opening lament in Ecclesiastes (1:2–2:23) contains only one reference to God, that allusion is central to the writer's overall purpose: God places a burden on humans to find meaning in life (Eccl 1:13)—an assertion that is repeated later in 3:10. In Eccl 2:24–26, we encounter the first of numerous and unannounced shifts in the writer's argument: God grants satisfaction, enjoyment, wisdom, and happiness to those who please him (v. 26). The burden or overarching task that weighs on every human being, as stated in Eccl 3:10, is qualified and clarified, however, by what follows: (1) God "has *made* everything beautiful in its time," and (2) he has ingrained within the human heart a sense of the eternal (3:11 NIV, emphasis added). A most curious—and significant, for our purposes—observation stands alongside the reality of the heart's sense of the divine: God gives the gift of contentment, part of which is satisfaction in human labor (3:13). Further qualification follows: what God does endures—nothing that humans might do can either add to or diminish this reality (3:14–15), the end result being that the Creator is to be revered. Moreover, God will judge all (3:15), the wicked and the righteous; and that judgment, significantly, will be according to our deeds (3:15–17). Inherent in this role of judging human actions is the reality of conviction and exposure of human motivations; hence, God "tests" human beings (3:18 NIV). Notice the presence in Eccl 3:1–22 of

---

[52] Similarities to my view, with some modification, can be found in Kidner, *A Time to Mourn*, 14–17, and Kidner, *The Wisdom of Proverbs, Job and Ecclesiastes*, 95–97.

the three interlocking themes previously noted: divine gifts to humanity, divine inscrutability, and divine judgment.

Following a renewed lament beginning in Eccl 4:1, a second shift occurs at the start of chapter 5. In this material, the reader learns that Creator God is to be approached, he is to be worshipped, and he is to be served (5:1–7). Human beings' approach before God, however, is strongly qualified, given the human tendency toward folly, haste, and impudence (5:1–2). Correlatively, God's nature is strongly qualified: he is "in heaven" (5:2 NIV), whereas human beings are part of the temporal order; that is, God is incommensurable and other, which should invoke in humans a sense of awe. The Creator is to be revered (5:7).

Following Qoheleth's proverbial observations about physical and material life in Eccl 5:8–17, we encounter material in which allusion to God once more, as in verses 1–7 of that chapter, is conspicuously dense (5:18–20). Here God is said to give. In verse 18, he gives life; in the next two verses, he gives temporal gifts such as wealth, satisfaction in work, and gladness of heart. Then, immediately again it is noted that God gives wealth, possessions, and honor (6:2).

Ecclesiastes 7 begins with material that describes the nature and character of wisdom. Wisdom, not infrequently, goes against human inclinations. In the end, it protects and shelters the human being from folly (see v. 12). This counterintuitive element is well illustrated in verses 13–14: the presence of wisdom, among other things, causes humans to ponder what God has done (7:13a) and what he has made or ordered (7:13b). Wisdom counsels us to be joyful when things go well and to be reflective when they do not; all told, it reminds us that we simply cannot penetrate the mystery of what God does (v. 14). In the end, God is to be revered (v. 18), and he is to be pleased (v. 26). The character of wisdom is such that it reminds us of the fallen nature of humanity: God created humanity upright, but we since have pursued wicked schemes and devices (v. 29; 8:11b).

The interlocking elements of what God has done, his giving gifts to humankind, and his inscrutable nature, all of which work to cultivate in human beings the fear of God, are recurring in the material of Eccl 8:11–9:1. Despite human wickedness, God is to be feared and revered—as we see in chapter 8, verses 12–13. Moreover, in the end, wickedness will not benefit the wicked, even when it often appears that the righteous get what the wicked deserve and the wicked get what the righteous deserve in this life (see vv. 13–14). In truth, God gives life and joy, and part of embracing contentment is linked to human labor (v. 15). Wisdom leads us to recognize that what God does and has done is unsearchable (vv. 16–17); wisdom causes us to acknowledge our limitations. This fact is immediately reiterated in the biblical text: the righteous and wise are in God's hands, and no one can penetrate the mystery of what God does (Eccl 9:1).

Ecclesiastes 9, which introduces the theme of humanity's common destiny, that is, the grave, contains one of the more fascinating passages in all of Wisdom literature. Mirroring a debt to other ancient Near Eastern sources, the material found in verses 7–10 contains several unusual and noteworthy declarations about God. Generally speaking, he is pleased by what we do in the moment (v. 7), and he grants life and satisfaction in all things, including in our work (v. 9).

It is unfortunate that most English translations of verse 9 cast it in a strongly negative light, which is counter to the very context in which the writer's admonitions are found. For example, after "Enjoy life with your wife, whom you love," the NIV reads, "all the days of this meaningless life that God has given you under the sun—all your meaningless days." This language is followed by the assertion, "[T]his is your lot in life and in your toilsome labor under the sun." Here a translation of "fleeting" rather than "meaningless" for *hebel* is more appropriate, since the "life that God has given you" cannot possibly be meaningless, nor is enjoyment of one's spouse meaningless, neither is our "lot" or "portion" (i.e., our "calling" or "vocation") meaningless. What is more, and in the same vein, the translation of "toilsome labor" for the generic Hebrew word *'āmāl* and its noun form in verse 9 is unfortunate, since this term, appearing thirteen times in Ecclesiastes, does not carry a sense of difficulty or burden elsewhere in the Old Testament.[53] "Labor" or "work" is the most appropriate rendering in English. "Toilsome," based on its common understanding in the English language, is almost uniformly negative and here discolors and distorts the present context. Finally, the very carpe diem that follows—"Whatever your hand finds to do, do it with all your might" (Eccl 9:10 NIV)—militates against any sort of negative understanding of labor. In fact, here we find the fullest acclamation of a life lived in faith and with gusto. Human potential here is unbounded; that is, the writer wishes to challenge the reader, in sheer freedom and exhilaration, to risk going beyond perceived human limitations—all, of course, in the awareness that we cannot predict or confine what God may do. This suggestion, that humans are remarkably free to take significant risks in faith, occurs again in the material found in Eccl 11:1–6.

In what serves as an introduction to the conclusion of the book (Eccl 11:1–12:1a), the interlocking themes of what God does, his inscrutable deeds, and his judging appear once more, as if to summarize the entire treatise's burden. God, the reader is reminded, has made everything, and his works are manifestly inscrutable (v. 5). Moreover, he calls human beings to account and he judges (v. 9). In this context, the reader is admonished to "banish anxiety from" his or her heart—advice that is accompanied in this material by similar (and in some respects, surprising) admonitions—for example, let your heart give you joy, follow the heart, enjoy your years, and enjoy your youth. All of these admonitions, significantly, appear alongside the counsel to "remember." We are to remember that God is judge (v. 9), we are to remember our Creator in the days of youth (Eccl 12:1), and we are to remember God before we grow old and near death (vv. 6–7). After all, it is the Creator who gave human beings the spirit of life.

---

[53] On the use of this term in the Old Testament, see David Thompson, "āmāl," in *New International Dictionary of Old Testament Theology and Exegesis*, ed. Willem VanGemeren (Grand Rapids: Zondervan, 2012), 3:435–37.

The work's conclusion, the "end of the matter," returns to two threads lacing their way throughout Ecclesiastes and unites them in a final reiteration.[54] God is to be revered, as evidenced by humans' willingness to keep his moral commands—an awareness that is stated to be universal ("the duty of all," NIV) and therefore binding (Eccl 12:13). In addition, God will judge, bringing every deed—good and evil, hidden and not—into accountability (v. 14).

Much commentary tends either to ignore, dismiss, or misconstrue the recurring admonitions or refrains in the book concerning life's enjoyment and God's gifts, which in and of themselves constitute "theological statements of faith in a just and loving God."[55] A thoughtful and coherent reading of Ecclesiastes, one that takes into account these intermittent refrains, leads to the firm conclusion that revering God and enjoyment in life are inextricably linked; the one does not mute or transmute the other. It needs emphasizing that the link between revering God and finding contentment is not only confirmed in the Old Testament's broader wisdom perspective (e.g., in Ps 31:19; 112:1; Prov. 19:23) but can be understood as a general biblical truth.[56]

The vocabulary of divine work or activity in Ecclesiastes, as already intimated, tends to receive scant attention among commentators. And where it does merit attention, writers are generally inclined to view the theology of Ecclesiastes as heterodox and deficient, under the assumptions that it (1) mirrors a harsh and distant God, (2) expresses a rejection of the traditional wisdom perspective, and (3) constitutes a denial of the

---

[54] Against much commentary, the epilogue does not represent a second theological position in Ecclesiastes, one distinct from or opposed to that of Qoheleth.

[55] Thus Graham S. Ogden, *Ecclesiastes* (Sheffield: JSOT Press, 1987), 26.

[56] One of the few to identify—and then develop—this linkage is Eunny P. Lee, *The Vitality of Enjoyment in Qohelet's Theological Rhetoric* BZAW 353 (Berlin: Walter de Gruyter, 2005).

theology of the New Testament.[57] But let us take one step back to ask, *How is the Creator God in Ecclesiastes mainly depicted?*

Lexical hints are suggestive: the verb "to give," appearing twelve times in the work, is indicative. God gives life, wisdom, joy, wealth and possessions, a sense of the eternal, as well as an awareness of limitations; and he assigns human beings their lot, portion, or reward. What's more, it is not insignificant that joy or life *is* the divine gift in eight of those twelve references.

Thus far we have argued that the structure of Ecclesiastes derives from recurring shifts in Qoheleth's argument, with meaninglessness and despair, to be sure, front and center. This literary-rhetorical strategy is intended to mirror an "under-the-sun" secular materialism, which as a life philosophy is bound to fail. Being contrasted with this dominant materialist outlook is a theistic view of ultimate reality in which human beings, motivated and undergirded by divine reverence, experience joy and satisfaction in life's endeavors.[58]

Given the shift between meaninglessness/despair and contentment, it behooves us to examine the so-called refrains alluded to above and identified below. Evidence for this literary-rhetorical strategy can be located in eight specific passages laced throughout Ecclesiastes that serve

---

[57] Note, however, the theological orientation of the apostle Paul: "Consider God's *kindness and severity*" (Rom 11:22, emphasis added). His orientation agrees with that of Ecclesiastes.

[58] My argument is not that we believers do not suffer, go through hardship, or experience seasons of excruciating pain; Old Testament Wisdom literature confirms that that is not the case. Rather, I wish to argue that one's basic approach to ultimate reality governs every dimension of the human experience—a significant part of which is human labor, wherein our lot, portion, or calling is to experience a deep measure of satisfaction in our labors. After all, we work because God works; we are created in the likeness of God and therefore find great contentment in the assignments apportioned to us by him.

as the antithesis to the pessimism and nihilism being lamented throughout the book. It is to these passages that we now turn.[59]

Human Labor in Ecclesiastes: A Wisdom Perspective

A common misperception about Ecclesiastes is that where particular passages refer to enjoyment, they merely speak of a lowest-common-denominator sort of experience, as if to say, "Get what you can, the little that you can," given the reality of surrounding despair.[60] However, upon closer examination, the evidence suggests otherwise. As the following discussion maintains, admonitions toward life's enjoyment surface throughout the treatise,[61] representing what one commentator describes as "climactic moments" in the book[62]—moments that will reach a crescendo in Eccl 11:1–12:1.[63]

---

[59] For a fuller treatment of wisdom and the work of God as it appears in Ecclesiastes, see chapter 1 of Charles, *Wisdom and Work*. Parts of that material have been used here with permission.

[60] For example, Tremper Longman III, *The Fear of the Lord Is Wisdom: A Theological Introduction to Wisdom in Israel* (Grand Rapids: Baker Academic, 2017), 35, writes that "It is hard to disagree with the majority of scholars who detect resignation, sadness and frustration in these [enjoyment] passages. In other words, the gist of Qohelet's thinking is that since life is difficult and then comes death, we should eke out of life whatever we can."

[61] Ryken identifies fifteen negative sections of material in the book and thirteen positive sections. Though greater length is devoted to the former, we are justified in calling enjoyment a prominent theme in terms of literary strategy. Leland Ryken, "Ecclesiastes," in *A Complete Literary Guide to the Bible*, ed. Leland Ryken and Tremper Longman III (Grand Rapids: Zondervan, 1993), 269–70.

[62] Graham S. Ogden, "'Vanity' It Certainly Is Not," *The Bible Translator* 38, no. 3 (1987): 301–6.

[63] In the present examination of these refrains, I am dependent on much fuller discussions appearing in Charles, "Wisdom and Work," 17–22, and *Wisdom and Work*, 99–124. Parts of that material are used here with permission.

The frequency of the term "meaningless"/"vanity" (Heb., *hebel*)—appearing almost forty times—would lend the strong impression of cynicism and despair on the part of the writer. What, then, can be an intrinsic good? Upon examination, we find the Hebrew *tôb* ("good") occurring with even greater frequency than *hebel* in the book—over fifty times.[64] Moreover, the writer employs the verb *śāmaḥ* ("to enjoy") or the noun form *śimḥâ* ("enjoyment," "joy") in the passages that are treated below (Eccl 2:24–26; 3:12–13; 5:18–19; 7:14; 8:15; 9:7–10; and 11:8–9). Together these indicators suggest a picture that departs considerably from conventional thinking about Ecclesiastes: there is indeed meaning, purpose, and satisfaction in life, *if* life—from a metaphysical standpoint—is viewed properly.

The presence of the enjoyment refrains presents the interpreter with a serious challenge. Not a few commentators assume that the message of Ecclesiastes is despair (or moderated despair) and the God depicted therein is harsh, cruel, tyrannizing, and despotic.[65] Taken together, the enjoyment statements would appear to rebut the meaninglessness thesis. These enjoyment refrains, which are no mere marginal comments tacked on by the writer, are notable because of several features: their common

---

[64] R. Norman Whybray, *The Good Life in the Old Testament* (London: T&T Clark, 2002), 186, as well as Graham S. Ogden and Lynell Zogbo, *A Handbook on Ecclesiastes* (New York: United Bible Society, 1997), 4, identify "good" as a catchword in Ecclesiastes.

[65] Lee, *The Vitality of Enjoyment in Qohelet's Theological Rhetoric*, is one of the few to have examined the enjoyment theme in Ecclesiastes with thoroughness while also reviewing the assumptions undergirding much professional commentary on the book. She observes that it is genuinely baffling to note a widespread interpretive resistance among Old Testament scholars along two lines: They resist (1) acknowledging the presence and the strategic importance of the enjoyment theme in the book and (2) linking the themes of joy and the fear of God as constitutive of—and informing—one another. In addition to Lee, exceptions include Whybray and Ogden, and more recently, Brian Neil Peterson, *Qoheleth's Hope: The Message of Ecclesiastes in a Broken World* (Lanham, MD: Lexington Books/Fortress Academic, 2020).

vocabulary, their common themes, their reference to God, and their strategic placement within the argument.

A further important piece of evidence needs explaining. In five of these statements the reader encounters an explicit connection between work (Heb. *'āmāl*)[66] and enjoyment. Moreover, eight times in Ecclesiastes the writer speaks of a human being's "lot" or "portion" (2:10, 21; 3:22; 4:9; 5:18; 9:6, 9; and 11:2) that has been "assigned" by God. Several of these appear in the positive context of one's delight in and through work.

We may view the eight passages or refrains speaking of enjoyment as representing eight intervals in the writer's argument.[67] These refrains help make some interpretative sense of a debate or dialogue that is being conducted.[68] They suggest a structure to the treatise that mirrors not so much a progression of thought as it does a cyclical pattern, by which two points of view are continually juxtaposed.[69] It turns out that there is more to reality—and to Qoheleth's position—than what is "under the sun."[70] In each of the

---

[66] In Ecclesiastes, the noun form occurs twenty times and the verb form fourteen. This high number of occurrences is significant.

[67] Whereas Whybray, *Ecclesiastes*, 64, and "Qoheleth, Preacher of Joy," *JSOT* 23 (1982): 87–98, points to seven allusions to enjoyment in the book, Lee, *Vitality of Enjoyment*, identifies eight. I follow Lee in terms of structure.

[68] On the dialogical element in the work's structure, see T. A. Perry, *Dialogues with Kohelet: The Book of Ecclesiastes* (University Park: Pennsylvania State University Press, 1993), 6–12.

[69] As already noted, no consensus whatsoever regarding the structure of Ecclesiastes exists among Old Testament commentators. And no proposed structural concept, it needs to be acknowledged, is airtight. Nevertheless, several individuals who propose a more or less cyclical pattern characterizing the framework of the writer's argument are Jacques Ellul, *Reason for Being*, 33–38, esp. 38; R. N. Whybray, *Ecclesiastes* NCBC (Grand Rapids: Eerdmans and Marshall, Morgan & Scott, 1988), 17; and Daniel J. Estes, *Handbook on the Wisdom Books and Psalms* (Grand Rapids: Baker Academic, 2005), 279. More recently, Douglas R. Fyfe, *Seeing What Qoheleth Saw: The Structure of Ecclesiastes as Alternating Panels of Observation and Wisdom* (Eugene, OR: Wipf & Stock, 2019), has described the writer's argument structurally in terms of "panels," i.e., alternating themes.

[70] Thus, his argument, in the words of Walter R. Steele, "Enjoying the Righteousness of Faith in Ecclesiastes," *Concordia Theological Quarterly* 74 (2010): 229, is "not a mess but a masterwork."

eight refrains, joy and contentment[71] are reaffirmed and linked to the "good" (*tôb*), which places them in contradistinction to the absurdities and meaninglessness characterizing a secular or materialistic perspective on existence. Each of these refrains calls for some interpretative comment.

> 1. There is nothing better for a man than to eat and drink and assure himself that *there is good in his labor*. Even this, I have seen, is from the hand of God. For who can eat and who can have enjoyment without Him? For to the person who pleases Him God gives wisdom, knowledge, and joy; but to the sinner He gives the work of gathering and collecting so that he may give to one who pleases God. This too is vanity and chasing after the wind. (Eccl 2:24–26, AMP, emphasis added)

With this material the reader encounters an initial, and in some ways unexpected, turning point. An alternative outlook is introduced, one that is theologically anchored in the reality of divine providence; a veil, as it were, is lifted. This alternative perspective is characterized by several notable features: multiple references to God; joyful contentment depicted as normative in the human experience; the commodities of wisdom, knowledge, and joy described as gifts from God to the one pleasing him; and satisfaction in work as a gift of God. These statements stand in conspicuous contrast to the previous lament of the utter inability of all things related to human striving to provide *any* meaning in life (see Eccl 1:12–2:23). They also provide a response to two rhetorical questions posed at the outset. First, the question, "What does a person gain [*yitrôn*] for all his efforts / that he labors at under the sun?" (Eccl 1:3) is reminiscent of Jesus's rhetorical question in Mark 8:36: "What does it benefit someone to gain the whole world and yet lose his life?" The answer, by both Qoheleth and Jesus, is nothing "under the sun." And

---

[71] The Hebrew noun *śimḥâ* is perhaps best rendered "contentment" in the rabbinic sense of being "happy with one's lot" (see, for instance, Eccl 5:19).

yet, at the same time, both acknowledge that there is an advantage or a "profit," but only in the context of pleasing and revering God. The second rhetorical question, which concerns what is "good" (Eccl 2:1),[72] finds its answer three times in Eccl 2:24–26. Indeed, apart from the Creator, there can exist no intrinsic good. This is the implied answer to the rhetorical question posed in Eccl 2:25: "Who can eat and who can enjoy life apart from [God]?"

These statements mirror the language and imagery of the psalmist, who declares such gifts as a sign of divine blessing:

> Blessed are all who fear the LORD,
> who walk in obedience to him.
> You will eat the fruit of your labor;
> blessings and prosperity will be yours. (Ps 128:1–2 NIV)

In line with this imagery, verse 24 of Ecclesiastes 2 contains the first of four "there is nothing better" rhetorical devices applied to work throughout the book and contextualized in the various joy refrains. A common wisdom technique,[73] this device combines a comparison and a verdict in a short but pregnant form, functioning to demonstrate or convince people of something contrary to conventional thinking.[74] The four "nothing better" statements serve as a key to understanding not only the overall structure of Ecclesiastes but the writer's own position and are to be understood in the sense that "there is no greater good," or, "it doesn't get any better." The suggestion is that eating, drinking, and working—norms

---

[72] The Hebrew *tôb* ("good") appears an astonishing fifty-two times in Ecclesiastes, more than any term. In terms of our interpretation, what might this suggest?

[73] See, for example, Prov 17:1; 21:9, 19; 27:5, 10; and Ps 37:16.

[74] Twenty-five "better than" statements are found in Ecclesiastes. On the writer's use of this device in the enjoyment refrains, see Graham S. Ogden, "Qoheleth's Use of the 'Nothing Is Better' Form," *Journal of Biblical Literature* 98, no. 3 (1979): 339–50.

of the human experience—are an intrinsic good, and therefore, a part of the way we are designed.[75]

2. I know that there is nothing better for them than to rejoice and to do good as long as they live; and also that every man should eat and drink and see and *enjoy the good [results] of all his labor—it is the gift of God*. (Eccl 3:12–13 AMP, emphasis added)

These statements follow on the heels of two important theological confessions. The first, one of the best-known of all scriptural passages, is framed in poetic verse and concerns the seasons of human life. Everything—*all* human endeavor, including recreation and labor—has its place, its purpose, and its time in the providence and economy of God. The second pronouncement, which also well affirms God's providence and superintendence of all things, is that God has set "eternity" (*'ōlām*[76]) in the human heart (Eccl 3:11). Insofar as the material in Ecclesiastes 3 concerns God's inscrutable purposes and works, there is much that human beings simply do not know.[77] If, in fact, there is a proper time

---

[75] See Ogden, *Qoheleth*, 62–63, Fredericks and Estes, *Ecclesiastes and the Song of Songs*, 100–101, and William P. Brown, *Ecclesiastes*, Interpretation (Louisville: John Knox, 2000), 62. It is intriguing that some commentators interpret the "nothing better" statements in the opposite direction of how they actually function—as a sort of last-resort concession by a melancholy cynic resigned to grabbing what he can since everything is futile. William H. U. Anderson, for example, vigorously denies the intent of the joy refrains, insisting that each refrain is "ironically invalidated" by surrounding pessimistic statements; see his "Philosophical Considerations in a Genre Analysis of Qoheleth," *Vetus Testamentum* 48, no. 3 (1998): 294–95. This sort of interpretation, unfortunately, is indebted to assumptions imported *to* the text from the outside rather than to careful exegesis and interpretation of the text itself. It also fails to discern the writer's literary-rhetorical strategy and the overall structure of his argument.

[76] This term appears seven times in the treatise—in Eccl 1:4, 10; 2:16; 3:11, 14; 9:6; and 12:5.

[77] The argument here is *not* that we know nothing of God, only that we cannot know his purposes, works, and ends. But what the Teacher does know is stated here. And the immediate context is important, for it helps interpret the

or season for everything (3:1; 8:6), everything cannot be "meaningless" (*hebel*). What is more, a sense of the eternal within the human heart gives vitality to our motivations and to our actions. Human beings, quite simply, would be incapable of revering God (3:14) without the sense of the eternal having been placed within their hearts, based on their design and the image of God.[78]

These statements also serve as a counterpoint to human inability to fathom what God has done and will do "from the beginning to the end" (Eccl 3:10–15). Divine inscrutability is not vexing for the believer, only for the secular materialist. Verse 22 of chapter 3 contains the second of four "nothing better" rhetorical devices applying to work in the book, while at the same time employing a wordplay on "good."

> 3. So I saw that there is nothing better than that all should *enjoy their work*, for that is their lot; who can bring them to see what will be after them? (Eccl 3:22 NRSV, emphasis added)

In this refrain, eating and drinking are absent, unlike in Eccl 2:24–26 and 3:12–13; thus, the accent is on human endeavor. This statement serves as a counterpoint to the finality of death and divine judgment mentioned in Eccl 3:16–22.[79] To rejoice in one's work is evocative of the Genesis creation account. Humans are creative, mirroring the *imago Dei*. Verse 22 contains the third of four "there is nothing better" rhetorical devices applied to work. Relatedly, the joy of human labor expresses itself both in the energy expended and the finished product. True contentment, it needs emphasizing, is to live with—and be satisfied in—one's "lot," "portion" or "allotment" (*heleq*), which we may regard as our particular

---

statements found in vv. 12 and 13: being suggested is the enduring, the transcendent, the permanent, and hence, the *meaningful*.

[78] In the words of Estes, *Handbook on the Wisdom Books and Psalms*, 313, though "bound by time," we still are "wired for eternity."

[79] That judgment, of both the wicked and the righteous, encompasses "every activity" and "every deed" done in this present life (Eccl 3:17) means it is a judgment according to works.

callings given by God. Elsewhere in the Old Testament, this term conveys a sense of "inheritance" or "reward."

4. Behold, what I have seen to be good and fitting is to eat and drink and *find enjoyment in all the toil with which one toils* under the sun the few days of his life that God has given him, for this is his lot. Everyone also to whom God has given wealth and possessions and power to enjoy them, and to accept his lot and *rejoice in his toil*—this is the gift of God. For he will not much remember the days of his life because God keeps him occupied with joy in his heart. (Eccl 5:18–20 ESV, emphasis added)

These statements signal another notable shift. They distinguish themselves by serving as a counterpoint to greed, the frustrations of wealth, and discontentment as are presented in Eccl 5:8–17 and 6:1–11. And notice the stark contrast between Ecclesiastes 5, verses 17 and 18: in the former, the human experience is "darkness," "frustration," "sickness," and "anger," where in the latter there is satisfaction. The fact that both the refrains of Eccl 2:24–26 and 5:18–20 shift from a bleak pessimism to joy suggests two possibilities: either they mirror an utter incongruence—a schizophrenia—on the part of the writer, or they are part of a literary-rhetorical strategy. Along with Eccl 3:10–15, these verses contain the most densely concentrated references to God in the entire treatise and establish the link between God and joy in the human heart.[80] Apart from a theocentric outlook on life, this sort of joy and satisfaction simply does not exist.

By twice connecting joy and our labor (Eccl 5:18–19) and then observing that God produces joy in the human heart, the Teacher underscores not merely the relatively good but the *genuine* good—something

---

[80] See Norbert Lohfink, "Qoheleth 5:17–19—Revelation by Joy," *Catholic Biblical Quarterly* 52, no. 4 (1990): 625–335, and Gianto, "The Theme of Enjoyment in Qohelet," 528–32.

that has been emphasized earlier, in Eccl 2:24; 3:12; and 3:22—and all of this mirrors a posture of contentment, a true gift of God. Moreover, the language of "lot"/"portion"/"allotment" (5:18), a reiteration of 3:22, suggests the writer is advocating a concept of grace. Wealth and possessions can be wonderful when enjoyed and used properly; their improper use is critiqued heavily in the material preceding. Neither gluttons nor misers (as described in 5:8–14) can truly enjoy and have real contentment; in truth, possessions and wealth have control of them.

Verse 20 of chapter 5 in particular speaks to the qualitative difference of happiness and contentment when compared to other outlooks on life; pessimism and despair are not what keep a believer occupied. The image created by this statement, moreover, suggests a state that comes as close to the "eternal" (the *ōlām*, v. 11) as is possible in the temporal realm; it also suggests that there are lasting fruits from our labor. Finding contentment in God's gifts, then, serves as the answer to the rhetorical question "What does a person gain for all his efforts?" that was posed at the outset (Eccl 1:3), essentially repeated after the poem of seasons (3:9), and reiterated here in what immediately precedes (5:16).

5. In the day of prosperity be joyful, and in the day of adversity consider: God has made the one as well as the other, so that man may not find out anything that will be after him. (Eccl 7:14 ESV)

The admonition to "consider," or contemplate the work of God, is intended to challenge the reader to alter his or her perspective, his or her worldview. Is it, for instance, possible to know true joy without experiencing sorrows and adversity? As the teaching in Ecclesiastes 3 makes clear, accepting various seasons of life is part of the faith commitment, thereby moderating human anxiety and fear and creating within us a deep trust, anchored in the awareness of divine providence. The fact that all human beings face bane and blessing does not negate the reality of joy in our experience. Good and evil, as well as prosperity and adversity, are mysteries; they are beyond human apprehension, though they will remain realities in a fallen world. Mystery and God's works, nevertheless, should produce reverence, for everything that God does has a redemptive quality about it, even though that quality might be hidden from human view.[81] This paradoxical statement serves as a counterpoint to potential disillusionment that arises from a lack of wisdom (see Eccl 7:1–8:1). It also hearkens back to the earlier argument, in Eccl 3:1–22, namely, that humans cannot fathom what God does. Here the writer is not arguing that God is the author of evil—a point missed by much commentary. The "crooked" in chapter 7, verse 13 refers not to evil but to the divine purpose—"what God has done" yet what does not fit human perception, that is, what is incomprehensible.[82]

These words, reminiscent of Job 8:3 and 34:12, are important in light of the human tendency to doubt God's omnipotence, his providence, and his goodness.[83] The secular materialist ignores death and dying and is incapable of accepting suffering. The God-fearer responds differently to changing fortunes, uncertainty, and suffering, anchored in an awareness that God has a purpose in adversity—a purpose that is hidden, to be sure. For this reason, the writer could observe earlier in proverbial form that "the heart of the wise is in a house of mourning" (Eccl 7:4). The fear of

---

[81] That everything God does has an essentially redeeming aspect to it, apart from our awareness, is part of the reality of divine providence. Hereby we observe that the doctrines of creation and redemption are inherently connected. Providence is not some periodic or rare intervention by God; rather, it is a moment-by-moment sustaining of all of creation. It corresponds to what we call common grace.

[82] Grasping a proper sense of these statements is Gutridge, "Wisdom, Anti-Wisdom, and the Ethical Function of Uncertainty," 291–92. Illustrating an improper interpretation of this text are Shields, *The End of Wisdom*, 236, who argues that Qoheleth indeed "ascribes evil to God," "accuses God," and "questions God's justice"; and Crenshaw, *Ecclesiastes*, 139, n. 105, who writes, "The twisted character of things also contradicts Qohelet's view in 7:29 that God made humankind straight . . ." What appears "crooked," it needs emphasizing, is a matter of human perception and expectation, not of divine creation.

[83] For this reason the psalmist writes, "Make us glad for as many days as you have afflicted us" (Ps 90:15 NIV).

God allows us to accept what we cannot control, even to the point of embracing suffering and sorrow, which is the spirit in which the proverbs of Eccl 7:2–4 are to be understood: "It is better to go to a house of mourning . . ."; "Grief is better than laughter"; and "The heart of the wise is in a house of mourning."[84] Again, mystery and divine sovereignty should have the effect of encouraging and not thwarting us. It should fashion reverence in human beings in light of the divine purpose; after all, it is divine counsel alone that stands (see Prov 21:1, 30). True wisdom, then, is sobriety amid uncertainty, an accepting of human limitations while affirming God's right to sovereignty and inscrutability.

6. I commended pleasure *and* enjoyment, because a man has no better thing under the sun than to eat and to drink and to be merry, *for this will stand by him in his toil* through the days of his life which God has given him under the sun. (Eccl 8:15 AMP, emphasis added)

These statements serve as a jolting contrast to what immediately follows in Eccl 8:16—awareness of wearisome labor—and what has immediately preceded—a description of life's seeming injustice (Eccl 8:11–14). The reader can be assured that "the righteous," with "their works," are "in God's hands" (Eccl 9:1). Once more in chapter 8, verse 15, we encounter reference to "the days . . . God has given"—a phrase that has been recurring. That joy and contentment are said to "stand by" us in our labors during the lifetime that God grants each of us is a remarkable statement. It suggests that contentment accompanies the God-fearer as a lifestyle, having an enduring quality that is both internal and external in nature.[85] The refrain also contains the fourth of four "there is nothing better" rhetorical devices applied to work, extending the pattern found in Eccl 2:24 and 3:12, for instance.

---

[84] Cf. Isa 53:3 and 1 Pet 2:21, 23.

[85] Unlike the ancient world, Scripture knows no dichotomy between physical and mental work, between intellectual and manual labor.

7. Go *then*, eat your bread in happiness and drink your wine with a cheerful heart; for God has already approved your works. Let your clothes be white all the time, and let not oil be lacking on your head. Enjoy life with the woman whom you love all the days of your fleeting life which He has given to you under the sun; *for this is your reward in life and in your toil* in which you have labored under the sun. *Whatever your hand finds to do, do it with all your might*; for there is no activity or planning or knowledge or wisdom in Sheol where you are going. (Eccl 9:7–10 NASB1995, emphasis added)

With this material, the reader encounters, once more, a conspicuous shift—both in content and in style. Stylistically, the shift moves from a descriptive to an imperative mood. These statements, which as a refrain reach a crescendo by employing multiple imperatives couched in exuberant—indeed, festive—imagery,[86] follow on the heels of the Teacher's reminder of death as the universal destiny of all (Eccl 9:2–6). They also constitute a powerful witness to human moral agency and the potential that humans have to seize the day when and where possible. This carpe diem is extended in the later admonitions to give and sow seed (11:1–6), for example, with no guarantees of what such efforts might yield. Thus seen, the present represents a theater of opportunity. The suggestion is that there is reward in the present: such is our "portion" and reward now.[87] The exuberant language in Eccl 9:7 that "God has already approved," regardless of how this language is parsed, suggests to the reader courage, hope, and confidence as he pursues whatever work is his to complete. The famous carpe diem here in v. 10—"Whatever your hand finds to do, do it with all your might" (NASB1995)—is confident,

---

[86] Comparable festive imagery can be found in Ps 23:5; 45:7–8; and Isa 61:3.

[87] Some versions of the Bible (for example, the NIV) translate *hebel*, which appears twice in Eccl 9:9 in its association with all the days of one's life, as "meaningless"; however, we have here an example of the term's multivalence. Here the context calls for a rendering that indicates not "meaningless" or even "futile" as NASB and CSB say, but "fleeting."

hopeful, and inspiring, not despairing, futile, and resigned. This refrain mirrors a life of energy, vitality, and delight—and, most important, meaning.[88] The imagery created suggests freedom and celebration, contentment, and fruitfulness or well-being, even when we cannot guarantee the success of our efforts (see Eccl 11:1–6).[89]

It is standard in virtually all commentary on Ecclesiastes to compare 9:7–10 with *The Epic of Gilgamesh*, an ancient Mesopotamian tale dating two millennia earlier that chronicles the weal and woe of a Sumerian king.[90] And indeed the similarities are striking. However, conspicuously absent from various parallels in ancient Near Eastern literature is the commendation of work in itself. Ancient cultures, as well as later classical Greco-Roman culture, did not view human labor in this way. Such a portrait of human labor is peculiarly Judeo-Christian and finds confirmation later in the Ecclesiastes treatise: skill applied will result in success (10:10b), but where a man is lazy, the roof sags (10:18a).

8. The light is pleasant, and it is good for the eyes to see the sun. Indeed, if a man should live many years, let him rejoice in them all, and let him remember the days of darkness, for they will be many. Everything that is to come will be futility. Rejoice, young

---

[88] This carpe diem, moreover, agrees with the teaching of the New Testament, for example, Eph 5:16 (". . . making the most of every opportunity . . .") and 2 Cor 9:6 ("The person who sows sparingly will also reap sparingly, and the person who sows generously will also reap generously").

[89] The divine approval depicted in Eccl 9:7 excludes the common interpretation that the God of Ecclesiastes is distant, arbitrary, harsh, or cruel. Fredericks and Estes, *Ecclesiastes and the Song of Songs*, 210, state the matter well: if all of life (including human labor) is meaningless, then the imperatives found in this material are a cruel joke; after all, why be diligent and creative about futility?

[90] For an English translation of *The Epic of Gilgamesh*, see James B. Pritchard, ed., *The Ancient Near East Volume 1: An Anthology of Texts and Pictures* (Princeton, NJ: Princeton University Press, 1958), 40–75, and James B. Pritchard, ed., *Ancient Near Eastern Texts Relating to the Old Testament* (Princeton, NJ: Princeton University Press, 1969), 72–98. The relevant passage, mirroring a correspondence with Eccl 9:7–10, is found in Tablet 10, section iii, lines 7–14.

man, during your childhood, and let your heart be pleasant during the days of young manhood. And follow the impulses of your heart and the desires of your eyes. Yet know that God will bring you to judgment for all these things. So, remove grief and anger from your heart and put away pain from your body, because childhood and the prime of life are fleeting. Remember . . . your Creator in the days of your youth. (Eccl 11:7–12:1a NASB1995)

In this refrain, which follows on the heels of multiple proverbs on wisdom and foolishness, the reader senses something of a call to decision,[91] given the inevitability and finality of death (Eccl 12:1b–8). The observation that light is good is a strong negation of meaninglessness (*hebel*); it communicates a sheer wonder over being alive. That youth is alluded to six times in these verses suggests that this stage or season of life is strategic; it is marked not only by impulsiveness but energy, creativity, and resourcefulness. Thus, youth is portrayed here as a divine gift and opportunity—a time of unbounded potential that is to be used creatively yet soberly. An alternative reading of these verses is not youth versus old age per se but youth versus "a time in which there is no longer the possession of pleasure" or energetic satisfaction.[92]

Life is to be cherished as a present possession, even when outcomes are out of our control and nothing is guaranteed (Eccl 11:1–6). In fact, the very open-endedness and lack of control in life depicted in vv. 1–6 serve as a prod, an impetus, toward energetically investing our time and abilities in what might possibly develop; it is in this light that we are to understand the imperatives "sow" or "cast" (v. 1, 6) and "give" (v. 2).[93]

---

[91] So, correctly, Eaton, *Ecclesiastes*, 139. Lee, *The Vitality of Enjoyment*, 72, describes this material as a "dramatic culmination" of the treatise.

[92] Graham S. Ogden, "Qoheleth XI.7–XII.8: Qoheleth's Summons to Enjoyment and Reflection," *JSOT* 34, no. 1 (1984): 33–34.

[93] In Jewish midrashic interpretation, casting bread on water (v. 1) serves as a metaphor for kindness or "moral investment"; see Larry Magarik, "Darshnut: Bread on Water," *Jewish Bible Quarterly* 28, no. 4 (2000): 268–70.

Simply because the farmer cannot guarantee a certain yield or result does not mean that he will not sow seed. Inactivity, alas, is worse than ignorance, for inactivity and idleness guarantee nothing.[94] After all, as the text of Eccl 11:6 points out, you just never know what will succeed. Which is to say, things happen in unlikely places and in unlikely ways; they occur in unlikely seasons and with utter unpredictability. You never know what God will do; therefore, don't wait for ideal conditions to sow, and "do not let your hand rest" in idleness (v. 6b). Thus, we may conclude from the sow-give-sow admonitions recorded in Eccl 11:1–6 that there is the possibility of profit in human labor, in response to the rhetorical question posed in Eccl 1:3; 3:9; and 5:16.[95] In fact, we might conclude that, based on Eccl 11:1b as translated in ESV, a reward is certain: "[we] will find it after many days."[96] Of course, the return may be slow in coming, but the principle is sure: blessing works invisibly but irresistibly, just as a child forms in the womb.[97] The condition of this gain, it needs reiterating, is that one "remember" one's Maker (Eccl 11:5 and 12:1). The imperatives found in Eccl 11:1–6, moreover, agree with the striking imperatives found in vv. 7–10—"rejoice" (twice), "be delighted," "follow your heart," "banish anxiety from your heart." While "meaninglessness" (*hebel*) leads to "vexation" of the heart (v. 10a), joy negates this. The difference between the two is lodged in the very source of human contentment, made abundantly clear by statements in Eccl 11:5, 9; and 12:1.

---

[94] See T. F. Glasson, "'You Never Know': The Message of Ecclesiastes 11:1–6," *Evangelical Quarterly* 55, no. 1 (1983): 43–48.

[95] True, we cannot be sure of what God is going to do, but it does not follow that there is no cause and effect.

[96] This agrees with Paul's affirmation to the Galatian Christians: "Let us not get tired of doing good, for we will reap at the proper time if we do not give up" (Gal 6:9).

[97] This is the language and the analogy used by Matthew Henry in "An Exposition, with Practical Observations, of the Book of Ecclesiastes," in *Matthew Henry's Commentary on the Whole Bible*, vol. 3, *Job to the Song of Solomon* (McLean, VA: MacDonald, 1710), 1042, 1044.

"Rejoice" and "remember" are the two admonitions receiving emphasis in this refrain. Life, though brief, is not meaningless; it can be utterly absorbing. These statements together call to mind the sort of disposition that undergirds the Augustinian maxim "Love God and do what you will."[98] All in all, this is wise counsel.[99]

Rethinking Human Endeavor in Ecclesiastes

The enjoyment refrains distributed throughout Ecclesiastes play a crucial role in identifying the structure of the writer's argument, and hence in properly understanding the book's message. They serve as interludes in the wider thesis between the bookends of Eccl 1:2 and 12:8 ("Meaningless! Meaningless! Everything is meaningless!" [NIV]). In their function, they are the antithesis of the meaninglessness theme. In Ecclesiastes, the reader encounters an argument in which the writer shifts back and forth, unannounced, between two diametrically opposed outlooks on life. On the one hand, he exposes the grimness of life lived not as a gift to be received from the Creator but as something to be gained by means of human striving. Consistent with this outlook is the basic assumption that, if life is pointless and meaningless, then work is an absurdity as well; therein one can expect only misery and toil, not satisfaction and meaning.

However, because the Teacher assumes and affirms a theology of creation and providence, though he does so indirectly as is common in Wisdom literature, important interlocking implications follow. All of life is to be received as a gift; therefore, it possesses meaning and purpose. Correlatively, practical wisdom in the affairs of life can be practiced and

---

[98] Joy in Ecclesiastes, most assuredly, is not "absurdly minimal," contrary to the position of William P. Brown, "Whatever Your Hand Finds to Do: Qoheleth's Work Ethic," *Interpretation* 55, no. 3 (2001): 281.

[99] Elsewhere I have developed a more extensive exegesis of these eight refrains in Ecclesiastes. See Charles, "Wisdom and Work," 17–22, and chapter 5 of Charles, *Wisdom and Work*. Parts of that material are used here with permission.

accrue, despite human limitations and even human wickedness. As a result, human endeavor—and labor itself—takes on a very different cast where it is done faithfully and with a view to please God. Moreover, that work can be understood as humanity's "assignment"—and hence itself a vocation or generalized calling—from God. Against much Ecclesiastes commentary, then, there *is* lasting profit in our endeavors and labor. Such is a gift of God to those who humbly acknowledge his providence and his inscrutable ways.

One external yet utterly fascinating clue to a proper interpretation of Ecclesiastes has received little—if any—attention by Old Testament commentators. The book of Ecclesiastes historically has been associated with Sukkot, the Feast of Booths (or Tabernacles), which is part of the Jewish celebration calendar.[100] As an annual, weeklong feast, the event commemorated God's provision in the wilderness following the exodus from Egypt. At the end of harvest, Israelites were to journey to Jerusalem to worship at the temple, giving thanks for divine sustenance and faithfulness. In consequence, Israel's gratitude for God's sovereign provision and gifts expressed itself, on an annual basis, in joy and celebration. Why, we may ask, would Ecclesiastes—of all things—play a role in Jewish celebration? The most natural answer is its invitation to rejoice. It most assuredly was *not* because life and human endeavor, including work, are meaningless. Israelites celebrated because they had received from God—which is a recurring theme throughout the treatise.

Work per se, it needs emphasizing, is never presented in the Old Testament as degrading, demeaning, or as something we should long to escape.[101] More specifically, Wisdom literature values, dignifies, and

---

[100] See Lev 23:33–4; Num 29:12–40; and Deut 16:13–17; cf. John 7:2–13.

[101] Furthermore, the enjoyment of our labor is not merely some momentary phenomenon—here one minute and gone the next. Rather, it has a residual effect in the believer's life. Recall the earlier refrains: "God keeps [a worker] occupied with the joy of his heart" (Eccl 5:20) and then satisfaction "will accompany [the person] in his labor during the days of his life that God gives him" (Eccl 8:15). What these texts suggest is that a God-given satisfaction is an intrinsic,

commends work.[102] In granting meaning and satisfaction in our labor, God sanctifies the ordinary.[103] And where some material in Ecclesiastes seems to suggest that the human person was not made for work and that our energies expended in labor are futile and wasted, it needs reiterating that the Teacher is mirroring—and responding to—conventional views of work and human activity. Correlatively, the Judeo-Christian tradition knows no split or dichotomy between manual and mental labor, in contradistinction to pagan thinking. The reason for this is that we are created in God's likeness (see Gen 1:26–27).

In summary, I argue that a double theme exists in Ecclesiastes.[104] The writer juxtaposes two contrasting views of reality—"all is meaningless" and "life comes as a gift from the hand of God, wherein true joy and contentment have their source"—before calling for a verdict. Based on the one perspective, there is no profit to any aspect of human endeavor and

---

qualitative good that is enduring and to be savored; work is not some painkiller, tranquilizer, or anesthetic to dull or distract us from the evil around us.

[102] Consider another wisdom saying: "There is profit in all hard work" (Prov 14:23a)—a "profit" that is measured not foremost in economic terms but in contentment. Wisdom literature also supports this perspective more broadly elsewhere: "The diligent hand will rule, / but laziness will lead to forced labor (Prov 12:24); "Do you see someone skilled in their work? / They will serve before kings . . ." (Prov 22:29 NIV); "For you repay each according to his works" (Ps 62:12); and "Let the favor of the Lord our God be on us; / establish for us the work of our hands— / establish the work of our hands" (Ps 90:17). The wisdom perspective on human labor, moreover, finds confirmation in Jesus's parabolic teaching. There is reward for our work(s), as he noted in Matt 25:21: "Well done, good and faithful steward. Because you have been faithful with smaller things, I will put you in charge of greater things. Come and share in your master's joy" (my translation).

[103] Compare this wisdom perspective with Paul's counsel to Timothy that "godliness with contentment is great gain" (1 Tim 6:6; cf. Phil 4:11).

[104] This double theme, then, necessitates that we recognize a double "framing" or "border" in terms of the writer's literary strategy: an "inner border" of "all is meaningless" (Eccl 1:2; 12:8) and an "outer border" that argues for life to be lived in the fear of God. Shead is one of the few to recognize this interpretive framework. Andrew G. Shead, "Reading Ecclesiastes Epilogically," *Tyndale Bulletin* 48, no. 1 (1997): 67–91.

labor; based on the alternative, theocentric outlook, life is to be received as a gift from the Creator, whereby human beings discover that there *is* profit in their efforts. That profit is qualitative in character, mirrored in a contentment that expresses itself both internally and externally, both in the heart and in activity.

Upon closer inspection, the book's message forces on us a reevaluation of human labor. Work might even be described as "the principal action through which humanity participates in creation."[105] Ecclesiastes addresses a material orientation toward life, misguided pursuits of happiness, conventional wisdom, the promise of success, seeking reputation and esteem, and living as if we will not die. Not only is work part of the writer's taxonomy of joy, but it is part of the Christian's as well. Hence, Ecclesiastes remains an important part of Christian ethical reflection, lodged at the very center of Christian vocation. This, properly understood, transforms our understanding of human labor and the trajectory of our lives.

Final Wisdom Reflection: The End of the Matter

The final piece of advice in Ecclesiastes, expressed in the last refrain (11:1–12:1a), is to pursue a life of joy or contentment that is tempered with sobriety. Hedonists, gluttons, and workaholics, after all, tend not to reflect on God's wisdom, providence, or gifts. So, it is on this note that the dialogue in Ecclesiastes ends. The writer's argument is summarized by a subtheme recurring in the treatise and characteristic of Old Testament Wisdom literature: humankind is to revere God.[106] In practical terms, the fear of the Lord moves human beings to acknowledge their limitations

---

[105] See Eaton, *Ecclesiastes*, 129. Eaton is one of the few to underscore not only the importance of the theme of work in Ecclesiastes but the writer's positive assessment of it in contrast to that of surrounding culture.

[106] The fear of God as a theme is at home in the wisdom tradition, as indicated by Job (6:14; 28:28) and Proverbs (e.g., 1:7, 29; 2:5; 8:13;10:27) as well as numerous Psalms (e.g., 19:9; 34:11; 111:10).

and be receptive to his works. Where human openness to the divine is absent, God's ways and work end up alienating us, rendering us cynical and skeptical.[107] If any true wisdom is to be found among human beings, it will lead a person *away from* the absurdity of secular materialism and *to* the acknowledgment of the mystery of divine providence. The call to fear God, in the end, is the final word in Ecclesiastes (12:13–14), fitting given the realities of divine providence, inscrutability, and human limitations. It induces us, in the words of the psalmist, to "be still, and know" that he is God (Ps 46:10 NIV).

Given Jesus's appropriation of both the content and form of Wisdom literature in his teaching, a final word of caution regarding standard interpretation of Ecclesiastes is in order. It issues from the widespread tendency among Old Testament commentators—and the average reader of Ecclesiastes, for that matter—to treat the writer of Ecclesiastes as a sort of foil or preparation for the Christian gospel, as if in Qoheleth the Teacher we are witnesses to a deficient person who is "in dire need of rehabilitation,"[108] and is confused, despairing, and resigned to life's misfortunes—a state or condition which is "resolved" in the new covenant through Christ.[109] A Christianized reading of Ecclesiastes, however, errs at several levels.

First, we do well to remember that Ecclesiastes was interpreted spiritually for much of the church's history until the Protestant Reformation.

---

[107] Roland E. Murphy, *Ecclesiastes* WBC 23A (Dallas: Word, 1992), 39, erroneously describes inscrutability in terms of "desperate trickery." But inscrutability, it needs emphasizing, is not injustice. Just because we cannot grasp God's works and God's purposes, it does not follow that God is harsh, malevolent, or distant.

[108] See Brown, *Ecclesiastes*, 121.

[109] Even the author of "Introduction to Ecclesiastes," which is part of the Theology of Work project, succumbs to this sort of misguided thinking. He writes, for example, "Unlike the Teacher, followers of Christ today see a concrete hope beyond a fallen world"; we have "a new Teacher. . . . The work we do as followers of Christ therefore does . . . have eternal value that could not have been visible to the Teacher." See www.theologyofwork.org/old-testament/ecclesiastes, accessed March 30, 2022.

That reading resulted in an interpretation of *contemptus mundi*, a contempt for the world. But to spiritualize or Christianize one's reading of Ecclesiastes is to wholly miss and distort its message. Relatedly, while the well-known maxim of Rom 8:28—namely, that all things have a divinely intended purpose—is certainly true, the apostle Paul is assuredly not stating that the Christian believer has "privileged insight" into God's works or his purposes.[110] Inscrutability is a biblical doctrine, not a facet of the divine nature restricted to the Old Testament. Our human need remains, just as it was over two millennia ago, to stand in awe of God and to accept our limitations.

In addition, a Christianized reading of the book fails to recognize the universality and enduring nature of Wisdom literature and the wisdom perspective. Wisdom literature is not intended to be read Christologically. When, for example, Proverbs entreats the reader or listener to eschew slothfulness and be diligent or seek wisdom or act justly or be a good steward or rescue the perishing, such advice is not a uniquely "Christian" insight that is only relevant to the days of the new covenant; it applies to all people everywhere at all times. The wisdom perspective, perennially true and necessary for life irrespective of time or social location, speaks to our design and our humanity, with its limitations. This is true whether we are Christian or non-Christian, whether we were born before the Christian advent or after.[111]

---

[110] See A. B. Caneday, "'Everything Is Vapor': Grasping for Meaning under the Sun," *Southern Baptist Journal of Theology* 15, no. 3 (Fall 2011): 28.

[111] While author Douglas Sean O'Donnell, in *The Beginning and End of Wisdom: Preaching Christ from the First and Last Chapters of Proverbs, Ecclesiastes, and Job* (Wheaton, IL: Crossway, 2011), 28–29, acknowledges that Wisdom literature teaches us of God as the source of wisdom, he adds, "But it also teaches us about the gospel, illustrating the wisdom of God in the sufferings of our Savior." Well, no; in fact, it does *not* teach this. Wisdom literature is not meant to be read Christologically, nor as "preparation" for the gospel, even when Christ is the fullness of wisdom. Such an interpretation must be read *back into the text* by the Christian reader.

Moreover, a Christianizing of particular parts of the Old Testament—not only Wisdom literature—fails to recognize that Old Testament saints indeed lived and were justified by faith. For this reason, through their works they pleased God. This, lest we forget, is the teaching of Hebrews 11 and of James. Work and vocation were not cursed up until the time of Christ, at which point they then suddenly became productive and meaningful; their meaning is anchored in creation, not the Christian advent.[112]

In truth, the Christian agrees with Ecclesiastes on its most important theological elements—its emphasis on the fear of God, the doctrines of creation and providence, divine inscrutability and hiddenness, our creaturely status, worldly versus godly wisdom,[113] the coexistence of divine sovereignty and human moral agency (that is, free will), joy and satisfaction in work and service, grace (that is, receiving everything as a gift from God), final judgment, and the futility of everything outside of a theocentric worldview.[114] The reality of divine providence, the goodness of creation, divine inscrutability, the fear of the Lord, human limitations, divine judgment, and the need for wisdom are every bit as true and vital in the new covenant era as they were prior. As it turns out, Ecclesiastes

---

[112] I am not arguing against the unfolding of salvation-history, which finds its culmination in Christ. However, the genre of Wisdom literature requires that we read these documents accordingly, and their purpose is not salvation-historical or Christological in nature.

[113] The New Testament agrees with this distinction. We see it, for example, in Jesus's teaching that God hides wisdom from some and gives it to others (see Matt 11:25; Luke 10:21); in Paul's teaching that God destroys "the wisdom of the wise," i.e., the wisdom of the world (1 Cor 1:18–25); and in James's teaching that there is a heavenly wisdom and an earthly wisdom (Jas 3:13–18).

[114] Echoes of this "futility" (*hebel*) in the New Testament abound—for example, in Acts 14:15 (Paul's preaching in Lystra to turn from "futile things"); Rom 1:21 (Paul's allusion to humanity's "futile" understanding); Rom 8:20 (Paul's observation that creation is subjected to futility); 1 Cor 3:20 (Paul's insistence that the wisdom of the world is "futile"); 1 Cor 15:17 (Paul's teaching that if Christ is not raised, our faith is "futile"); Eph 4:17 (the "futility" of the unbeliever's thinking); and Titus 3:9 (Paul's warning to avoid what is unprofitable and "futile").

serves, in an *abiding* way, as an effective apologetic. It presents a dialectic that continually informs people of faith in God while challenging misplaced "faith" and values.[115] When we listen to the Teacher's argument, we get a sense of the cultural mindset with which he was in dialogue, but we also get a sense of our own, with its "counterfeit gifts, forged advantages, and illusory pleasures."[116]

Ecclesiastes surely confronts us with what human beings resist the most. It is withering in its exposure of life's absurdity when and where human existence has been bleached of an acknowledgement of God, whose ways are inscrutable. A literary product of antiquity, Ecclesiastes is utterly remarkable in its relevance to any age, particularly ours. It mirrors contemporary debates on the meaning of life, with the writer engaging those debates in wholesale fashion, laying waste to a dominant outlook on life. In its own unique way, Ecclesiastes is an invaluable guide to living faithfully in a culture that at best is agnostic and at worst is hostile to the One who is Creator, sustainer, and judge of all things. Ecclesiastes confronts us with our own ills; and listening attentively to its argument permits us not only to hear the cultural mindset of the writer but our own. "Where will wisdom be found?" cried Job to his three visitors (see Job 28:12). We do well to ask and ponder the same question.[117]

---

[115] See Iain W. Provan, "Fresh Perspectives on Ecclesiastes: 'Qohelet for Today,'" and Daniel C. Fredericks, "Preaching Qohelet," in *The Words of the Wise Are like Goads: Engaging Qohelet in the 21st Century*, ed. M. J. Boda et al. (Winona Lake: Eisenbrauns, 2013), 401–16 and 417–42 respectively.

[116] Zack Eswine, *Recovering Eden: The Gospel According to Ecclesiastes* (Phillipsburg: P & R, 2014), 13.

[117] Ecclesiastes and Wisdom literature in general are desperately needed in our foolish age—an era in which time-tested, age-old wisdom is ridiculed, mocked, muzzled, or ignored. And one need not profess Christian faith to recognize this latter sobering reality.

Young adults, who lack life experience, are in special need of wisdom. They need a proper sense of moral accountability and moral priorities, of nonmaterial reality that can help shape their values and priorities in the material world—one that provides a proper perspective even on death. It is a metaphysical outlook that

Embracing the idea of vocation—or, as expressed in Ecclesiastes, one's "allotment," "placement," or "reward" (*heleq*)—has the effect of recalibrating our sense of duties within the context of God's providential care and his wider design. In its essence, work is lodged at the center of calling.[118] The teaching of Ecclesiastes is that work is a satisfying gift coming from the hand of God. It is only meaningless when and where it is measured by a wrong metaphysical outlook. If human labor truly is a satisfying gift, but the believer's day-to-day experience in the marketplace is neither satisfying nor viewed as such, something is askew and we have failed to realize our design. Theological recalibration is then in order, at the heart of which stands the concept of vocation.

In the following chapter we intend to probe vocation or calling in a fuller way, exploring its religious meaning and its significance for the individual Christian.[119]

---

alone provides joy, contentment, and satisfaction in human endeavor. Even as we enter the third decade of the 21st century, what "the Teacher" wrote remains "truth" (Eccl 12:10). The statement that follows, namely, that the words of the wise are like "cattle prods" and "firmly embedded nails" (v. 11), speaks of the effects of wisdom as it enters the heart of the listener. It can disturb the conscience and unsettle pride. This is as it should be, and the Teacher, if he was truly wise (v. 9), sought to evoke a "conversion" in terms of the reader's/listener's outlook

[118] This is true even when faithfully undertaking a particular job does not represent the totality of that calling.

[119] Elsewhere I have examined more completely the enjoyment theme in Ecclesiastes as it relates to work as well as the "the end of the matter." See chapter 5 of Charles, *Wisdom and Work*. Parts of that discussion have been used and developed in the present chapter by permission of Wipf and Stock Publishers, www.wipfandstock.com.

CHAPTER
6

A "Wisdom" Perspective on Vocation
Uniting God's (Providential) Calling and Our Response

The preceding chapter ended on a critical note: a proper grasp of the notion of vocation has the effect of clarifying, adjusting, or recalibrating our sense of duties and obligations within the larger ethical framework of God's providential care and purpose. Without question, the operative word here is providential, for it is in a proper grasp of divine providence—and only therein—that vocation (or calling) can be understood and experienced. Recall once more the presentation of human labor in Ecclesiastes where it expressed a theocentric outlook on reality in contrast to a *self-* or *culture-*centered perspective (the latter yielding "meaninglessness"): work is both satisfying and a gift of God. This, the writer affirms repeatedly, is one's *heleq*, one's "lot," which can also be translated "portion," "allotment," or "reward." That divine providence, sovereignty, and inscrutability underpin the theology of Ecclesiastes is unmistakable.

And as was observed in chapter 5, Ecclesiastes 3 is perhaps the clearest and most forceful declaration of providence anywhere in Scripture.

In this present chapter I will argue not only that vocation is a theme whose time again has come but that (1) our callings are discernible, in accordance with God's fundamental nature—he speaks, communicates, reveals, initiates, confirms, prods, and works—and (2) a sense of direction and confidence, joy and satisfaction, are the by-products of vocation properly understood.[1] This view proceeds under the assumption that vocation is a gift—a heavenly gift—which is not chosen but is to be received in gratitude; in the language of Ecclesiastes, it is our "portion" or "allotment," which providence has bestowed. Our responses to God constitute our vocation, and without a sense of vocation, of calling, we personally are adrift.

The Disappearance of Vocation

Vocation is a central doctrine of the faith, notwithstanding its relative neglect in the church's teaching and preaching. In classic Christian formulation, vocation, at least since the early sixteenth century, may be

---

[1] According to a global Gallup poll published in 2017 and data taken from 160 countries, only 15 percent of the world's roughly one billion full-time workers have a sense of "engagement" at work. See Jim Clifton, "The World's Broken Workplace," Gallup, June 13, 2017, news.gallup.com/opinion/chairman/212045/worl-broken-workplace.aspx. If 85 percent are so dissatisfied, that suggests most of the world's workers lack a sense of calling, and that means most people are not flourishing. According to this same poll, in fact, a whopping 94 percent of Japan's workers indicate that they are "not engaged." The nation's accompanying high suicide rates verify this tragic reality. In the US, 30 percent indicated satisfaction in the workplace. But the truth is that a 70 percent dissatisfaction rate is cause for concern; again, people are not flourishing. And according to current U.S. Department of Labor statistics, in April 2021 workers who left their jobs constituted 2.7 percent of the total labor force—a jump from 1.6 percent a year earlier. Lauren Weber, "Forget Going Back to the Office—People Are Just Quitting Instead," *Wall Street Journal*, June 13, 2021, https://www.wsj.com/articles/forget-going-back-to-the-officepeople-are-just-quitting-instead-11623576602.

described as "that place in the world of productive work that one was created, designed, or destined to fill by virtue of God-given gifts and talents and the opportunities presented by one's station in life."[2] The concept of vocation was a driving force in Protestant thought from the beginning. And because of vocation's central importance, its loss in the church—and we must acknowledge that its emphasis *has* been *utterly* lost—is unspeakably tragic. The concept of calling, in the words of one writer, has become "alienated" and "dearly missed,"[3] and surely another writer does not overstate the matter in declaring that the notion of vocation has "slipped away . . . into near oblivion."[4] Tragically, vocation (properly understood) has been banished from human labor.[5]

Yet, this disappearance is not *merely* a case of secularization, which indeed is part of the story. To be sure, in religion-dominated societies of the past, people generally sensed that they were "called" to a task. Today, absent any transcendent metaphysical aim that guides a sense of "calling" and day-to-day living, the driving motivation is self-interest. Indeed, once the notion of "calling" or "vocation" was stripped of its religious meaning, it devolved into "vague moral idealism" and "flabby pietism" as well as "career-" and "job-training."[6] As correctly noted by one theologian, work

---

[2] J. Stuart Bunderson and Jeffery A. Thompson, "The Call of the Wild: Zookeepers, Callings, and the Double-Edged Sword of Deeply Meaningful Work," *Administrative Science Quarterly* 54, no. 1 (2009): 33.

[3] So Hans Dirk von Hoogstraten," Reclaiming the Concept of Calling," in *Finding Meaning in Business: Theology, Ethics, and Vocation*, ed. Bartholomew C. Okonkwo (New York: Palgrave Macmillan, 2012), 19.

[4] D. H. Williams, "Protestantism and the Vocation of Higher Education," in *Revisiting the Idea of Vocation: Theological Explorations*, ed. John C. Haughey (Washington, DC: Catholic University of America Press, 2004), 141.

[5] Although Douglas J. Schuurman, *Vocation: Discerning Our Calling in Life* (Grand Rapids: Eerdmans, 2004), 1–16, identifies as many as six modern challenges to vocation rightly understood—secularist materialism, consumerism, technology, specialization of labor, religion as a "consumer good," and radical pluralism—I would subsume most of these under "secularization" broadly construed.

[6] Williams, "Protestantism and the Vocation of Higher Education," 141–62, traces this secularizing process over the last century as it gutted university

and vocation typically have not been treated as theology proper; usually they are subsumed under historical or sociological analysis or organizational psychology.[7] However, the *far sadder* truth is that the utter disappearance of vocation properly understood has been the result of a certain *religious* thinking that has been dominant in our own circles. And this has been true of *Protestants*, not merely Catholics.[8]

In fact, it is a sad truth that for most of the church's history (well over a millennium), the notion of vocation had been distorted and obscured—so much so that a "reform of protest" in the early sixteenth century was needed to expose and counter its many abuses. For this reason, the Lutheran breakthrough was—and remains—an important milepost in the church's history. The Latin *vocatio* and *vocare* ("to call") indeed entered English language, at least in more common usage, in the early sixteenth century as a result of Protestant—and specifically Lutheran—reform, mirrored in an anti-clerical shift by Luther and fellow Reformers to follow. Luther's emphasis on *vocatio* was necessary in rectifying over a millennium of wrong thinking about work and vocation, for it helped collapse the insidious and false dichotomy between the "sacred" and "secular" realms of temporal existence—a distortion that continually arises in every generation. In our day, this distortion is typically found among more pious believers of *both* Protestant and Catholic traditions

---

education, emptying colleges and universities of their original confessional commitments.

[7] Gary D. Badcock, *The Way of Life: A Theology of Christian Vocation* (Grand Rapids: Eerdmans, 1998), 29.

[8] In chapter 3 we already noted Christian thinkers—for example, Jacques Ellul, Stanley Hauerwas, and Miroslav Volf—who either reject the Protestant notion of vocation as unbiblical, reject Luther's view of vocation because of the Reformer's anchoring the doctrine in creation, or reject the idea of human beings "co-creating" with God. Offering a thorough and much-needed rebuttal of this line of thinking, to his great credit, is Douglas J. Schuurman, "Creation, Eschaton, and Social Ethics: A Response to Volf," *Calvin Theological Journal* 30, no. 1 (1995): 144–58.

who earnestly wish to serve God.⁹ And while since 2000 there have been signs of increased interest in vocation as a result of initiatives such as the Lilly project "Programs for the Theological Exploration of Vocation" (PTEV), it is supremely difficult more than two decades later to measure the effects of such initiatives.¹⁰ Today there exists, in a Christian context, very little serious discourse on vocation. Where it does receive attention, that context tends to be journals of organizational psychology, business ethics, and organizational behavior. Moreover, most students today, even in a Christian liberal arts environment, will not learn the difference between vocation and occupation. This unfortunate state of affairs needs to be challenged.¹¹

Recall from chapter 4 the observations of noted German theologian Jürgen Moltmann—vocation is "the third great insight" of the Reformation (after Word and sacrament)—and Lutheran theologian Kenneth Cherney—vocation is "the second most frequent emphasis" in Luther's writings. It is surely difficult to understand, if Moltmann and Cherney are correct, why the Christian church is largely silent now, in its efforts in education and spiritual formation, on a doctrine of such crucial importance—a doctrine that flows out of justification by faith and

---

⁹ In my own generation and in more "evangelical" circles, the exhortation "Every Christian should be headed toward the mission field unless otherwise directed by God" was commonly heard. While I do not doubt the sincerity of those making such pronouncements, the "call" to (foreign) "missions" was typically and mistakenly viewed as a "higher calling" (if not by those "called" to it then by multitudes of laypersons). In its own Protestant manner, it replicated the dualism that Luther rejected in the early sixteenth century.

¹⁰ See chapter 1, n. 26. As of 2015, based on eighty-eight participating "church-affiliated" colleges and universities that sought conversations around a "theology of vocation," the results evade measurement. Tim Clydesdale, *The Purposeful Graduate: Why Colleges Must Talk to Students about Vocation* (University of Chicago Press, 2015).

¹¹ Schuurman is surely right: churches and church-affiliated colleges should "lead the way in recovery of life as vocation" (*Vocation*, xiii). To these two I would add a third: seminaries and divinity schools.

the priesthood of every believer and is emphasized by Luther as much as scriptural authority and the sacraments. Given Christianity's waning influence in our post-Christian world, it is reasonable to ask whether the Reformation understanding of vocation might not be a proper (and much-needed) antidote to the compartmentalizing of faith that contemporary Christians sense and experience.

Indeed, we do well to be reminded of the radical—that is, basic[12]—ramifications of Luther's emphasis on universal priesthood. First, "vocation" properly understood collapses any distinction between the spiritual and temporal, between the sacred and the secular. Next, all work has intrinsic dignity; no work is insignificant, and all believers have a calling or vocation that is specific to their individual giftings, inclinations, burdens, and stations in life. Vocation, then, joins faith to both *work* and *works*—another insight owing to Luther. While the New Testament contains no blueprint for finding a particular occupation, it needs emphasizing—for example, through its accent on work and works—that it does not call us *away* from society; rather, it calls believers *to* it in new, creative, and redemptive ways. As one theologian observes, a bad "theology of works" leads to a bad "theology of work."[13] Foundationally, our work should be an outpouring of who we are—people created in the divine image who are also grateful that God has justified us.

My own experience through the years as a teacher, advisor, and mentor (and as a father) in attempting to guide students at the university level and even adults beyond the university level who are already in the workforce has confronted me again and again with the significance of the concept of vocation; it is a "doctrine" that lies at the heart of Christian faith. And as prior chapters have suggested, vocation is not merely relevant to those entering the job market for the first time. It is a matter that perplexes and is relevant to believers who have been in the

---

[12] The word "radical" derives from the Latin *radix* ("root" or "base").

[13] Darrell Cosden, *The Heavenly Good of Earthly Work* (Bletchley, UK: Paternoster, 2006), 107.

workforce for years, just as it is relevant to those of retirement age who wrestle with meaningful service and endeavor beyond their "careers" or "occupations."[14] Guided by a sense of vocation, the believer—regardless of age-group—is not consigned to groping blindly or being plagued by a sense of uneasiness about the future. But given the considerable confusion that surrounds the term "calling," at least among those who presuppose a caller, we will need to unpack a proper understanding of vocation to grasp its full weight and significance.

An Anatomy of Vocation

In the wonderfully insightful volume *Business as a Calling*, Michael Novak shares the stories of a litany of businessmen who have been remarkably gifted and successful in terms of their calling to the marketplace. Not all were headed there early in their lives; remarkably, several were seminarians or wished to become foreign missionaries.[15] Novak describes the path that led each of these individuals, over time, in the direction of their specific callings—which, interestingly, did not involve work as career clergymen. He then summarizes what he believes to be four important characteristics of calling or vocation:

---

[14] Retirement so-called, as we have sought to argue in previous chapters, does not bring an end to vocation; it simply begins a new phase or chapter of our calling.

[15] Michael Novak, *Business as a Calling: Work and the Examined Life* (New York: The Free Press, 1996), 20–34. One of these vignettes is devoted to John Templeton. According to Novak (20–21), who later in life became a personal friend of this remarkably successful businessman and visionary, early on Templeton had aspired to be a missionary. But while studying at Yale and Oxford, he struggled with doubts, eventually recognizing that he did not have "the right stuff" for such a role. In the long run, he decided to pursue his more natural bent toward business. And in so doing, he found himself able to devote much to assisting career missionaries financially.

- Calling is unique to each individual. Each person mirrors a unique—and beautiful—aspect of the created order.
- Calling involves certain preconditions. That is, it requires more than desires; it requires talent.
- A true calling reveals its presence by the satisfaction and sense of renewed energy that comes with its practice. The test of a vocation, as both wisdom and human experience confirm, is the love of drudgery that is associated with that particular line of work. For unless one welcomes with a certain satisfaction the tedium, frustrations, and obstacles, and (typically) small steps forward, the claim that this is a "calling" has a hollow ring.
- Calling is not always immediately or readily apparent. It is not easily uncovered but often is discerned as a result of setbacks, disappointment or surprises, prayerful discernment, and patience.[16]

"You can be anything you want to be!" "Be all that you can be!" "No limits!" How often in the American cultural context, owing chiefly to pop psychology and Disney films, have we heard these (and similar) mantras? For decades, parents and teachers, wishing to avoid contributing to a child's sense of low self-esteem, have been parroting such phrases. After all, at least in the context of raising children, this sounds like liberated parenting, right? And perhaps not a few Christian parents would insist that faith *does* enable us to believe that there really are *no limits* to what our children might become. While the thoughtful (and faith-filled) believer refuses to limit God and his work in the human experience, at the same time that thoughtful Christian and parent, if he or she is theologically grounded, is forced to respond, "*No*, dear child, you *can't* be anything you want to be, and it's a very good thing that you can't!"[17]

---

[16] Novak, *Business as a Calling*, 34–36.

[17] Worth reading is the provocative essay by William T. Cavanaugh, "Actually, You Can't Be Anything You Want (And It's a Good Thing, Too)," in *At This Time and in This Place: Vocation and Higher Education*, ed. David S. Cunningham (Oxford: Oxford University Press, 2016), 25–46.

Clearly, some readers will be put off by this assertion. Aren't we *limiting* our children (or our students, especially younger children) by not teaching them, *You can be anything you want to be!*? The claim that we cannot be anything we wish begs a question. What possible theological rationale might stand behind such an assertion?

The rationale, as it turns out, is anchored in an awareness of divine providence. Life, and everything in it, is *received* from the Creator, as chapter 5 and our examination of Ecclesiastes reminded us. The entire biblical witness is that God creates, God initiates, God calls, God acts in the world, and God redeems and transforms. For this reason, a logical and authentically Christian response to divine providence will maintain that indeed we *cannot* be *anything* we wish; such would be a flagrant violation of God's sovereign purposes as well as a prostituting of human freedom.

A qualification is in order here. Divine sovereignty properly understood does not mean the absence or negation of human moral agency and free will; such, most assuredly, is not what this volume wishes to argue. But it does require of human creatures that we acknowledge the source of all life, and therefore, that we order our lives accordingly. Everything in life is *received*, and this is the message of not only Ecclesiastes but the entire Judeo-Christian tradition. God equips us with specific giftings and abilities and plants within each of us unique burdens for the purpose of serving him and serving others. This ethical mindset negates any carte blanche approach to vocation. Desires are legitimate to the extent that they are guided by a desire to serve God, serve others, and contribute to the common good. But a common question with which many struggle is this: *How do I know which desires are legitimate and from God?* Our answer is this: it is those desires that are enduring and do not fade with the passage of time that are divinely instilled.[18] Nevertheless, more needs to be said about divine providence as it relates to the notion of vocation.

---

[18] These, of course, stand in contrast to selfish or corrupting desires that are often the result of misplaced priorities.

Providence implies purpose and meaning behind, as well as direction and guidance for, each believer's life journey. The concept of redemption, where grasped correctly, has the effect of personalizing that purpose and direction.[19] Previously in this volume I argued that it is a distortion to view the hand of providence as a rare phenomenon or intervention in normal affairs; it is, rather, a daily, hourly, and moment-by-moment presence of the Creator in human affairs. God is "ceaselessly active" both among human beings and within the person.[20] Because of this, it follows that both human affairs, at the cosmic level, and my individual life, at the personal level, work toward a greater design. God's design is both general (in a wider sense) and specific (to each of us). It also follows, therefore, that God "wishes us to experience, in full awareness, the joy of his service" and "to realize, in some measure at least, the part we are playing in his great design."[21]

Not only does a proper understanding of providence provide a sense of meaning in the mundane and in daily life, but it also frees us to step out in faith, to take risks—even make mistakes!—and use our glorious freedom in creative though responsible ways. A wrong view of providence and vocation, by contrast, is to think that there is one plan for your life that has been predetermined and mapped out in detail, which you must now discover or become a failure. This "discovery" process is often thought to resemble stumbling through a maze, with no markers, and

---

[19] Here we must distinguish between "purpose" as portrayed in best-selling examples of the "self-help" or pop-psychology genre—for example, Richard J. Leider, *The Power of Purpose* 3rd ed. (Oakland: Berrett-Koehler, 2015)—and "purpose" as defined by Christian theology and anchored in the doctrine of creation. Leider, to illustrate, defines purpose as "that deepest dimension within us," "our central core or essence," and the sense of "where we came from . . . and where we're going" (1). While in chapter 4 he acknowledges the importance of a generic "spiritual dimension," he remains generally pantheistic in speaking of "a deeper call." For him, the source of the spiritual realm and purpose, ultimately, lies within; it is not anchored in the transcendent.

[20] Harry Blamires, *The Will and the Way* (New York: Macmillan, 1957), 43, has stated this with utmost clarity.

[21] Blamires, 44.

with only "one way out." This "plan," moreover, is one I can "miss" if I take a "wrong turn." But that false stereotype needs collapsing. In fact, since most occupations or careers in our day are not guaranteed, irrevocable, or unchanging, it is possible that one might need to experiment or try out a job to know whether it's a good fit. Career paths, after all, are rarely straight; often they are marked by detours, unmarked intersections, and surprises. Not infrequently one may discover that a certain type of work or even a particular job is simply not the "right fit." That, however, does not render it a "wrong choice," since *we learn* from the experience (at least, if and where our intention is to learn). "Wrong choices" (or, "missing the boat") are, quite simply, a wrong way of viewing divine sovereignty; they are not a possibility where faith is operative and we trust the sovereign God to lead us and use all things in that process.

In fact, working a normal job—*any* job—for a season is often healthy, causing our desires, goals, and priorities to settle and take shape. I have frequently offered this advice over the years to students, including my one son who decided to step out of his undergraduate education midstream to gain clarity in terms of his own wider calling. Today that son would return and thank me for that advice, for that year away—which entailed him taking a job that had seemingly nothing to do with his overall life calling or his present occupation—ended up being invaluable, in his estimation.

Our trust is in a God who is sovereign; therein we find the place of rest. God guides us at every step of the way if we have committed ourselves to him. Hence, *we need not feel paralyzed* when we are agonizing over whether we have chosen "the right path" by changing careers or accepting a major move or taking a pay cut. After all, our nature is such that anxiety, regret, and guilt have a way of haunting us throughout (as well as after) the process of decision-making. A sense of calling can help prevent needless agonizing, allowing us to be at peace with our limitations and our lack of clarity, and assisting us in establishing our priorities.[22]

---

[22] Helpfully distinguishing between these two is John P. Neafsey, "Psychological Dimensions of the Discernment of Vocation," in *Revisiting the Idea of*

Providence and vocation are mutually dependent; they go hand in hand. Whereas providence, as I have argued, stresses the ceaseless operation of God in human affairs, vocation defines the mode of that operation in ways that are *person-specific*. As one writer has defined it, vocation is what providence asks of us.[23] Or, as another writer describes it, vocation sets (or resets) our obligations and duties within the larger ethical framework of God's purposes.[24] For this reason, we sense that God honors us by choosing us and using us. And it is why we pray that God will guide our steps and bless the work of our hands. This outlook, which assumes God's providential care and guidance at the personal level, helps us to avoid both pride and despair, both fatalism and the heresy of absolute autonomy.

Where does all this lead us? We do not choose our vocations; rather, they choose us. Just as none of us choose the families into which we are born or the children we are given, so we do not get to select but instead receive our vocations from God ("Providence"). Moreover, reception typically occurs in increments: we discover our vocations through a progressive and gradual process, which entails the various seasons of our lives. For this reason (and others), doing "the will of God," as we discover through Christian discipleship, is not a one-step matter that occurs through blind-light revelation.[25] Instead, it occurs in the context of our relationship to God. "The will of God," then, needs demystifying, for doing God's will—that is, cooperating with his purposes and walking in communion with him—is a moment-by-moment reality and progressive journey.[26] God's will, alas, is neither geographical nor circumstantial; it

---

Vocation: Theological Exploration, ed. John C. Haughey (Washington, DC: The Catholic University of America Press, 2012), 188.

[23] Blamires, *The Will and the Way*, 67.

[24] Schuurman, *Vocation*, xii.

[25] As will be argued in the following chapter, Gideon's fleece (Judges 6) as a method of guidance is not normative, nor is religious superstition or Christian "magic" a mode of genuine faith.

[26] Consider the journey depicted in John Bunyan's *Pilgrim's Progress*.

is relational, occurring in communion with the living God who leads us step-by-step, regardless of where we may find ourselves.

At the same time, as our reflections on the book of Ecclesiastes in chapter 5 suggested, "God's will" remains a mystery and is impenetrable, to the extent that God's ways and purposes are inscrutable. We simply cannot know *the entirety* of God's will for our lives—inasmuch as we walk by faith, knowing only "in part" (see 1 Cor 13:12). In truth, not even the heroes of the faith, as chronicled in the New Testament in Hebrews 11, knew God's complete will for their lives. All had to walk by faith, and, we are told, they were commended for their faith; yet they did not receive—in fullness—the promise (Heb 11:39). Thus, a demystifying of God's will, called for in the previous paragraph, exists alongside the fact that God's will and purposes remain inscrutable. No one can claim to know the mind of the Lord.

But in our attempts to adopt a proper understanding of vocation, let us step back again into Christian history, which is instructive here. In chapter 4 we noted the late-medieval context in which Luther's revolt occurred: his was a reaction against monasticism, which had endured for well over a millennium. The monastery, an expression of a two-tiered understanding of *vocatio*, had come to be viewed as a straighter or higher path to holiness than one could walk elsewhere. Undergirding this view, at least as Luther experienced it, was the wider assumption that grace is dispersed by the Church, not by God. According to such an outlook, works and work become good only when they are meritorious.

Undergirding Luther's revolt against this outlook was the discovery—or more accurately, the *re*discovery—of God's gracious and providential care, whereby the Christian believer recognizes God's provision and guidance in all of life. Most significantly, human beings are justified before God not by meritorious works but by God's own redeeming work. Hence, all have equal standing before God (see 1 Pet 2:5, 9). The ramifications of the priesthood of every believer, as Luther sought to emphasize in response to the false dichotomy of the sacred-versus-secular mindset, has far-reaching implications for everyday life. *Vocatio*, as Luther propounded the concept, has the effect of collapsing any distinction between the spiritual and temporal spheres, since *all* spheres of the created order require our participation and *all* Christians are "priests,"[27] thereby mediating God's good purposes and work through their own vocational callings. Accordingly, although we all have different offices and stations in life, there are no differences in terms of status; all manner of work is noble and sacred, possessing an intrinsic dignity. Vocation rightly understood issues out of our awareness of divine providence: God calls each of us to specific avenues of work that serve the needs of our neighbors. Human history has been richly served by the Protestant concept of vocation, and, as Gilbert Meilaender aptly reminds us, in order to love our neighbors we need not become Franciscans.[28]

Recall the ancient roots of the medieval mindset against which Luther was reacting. "Unemployment," if we may use the term, was the intended goal, in order that one might contemplate the deeper things of life. For Plato, the body was understood to enslave us, preventing us from seeing truth. For Aristotle, contemplation was viewed as the highest pursuit in life. Early Christian and medieval thinking, as already noted, shared this basic dualism between the physical/material and the mental/spiritual, as on display in monastic life. This mindset was perceived as a "call" to withdraw *from* the world.

Luther's revolt, then, can be appreciated at (at least) three vocational levels. (1) It dignified and ennobled work—*all* manner of work. (2) It democratized the idea of calling inasmuch as it affirmed that *all* people,

---

[27] Luther notes, "Those who are now called 'spiritual,' that is, priests, bishops, or popes[,] are neither different from other Christians nor superior to them, except that they are charged with the administration of the word of God and the sacraments, which is their work and office." *To the Christian Nobility of the German Nation*, in *Luther's Works*, ed. James Atkinson (Philadelphia: Fortress, 1966), 44:130.

[28] Gilbert Meilaender, "Friendship and Vocation," in *Leading Lives That Matter: What We Should Do and Who We Should Be*, ed. Mark R. Schwehn and Dorothy C. Bass (Grand Rapids: Eerdmans, 2006), 206.

not just clergy and monks, had a vocation. And (3) it aimed to liberate the Christian to serve the neighbor and the community—that is, all of society.[29] If we fast-forward from Luther's day to our own, we are confronted by the same secular-versus-sacred dichotomy; the cultural context, however, has changed the specific nature of this tension. Today we face a massive and thoroughgoing tendency toward secularization, by which the religious meaning of *vocatio* has been stripped. Standard use of "vocation" in contemporary society mirrors this evolution. The term is typically understood as a synonym for job, occupation, trade, job training, career, profession, or what one does for a living. Emptied of its inherently religious meaning, "vocation" becomes an expression of self-interest. Left to itself, it is concerned not only with one's skills and interests but, perhaps chiefly, with matters of pay and compensation, benefits, and leisure and status.

Concomitantly, attending the deterioration of moral values in the contemporary world is a widespread crisis of meaning. Where spiritual values have dissipated and are neglected, people must create their own meaning. This will typically be achieved by material and not social or spiritual means. At the same time, however, even in a deeply secularized society many people sense that "calling" entails something *more than* the mere material. In fact, one might even argue that despite secularization, the concept of calling has not completely disappeared; it has simply morphed into best-selling "self-help" books like those noted in chapter 3, of which Stephen Covey, Eckhart Tolle, Deepak Chopra, Oprah, and Joel Osteen are merely representative. Even where little to no public "instruction" or "pointers" exist and where little to no teaching and preaching or religious education in our churches address the subject, most vaguely religious people intuit—however imperfectly—that (1) something outside mere self-interest, (2) an inner sense of direction and purpose, and (3) a duty to contribute to the needs of others are part of life's obligation.

---

[29] On the effects of Luther's revolt as it concerns vocation, see Chris R. Armstrong, "Refocused Vocation," *Leadership Journal* (Winter 2013): 44–48.

Is it perhaps possible, then, that vocation could be a helpful antidote in "combatting secular disenchantment" in Western societies?[30]

A basic question raised by the present volume and directed to the confessional Christian reader is this: Do we (or can we) serve God in and through our individual work on an everyday basis, and is this a high and noble calling? That, of course, is to ask, is our work merely extrinsic and tangential to (or perhaps even separate from) our salvation and redemption by Christ, or is human labor—the Monday through Friday—a sanctifying and satisfying "working out" of that salvation and redemption and hence our "highest calling"?[31] How we answer that question is determined by how we understand the doctrine of vocation.

A Theology of Vocation

A theology of vocation, I have argued, is anchored in the cardinal doctrines of biblical theology. These include:

- the doctrine of creation (*ex nihilo* creation shows that God brings the new into existence and that he is the source of all that is good and purposeful);[32]

---

[30] Such is suggested by John Carroll, "Is the Vocation Paradigm under Threat?" *Journal of Sociology* 56, no. 3 (2020): 282–96.

[31] As a Protestant I can say that work, by divine design, sanctifies the human being—not in a *salvific* sense but in terms of developing human potential. Fittingly, in his 1981 papal encyclical *Laborem exercens* ("On Human Work"), John Paul II describes the "sanctifying" nature of work in this way: "Through work man *not only transforms nature*, adapting it to his own needs, but he also *achieves fulfillment* as a human being and indeed, in a sense, becomes 'more a human being'" (no. 9); See https://www.vatican.va/content/john-paul-ii/en/encyclicals/documents/hf_jp-ii_enc_14091981_laborem-exercens.html, accessed April 1, 2022. Emphasis in original.

[32] This guards us from accepting materialistic reductionism (metaphysical naturalism), a recurring temptation in human history.

- the *imago Dei* and human dignity (which inform the value and worth of human labor, thereby underscoring the fact of work as both co-creation and stewardship);
- the doctrine of redemption (which reasserts Christ's reign over the entire created order—over things material and nonmaterial—and which is inseparable from creation);[33] and
- the doctrine of incarnation (by which the church continually embodies the life of Christ in the world).[34]

In sum, humans are given "stewardly dominion" over the created order to develop human culture.[35] Our English word "culture," after all, derives from the Latin term *colere*, which signifies "grow," "tend the earth," "cultivate," and "nurture." For this reason, in fact, we refer to yeast prepared for bread-making as a culture.

These doctrinal foundations, where taken seriously, will inform—and cause us to redefine, as was argued in chapter 2—what we understand to constitute "mission(s)." The church's mission in and to the world, in the words of Lesslie Newbigin, is "a participation in the work of the triune

---

[33] Christ's resurrection reaffirms his lordship over creation, as Oliver O'Donovan, *Resurrection and Moral Order: An Outline for Evangelical Ethics* (Leicester, UK: Eerdmans, 1986), has argued.

[34] In his book *How Then Should We Work?: Rediscovering the Biblical Doctrine of Work* (Bloomington: Westbow, 2012), Hugh Welchel acknowledges the effects of a lack of teaching and understanding on vocation. Generations of well-meaning Christians have suffered from reducing the biblical "grand narrative" to a truncated version of fall and redemption, by which he means "fall-salvation-heaven"—a theological outlook that mirrors a lack of vision, pessimism toward cultural engagement, and a resultant escapist mindset. Albert M. Wolters, *Creation Regained: Biblical Basics for a Reformational Worldview*, 2nd ed. (Grand Rapids: Eerdmans, 2005), 91, helpfully summarizes a more accurate understanding of the grand narrative: "formation—deformation—reformation."

[35] "Stewardly dominion" is the phrase of Max Stackhouse, "Vocation," in *The Oxford Handbook of Theological Ethics*, ed. Gilbert Meilaender and William Werpehowski (Oxford: Oxford University Press, 2005), 189.

God."[36] While in the late 1800s and early 1900s "missions" was reduced to refer to "foreign" (i.e., cross-cultural) evangelism, developments over the last several generations have demonstrated that "missions" is not merely attempting to evangelize our coworkers, our neighbors, our cities, or other people groups with the good news about Jesus.[37] Rather, "missions" is (or should be) an obedience to God's purposes in all of creation as expressed through our individual and various vocations. The Monday–Friday indeed *is* "the Lord's work." Why? Because the idea demonstrates "Christ's cosmic lordship" over all realms of the created order.[38] In the past, in our thinking about missions, we have seldom included the arts, the sciences, technology, and the varied dimensions of secular life; thereby, we have denied "the splendor of [much of] God's work in creation."[39] As Newbigin observes, we have viewed "men in politics or social service or research as having a *less central part in God's purposes* than the man who gives full-time service to the church."[40] But mission, properly understood, concerns the rule of God over everything that exists.[41] Vocation, for the Christian, includes all aspects of cultural and social life; it is comprehensive.[42] If we fail in this understanding, we will fail—I believe—in the Christian's primary task. After all, the laity now represents the frontline of the church's efforts at cultural engagement. The real frontier work is in the marketplace.

---

[36] Lesslie Newbigin, *Trinitarian Doctrine for Today's Mission.* repr. (Carlisle, UK: Paternoster, 1998), 54.

[37] My argument is not to dismiss evangelism; it is only to widen our understanding of God's purposes in the created order.

[38] Newbigin, *Trinitarian Doctrine,* 62, 203.

[39] Newbigin, 27.

[40] Newbigin, 27, emphasis added.

[41] Even the introductory remark by the editor of a recent volume on work and mission—"God calls us both to work and mission"—suggests a false, unnecessary distinction between the two terms. See Steve Lim, ed., *Your Call to Work & Mission* (Springfield: Assemblies of God Theological Seminary, 2015), 4.

[42] Schuurman, *Vocation,* 51, rightly captures this recognition of mission.

Historically, Christian teaching has emphasized two types of vocation: a general calling and a more specific, personal calling.[43] By the former it is understood that we are called to God in Christ, that we believe through faith and commit our lives to him, and that through his justifying work we therefore belong to his kingdom. Hence the significance of the church as the *ekklēsia*, the "called out" ones who have been called out for a unique purpose. As refracted through the New Testament, this calling to Christ is a calling to "eternal life" (1 Tim 6:12); to an "eternal inheritance" (Heb 9:15); to justification (Rom 8:30); into "fellowship with . . . Jesus Christ our Lord" (1 Cor 1:9); to "the peace of Christ" (Col 3:15); into God's "kingdom and glory" (1 Thess 2:12); to "eternal glory" (1 Pet 5:10); "out of darkness and into his marvelous light" (1 Pet 2:9); to holiness (1 Thess 4:7); to freedom (Gal 5:13); and to peace (1 Cor 7:15). By the latter, a more specific calling, it is understood that we are summoned to specific, concrete stations,[44] tasks, and avenues of service during various seasons of life as we steward the created world and meet human need through our God-given abilities and talents. Calling, in this second sense, which assumes that the general call of God to Christ will take a specific form and shape in each Christian's life, may be defined as "the historical and circumstantial particularizing of God's purposes in the

---

[43] Some would add a third: the calling to daily obligations. I take the position that this third element is implicit in both our general calling to Christ and our specific personal callings.

[44] I understand "stations" as referring to our context, circumstances, our jobs, and our relationships—not to social privilege or status. In discussing vocation, I prefer to speak of various "seasons" of life rather than "stations" (as Luther does). One reason is the simple fact of changes and differences that separate society in Luther's day from ours. Another is that "seasons" and "stations" change, whereas vocation does not. Relatedly, some would hold the position that we have multiple vocations throughout life, or at any one time. I prefer to view vocation as overarching and lifelong, not ceasing or changing even when employment, occupations, and seasons do change. So, for example, the vocation of marriage ceases if and when someone's spouse dies. Vocation, then, is abiding, anchoring us when seasons change.

life of an individual."[45] Calling or vocation, hence, represents the specific *form* of one's service to God and to others, by extension. It might also be described as a "dialogue," by which God initiates and one responds.[46] Properly viewed, vocation is neither a goal nor a dream that I pursue but something that I sense, a divine call to which I respond.

Not merely the fact that we belong to Christ in general terms but his commissioning every individual with specific tasks, obligations, and burdens in particular spheres of life and places of service is what gives meaning, purpose, and direction to the Christian believer.[47] And where this awareness is present in believers' lives, whereby we understand that we are both stewards of our talents and donors of our labors, we are able to endure even seasons of being unemployed, for unemployment does not mean that we are without a vocation. Vocation, then, is properly understood as a *way of life* and not merely a job, occupation, or even a "career."[48] Vocation encompasses the *totality* of our lives, not merely our careers, occupations, present jobs, or so-called retirement—even when vocation encompasses all of those, yet more. And because of the overarching nature of our calling to follow Christ, it makes senses that this specific calling is expressed through our careers, our occupations, our jobs, and our various endeavors. One thoughtful writer expresses it this way: the general call

---

[45] See Gary L. Chamberlain, "The Evolution of Business as a Christian Calling," in *Finding Meaning in Business: Theology, Ethics, and Vocation*, ed. Bartholomew C. Okonkwo (New York: Palgrave Macmillan, 2012), 33–56.

[46] See Mark A. McIntosh, "Trying to Follow a Call: Vocation and Discernment in Bunyan's *Pilgrim's Progress*," in *Revisiting the Idea of Vocation: Theological Explorations*, ed. John C. Haughey (Washington, DC: The Catholic University of America Press, 2012), 120.

[47] Novak, in *Business as a Calling*, 34–36, lists three basic elements that are normally required in identifying one's calling: (1) God-given talents or abilities; (2) both a desire and a satisfaction in performing the task; and (3) a patient discernment, given inevitable detours, roadblocks, or disappointments.

[48] As one writer puts it, we are "care-takers"—i.e., stewards of the world around us—rather than "career-seekers." See Quentin J. Schultze, *Here I Am: Now What on Earth Should I Be Doing?* (Grand Rapids: Baker Books, 2005), 9.

of God to Christ will take specific shape in each Christian's life, just as a prism refracts light into an endless variety of colors.[49]

Every believer, then, has a particular calling—a vocation—even when he or she may not have a clear sense of it, or even a clearly defined career or occupation. This means that even should my work, my job, or my career come to an end, my calling (my *vocatio*), which is all-encompassing and broader, does not.[50] Moreover, there may be different seasons within my calling—seasons that might even seem to involve unrelated jobs, responsibilities, or duties. And along the way, I might encounter detours, changes, and transitions. The sheer mystery of walking by faith requires that we employ basic discernment, which will stabilize us in an awareness of our wider calling and in God's providential care. In this light it is helpful to keep in mind John Bunyan's *Pilgrim's Progress*, for the Christian pilgrim dramatizes the believer's journey as he deals with ambiguity, encounters doubt and dead-ends, unmasks deception, and learns the value of discernment. Pilgrim was initially called to his journey by Providence, and Providence sustains him along the way.[51] Moreover, because calling operates based on our response, through *affection* rather than *coercion*, it follows that we can deny, resist, or negate our calling.[52] This, of course, can occur by several means—for example, through insensitivity, indifference, or disobedience.

Vocational questions, it needs emphasizing, follow us through various stages of life—not just when we head off to college or enter the workforce after graduation. They confront us in middle adulthood and later adulthood as well. In any case, the Christian wrestles with—and keeps

---

[49] Schuurman, *Vocation*, 47.

[50] The word "career" comes from the same root as our word *car*, indicating travel. The Latin *carrus* signified "chariot" or "carrier," suggesting a short, though fast, gallop, as in a racecourse.

[51] See the thoughtful essay by McIntosh, "Trying to Follow a Call," 119–40, which charts the Christian pilgrim's journey in terms of having to learn discernment.

[52] So Elton Trueblood, *Your Other Vocation* (New York: Harper, 1952), 65.

in tension—two basic vocational questions: *How is God calling me to serve him at this time, in this present season of life?* and *What is my wider calling in life, for which I have been made a steward of particular gifts, abilities, capacities, and burdens?* Having a sense of the latter—an awareness of my wider vocational calling in life—will give at least a modicum of personal peace in each particular season in which I find myself (even should I lack a clear sense of how to live out that purpose in a particular moment).[53]

Permit me to illustrate with some further self-disclosure. Two seasons of my own life, having seemingly *nothing* to do with each other, help anchor the awareness of personal calling in my own life not only to teach and to write but, specifically, to relate Christian faith to public policy and address issues of justice. During one season (in the 1980s) I was living for several years in former West Germany, the result of having married a German citizen. My German father-in-law, as it happened, had spent all five years of the Second World War serving with the German military, the *Bundeswehr*, in Poland. Not only that, he had spent all five years of the war working as a railroad-car switcher—again, in Poland. Think of the notorious death camps in that country—for example, Auschwitz-Birkenau, Sobibor, Warsaw, or Treblinka. One does not need much imagination to wonder what Papa witnessed. Hence, having married into German culture I am wed to more recent German history, a responsibility which I do not take lightly.

The second season of life that was formative and confirming of my own calling in terms of faith and policy and issues of justice was the early-to-mid 1990s, during which time I was doing criminal justice research in Washington, DC. There I saw again and again not only the necessity of theological conviction but also the need to be able to translate those

---

[53] While I have no inherent bias against the use of "personality tests" that measure or assess our strengths and weaknesses or our personal inclinations, I would maintain that having a sense of how God is calling us to serve him in a particular season of my life cannot be solved by such a tool. Such is foremost a matter of discernment, and discernment must grow within us.

convictions, both philosophically and practically, in compelling ways in the public arena. Our wider vocational calling, then, unites various seasons of our lives, even when we have difficulty making sense of them at the time or connecting the dots.

Perhaps at this point you are thinking, *Daryl, all well and good, and very interesting, but what do we mean in practical terms by vocation? What does it mean to think vocationally?* Perhaps we can answer in the form of several qualifying definitions of the concept of vocation. Properly (and biblically) understood, vocation can be measured in the following ways.

1. Vocation lies at the *very heart* of an integrated, holistic faith.
2. Vocation entails the basic awareness that, based on the image of God within us, we are created for work, which can be a form of worship.
3. Vocation entails the awareness that we do not choose our callings; rather, they choose us—or rather, God chooses them. Just as none of us get to select our own DNA coding, our birthdates, or our children, our vocations are ultimately up to him. In fact, it is more accurate to say that we discover rather than receive our vocations, and that discovery tends to come through a gradual process.
4. Vocation entails a willingness to serve others and thereby serve the common good. What is the Great Commandment as identified in the Old Testament and reiterated by Jesus in the New? Love God and love thy neighbor.[54] *That* is the heart of the specific calling given to every believer. Vocation is intrinsically related to the common good and the needs of others.
5. Relatedly, vocation entails the meeting of genuine human need. While none of us can meet every need, we each are equipped in such a way as to be able—through our giftings, energy, and influence—to meet *some* need(s) in a strategic and practical sense.

---

[54] Lev 19:18; Matt 22:36–40; Mark 12:28–34; and Luke 10:25–28.

6. Vocation also entails our recognition of skills, talents, and abilities that have been given to us by God and of which we are stewards; moreover, it presumes an intentional and guided development of those skills and talents.
7. Vocation entails the recognition that we were placed in the world strategically, within a particular sociocultural context. Culture, therefore, is to be taken seriously.
8. Vocation entails social commitment; it cannot be actualized apart from community. Service to God will translate into service to others and building the common good, whether that involves the Christian community or the wider communities in which we live. A secularizing of the concept of vocation has the effect of removing the core communal element and placing the focus on the individual. No vocation is fulfilled in a vacuum.[55] We are social beings, created for community.[56]
9. And finally, vocation entails the recognition of work's intrinsic worth, dignity, and value; therefore, work is its own reward in terms of a certain level of satisfaction. Work must not be our identity, and the rhythm of work followed by rest is the divine rhythm that human creatures are to follow.[57] Nevertheless, properly viewed, work offers a distinct measure of joy and satisfaction.

---

[55] See Gordon T. Smith, *Courage and Calling: Embracing Your God-Given Potential*, rev. ed. (Downers Grove, IL: InterVarsity, 2011), 256.

[56] In Bunyan's *Pilgrim's Progress*, community, Pilgrim comes to realize, is very important. Figures such as Hopeful, Charity, Prudence, Piety, Watchful, and Discretion remind the reader of the importance of virtues, which are inculcated in and through community. In Pilgrim's journey, if you travel alone, you die or become utterly confused and lost; self-deception and self-indulgence are ruinous.

[57] Readers of this volume might legitimately complain that I have not given sufficient attention to the common problem of people being "workaholics." Nevertheless, I am assuming the fundamental difference between hard work and the vice of "workaholism"; the latter is idolatry.

Notice that all of these insights into vocation/calling have their foundation in theological truth. I refer specifically, once more, to the doctrines of creation, providence, redemption, and incarnation, all of which are interlocking and inform one another. A few related comments bearing upon the doctrine of vocation are in order.

In creation we see God calling into existence what he had purposed before the foundations of the created order appeared. And the centerpiece of creation is the human person, in whom is found the *imago Dei*, the very likeness of God. Moreover, based on this likeness, humans are co-regents of creation; their role is to co-create, mold and shape, and extend the created order as vice-regents, if you will, and as stewards.

Divine providence, as argued thus far, implies meaning and purpose, and it also implies redemption and restoration. It is a distortion to view the hand of providence as some rare intervention; rather, it is a moment-by-moment, hour-by-hour, day-by-day presence and guiding of human affairs. Providence is ceaselessly, not occasionally, operative in the affairs of people and nations. This in itself renders daily life—the mundane—meaningful. It follows, then, that human affairs and one's individual life work together toward a greater, broader design. We must train ourselves to think in those terms.

At the same time, it is important to remember that this doctrine implies neither some form of fatalism nor a sort of determinism to which we all must submit. Rather, it suggests purposefulness, which offers hope rather than resignation. Recall, again, the literary strategy and purpose of the book of Ecclesiastes. Resignation—that is, "Everything is meaningless!"—is being contrasted with satisfaction that is anchored in the fear of God and divine providence. Correlatively, providence does not cancel out the marvelous realm of human freedom and moral agency. Judas's treachery, we do well to remember, did not negate Jesus's work and redemption. Mysteriously, even it was used by God toward his redemptive purpose (see Matt 26:24). This should produce within us not only wonder but hope.

Relatedly, we must also insist that redemption is part of God's character, not an exception to it or some novel or wildly abstruse intervention that God has concocted. Undergirding much of the argument presented in this volume is the conviction that redemption is to be understood not as a replacement but as a restoring of creation, the distinction between these two being theologically critical. And incarnation, which is part of the redemptive process, is part of God's character as well; it is his very nature, as the prologue to the Fourth Gospel makes clear: "In the beginning . . . the Word was with God . . . [and] the Word became flesh and dwelt among us" (John 1:1, 14). God creates, God communicates, God restores, God sustains, God guides. What's more, this creative redemptive program applies to "all things"—things material and nonmaterial, things visible and invisible.[58] Christian vocation at the macro level, therefore, includes all aspects of the created order and all aspects of human cultural and social life; at the micro level it takes shape, in unique and wonderful ways and within myriad contexts specific to individuals, through the offering of one's talents and gifts—indeed, of his or her everything—to the Lord of creation.

Creation, providence, redemption, incarnation, *and* vocation, then, go hand in hand. They are mutually dependent on one another. Together they furnish our theological baseline for all of life—that is, for our *vocation*. In this regard, an important distinction needs emphasizing: vocation begins with creation, not Christology. The failure to make this distinction is surely one reason why the church, past or present, has had a deficient view of vocation. Vocation develops and transforms the created order through our service to others.[59]

The benefits of thinking vocationally, it should be emphasized, are many; and they are both profound and quite practical. Thinking

---

[58] Col 1:15–20.

[59] Tragically, one searches in vain, among both Protestants and Catholics, to find teaching that affirms this basic truth.

vocationally, first and fundamentally, collapses and dispels the insidious dualism that has plagued the church since time immemorial, namely, the divide between the "sacred" and the "secular." We have harped on this false dichotomy in virtually every chapter, at the risk of being redundant.

In practical terms, thinking vocationally will prevent us from a sort of chaotic, out-of-control, meaningless, day-to-day lifestyle that can plague us when we have no sense of direction. That mode of living, of course, takes its toll on us spiritually, mentally, and psychologically. For some of us, it can even lead to despair. For this reason, John Calvin describes the importance of having a sense of vocation in our lives: "Each individual has his own kind of living assigned to him by the Lord as a sort of sentry post so that he may not heedlessly wander about throughout life."[60]

Relatedly, thinking vocationally liberates us from what is often called the tyranny of the urgent. This expression was coined by writer Charles Hummel in the late 1960s to depict the frustration that mounts from jumbled priorities, unfinished business, and lack of time.[61] In addition, it keeps us from a false sense of duty and conformity to the world with its standards, while also freeing us from the enslavement of comparing ourselves with others and becoming people pleasers. Living in the reverential fear of God, as Ecclesiastes reminds us, rather than in fear of what others think, is utterly liberating, causing us to be at peace with ourselves and giving us boldness and confidence.[62]

---

[60] John Calvin, *Institutes of the Christian Religion*, ed. John T. McNeill, trans. Ford Lewis Battles (Louisville: WJK, 2006), III.10.6.

[61] See Charles E. Hummel, *Tyranny of the Urgent*, rev. ed. (Downers Grove, IL: InterVarsity, 1994).

[62] Few have expressed the benefits of having a vocational mindset more helpfully than Smith, *Courage and Calling*, 128–47.

Further Reflections on the Implications of Vocation

"Most of us are looking for a calling, not a job."[63] This well-worn insight, however trite and intuited by many, needs repeating, particularly in the present age. The ramifications of the doctrine of vocation, regardless of how utterly foreign to the church's standard teaching and preaching this doctrine may be, are significant and far-reaching.

At the most basic level, the doctrine of vocation is inherently "this-worldly."[64] It collapses any supposed dichotomy between the spiritual and the temporal, between a sacred-versus-secular understanding of human labor, while elevating, sanctifying, and ennobling almost every line of work. This was perhaps the foremost application of Luther's understanding of justification, and hence, the priesthood of every believer. Because of the doctrine of creation and because all things have been redeemed through God in Christ, every endeavor, every labor, every task has meaning and purpose when done to honor God and serve the neighbor. The "great misnomer" going by the name of "full-time Christian service" raises a false division between clergy and laity and is unscriptural.[65] For this reason it was forcefully opposed and rejected by Luther. And yet, the sad fact is that this false dualism continually resurfaces—among Catholics and Protestants, it is a perennial problem.

It does need acknowledging, however, that in the mid-twentieth century Catholic social teaching began to shift in important ways. The initial

---

[63] While not original to the authors, this maxim can be found, for example, in Kevin and Kay Marie Brennfleck, *Live Your Calling: A Practical Guide to Finding and Fulfilling Your Mission in Life* (San Francisco: Jossey-Bass, 2005), 3.

[64] See Donald R. Heiges, *The Christian's Calling* (Philadelphia: Fortress, 1984), 38.

[65] Edward Deratany, *When God Calls You* (Nashville: Thomas Nelson, 1976), 30, uses the language of "great misnomer" in referring to "full-time Christian service" and the unnecessary cleft between clergy and laity. Luther's position, in fairness, was not that some (i.e., priests) should not be preaching the Word and administering the sacraments. However, he realized that very few are called to this role in terms of full-time service to the church.

impetus came from Pope John XXIII, whose 1961 encyclical *Mater et Magistra* expanded the idea of vocation beyond the priesthood—a move that would have been unthinkable previously. Thereafter, Pope John Paul II contributed to this noteworthy development. His 1981 encyclical *Laborem exercens* examined the ethical meaning of work, observing work to be a fundamental dimension of our earthly existence and considering its role in one's fulfillment. His 1991 encyclical, *Centesimus annus*, extended John Paul's own thinking of ten years prior: work possesses a social dimension that contributes to the common good. In John Paul's writings, readers witness a grasp of vocation that is moving toward a more Protestant understanding. In fact, consistent with Reformed Protestant thinking, vocation for John Paul entails participation, co-creation, and partnership with God in all facets of life in God's world. And mirroring John Paul's notable influence, the *Catechism of the Catholic Church* speaks of the "vocation of lay people" (nos. 898–900), even to the acknowledgment of lay believers as "the front line" of the church's life.[66]

In any event, the effects of a professionalizing of clergy, regardless of context, are detrimental, impairing the body of Christ insofar as all are "priests" (see 1 Pet 2:5, 9).

A second implication of vocational calling is that it gives the Christian believer a sense of identity. Within this volume I have presented the tendency of therapeutic society to reinforce self-interest and promote an excessive individualism in our understanding of work and career.[67] And indeed, one legitimate criticism that might be leveled against some of the existing literature on vocation is its highly individualistic nature, with its emphasis on personal significance and discovering one's passion

---

[66] *Catechism of the Catholic Church* no. 899, accessed April 4, 2022, http://www.scborromeo.org/ccc/para/899.htm.

[67] I do not wish to place Christian faith and psychology in opposition; after all, two of my three children are professional therapists. What I do wish to stress, however, is that any psychological method, if it is to truly help, will presume that every person is designed in the image of God. A proper anthropology as a starting point is crucial if we truly wish to help in redemptive ways.

that also tends to downplay service to others. The claim that we find personal significance in our work or in our vocation, therefore, needs severe qualification.

If we understand vocation or calling properly, our starting point must be the One who calls, not self-interest, self-actualization, and excessive individualism. After all, most types of meaningful work are those that have as their goal a serving of others; typically, these avenues of work are not glamorous or sexy but entail the meeting of genuine human need, which will require the virtues of discipline, patience, endurance, and forbearance. If we wrongly perceive "significance," we will not find meaning and satisfaction in the ordinary, in the nine to five, in the Monday-through-Friday. That said, it needs reiterating that we *can* expect joy and satisfaction to attend our callings, even when we do not make personal significance our primary focus. Such is the Teacher's response to "all is meaningless" in Ecclesiastes. And in truth, as human creatures we have a built-in psychological need for "calling," based on our design.[68] One writer has helpfully summarized the essence of calling: we grasp a sense of vocational calling in our lives "when the heart of faith joins opportunities and gifts with the needs of others."[69]

Alas, personal identity, as unveiled through the lens of Christian faith, is not understood in the sense of much modern psychology and the therapeutic model. Calling contributes to one's self-fulfillment—or more accurately, *fulfillment*—only in the sense of an uncovering of one's personal *destiny*, a purpose *larger* than self.[70] Personal identity, then, proceeds out of our understanding of—and relationship to—the Creator, in whom and from whom we comprehend human design. In response to the concern of workaholism, or work as idolatry, we may insist that vocation

---

[68] A healthy approach to understanding personal significance can be found in David W. Loy, "Luther, Vocation, and the Search for Significance," *Lutheran Quarterly* 35 (2021): 50–72.

[69] Schuurman, *Vocation*, 4. See also Robert Benne, "Vocations?" *Lutheran Quarterly* 35 (2021): 73–79.

[70] Novak, *Business as a Calling*, 18, grasps this important qualification.

and our calling in Christ determine a person's identity, *not* what we do or achieve. Worth and identity come from the Creator and our having been fashioned in his image. Vocation should not be defined in terms of satisfaction; at the same time, satisfaction and fulfillment issue out of—and confirm—our vocation and thus can be viewed as by-products.

Correlatively, our identities, if anchored in a theistic understanding of reality, aim at *service*. "Love God and love [that is, serve] others" is the Great Commandment.[71] As I have already suggested, much literature on calling or vocation tends to be more *self*-oriented than *theo*- and others-oriented.[72] Any teaching on vocation that emphasizes—or overemphasizes—the benefits to self and minimizes (or ignores) the central component of service to others is counter to the Christian moral tradition. In addition, it will likely gloss over, if it does not wholly avoid, the fact of hardship and suffering which attend the normal Christian life.

A third ramification of this important doctrine is that every believer has been equipped with gifts and enablements for his or her specific calling in the marketplace. The apostle Paul writes to the Corinthians that each person has been assigned a place in life to which God has specifically called him or her (see 1 Cor 7:17–24; cf. 12:4–6). The Lutheran notion of having a "station" of life (and for Calvin, a "sentry post") *assigned*—i.e., a particular calling in terms of *context* for work and service—points to the

---

[71] Matt 22:37–39; Mark 12:30–31; and Luke 10:27.

[72] See, for example, Shoshana R. Dobrow and Jennifer Tosti-Kharas, "Calling: The Development of a Scale Measure," *Personnel Psychology* 64 (2011): 1005, who define "calling" as "a consuming, meaningful passion [that] people experience toward a domain" and "a primarily psychological construct." Even works such as Bryan J. Dik and Ryan D. Duffy's *Make Your Job a Calling: How the Psychology of Vocation Can Change Your Life at Work* (West Conshohocken: Templeton Press, 2012) assiduously avoid religious language and categories. At most, Dik and Duffy refer to a "transcendent summons" to describe "calling," and in chapter 4 ("Making Meaning"), the closest to "transcendence" that the authors find themselves, they focus on non-religious elements such as "finding work that matters" and work that is "meaningful," "using one's strengths," finding a "good fit," and being able to "adapt to change."

doctrine of Divine providence, as I have argued.[73] And to the Christians living in the imperial seat of Rome, Paul writes that *all* have different gifts, according to the measure of grace given to *all* (Rom 12:3–8). Furthermore, Peter tells us that we should steward the gifts that God has given us, inasmuch as we are simply passing on, through "a variety of forms," God's grace (1 Pet 4:10).[74]

Here we might pause for a moment and reflect. What is the question that virtually every college student dreads? Whether coming from family or friends, it is likely the question "What are your plans after graduation?" I shall never forget one such conversation I had with a former student of mine. This precious young woman whom I had had in my theology class during her senior year knocked on my office door two weeks before graduation. Sheepishly she asked if she might discuss a matter that had been vexing her. Once inside the office she poured out her heart, weeping and confessing that she absolutely *dreaded* heading back home in two weeks following commencement exercises. Why? Because she could not answer the two big questions that her parents—confessing Christians—would be asking of her upon graduation: "What do you expect to be doing now that you've graduated?" and (oh, by the way) "Have you met anyone special [after four years at a Christian institution]?"

---

[73] My argument is not that early-modern society as the Protestant Reformers experienced it is comparable to twenty-first century society; only that the matter of vocational calling, service to others, and—most importantly—the awareness of divine providence are perennial questions that are specific to each believer, regardless of cultural context.

[74] While it is true that "calling" in the New Testament does not address occupation, profession, education, or specific avenues of work—after all, such questions were rarely part of the ancient world—the fact of God's gifting individuals with unique abilities and talents for service rendered to others is thoroughly underscored in the New Testament. What is true of the body of Christ—i.e., individuals have been variously (and uniquely) equipped for service—applies equally to wider society and the marketplace.

While the dread in her case was twofold, I shall not address here the second question (even when I am the parent of three children who have passed through the same portal!). But why the dread regarding her first burden—a dread that by no means is to be found solely among college graduates set to enter the job market? In fact, I have found personally that not just students on the eve of gradation but older Christians as well, even retirement-age folks, struggle with the same concern (even when they do not vocalize it), namely, identifying their vocational calling—a calling that includes work, occupation, or employment but which also transcends it. What petrified this student was the lack of any sense of vocation or calling. But this absence is nothing new. "Vocation," alas, has disappeared from our Christian vocabulary; she is no more.

Going hand in hand with our gifts and the way God has uniquely equipped each believer is the matter of service to others and the meeting of human need. A further ramification of vocation is that, properly conceived, it is aimed at meeting authentic needs in my neighbor and not merely my own sense of fulfillment; vocations given by God contribute to the common good.

Here a cautionary word concerning the needs of others is in order. That we should factor surrounding human need into our vocational decision-making goes without saying. But the more important matter is how to judge those needs around us in order to figure out the role they should play in our individual callings. If people simply try to choose their calling by how many needs surround them, or how severe the needs happen to be, they are likely to become overwhelmed, confused, and frustrated. How, then, can we discern others' "needs" correctly and our unique roles in meeting them?

A simple, though general, rule of thumb might be this: The surrounding need does not determine the call, even when it may contribute to that call in some way. The truth is that we all are generally unsuited to meet most needs around us, which should not be interpreted as an excuse for indifference or cold-heartedness. Therefore, we each must be discerning and will have to say no when confronted with some needs around us. If, by way of illustration, you pass fifteen homeless people in the downtown sector of your city, you probably are not "called" to help them all; in fact, you will be unable to help them. Jesus's own example might be instructive: the needs all around him—endless needs—did not determine his mission or his strategy in the three years of his "messianic" service, yet he completed his mission, his *vocation*, while attending to needs along the way.[75]

Finally, because much of the literature concerning vocation, as was noted earlier, tends to highlight self-interest and self-fulfillment while downplaying service to others, another element associated with a proper understanding of vocation requires some comment. I refer here to the element of hardship and suffering, which is basic to a proper understanding of Christian discipleship. The Christian's general call to follow Jesus will entail taking up one's cross, whatever that may mean and however that may translate in an individual's life. Suffering, then, no matter one's vocation, is part of each Christian's calling (see 2 Cor 1:5; Phil 1:29; 2 Thess 1:5; 1 Pet 2:21; 3:14, 17; 4:13, 19; and 5:10).

The topic of suffering, of course, which is virtually absent from our Western pulpits, engenders very different types of discourse and responses, depending on context. In general terms, the North American—and, yes, very human—way of responding to hardship and suffering is to assume (and cry) that we are victims, innocent and undeserving of whatever difficulties have befallen us. We thus are inclined to live with self-pity, anger or resentment, and a sense of entitlement. At the academic and theological level, the focus of much study and discourse is the meaning of suffering and the question of theodicy. How are we to reconcile human pain, suffering, and evil with a just and loving God? At the more clinical and pastoral level, the focus is far less abstract; it is existential and a question of survival.

---

[75] Here I am particularly appreciative of—and indebted to—Smith's helpful discussion of "need" and "calling" in *Courage and Calling*, 75–77.

I noted earlier that two of my children are professional therapists. Daily they are witnesses to people for whom pain, hardship, and suffering are simply a matter of survival. How do they respond to them? As professionals, they are first obligated to listen, to empathize with those sharing their stories, and to understand as best they can. After listening, part of their responsibility is to discern what level of suffering within the client might be the result of sinful, misguided, or otherwise unhealthy choices they have made. At the same time, as every Christian at least intuits, they remain aware that not all suffering occurs because of personal sin; not all suffering is the fruit of my wrong choices. And here is where things get tricky, and the role of the pastor, the counselor, or the therapist at this point is crucial, even when it defies any set pattern in terms of charting a response.[76] Job, after all, was assessed by his three "friends" in light of their "theology of retribution." They therefore concluded that Job surely must have sinned, for no righteous person would be (or should be) suffering as he. And, in the end, to the reader's great dismay, Job never does learn the *why* of his tribulation, even after his three friends had to repent and offer atonement for their callousness. Suffering, alas, remains impenetrable. God's ways, as Ecclesiastes teaches, are inscrutable. Hardship and suffering remain incomprehensible, hence the need to read the psalms of lament.

Few have treated this important—though difficult—topic with the sensitivity and insight that John Paul II did while serving as supreme pontiff of the Catholic Church. In his 1984 apostolic letter *Salvifici Doloris*,[77] John Paul argued, quite eloquently though with pastoral sensitivity, that in Christian discipleship there is the reality, to which every Christian believer is called, of redemptive suffering. By describing the

---

[76] And, of course, any confession of Christian faith in the client will affect the counselor's response in terms of strategy.

[77] "Salvifici doloris" translates literally to "redemptive suffering." See John Paul, *Salvifici Doloris*, accessed April 4, 2022, https://www.vatican.va/content/john-paul-ii/en/apost_letters/1984/documents/hf_jp-ii_apl_11021984_salvifici-doloris.html.

category of hardship as "redemptive," he intended to argue that through our suffering we (1) draw near to Christ, who suffered on our behalf, and (2) draw near to fellow human beings, whose suffering needs our attention, out of which Christ's love is then manifest on their behalf. Redemptive suffering, according to John Paul, represents a powerful witness to the world—one that authenticates the gospel.

My argument here is not that certain vocations promise more or less suffering or hardship than others. Nor am I intending to develop a "theology of suffering." I only wish to emphasize that being faithful to God's specific calls in our lives will entail disappointment, detours, seasons of doubt or confusion, seemingly unanswered prayer, hardship, and—yes—suffering, a suffering that is promised to all who enter the kingdom and who wish to follow Christ. Consider the example of John Bunyan (1628–1688), who was thrown in jail—and remained there for twelve years—simply because he was a Baptist dissenter at the time. It was during the years of imprisonment that Bunyan wrote *Pilgrim's Progress*. And as it would turn out, aside from the Bible, *Pilgrim's Progress* became the most widely read book in America up to the Civil War.[78]

When we contemplate the role of suffering and hardship in the context of vocation and Christian discipleship, we do well to recall the wisdom perspective on display in Ecclesiastes: to everything there is a time and a season (3:1–8). Wisdom acknowledges this reality, even when human beings cannot penetrate the mystery of divine providence. There will be closed doors, disappointments, ambiguities, and different seasons; there will be no straight line or guarantees along the way—but all of this is based on God's providence and inscrutability. This is not to argue, however, that there will be no clarity regarding one's calling; only that discernment along the way will be needed.

---

[78] According to *Christianity Today's* website, 100,000 copies of the book were already in print by 1692, four years after Bunyan's death. See https://www.christianitytoday.com/history/people/musiciansartistsandwriters/john-bunyan.html, accessed April 4, 2022.

While Christian bookstores tend to be filled with best sellers like *How to Know God's Will*, *How to Hear God's Voice*, *How to Be the Real You*, and *How to Prosper and Succeed*, there remains a desperate need to demystify certain aspects of calling on the one hand while developing the qualities of wisdom and discernment on the other. This leads us to the knotty problem of guidance, to which we shall now turn.[79]

---

[79] A version of the discussion in this chapter has appeared in J. Daryl Charles, *Wisdom and Work: Theological Reflections on Human Labor from Ecclesiastes* (Eugene, OR: Cascade Books, 2021), 99–129. This material is used with permission of Wipf and Stock Publishers, www.wipfandstock.com.

CHAPTER
7

The Matter of Guidance

How does God speak? How does he call? Is it a lack of faith if I don't hear an audible voice? Can I miss my call? What if I've already made a wrong choice? Could I be stuck in the wrong occupation? How do I reconcile my present job and my true desires? What do I do if the present job or season of life seems like a detour? How do I know if my desires are from God? To hear from God, should I be laying out fleeces? How do I recognize a call, anyway? Should I take any open door? And what about closed doors?

These and related questions plague believers of every age group—not only those graduating into the workforce but those at mid-career and even those approaching or entering "retirement" age. A great deal of confusion exists as to how each believer comes to discern his or her personal calling. Sadly, little or no teaching and preaching and education proceeds from the church to address such matters. As an educator, I can confirm that worry or doubt about guidance is palpable among students and young adults. But older Christians struggle in this domain as well, even when their questions are rarely vocalized.

Personal anxiety over the matter of guidance is not confined to our own time. It is a recurring phenomenon and abiding issue, visiting every generation and challenging every individual. Uncertainty and worry, of course, abound if and where we expect to hear God "speaking" and "calling" by extraordinary means. Hearing an audible voice from heaven, alas, is not normative, as the believer's experience will confirm, yet we still wish for the exception, do we not? How, then, *does* God call? Which is to ask, *How does God lead?*

What *is* normative—and foundational—in the Christian experience is that we must learn to listen. For this reason, in fact, the psalmist implores the godly to "Be still, and know that I am God" (Ps 46:10 NIV). Note the context here as mirrored in the psalm: amid turmoil, turbulence, and terror, the heart must choose a place of stillness. The contrast could not be sharper. And despite the many Old Testament accounts in which God seems to speak audibly to his servants, one narrative is particularly instructive, for it is akin to the experience of most believers, and thus normative: God often speaks to his servant not through a "mighty wind," nor through an "earthquake," nor through a "fire," but through a "soft whisper" (see 1 Kgs 19:11–12). Such whispers are often internal promptings. The predisposition of having a listening heart, an attentive mindset, and a discerning attitude can be said to constitute the core of bona fide faith. Is it possible that most Christians are more concerned with decision-making and finding "blueprints" for "guidance" than with cultivating virtue, wisdom, and communion with their Creator (out of which discernment arises)?

This leads us, then, to reconsider the very essence of vocation, which possesses two key components: (1) God initiates and (2) we respond. God's acts and God's initiating, of course, are always a mystery. That is, his works and his ways are inscrutable and unique (recall the message of Ecclesiastes); they can never be predicted, understood, or duplicated. Does God guide? Of course. He leads guidable, teachable people. But there exists no divine pattern or blueprint for *how* he does it. God's methods are limitless, as the introduction to the letter of Hebrews suggests: "In *many and various* ways God spoke of old to our fathers . . . but in these last days he has spoken to us by a Son" (Heb 1:1–2 RSV, emphasis added). This infinitely variegated characteristic of divine speaking requires of human beings an ever listening and discerning disposition, so that we do not presume that God always or even regularly acts, speaks, or leads in a particular way. God's ways and means, as Ecclesiastes teaches perhaps more than any biblical book, are inscrutable. Hence, as Qoheleth the Teacher admonishes us, we are to approach God with reverence, awe, and silence (Eccl 5:1–2). This very disposition, strange as it might strike the average Christian, is crucial as it applies to the matter of discernment. Learning discernment is a matter of wisdom. At the same time, it needs accentuating that this disposition mirrors our trust and confidence in God, a confidence that God in fact *does* lead and guide us, however veiled or "unpredictable" that leading is.

In this light, a word on the present cultural moment is in order. Contemporary culture is at war with our souls. What do I mean? I am referring not to the ideological battles facing Christian believers in our day—battles on virtually every front that are very real and in some ways escalating even as I write. What I mean is that in Western culture (and especially within the American context) we are, quite simply, surrounded all day long—every day of our lives—by noise, impulses, voices, volume, stimulation, agitation, and bombast—that is, with a veritable flood of sensory phenomena. And without mitigation, these can dull or deaden our souls. Because God is not calling most of us out of the world and to monastic life, wherein silence and contemplation are thought to govern the inner person, we must fight—indeed, it is no exaggeration to say that we must truly *fight*—to find those places, those times, and those disciplines that permit us to be "still," be quiet, and learn (or relearn) the discipline of listening. This battle will prove ongoing and unrelenting for all who choose not to withdraw from the world.

On Listening and Developing a Sense of Discernment

Given our social and cultural surroundings, a basic question confronts us: What does it mean to be still or quiet? And for that matter, how does one develop a listening heart? A key place to start is to learn the art of being free from distraction, of being attentive. One thoughtful commentator offers a helpful explanation on this point. He writes that being "attentive" means being

- teachable (i.e., malleable without being gullible or naïve);
- open (i.e., receptive without being uncritical);
- discerning (i.e., discriminating without being cynical or hypercritical);
- vigilant (i.e., alert or perceptive without being overly analytic or rationalistic); and
- morally honest (i.e., conscious of the temptation toward sin without being overly introspective).[1]

Attentiveness, as this wise commentator intuits, is really a synonym for what we might call discernment. As most serious Christians can attest, we learn over time to develop a sense of spiritual discrimination—that is, discernment—as we walk by faith. This sense materializes, in fact, as a result of both objective and subjective phenomena and as we choose ongoing fellowship with the triune God, based on his providential care and guidance. The same indwelling Spirit who bears witness that we are children of God (see Rom 8:16) is at work in an abiding fashion to assist us in processing our thoughts, our impulses, and our reflections on our own experiences as we live out our lives. That awareness, it needs emphasizing, issues out of both internal promptings and external circumstances, the sum total of which is shaped by prayerful reflection on scriptural

---

[1] A. J. Conyers, *The Listening Heart: Vocation and the Crisis of Modern Culture* (Dallas: Spence, 2006), 10–67.

truth, an attitude or predisposition of willingness and obedience, and a commitment to live in the context of Christian community.²

How does God call? How does God speak? In our wrestling with these questions, we may say that God will use reason, emotions, circumstances, impressions, and prodding, the subjective and the objective, the internal and the external. He will use direct and indirect influences, personal inclination and the counsel of others, our giftings, and others' needs. But as we process all of this, a danger—and it is unquestionably a universal tendency—is to expect or to normalize the extraordinary: for example, the burning bush, the audible voice, the fleece, or the blind-light revelation. We expect (or at least wish) to hear God speaking as he seemed to do with Abraham, Moses, David, and the prophets of old; or perhaps we rely on the "Gideon's fleece" method, which seems to retain strangely popular appeal.

Allow me, at this point, to put the idea of Gideon's fleece (as the concept appears in Judges 6) into proper (that is, new covenant) perspective in terms of the matter of guidance. In that narrative, Gideon asks that a fleece on the ground remain free of the night's dew as a sign that God really wants him to take a certain course of action; the narrative concerns the fledgling nation of Israel, who had done "what was evil in the sight of the LORD" to the point that God had handed them over to their enemies (Judg 6:1). The context of the fleece thus concerns theocratic Israel and God's necessarily extraordinary intervention, as mediated by a mysterious Old Testament figure called "the angel of the LORD" (Judg 6:11). In the end, his instruction was to have 300 trumpeters blow their instruments at a set point, which resulted in chaos for and the destruction of the

---

² By "Christian community" I am referring not to a cloistered or isolated living arrangement but to a tangible expression of the body of Christ wherein believers experience some measure of accountability and service. The "Christian Lone Ranger" is a contradiction. Our new birth is designed to bring us into the body of Christ, where we grow, are nourished, find accountability, and are equipped for service. As a Protestant, I can say without equivocation that the church in a very real sense is our "mother."

Midianites' invading army (7:22). Most new covenant believers readily acknowledge that the method of blowing 300 trumpets is not a normative plan in terms of taking down an enemy. When Gideon is praised in Hebrews 11:32, then, it cannot be because the writer to the Hebrews simply wishes believers to follow Gideon's methodological example (an approach occurring just that one time in Israel's theocratic history). Rather, Gideon is praised because of his overall willingness to trust the Lord amid Israel's apostasy. Few Christians, upon reading Judges 6–7 in light of its context, would take all of the events described in this narrative and apply them as normative for the Christian life. Gideon's use of the fleece, in fact, is just a part of this extraordinary working of God in a unique period of Israel's history. Gideon's *trust in God* is what we should emulate, not his use of a fleece. From a Christian standpoint, the problem with relying on fleeces in order to make vocational and other decisions is that it is presumptive, insofar as it attempts to force God's hand and is dependent on signs rather than God's indwelling presence and providential care. As one commentator observes, it is a shortcut, ignoring the relational aspect of one's walk with God and the importance of growing in maturity and perseverance.[3]

Recall the prior suggestion: God's speaking comes to us through whispers. For almost all of us, in fact, vocation and God's leading occur unspectacularly, as a process of piece-by-piece discovery over time.[4] All of the factors cited above, mixed with our willingness, availability, and

---

[3] Gordon T. Smith, *Listening to God in Times of Choice: The Art of Discerning God's Will* (Downers Grove, IL: InterVarsity, 1997), 15–23. In the related argument here I am *not* denying that some people have a more dramatic sense of call.

[4] Most of us, though, have used the language of "I felt led . . ." or "I believe that the Lord . . ." On occasion we might be justified in employing such language. But doing so might also reflect either a tinge of spiritual pride or an unwillingness to admit an error of judgment. Not infrequently, this sort of language is used by those who are young in the faith or who wish to exhibit an aura of the supernatural (for example, televangelists). One of the more useful resources on this topic is a collection of essays by Joseph Bayly, ed., *Essays on Guidance* (Downers Grove, IL: InterVarsity, 1973).

obedience, as well as our deepest sanctified desires, to which then are added the influence of friends, circumstances, seasons of life, and our increase in wisdom—all of these contribute to our growth in spiritual discernment. To our ability to know what God wants of us.

In our attempts to understand discernment, it needs stating that callings and an ability to discern grow out of the same source—communion with God. For this reason the psalmist wrote, "I will instruct you and show you the way to go; / with my eye on you, I will give counsel" (Ps 32:8). Herewith we get the proper sense of how to discern calling: it is not first and foremost a matter of what we *do*; rather, it is the by-product or fruit of our communing with God. Therein lies the essence of discernment. "Calling," as the authors of the volume *Listening Hearts* remind us, never comes with a road map.[5]

But what, actually, is discernment? Our English word derives from the Latin *discernere*, which means "to separate, set apart, or distinguish, and therefore, to determine or recognize." Discernment, thus, has to do with listening and distinguishing. It is, moreover, both a spiritual gift from God—for example, a gift that some individuals will manifest in notable ways within the body of Christ[6]—as well as a virtue intentionally and deliberately cultivated as a result of discipline and maturity on our part. Without spiritual discernment, finding God's guidance will be a constant source of frustration for the Christian—a "crapshoot," so to speak. It needs reiterating that vocation and discernment are anchored in the same foundation—a relationship with God.

The roots of discernment may be understood as psychological in nature, though we must resist the temptation to collapse our understanding of discernment into psychological method. Here I am refusing to place spirituality and psychology (properly understood) in opposition,

---

[5] Suzanne G. Farnham et al., *Listening Hearts: Discerning Call in Community*, rev. ed. (Harrisburg: Morehouse, 1991), ch. 1.

[6] This seems to be the nature of the gift identified as "discerning between spirits" in 1 Cor 12:10.

since the root meaning of "psychology" is "the study of the soul." Hence, there is an inherent dialogue between spirituality and psychology, given the fact of our integrated nature as humans and our being fashioned in the image of God. For this reason and more, it is important to develop a listening inner posture as we grow in the faith. Again, however, I am not arguing that faith and spirituality simply reduce to mere psychotherapy or technique. Rather, we are unitary beings; we are composite, integrated emotional-spiritual-rational creatures.[7] After all, God can and does guide us through various thoughts, impressions, emotions, and images in the inner person. At the same time, the objective guide of Scripture constantly admonishes us to renew and sanctify this inner person, so that our desires and priorities are God-honoring. Prayer, reflecting on the Word, and the indwelling Spirit combine in this ongoing renewing process.

There is a tendency among the authors of some of the existing literature on vocation to refer to an "inner voice," but without qualifying that voice or anchoring it in the transcendent, let alone God's indwelling Spirit. Examples of this range from Quaker writer Parker Palmer's *Let Your Life Speak*,[8] to more popular and less religiously motivated works such as Richard J. Leider's *The Power of Purpose*—which speaks of "that deepest dimension within us" and "our central core."[9] Even in some of the more technical literature, we find calling being identified as "a consuming, meaningful passion" and "a primarily psychological construct."[10] All of this raises the question, Which voice? After all, there are myriad voices competing for our attention. Moreover, how can we distinguish between

---

[7] Here I acknowledge modern psychology's resistance to religious faith without throwing out the insights of psychology per se.

[8] Parker J. Palmer, *Let Your Life Speak: Listening for the Voice of Vocation* (San Francisco: Jossey-Bass, 2000).

[9] Richard J. Leider, *The Power of Purpose: Find Meaning, Live Longer, Better* (San Francisco: Berrett-Koehler, 1997), 1.

[10] See Shoshana R. Dobrow and Jennifer Tosti-Kharas, "Calling: The Development of a Scale Measure," *Personnel Psychology* 64 (2011): 1005.

the voice of God's indwelling Spirit and other competing inner voices? After all, following my passion might be God-honoring, but it might also be the result of misplaced priorities.

Paul, in his teaching on the fruit of the Spirit in Gal 5:16–26, describes the inner person as well as the inner battle that rages within every believer. Given the "flesh" and our sinful nature, the apostle's exhortation is unambiguous: we are to be "led by the Spirit" (vv. 18 and 25), and we are to "keep in step with the Spirit" (v. 25). The implication of this is that our inner psychology needs to be tempered by God's indwelling influence, given our fallen inclinations. The daily goal of authentic faith and spirituality, after all, is not simply to "feel good" or even to "be true to ourselves," as is popularly understood. Our feelings vacillate, and for this reason the spiritual disciplines necessarily assist us. As one Christian psychologist has aptly noted, a commitment on our part to develop both virtuous habits and a "listening" posture will produce internally a godly peace that, in contrast, transcends the vacillations and vicissitudes of everyday life. While the "ego" can indeed defensively avoid or resist the demands of spiritual growth and discernment, it can willingly submit to them as well. Being freed from the fears, defenses, and resistance that rob the soul can liberate the Christian for his or her calling.[11]

Vocation thus mirrors a working out of our relationships with God on the journey of life. In processing all of the events, circumstances, and seasons that visit us, we grow in our discernment. And as we enter various seasons of life (wherein we learn the importance of timing), we aim to be attentive, which means that we are teachable, willing, and in the end obedient to God's call, wherever that might lead. After all, the disciple's attitude should be modeled after our Lord's—"not my will, God, but yours

---

[11] A helpful and balanced discussion of the psychological characteristics of discernment can be found in John N. Neafsey, "Psychological Dimensions of the Discernment of Vocation," in *Revisiting the Idea of Vocation: Theological Explorations*, ed. John C. Haughey (Washington, DC: Catholic University of America Press, 2012), 163–95.

be done"[12]—a predisposition that will consistently meet the challenge of misplaced or improper motivations.

As we contemplate God's leading and guidance, some additional commentary is needed with respect to our personal gifts, talents, inclinations, and interests. In this discussion I am assuming the interchangeability—and hence the equation—of God-given gifts," "natural gifts," "apparent strengths," and "spiritual gifts." Reasons for this equation are simple. Each of these expressions conveys the same basic truth: as unique creations of God, we each have been uniquely gifted by God. Those giftings may be physical, mental, intellectual, spiritual, psychological, or social. And because we are *integrated* creatures, any strict dichotomy between physical and mental or social and psychological, for example, collapses. Moreover, nowhere in Scripture is a strict separation or distinction suggested. Even in the matter of spiritual giftings, the fact that some individuals have gifts, say, in the area of teaching or encouragement or generosity or leadership or mercy (Rom 12:6–8) is to presume that they can exercise these—or at least that they may have the opportunity to exercise them—in broader life and in countless ways, and not merely within the context of congregational life. In Pauline teaching, the question being entertained seems to be whether people's gifts will contribute to the building of Christ's body, not their delimitation and usefulness in a purely ecclesial context.

Moreover, most parents, in assessing their child's abilities, will not distinguish between the categories of "spiritual" or "natural." Most parents observe particular sensitivities or giftings in their children when they are very young. A child's giftedness does not begin at a certain age, even when we can acknowledge that it grows steadily with the child's maturation. Theologically speaking, this may suggest that God has created human beings in a manner such that no natural versus spiritual dichotomy exists in the matter of gifts. Regardless, any giftings we have are God-given and therefore organically united, applicable to all of life.

---

[12] See Matt 26:39; Mark 14:36; and Luke 22:42.

This places the onus on parents to assess sensitively their children's giftings, inclinations, and aptitudes, and then encourage these in natural ways over time.

In addition, I must note that there is no need on our part for a false humility or worry about pride as we attempt to assess the gifts and talents that God has given us. These abilities come to us through divine grace, just as every good thing coming to human beings reflects God's grace. This, then, is a given: we live by grace and by what God gives. To be overly introspective as we assess our strengths and weaknesses is no virtue in the Christian life;[13] we must simply acknowledge what God has given to us and then respond.

It also needs stating that some gifts in our lives might be present, albeit dulled or veiled, when we are still unbelievers and then renewed and sanctified as a result of Christian faith. Relatedly, some gifts or abilities might have the appearance of being new, that is, birthed out of our new birth in Christ and thus expressing themselves only later in our lives, after conversion has perhaps occurred in adulthood. Most of us who have experienced adult conversions to the faith very likely have witnessed *both* of these perceptions in our lives. My own story illustrates the latter possibility.

From the time I was a child, I tended to be athletic, and my interests followed. Hence, upon going to college, I chose to major in health and physical education, even competing at the university level in two sports (almost unthinkable today, given the university demands on athletes in one sport alone). Why this choice? At the time, based on my priorities in life, "health and physical education" represented the path of least resistance to me; I had no meaningful life orientation. My interests were lodged in sports alone. I came to Christian faith, however, in my twenties as I was leaving the university. Up to that point, I had no intellectual

---

[13] I am assuming the fundamental difference here between true humility—that basic disposition of attentiveness to the Lord—and a false sense of humility, which is rooted in self-righteousness or pretense.

appetite and was not much of a reader. But spiritual transformation, getting to know the Lord through his Word and prayer and gathering with other believers, began to change me in both subtle and profound ways. Spiritual transformation, however, changed my appetites over time, post-university and post-conversion, in both subtle and profound ways.

Compounding this process of change was the subsequent experience of living in Europe for almost four years. There I discovered my acumen for language learning, and—as it turned out—for wider learning. By the time I returned to the States in my mid-thirties, I'd decided to embark on the path of graduate education. Today, after thirty years of teaching religion and philosophy at the university level and doing public-policy research, I can say with gratitude that God changed both my giftings and *my awareness* of my giftings after I came to faith. I grant, of course, that this is not the experience of the majority.

Someone might wonder how we should interpret the role of personal desires and interests. How do we know what desires are legitimately from God, and thus worthy of pursuit? Again, a measure of demystification is in order. A useful principle, and one borne out by human experience, is that we can trust those desires that have an abiding quality about them; those that endure and do not fade with the passing of time generally are instilled by God. Moreover, these stand in sharp contrast to selfish or corrupting desires, with which every human being struggles. Biblically speaking, the most common of those desires that corrupt the human spirit issue out of and mirror misplaced or false priorities—for example, the lust for self-gratification, material wealth, power or influence, and reputation. Hence, in the Western cultural context one must constantly guard against narcissistic tendencies and the effects of a totalitarian consumerism, all of which surround us at myriad levels. True joy and satisfaction, as Ecclesiastes reminds us, are gifts of God; seeking after the world's warped and false priorities will leave us with a sense of life's meaninglessness.

Correlatively, we may assume that our deepest desires align themselves with our God-given gifts. There exists a correlation between the two, and this unity is part of our being created in the image of God. Remarkably, in forty-five years of being a Christian I cannot *once* recall hearing a sermon or teaching on this most basic of truths. This simply should not be. Here, of course, I am assuming that we have been regenerated and are in communion with God; that is, we have responded to the first or "general" call—to Christ himself. When we belong to Christ and are seeking to please him, we need not treat all of our desires as dirty laundry or spoiled goods. The oft-repeated Augustinian saying, mentioned earlier, remains true: "Love God and do what you will." The simple truth undergirding this admonition is that when we have committed our all to Christ, we can trust that our deepest desires will be pleasing to God and have a redemptive quality. In fact, the psalmist can say that the Lord "satisfies [our] desires with good things" (Ps 103:5 NIV); "He fulfills the desires of those who fear him" (Ps 145:19). Having such awareness is liberating, for it frees us from a false and legalistic tendency that can rob believers of joy, purpose, and peace of mind.

Let it be clearly stated, then, that there is a direct correlation between our giftings and propensities, our deepest burdens, and our vocations.[14] None of God's people in Christ need blind-light revelations or the laying out of fleeces to recognize the way God has equipped them. And where we lack clarity, others who know us, in the context of community, can help us identify these giftings. Simply asking those who know us intimately, in fact, will confirm where our giftings and inclinations lie. This, of course, does not mean that there won't be seeming detours or seasons of our lives in which we struggle with a lack of clarity of perspective as to how to live out our calling. It is only to affirm that discernment comes to us as whispers, unspectacularly and amid a variety of phenomena, as we walk forward—trusting God, being in community, and desiring to serve others.

---

[14] It is wisdom to acknowledge that those desires or deepest interests or burdens that are enduring come from the heart of God and therefore contribute to our callings.

One helpful summary of God's guidance to the Christian as he or she seeks to respond to God's call was laid out by Horace Bushnell (1802–1876) in his sermon "Every Man's Life a Plan of God." In it, Bushnell attempted to outline "where duties lie" for individual Christian believers as they seek to respond to God's calling. His advice was this:

- Be anchored in God's character.
- Recognize that your will is at rest in God's will.
- Follow your conscience, given to you by God.
- Trust God's moral law to guide you.[15]
- Be aware of God's providential guidance along the way.
- [Seek] the advice of faithful friends and Christian community.
- Seek your calling with an expectant attitude.[16]

Bushnell is summarizing what should be obvious and commonsensical to the average Christian, even when on occasion it needs reiterating. Discernment in terms of our callings is foremost a matter of *listening*, and that does not reduce to a magical formula; it must be learned.

On Quiet and Christian Community

Earlier I stressed the importance of "fighting" for quiet and solitude in the normal Christian life, given the surrounding cultural "bombast" that threatens to dull or deaden the soul. If we do not learn how to quiet the

---

[15] God's general will concerning all of human life is revealed in the form of the Ten Commandments, even when this revelation needs contextualizing in varied social-cultural environments. In addition, we have the natural moral law—the law "written on the heart," as Paul describes it, which agrees with the Commandments and witnesses to basic moral truth having been planted within in the human heart (see Rom 2:14–15).

[16] Horace Bushnell, "Every Man's Life a Plan of God," in *Sermons for the New Life* (New York: Charles Scribner, 1858), 21–23. Bushnell's sermon has been reproduced in William C. Placher, ed., *Callings: Twenty Centuries of Christian Wisdom on Vocation* (Grand Rapids: Eerdmans, 2005), 353–58.

soul and develop a "listening" posture, we will struggle in the realm of discernment. But learning to be still is profoundly countercultural. We can expect no help from our noisy surroundings; that much is certain.

Our need for quiet and solitude, however, should not be interpreted as an excuse or rationale either for being unattached to a local expression of the body of Christ, and thus to community, or fleeing the culture. It is in the context of Christian community that we grow, are nourished, find accountability, and are equipped for service. Above I had confessed as a Protestant what is often associated with Catholic theology: in a very real sense the Church *is* our "mother." Just as we are physically birthed into families, and not left to ourselves to survive or grow, so too we are spiritually birthed into God's family, the body of Christ, without which there will be no nurture, no growth, and no direction or purpose.[17] We humans are inescapably social and relational in our constitution, which is another expression of the image of God. Where individuals deny or negate this reality, they inevitably struggle with despondency, even suicidal tendencies.

Thinkers as different as Aristotle and John Calvin emphasize our inherently social nature, that we are social creatures by design. The New Testament confirms this presupposition; its teaching on the body of Christ is instructive—and emphatic—on various levels. Most obvious is the implication that the many and extremely varied members or parts of the body do not—indeed, cannot—exist alone. One need only imagine the monstrosity of hands and ears and kidneys and eyeballs and toes severed from the rest of a physical body to understand why. Spiritually speaking, all true Christians are connected to the same Head, without whose direction they cannot function (see Eph 4:15–16).

Given our design, then, we are created for community. This is true not merely as it applies to the faith, and thus the body of Christ, but on all social levels. We seek to serve the community—whether that community

---

[17] "Where there is no guidance, a people falls, but in an abundance of counselors there is safety" (Prov 11:14, ESV).

is the family as the most basic social unit, the neighborhood, the city, or the community of nations. By implication, we are to serve *the common good*. "The common good"—how does this expression strike most Protestants? More than likely, it strikes us as a "Catholic" thing, or as something with which only policy wonks concern themselves. Almost never do we hear from the pulpit (at least explicitly) of "building the common good." Rarely is faith translated in meaningful ways that would seek to build the common social good. Perhaps this is partly the result of the wider culture, which is in captivity to a "me first" and entitlement mindset. But perhaps it is also the fruit of a view of Christian faith that, as earlier chapters noted, is limited to what God does *in* me rather than what God intends to do *through* me.

In a most enlightening way, author Gordon Smith devotes the final chapter of his important work *Courage and Calling* to the balance we need in our personal and social lives. The title of this chapter—"The Ordered Life: Between Solitude and Community"[18]—suggests that true freedom is the fruit of discipline and order in our lives. Thereafter Smith describes solitude and being in community as two anchors that work in symbiosis. In solitude, we find God and are renewed—spiritually, mentally, intellectually, and psychologically. On the other hand, we are members of Christ's body, made for community. No vocation, therefore, is fulfilled on an island. Vocation and vocation-related decisions, though requiring quiet contemplation, usually are confirmed in community through the body of Christ.

On the Importance of Timing: Vocation and Personal Detours

When I went to live in West Germany in 1980, I had no idea how long I would be living there; as it turned out, it was nearly four years. What

---

[18] Gordon T. Smith, *Courage and Calling: Embracing Your God-Given Potential*, rev. ed. (Downers Grove, IL: InterVarsity, 2011), 251–64.

I *did* know at the time was that I needed to learn the language, for up to that point I scarcely knew any German.[19] Before I found an opening in a language school, my wife and I needed income, which meant that I needed a job—*any* job.

At the time, West Germany had a 13 percent unemployment rate, which by their standards was catastrophic. Nevertheless, I went to the *Arbeitsamt* (the employment office) in the city where we lived. There I was informed of three available possibilities, two of them requiring training, which seemed out of the question at the time. The third did not and was temporary. It was a three-week gig at a large cemetery. My long-term sense of calling, I assure you, did not include digging graves. Yet, not having any alternatives and needing money, I took the job, thinking, *God, I cannot believe it. You lead me to Germany for who knows how long, and this is what I get in response!*

To make a long story short, a three-week temporary position grew into a more permanent role (to my surprise and moderate consternation), after which deliverance came and I was granted a *Studienplatz* (student seat) at the university to begin language study. That season of working in a cemetery turned out to be important, painful as it was, and God in his providence had a purpose behind it; I simply could not see it. After spending several years studying language and linguistics, and enjoying education as never before, I eventually became proficient in the language—proficient enough to translate a book written by a famous German Old Testament

---

[19] Subsequently, in the university classroom through the years I have exhorted my students, if they sensed that they might be living abroad for an extended length of time, to study the language of the country to which they feel called for a *minimum* of two years before entering the foreign culture for service. The simple reason, which I learned as an American living abroad, is that the host culture will take you *far more seriously* if you speak the language, or at least are attempting to learn the language. The implication is clear: as Christians, our witness is far stronger if we demonstrate a willingness to identify with the culture in which we have been placed. The first step—the most basic step—to demonstrate our appreciation of the culture is to learn its language. This is true both literally and figuratively.

scholar into English once I was back in the States.[20] But was I able to connect the dots while I was digging graves? Hardly.

I later returned to the US for graduate school, after which I did public policy work in Washington, DC, before entering the university classroom, where for several decades various threads of my calling have been united.

Regardless of the hardship (and many questions!) I experienced upon arriving in a foreign culture, I understand my own vocational calling—which not only includes my job but extends beyond it—as a call to the academy and to the church as a teacher and writer, for the purposes of bringing Christian faith to bear on public life, including social and public policy. Looking back, I can say without equivocation that the lessons learned while living in a foreign culture contribute enormously—and providentially—to my perception of faith and to my own calling. Living abroad was by far the most formative season of my life. The experience of learning and living in a foreign culture forces a person to wrestle with the essence of Christian faith, with basic meaning in life, and with appropriate ways of clothing Christian truth in a cross-cultural context. These lessons are simply invaluable.

To describe events, circumstances, and situations that affect vocation as "detours," however, raises an important and related matter. It is the matter of *timing*. Not all decision-making, of course, is freighted with moral implications. Where we buy our groceries, what kind of car we drive, and what our individual tendencies and tastes might be are not matters that (usually) require "discernment." Other decisions, however, do carry with them far-ranging consequences as well as spiritual or moral significance, particularly vocational decisions. Moreover, not merely *what* should be done but *how* it is to be done and *when* it is to be done are important matters. How and when, in fact, are matters of wisdom, as the Teacher in Ecclesiastes observes: The "wise heart knows the right time

---

[20] See Claus Westermann, *Roots of Wisdom: The Oldest Proverbs of Israel and Other Peoples*, trans. J. Daryl Charles (Louisville: WJK, 1995).

and procedure. For every activity there is a right time and procedure" (Eccl 8:5–6). The latter statement needs several remarks.

The element of divinely orchestrated timing is well illustrated by our Lord himself in his earthly vocation. At several points in the Gospel narratives, Jesus states, "My time has not yet come" (see, for instance, John 2:4; 7:6).[21] His messianic work and movement, though not avoiding Jerusalem, were orchestrated in such a way that he moved toward or away from the city strategically. And we are told that as he approached the time of his sacrificial "offering," his movements corresponded with a most important feast time in the Jewish calendar, in order to fulfill certain messianic prophecies. Even salvation history unfolds with a sense of proper "timing." Jesus moves and operates according to the will of the Father. Time and timing, therefore, are everything.

But one need not look only to our Lord for confirmation of the important "wisdom" element of timing. Consider the farmer's work. His sowing of seeds, their cultivation, and even the harvest are all matters of timing. Weather and circumstances may or may not cooperate. However, the farmer does not depend on or look to these variable conditions to know the "season." Nor does he let inclement weather or repair of broken farm equipment or lack of laborers prevent him from acting when the season calls for appropriate action—whether that be planting, cultivating, or harvesting. Agriculture is based on knowing what the current season is and what it calls for. Here the lessons are basic. To intend to "do the right thing" in the wrong season would be inappropriate and foolish. Conversely, to not act when the season seems to call for action would also be equally inappropriate and foolish.

As it applies to Christian discernment and "guidance," an "open door" may or may not be appropriate to one's situation. But the same may be said of a "closed door" as well. The critical issue here is that of timing. What does the season in which we find ourselves call for? Once

---

[21] See also Matt 26:18; Mark 1:15; John 7:8, 30; 8:20; 13:1.

again, we return to that wondrous, life-giving theological reality of divine providence: we can rest in the fact of God's providential care for our lives. "Open doors" can be invigorating when we sense by faith that the timing is right to enter. In the same vein, not infrequently we get a sense of peace when we encounter "closed doors," and the reasons for that "peace" are anchored in our awareness of God's providential leading and guiding, at all junctures along life's path. We sense then, again and again, that timing is critical.

Recall, once more, the wisdom of Ecclesiastes: there is a time and season for everything under heaven (3:1, 17), and the wise man's heart will discern both the proper time and procedure (8:5–6). As was observed earlier in this volume, the wisdom perspective calls human beings not to attempt to "understand" God's works and God's ways—after all, they are inscrutable—but to allow for divine providence in the ordering of our lives. Only the fear of God, as Ecclesiastes makes so abundantly clear (and note its strategic placement in 3:14), allows us to put the impenetrable and inscrutable in proper perspective.

Take birth and death as an illustration of this point (see Eccl 3:2). While we humans universally rejoice over births and would prefer to avoid death, we acknowledge and find rest in the fact of Providence: death is a reality that comes to all; after all, we are human *creatures*. The reason for this rest is explained by both the writer of Ecclesiastes, in implicit terms, and the apostle Paul, in expressly theological terms. As mirrored in Ecclesiastes, death reminds *all* people—not just the "covenant community"—that a life lived and deeds done are "meaningless" apart from the fear of a Creator God and the acknowledgment of transcendent realities. In Pauline literature, the portrayal of death is presented in expressly theological categories; it is defined in terms of what Christ, lord over life and death, has revealed with a view of eternity in mind.[22] There is continuity between how we live our lives in the temporal world and the eschaton.

---

[22] See 1 Corinthians 15.

Or we might reflect for a moment on the polarities in Ecclesiastes 3 that follow the observation that there is a time to live and a time to die: planting and uprooting, killing and healing, tearing down and building, weeping and laughing, and mourning and dancing (vv. 2–4). What might be said of these opposites? The examples of planting and uprooting are readily understood if we consider the nature of agriculture, as noted above. Killing and healing, however, given our varied ideological dispositions, require a bit more explanation. A "time to kill" suggests that on rare occasion killing is necessary—when, for example, someone with criminal intent wishes to jeopardize the common good and take the lives of others (who, in relative terms, are innocent), it is not only appropriate but morally necessary. This principle would apply to both domestic contexts—for example, to law enforcement—and to international affairs—for example, to dealing with terrorism, rogue nations, or cases of genocide.[23]

Or take the contrast in Eccl 2:4 of weeping or laughing and mourning or dancing. What would wisdom (and Christian faith) do in the context of sadness or trauma induced by catastrophe or death? As Paul observes in his letter to the Roman Christians, faith and common sense require that we "weep with those who weep" and "rejoice with those who are rejoicing" (Rom 12:15). What, after all, would be the reaction if we were to bring levity, joking, or manufactured joy into an environment in which people are suffering and grieving due to egregious loss, catastrophe, or death? Such would be unthinkable; such would be inhumane.

What, then, does this suggest, and how does this bear on the topic of "discernment"? In sensitivity to others, we "honor" the particular season, whether it is sadness or joy, mourning or rejoicing. We do not dance when people are dying, but we should also not be mourning in an environment of genuine joy and rejoicing that surrounds us. And even when we might

---

[23] Because of the image *of God in others*, the Genesis account declares that death for the murderer is just (Gen 9:6), much to our consternation. Human life is sacred, which is why punishment for the sins of humanity required death on a cross. This moral principle abides.

personally be experiencing a season of deprivation or sadness, we do not bring that disposition into an environment in which others have true reason to rejoice and be glad. This, in the end, is wisdom, and this wisdom is spelled out in Ecclesiastes 3.

Seeking wisdom as we confront vocational decisions will require that we deal with setbacks, seemingly unanswered prayers, obstacles, and even suffering, as we have attempted to argue in both this chapter and chapter 6. Our theological foundations will anchor us as we confront these various seasons of life. *For everything under heaven there is a time and a season.*

CHAPTER

8

Conclusion: The Impact of the Ordinary

Taking Seriously Our Calling to the World

Important as theological and philosophical reflection might be for the Christian community and particularly for those called to do the work of Christian scholarship, moral principle must find application to society's quandaries in ways that do not reduce merely to philosophical abstraction. This must occur in the church's social witness in practical ways. Given that humans are by nature social beings, this application will occur through relationships, in community, and in the marketplace, where people spend most of their waking hours. Although the argument presented in this volume does not exclude "evangelism" (narrowly construed) as a strategy of cultural persuasion, it does assume that there are other foundational aspects of the church's witness to society. It assumes that our work and our vocational callings, the Monday-through-Friday jobs that we do and interactions we have, are the primary means by which we speak to the culture. It assumes that engaging the marketplace, to which 99 percent of us in the body of Christ are called, is an essential part of "doing the Lord's work."

At the outset of this volume, it was argued that the church has a responsibility for society. For some believers, however, it will remain unclear—perhaps even doubtful—whether Christians have a stake in how society operates. And if we do not propose a "Christian society" per se, how *do* we leaven culture, bringing moral truth to bear without succumbing either to the isolationist, the accommodationist, or the theocratic triumphalist distortion?

At the most basic level, the Christian community enters into voluntary yet open-hearted engagement of the culture in all aspects of social interchange—that is, where society is relatively free and open to such engagement.[1] Where this is possible, it is necessary that all participate, each person in various ways according to his or her abilities and role, without which it is impossible to promote the common good of the culture. From a Christian standpoint, this obligation inheres in two theological realities: the very dignity of fellow human beings around us based on the image of God within them and the creation mandate that we, as stewards, are to cultivate every aspect of the created order. Cultural separatists, activists, and anarchists, in every age, need reminding of this obligation, regardless of their rationale for retreating from or denouncing the culture of which they are a part.

Basic to Christian witness is for the church to work for the common good of that cultural context in which she finds herself. The "common good," as I am using the expression, may be defined as "the sum total of social conditions which allow people, either as groups or as individuals, to reach their fulfillment" as human beings within society and allow

---

[1] What made the American "experiment in ordered liberty" unique was its commitment not only to avoid the excesses or failed experiments in the European context but to strive for an "ordered liberty," by which the founders and fathers understood that certain moral laws govern the universe, and that to be truly free is to be guided by those laws. They perceived that liberty can be readily lost. And indeed this "ordered liberty" in our day seems to have been lost.

them at the same time to be protected as humans.² We do this—we *work* for this—in the awareness, as argued, that people are created in the image of God.

The *Catechism of the Catholic Church* helpfully identifies three components that comprise the common good. These elements are worthy of consideration. First, "the common good presupposes *respect for the person* as such. In the name of the common good, public authorities are bound to respect the fundamental and inalienable rights of the human person."³ Second, "the common good requires the *social well-being* and *development*" of both individuals and groups within society. Development, after all, "is the epitome of all social duties." At the most basic level, society must safeguard what is needed for people to live; needs include not only the most basic elements such as food, clothing, and shelter but "health," opportunities for work, "education" and cultural growth, "the right to establish a family" (that is, a family as informed by cultural history and not contemporary social activism), as well as the basic freedoms of worship and speech.⁴

Finally, "the common good requires *peace*" and stability, that is, "the security of a just order" that is underpinned by moral law. "It presupposes that authority should ensure by morally acceptable means the security of society and its members," providing an environment in which human beings might flourish.⁵ Hereby the *Catechism* is underscoring the basis of the right to legitimate personal and collective protection.

The common good is always oriented toward others; it is motivated by our desire to see human beings flourish. God has designed human community with this goal in mind. The nature of human community, as the *Catechism* spells out, respects the dignity of the person, the

---

² *Catechism of the Catholic Church* (Washington, DC: United States Catholic Conference, 1994), no. 1906, accessed April 5, 2022, https://www.vatican.va/archive/ENG0015/__P6K.HTM.

³ *Catechism of the Catholic Church*, no. 1907 (emphasis in original).

⁴ *Catechism*, no. 1908 (emphasis in original).

⁵ *Catechism*, no. 1909 (emphasis in original).

development of social well-being, and a stable, lawful order of security and peace. Where these elements are valued, people will be inclined toward flourishing. Such an environment—what we might call civil society—is "founded on truth, built up in justice, and animated by love."[6] Where they are demeaned or dismissed, social and cultural chaos ensue.

In his thoughtfully written and engaging volume *Ordinary Saints*, Lutheran theologian Robert Benne has identified at least four "duties" people "owe their society if they are to be responsible citizens." These duties, which work toward the common good and are necessary for civil society, are worthy of our attention. They are (1) self-reliance and self-government; (2) civility; (3) informed participation in political life; and (4) a willingness to serve.[7] All of these predispositions are public virtues. And they presume that Christians are indeed, in a very tangible way, responsible for the societies of which they are a part. Moreover, they disqualify much current social activism (at least, as popularly understood) as a duty of citizens, since very often—especially in our day—social activists are motivated by a sense of *rights* and *entitlement*, not by a desire to *serve* others or build the common social good.[8]

The language of contributing to the common good may seem abstract, even academic, to most believers. However, our grasp of work's fundamental dignity and our finding clarity in our vocational callings are not abstract entities. Take, for example, the qualification of our willingness to serve, which is a core feature of vocation. "Service to others," while almost universally laudable, often is ranked low on the list of motivations for many people as they weigh vocational decisions. Aside from pay and personal benefits, perhaps the highly specialized nature of much industry today and the workforce is what causes some to rank "service to others"

---

[6] *Catechism*, no. 1912.

[7] Robert Benne, *Ordinary Saints: An Introduction to the Christian Life* (Minneapolis: Fortress Press, 2003), 189.

[8] Where relatively free Western societies take the responsibilities of citizenship for granted, or simply ignore them, they tend to become increasingly lawless and move toward either a softer or harder form of totalitarianism.

as less important. And in some industries one's place surely may seem like only a cog in the wheel in terms of how one might contribute to the common good. But it should be said that in relatively free societies a wide variety of professions, businesses, and enterprises permit a wide range of using one's skills and aptitudes to contribute to the common good.

Work that is intrinsically satisfying, as Benne points out, contributes either indirectly or directly to the needs of others, thereby taking on a deeper meaning and expressing in concrete terms the "priesthood of all believers," as Luther understood it. All useful work shares in what Benne calls a "holy secularity," resulting in blessing to the worker and pleasure to God.[9] While the cultural climate of which we are a part might be considered postmodern and post-Christian, it is surely not—nor will it become—post-vocational. Churches, seminaries, and divinity schools, whether or not they are attuned to this reality, should be preaching this message with unmitigated authority. After all, most of the church is called to the marketplace. We are thus called, in Benne's words, to a "holy secularity."

Let us focus, for the moment, on service to others, what Jesus (and Luther) called "neighbor-love." A commitment to loving our neighbors (see Lev 19:18; Prov 14:21; Matt 19:19; 22:39; Mark 12:31, 33; Luke 10:27; Rom 13:10) will have the effect of causing our vision to be external rather than merely internal. It will move us to ask whether our work really does contribute to the common social good rather than to mere self-preservation and "making a living." In asking this question, Christians find help in discerning whether the work—as well as the wider vocation—that they ponder has lasting value.[10] Most occupations and professions do not raise obvious questions of moral legitimacy. Today, however, the lines might be blurred by any number of social, economic, and cultural factors: for

---

[9] Benne, *Ordinary Saints*, 171.

[10] And as I suggested in chapter 3, this will help establish for the believer the moral limits of not only the type of work to be undertaken but the type of employer with which to be associated.

example, by economics interests controlled by totalitarian regimes (China, for example), by specialization and division of labor in some industries, by the world of advertising (whose moral standards have dropped precipitously), by the entertainment industry, whether stage or screen (whose standards and output are overwhelmingly oriented toward blurring or crossing moral and sexual lines), or by pharmaceutical companies (whose biomedical orientation in the laboratory might be questionable, such as in the service of genetic engineering or in its potential to use fetal tissue or extracts in the process of experimentation). Because these and other workplace dilemmas are public and ethical in nature, they will require active Christian participation and expressed conviction in the public arena.

Earlier in this book's discussion of vocation it was noted that, because of the wondrous realm of divine providence, the believer is free to step out and take risks—not in a foolish or haphazard way but in the awareness (and a confident hope) that our lives, our vocations, and our work truly can contribute to something lasting, even when we cannot immediately or readily measure their value. On occasion this might mean taking a new line of work that increases our service to others. Such a decision will not normally be predicated on income or financial factors or other immediate and measurable reward; in fact, often it will seem to go against the grain of personal interest and gain. And in truth, such venturesome steps are often met by resistance around us. Again, Robert Benne: "The world is not always ready for reform. But reforms are made by those willing to risk, and Christians should be at the forefront of the willing. They should act on the discomfort that love creates."[11]

And *act* we must. Recall the open-ended admonitions of the Teacher in Ecclesiastes:

- "Whatever your hands find to do, do with all your strength." (9:10)
- "Send your bread on the surface of the water." (11:1)
- "Give a portion to seven or even to eight." (11:2)

---

[11] Benne, *Ordinary Saints*, 176.

- "Sow your seed." (11:6)
- "Banish anxiety from your mind." (11:10 NRSV)

Recall as well, in this vein, that we simply "do not know what might succeed, whether this enterprise or that venture, or whether both undertakings might equally flourish" (11:6, my translation). The sheer mystery of God's purposes and God's works is intended to exhilarate us, causing us to live daily life with gusto rather than be paralyzed by doubt and indecision.

Dorothy Sayers was correct to note that the end or goal of our work "will be decided by our religious outlook." The same applies to our individual callings, our vocations; these will be determined by our religious convictions, our theological bearings. Surely our work and our vocational callings, then, must be "the [true] expression of ourselves."[12] Life—yes, ordinary life—takes on a very different, and far richer, cast when we view our faith in terms of "divine vocation," inasmuch as vocation calls forth "a person's entire range of capacities and skills into worship and devoted work for the common good, by a power not only greater than [us] but greater than the whole world in which [we live]."[13]

"If work is to find its right place in the world," Sayers concludes, "it is the duty of the Church to see to it that the work serves God"[14] Surely Sayers is not far from the mark: it is the church's duty to equip the body of Christ for responsible and redemptive service in the marketplace. Given work's inherent dignity and the fact that, based on our design, we mirror the very likeness of God, our vocation is *to*—rather than *away from*—social and cultural institutions. We are stewards of the entire created order. And in this task, we indeed share in a "holy secularity," which results in blessing and satisfaction to the worker as well as pleasure to God.

Who will equip us for this noble task?

---

[12] See Dorothy L. Sayers, "Why Work?," in *Creed or Chaos?: Why Christians Must Choose either Dogma or Disaster; or, Why It Really Does Matter What You Believe*, repr. (Manchester: Sophia Institute Press, 1974), 114–15.

[13] Robert Lowry Calhoun, in *God and the Day's Work: Christian Vocation in an Unchristian World* (New York: Association Press, 1957), 9.

[14] Sayers, 116.

BIBLIOGRAPHY

Adams, Samuel. *Wisdom in Transition*. SJSJ. Leiden: Brill, 2008.

Ahn, Jina, et al. "A Cross-Cultural Study of Calling and Life Satisfaction in the United States and South Korea." *Journal of Career Development* 20, no. 10 (2019): 1–15.

Alter, Robert. *The Wisdom Books: Job, Proverbs, and Ecclesiastes*. New York: W. W. Norton, 2010.

Anderson, William H. U. "The Curse of Work in Qoheleth: An Exposé of Genesis 3:17–19 in Ecclesiastes." *Evangelical Quarterly* 70, no. 2 (1998): 99–113.

———. "Philosophical Considerations in a Genre Analysis of Qoheleth." *Vetus Testamentum* 48, no. 3 (1998): 289–300.

———. *Qoheleth and His Pessimistic Theology*. MBPS 54. Lewiston: Edwin Mellen, 1997.

Apology of the Augsburg Confession in *The Book of Concord: The Confessions of the Evangelical Lutheran Church*, edited by Theodore G. Tappert. Minneapolis: Fortress, 1979.

Aquinas, St. Thomas. *Summa Theologica*. Translated by the Fathers of the English Dominican Province. Westminster: Christian Classics, 1981.

Aristotle, *Nicomachean Ethics*. 2nd ed. Translated by Terence Irwin. Indianapolis: Hackett, 1999.

Armstrong, Chris R. "Refocused Vocation." *Leadership Journal* (Winter 2013): 44–48.

Athas, George. *Ecclesiastes, Song of Songs.* SGBC. Grand Rapids: Zondervan Academic, 2020.

Atkinson, Tyler. *Singing at the Winepress: Ecclesiastes and the Ethics of Work.* London: T&T Clark, 2015.

Badcock, Gary D. *The Way of Life: A Theology of Christian Vocation.* Grand Rapids: Eerdmans, 1998.

Balantine, Samuel E. *Wisdom Literature.* CBS. Nashville: Abingdon, 2018.

Bartholomew, Craig. *Ecclesiastes.* BCOT. Grand Rapids: Baker Academic, 2009.

———. "Qoheleth in the Canon?! Current Trends in the Interpretation of Ecclesiastes." *Themelios* 24, no. 3 (May 1999): 4–20.

Bayer, Oswald. *Martin Luther's Theology: A Contemporary Interpretation.* Translated by Thomas H. Trapp. Grand Rapids: Eerdmans, 2008.

Bayly, Joseph, ed. *Essays on Guidance.* Downers Grove, IL: InterVarsity, 1973.

Beckett, John D. *Mastering Monday: A Guide to Integrating Faith and Work.* Downers Grove, IL: InterVarsity, 2006.

Bellah, Robert, et al., *Habits of the Heart: Individualism and Commitment in American Life.* Berkeley: University of California Press, 1985.

Benne, Robert. *Good and Bad Ways to Think about Religion and Politics.* Grand Rapids: Eerdmans, 2010.

———. *Ordinary Saints: An Introduction to the Christian Life.* Minneapolis: Fortress, 2003.

———. "Vocations?" *Lutheran Quarterly* 35 (2021): 73–79.

Berger, Benjamin Lyle. "Qohelet and the Exigencies of the Absurd." *Biblical Interpretation* 9, no. 2 (2001): 141–55.

Bergsma, John. "The Creation Narratives and the Original Unity of Work and Worship in the Human Vocation." In *Work: Theological*

Foundations and Practical Implications, edited by R. Keith Loftin and Trey Dimsdale, 11–29. London: SCM, 2018.

Blamires, Harry. *The Will and the Way: A Study of Divine Providence and Vocation.* New York: Macmillan, 1957.

Bloom, Harold. *Where Shall Wisdom Be Found?* New York: Riverhead, 2004.

Bolin, Thomas M. *Ecclesiastes and the Riddle of Authorship.* BW. New York: Routledge, 2017.

Borgman, Brian. "Redeeming the 'Problem Child': Qoheleth's Message and Place in the Family of Scripture." *Southern Baptist Journal of Theology* 15, no. 3 (Fall 2011): 62–71.

Bornapé, Allan. "'Fear God and Keep His Commandments': The Character of Man and the Judgment of God in the Epilogue of Ecclesiastes." *DavarLogos* 17, no. 2 (2018): 37–59.

Brecht, Martin. *Martin Luther: The Preservation of the Church, 1532–1546.* Translated by James L. Schaaf. Minneapolis: Fortress, 1993.

———. *Martin Luther: His Road to Reformation, 1483–1521.* Translated by James L. Schaaf. Minneapolis: Fortress, 1985.

———. *Martin Luther: Shaping and Defining the Reformation, 1521–32.* Translated by James L. Schaaf. Minneapolis: Fortress, 1994.

Brennfleck, Kevin, and Kay Marie Brennfleck. *Live Your Calling: A Practical Guide to Finding and Fulfilling Your Mission in Life.* San Francisco: Jossey-Bass, 2005.

Brown, William P. "Character Reconstructed: Ecclesiastes." In *Character in Crisis: A Fresh Approach to the Wisdom Literature of the Old Testament*, 120–50. Grand Rapids: Eerdmans, 1996.

———. *Ecclesiastes.* Interpretation. Louisville: John Knox, 2000.

———. "Whatever Your Hand Finds to Do: Qoheleth's Work Ethic." *Interpretation* 55, no. 3 (2001): 271–84.

Brunner, Emil. *The Divine Imperative: A Study in Christian Ethics.* Translated by Olive Wyon. Philadelphia: Westminster, 1947.

Bunderson, J. Stuart, and Jeffery A. Thompson. "The Call of the Wild: Zookeepers, Callings, and the Double-edged Sword of Deeply Meaningful Work." *Administrative Science Quarterly* 54, no. 1 (2009): 32–57.

Burtless, Gary, and Joseph F. Quinn. "Retirement Trends and Policies to Encourage Work among Older Americans." In *Ensuring Health and Income Security for an Aging Workforce*, edited by Peter P. Budetti et al., 375–415. Kalamazoo, MI: Upjohn Institute, 2001.

Bushnell, Horace. "Every Man's Life a Plan of God." In *Sermons for the New Life*, 21–23. New York: Charles Scribner, 1858.

Buttrick, George A. *The Parables of Jesus*. New York: Harper & Bros., 1928.

Cahalan, Kathleen A., and Bonnie J. Miller-McLemore, eds. *Calling All Years Good: Christian Vocation throughout Life's Seasons*. Grand Rapids: Eerdmans, 2017.

Calhoun, Robert Lowry. *God and the Day's Work: Christian Vocation in an Unchristian World*. New York: Association Press, 1957.

Calvin, John. *A Harmony of the Gospels: Matthew, Mark and Luke; and James and Jude*, edited by Thomas F. Torrance and David W. Torrance. Translated by A. W. Morrison and T. H. L. Parker. Grand Rapids: Eerdmans, 1995.

———. *Institutes of the Christian Religion*, Volumes 1 and 2, edited by John T. McNeill. Translated by Ford Lewis Battles. Philadelphia: Westminster, 1960.

Caneday, A. B. "'Everything Is Vapor': Grasping for Meaning under the Sun." *Southern Baptist Journal of Theology* 15, no. 3 (Fall 2011): 26–40.

Carroll, John. "Is the Vocation Paradigm under Threat?" *Journal of Sociology* 56, no. 3 (2020): 282–96.

Catechism of the Catholic Church. Washington, DC: United States Catholic Conference, 1994. https://www.vatican.va/archive/ENG0015/_INDEX.HTM.

Cavanaugh, William T. "Actually, You Can't Be Anything You Want (And It's a Good Thing, Too)." In *At This Time and in This Place:*

Vocation and Higher Education, edited by David S. Cunningham, 25–46. Oxford: Oxford University Press, 2016.

Chamberlain, Gary L. "The Evolution of Business as a Christian Calling." In *Finding Meaning in Business: Theology, Ethics, and Vocation*, edited by Bartholomew C. Okonkwo, 33–56. New York: Palgrave Macmillan, 2012.

Chanoff, Sasha, and David Chanoff. *From Crisis to Calling: Finding Your Moral Center in the Toughest Decisions*. San Francisco: Berrett-Koehler, 2016.

Charles, J. Daryl. "The Kuyperian Option: Cultural Engagement and Natural Law Ecumenism." *Touchstone* (May-June 2018): 22–28.

———. "Natural Law and Protestant Reform: Lessons from a Forgotten Reformer." In *Wisdom's Work: Essays on Ethics, Vocation, and Culture*, 61–87. Grand Rapids: Acton Institute, 2019.

———. "Post-Consensus Culture, Natural Law, and Moral Persuasion: Translating Moral Conviction in a Disbelieving Age." In *Wisdom's Work: Essays on Ethics, Vocation, and Culture*, 1–26. Grand Rapids: Acton Institute, 2019.

———. "Toward Restoring a Good Marriage: Reflections on the Contemporary Divorce of Love and Justice and Its Cultural Implications." *Journal of Church and State* 55, no. 2 (2013): 367–83.

———. *Wisdom and Work: Theological Reflections on Human Labor from Ecclesiastes*. Eugene, OR: Wipf & Stock, 2021.

———. *Wisdom's Work: Essays in Ethics, Vocation, and Culture*. Grand Rapids: Acton Institute, 2019.

Cherney, Kenneth A., Jr. "Hidden in Plain Sight: Luther's Doctrine of Vocation." *Wisconsin Lutheran Quarterly* 98, no. 4 (2001): 287–88.

———. "Uncovering Our Calling: Luther's Reformation Re-Emphasis on Christian Vocation." https://www.abidingpeace.org/home/140000215/140000215/files/Uncovering%20Our%20Calling.pdf.

Christianson, Eric S. *A Time to Tell: Narrative Strategies in Ecclesiastes*. JSOTSS 280. Sheffield: Sheffield Academic, 1998.

———. "Ecclesiastes in Premodern Reading." In *The Words of the Wise Are like Goads: Engaging Qohelet in the 21st Century*, edited by Mark J. Boda et al., 3–36. Winona Lake, IN: Eisenbrauns, 2013.

———. "Qoheleth and the Existential Legacy of the Holocaust." *HeyJ* 38, no. 1 (1997): 35-50. (1997): 35–50.

Cilliers, J. "The Absence of Presence: Homiletical Reflections on Luther's Notion of the Masks of God (*Larvae Dei*)." *Acta Theologica* 30, no. 2 (2010): 36–49.

Clifton, Jim. "The World's Broken Workplace." Gallup. June 13, 2017, https://news.gallup.com/opinion/chairman/212045/world-broken-workplace.aspx.

Clydesdale, Tim. *The Purposeful Graduate: Why Colleges Must Talk to Students about Vocation*. Chicago: University of Chicago Press, 2015.

Conquest, Robert. *Reflections on a Ravaged Century*. New York: W. W. Norton, 2000.

Conyers, A. J. *The Listening Heart: Vocation and the Crisis of Modern Culture*. Dallas: Spence, 2006.

Cosden, Darrell. *The Heavenly Good of Earthly Work*. Bletchley, UK: Paternoster and Hendrickson, 2006.

———. *A Theology of Work: Work and the New Creation*. PTM. Bletchley, UK: Paternoster, 2004.

Courtois, Stéphane, et al. *The Black Book of Communism: Crimes, Terror, Repression*. Translated by J. Murphy and M. Kramer. Cambridge: Harvard University Press, 1999.

Crenshaw, James L. *Ecclesiastes: A Commentary*. OTL. Philadelphia: Westminster, 1987.

———. "Ecclesiastes (Qoheleth)." In *Urgent Advice and Probing Questions: Collected Writings on Old Testament Wisdom*, 499–519. Macon: Mercer University Press, 1995.

———. *Old Testament Wisdom: An Introduction*. Rev. ed. Louisville: WJK, 1998.

Crosby, John F. "Education and the Mind Redeemed." *First Things* 18 (December 1991): 23–28.

Davidson, James C., and David P. Caddell. "Religion and the Meaning of Work." *Journal for the Scientific Study of Religion* 33, no. 2 (1994): 135–36.

de Jong, Stephan. "A Book on Labour: The Structuring Principles and the Main Theme of the Book of Qohelet." *JSOT* 54 (1992): 107–16.

DeKoster, Lester. *Work: The Meaning of Your Life: A Christian Perspective.* Grand Rapids: Christian's Library Press, 1982.

de Kruijf, Gerrit G. "The Christian in the Crowded Public Square: The Hidden Tension between Prophecy and Democracy." *Annual of the Society of Christian Ethics* 11 (1991): 21–42.

———. *Ethiek onderweg: Acht Adviezen.* Zoetermeer: Meinema, 2008.

———. "Is Prophetic Witness the Appropriate Mode of Christian Participation in Public Discourse in the Netherlands?" HTS *Teologiese Studies* 66, no. 1 (2010). https://hts.org.za/index.php/hts/article/view/781/1151.

Dell, Katherine J. *Interpreting Ecclesiastes: Readers Old and New.* Winona Lake, IN: Eisenbrauns, 2013.

———. "A Wise Man Reflecting on Wisdom: Qoheleth/Ecclesiastes." *Tyndale Bulletin* 71, no. 1 (2020): 137–52.

DeLoach, Albertus L. "The Concept of Work in Ecclesiastes." MST thesis, University of the South, 1972.

Dempster, Stephen G. "Ecclesiastes and the Canon." In *The Words of the Wise Are like Goads: Engaging Qohelet in the 21st Century*, edited by Mark J. Boda et al., 387–400. Winona Lake, IN: Eisenbrauns, 2013.

Deratany, Edward. *When God Calls You.* Nashville: Thomas Nelson, 1976.

Diehl, William E. *Christianity and Real Life.* Philadelphia: Fortress, 1976.

Dik, Bryan J., and Ryan D. Duffy. "Calling and Vocation at Work: Definitions and Prospects for Research and Practice." *The Counseling Psychologist* 37, no. 3 (2009): 424–50.

———. *Make Your Job a Calling: How the Psychology of Vocation Can Change Your Life at Work*. West Conshohocken, PA: Templeton Press, 2012.

Dillard, Raymond B., and Tremper Longman III. *An Introduction to the Old Testament*. Grand Rapids: Zondervan, 1994.

Dobrow, Shoshana R., and Jennifer Tosti-Kharas. "Calling: The Development of a Scale Measure." *Personnel Psychology* 64 (2011): 1001–49.

Doyle, Sir Arthur Conan. "The Sign of the Four." In *Working: Its Meaning and Its Limits*, edited by Gilbert C. Meilaender, 47–48. Notre Dame: University of Notre Dame Press, 2000.

Dreyer, Wim A. "The Priesthood of Believers: The Forgotten Legacy of the Reformation." *HTS Teologiese Studies* 76, no. 4 (2020), https://hts.org.za/index.php/hts/article/view/6021/16223.

Duffy, Ryan D., and William E. Sedlacek. "The Presence of and Search for a Calling: Connections to Career Development." *Journal of Vocational Behavior* 70, no. 3 (2007): 590–601.

Duncan, Julie Ann. *Ecclesiastes*. Abingdon Old Testament Commentary Series. Nashville: Abingdon, 2017.

Eaton, Michael A. *Ecclesiastes: An Introduction and Commentary*. TOTC. Leicester, UK: InterVarsity, 1983.

Edgar, William. *Created and Creating: A Biblical Theology of Culture*. Downers Grove, IL: IVP Academic, 2017.

Eliason, Eric J. "*Vanitas Vanitatum*: 'Piers Plowman,' Ecclesiastes, and Contempt of the World." Unpublished PhD diss., University of Virginia, 1989.

Ellis, Peter F. *The Men and the Message of the Old Testament*. Collegeville: Liturgical, 1963.

Ellul, Jacques. *The Ethics of Freedom*. Grand Rapids: Eerdmans, 1976.

———. *Reason for Being: A Meditation on Ecclesiastes*. Translated by Joyce M. Hanks. Grand Rapids: Eerdmans, 1990.

Ellul, Jacques, and David Lovekin. "From the Bible to a History of Non-Work." *Cross Currents* 35, no. 1 (1985): 43–48.

Enns, Peter. "The Contribution of Ecclesiastes to Biblical Theology." In *The Bible as a Human Witness to Divine Revelation: Hearing the Word of God through Historically Dissimilar Traditions*, edited by Randall Heskett and Brian Irwin, 185–201. New York: T&T Clark, 2010.

———. *Ecclesiastes*. Grand Rapids: Eerdmans, 2011.

Estes, Daniel J. *Handbook on the Wisdom Books and Psalms*. Grand Rapids: Baker Academic, 2005.

Eswine, Zack. *Recovering Eden: The Gospel According to Ecclesiastes*. Phillipsburg: P&R, 2014.

Farnham, Suzanne G., et al. *Listening Hearts: Discerning Call in Community*, Rev. ed. Harrisburg: Morehouse, 1991.

Fee, Gordon D., and Douglas Stuart. *How to Read the Bible for All Its Worth*. Grand Rapids: Zondervan, 1982.

Fox, Michael V. *Ecclesiastes*. JPS Bible Commentary. Philadelphia: The Jewish Publication Society, 2004.

———. "Frame Narrative and Composition in the Book of Qoheleth." *Hebrew Union College Annual* 48 (1977): 83–106.

———. *Qohelet and His Contradictions*. JSOTSup 71. Sheffield: Sheffield Academic, 1989.

———. *A Time to Tear Down and A Time to Build Up*. Grand Rapids: Eerdmans, 1999.

———. "Wisdom in Qohelet." In *In Search of Wisdom*, edited by Leo G. Perdue et al., 115–31. Louisville: WJK, 1993.

Frankl, Viktor E. *Man's Search for Meaning*. Boston: Beacon, 1959.

Fredericks, Daniel C. *Coping with Transience: Ecclesiastes on Brevity in Life*. Sheffield: JSOT Press, 1993.

———. "Preaching Qohelet." In *The Words of the Wise Are like Goads: Engaging Qohelet in the 21st Century*, edited by M. J. Boda et al., 417–42. Winona Lake, IN: Eisenbrauns, 2013.

Fredericks, Daniel C., and Daniel J. Estes. *Ecclesiastes and the Song of Songs*. AOTC 16. Nottingham, UK: Apollos and InterVarsity, 2010.

Frydrych, Tomaś. *Living under the Sun: Examination of Proverbs and Qoheleth.* VTSup 90. Leiden: Brill, 2002.

Fuerst, Wesley J. *The Books of Ruth, Esther, Ecclesiastes, the Song of Songs, Lamentations.* CBC. Cambridge: Cambridge University Press, 1975.

Fyfe, Douglas R. *Seeing What Qoheleth Saw: The Structure of Ecclesiastes as Alternating Panels of Observation and Wisdom.* Eugene, OR: Wipf & Stock, 2019.

Galles, Jacob A., and Janet G. Lenz. "Relationships among Career Thoughts, Vocational Identity, and Calling: Implications for Practice." *Career Development Quarterly* 61, no. 3 (2013): 240–48.

Genung, John Franklin. *Words of Koheleth.* Boston: Houghton, Mifflin, 1903.

Gericke, J. W. "Axiological Assumptions in Qoheleth: A Historical-Philosophical Clarification." *Verbum & Ecclesia* 33, no. 1 (2012): 1–6.

Gese, Helmut. "The Crisis of Wisdom in Koheleth." In *Theodicy in the Old Testament*, edited by James L. Crenshaw, 141–53. Philadelphia: Fortress and SPCK, 1983.

Gianto, Agustinus. "The Theme of Enjoyment in Qohelet." *Biblica* 73 (1992): 328–32.

Glasson, T. F. "'You Never Know': The Message of Ecclesiastes 11:1–6." *Evangelical Quarterly* 55, no. 1 (1983): 43–48.

Greene, Mark. "Preface." In *Transforming Vocation: Connecting Theology, Church, and the Workplace for a Flourishing World*, edited by David Benson et al., xiii–xxiii. Eugene, OR: Wipf & Stock, 2021.

Greidanus, Sidney. *Preaching Christ from Ecclesiastes.* Grand Rapids: Eerdmans, 2010.

Gutridge, Coralie Ann. "Wisdom, Anti-Wisdom, and the Ethical Function of Uncertainty: The Book of Qoheleth/Ecclesiastes in the Context of Biblical and Greek Wisdom Theory." PhD diss., University College London, 1998.

Hahnenberg, Edward P. *Awakening Vocation: A Theology of Christian Call.* Collegeville: Liturgical, 2010.

Hall, Douglas T., and Dawn E. Chandler. "Psychological Success: When the Career Is a Calling." *Journal of Organizational Behavior* 26 (2005): 155–76.

Hall, Stephen S. *Wisdom: From Philosophy to Neuroscience.* New York: Alfred A. Knopf, 2010.

Hardy, Lee. *The Fabric of This World: Inquiries into Calling, Career Choice, and the Design of Human Work.* Grand Rapids: Eerdmans, 1990.

Hauerwas, Stanley. "Work as Co-Creation: A Critique of a Remarkably Bad Idea." In *Co-Creation and Capitalism: John Paul II's Laborem Exercens*, edited by John Houck and Oliver Williams, 42–58. Washington, DC: University Press of America 1983.

Heiges, Donald R. *The Christian's Calling.* Philadelphia: Fortress, 1984.

Hendry, G. S. "Ecclesiastes." In *New Bible Commentary*, edited by Donald Guthrie and J. A. Motyer, 570–71. Rev. ed. Grand Rapids: Eerdmans, 1970.

Hengel, Martin. *Judaism and Hellenism: Studies in Their Encounter in Palestine During the Early Hellenistic Period.* 2 Volumes. Translated by John Bowden. Philadelphia: Fortress, 1974.

Henry, Matthew. *Matthew Henry's Commentary on the Whole Bible*, vol. 3, *Job to the Song of Solomon.* McLean, VA: MacDonald, 1710.

Hildebrandt, Franz. *Melanchthon: Alien or Ally?* Cambridge: Cambridge University Press, 1946.

Hill, R. Charles. *Wisdom's Many Faces.* Collegeville: Liturgical, 1996.

Hillman, Os. *The 9 to 5 Window: How Faith Can Transform the Workplace.* Ventura: Regal Books, 2005.

Hirschman, Marc. "The Greek Fathers and the Aggada on Ecclesiastes: Formats of Exegesis in Late Antiquity." *Hebrew Union College Annual* 59 (1988): 137–65.

Holm-Nielsen, Svend. "On the Interpretation of Qoheleth in Early Christianity." *Vetus Testamentum* 24, no. 2 (1974): 168–77.

Holmstedt, Robert D., et al. *Qoheleth: A Handbook on the Hebrew Text.* BHHB. Waco: Baylor University Press, 2017.

Horne, Milton F. *Proverbs-Ecclesiastes.* SHBC. Macon: Smyth & Helwys, 2003.

Hummel, Charles E. *Tyranny of the Urgent.* Rev. ed. Downers Grove, IL: InterVarsity, 1994.

Hunter, Archibald M. *The Parables Then and Now.* Philadelphia: Westminster, 1971.

Jensen, David H. *Responsive Labor: A Theology of Work.* Louisville: WJK, 2006.

Jenson, Robert W. "The Church's Responsibility for the World." In *The Two Cities of God: The Church's Responsibility for the Earthly City*, edited by Carl E. Braaten and Robert W. Jenson, 1–10. Grand Rapids: Eerdmans, 1997.

Jerome, St. *Commentary on Ecclesiastes*, edited and translated by Richard J. Goodrich and David J. D. Miller. New York: Newman, 2012.

John Paul II. *Laborem exercens.* Papal encyclical, September 14, 1981. https://www.vatican.va/content/john-paul-ii/en/encyclicals/documents/hf_jp-ii_enc_14091981_laborem-exercens.html.

———. *The Meaning of Vocation.* Princeton: Scepter, 1998.

———. Meeting with the Bishops of the United States of America (September 16, 1987). https://www.vatican.va/content/john-paul-ii/en/speeches/1987/september/documents/hf_jp-ii_spe_19870916_vescovi-stati-uniti.html.

———. *Salvifici Doloris.* Apostolic letter, February 11, 1984. https://www.vatican.va/content/john-paul-ii/en/apost_letters/1984/documents/hf_jp-ii_apl_11021984_salvifici-doloris.html.

Johnson, Raymond E. "The Rhetorical Question as a Literary Device in Ecclesiastes." PhD diss., The Southern Baptist Theological Seminary, 1986.

Joint Declaration on the Doctrine of Justification. The Lutheran World Federation and the Roman Catholic Church. Grand Rapids: Eerdmans, 2000.

Kaiser, Walter C., Jr. *Ecclesiastes: Total Life.* Chicago: Moody, 1979.

Kallas, Endel. "Ecclesiastes: *Traditum et fides evangelica:* The Ecclesiastes Commentaries of Martin Luther, Philip Melanchthon, and Johannes Brenz Considered within the History of the Interpretation." PhD diss., Graduate Theological Union, 1979.

Keller, Timothy, and Katherine Leary Alsdorf. *Every Good Endeavor: Connecting Your Work to God's Work.* New York: Riverhead Books, 2012.

Kidner, Derek. *A Time to Mourn, A Time to Dance.* Leicester, UK: InterVarsity, 1976.

———. *The Wisdom of Proverbs, Job and Ecclesiastes.* Leicester, UK: InterVarsity, 1985.

Kiel, Micah D. "Ecclesiastes." In *Wisdom, Worship, and Poetry,* edited by Gale A. Yee et al., 627–42. FCB. Minneapolis: Augsburg Fortress, 2016.

Kim, Jimyung. *Reanimating Qoheleth's Contradictory Voices.* Leiden: Brill, 2018.

Klein, Christian. *Kohelet und die Weisheit Israels.* BWANT 132. Stuttgart, Berlin: Kohlhammer, 1994.

Kleinhans, Kathryn. "The Work of a Christian: Vocation in Lutheran Perspective." *Word & World* 25, no. 4 (2005): 394–402.

Knapp, John C. *How the Church Fails Businesspeople (and What Can Be Done about It).* Grand Rapids: Eerdmans, 2012.

Knopf, Karl Sumner Knopf. "The Optimism of Koheleth." *Journal of Biblical Literature* 49, no. 2 (1930): 195–99.

Kolden, Marc. "Work and Meaning: Some Theological Reflections." *Interpretation* 48, no. 3 (1994): 262–71.

Kuyper, Abraham. *Common Grace: God's Gifts for a Fallen World.* 3 volumes. Edited by Jordan J. Ballor, Stephen J. Grabill, and J. Daryl Charles. Translated by Nelson D. Kloostermann and Ed van der Maas. Grand Rapids: Acton Institute and Lexham, 2015, 2019, 2020.

———. *Lectures on Calvinism.* Repr. Grand Rapids: Eerdmans, 1987.

———. "The Social Question and the Christian Religion." In *Makers of Modern Christian Social Thought: Leo XIII and Abraham Kuyper on the Social Question*, edited by Jordan J. Ballor, 47–117. Grand Rapids: Acton Institute, 2016.

Lane, Jason D. *Luther's Epistle of Straw: The Voice of St. James in Reformation Preaching.* HHSS 16. Berlin: Walter de Gruyter, 2018.

Lee, Eunny P. *The Vitality of Enjoyment in Qohelet's Theological Rhetoric.* BZAW 353. Berlin: Walter de Gruyter, 2005.

Lehmann, Karl, ed. *Justification by Faith: Do Sixteenth-Century Condemnations Still Apply?* Translated by Michael Root and William G. Rusch. New York: Continuum, 1997.

Lehmann, Karl, and Wolfhart Pannenberg, eds. *The Condemnations of the Reformation Era: Do They Still Divide?* Translated by Margaret Kohl. Minneapolis: Fortress, 1990.

Leider, Richard J. *The Power of Purpose: Find Meaning, Live Longer, Better.* 3rd ed. Oakland: Berrett-Koehler, 2015.

Leider, Richard J., and David A. Shapiro. *Work Reimagined: Uncover Your Calling.* San Francisco: Berrett-Koehler, 2015.

Lewis, C. S. "Good Work and Good Works." In *The World's Last Night.* New York: Harcourt Brace, 1952.

Lim, Steve, ed. *Your Call to Work and Missions.* Springfield, MO: Assemblies of God Seminary, 2015.

Lindberg, Carter. *Beyond Charity: Reformation Initiatives for the Poor.* Minneapolis: Fortress, 1993.

———. *The European Reformations.* 2nd ed. London: Wiley-Blackwell, 2010.

———. "Luther and the Common Chest." In *The Forgotten Luther: Reclaiming the Social-Economic Dimension of the Reformation*, edited by Carter Lindberg and Paul Wee, 9–29. Minneapolis: Lutheran University Press, 2016.

———. "Luther on a Market Economy." *Lutheran Quarterly* 30 (2016): 373–92.

Lindberg, Carter, and Paul Wee, eds. *The Forgotten Luther: Reclaiming Social-Economic Dimension of the Reformation.* Minneapolis: Lutheran University Press, 2016.

Loader, J. A. *Ecclesiastes: A Practical Commentary*. Text and Interpretation. Translated by J. Vriend. Grand Rapids: Eerdmans, 1986.

———. *Polar Structures in the Book of Qohelet*. BZAW 152. Berlin: Walter de Gruyter, 1979.

Loewe, Andreas, and Katharine R. Firth. "Martin Luther's 'Mighty Fortress.'" *Lutheran Quarterly* 32, no. 2 (2018): 125–45.

Loftin, R. Keith, and Trey Dimsdale, eds. *Work: Theological Foundations and Practical Implications*. London: SCM, 2018.

Lohfink, Norbert. *Qoheleth*. CC. Translated by Sean McEvenue. Minneapolis: Fortress Press, 2003.

———. "Qoheleth 5:17–19—Revelation by Joy." *Catholic Biblical Quarterly* 52, no. 4 (1990): 625–35.

Lohse, Bernhard. *Mönchtum und Reformation*. Göttingen: Vandenhoeck & Ruprecht, 1963.

Longman, Tremper, III. *The Book of Ecclesiastes*. NICOT. Grand Rapids: Eerdmans, 1998.

———. "The 'Fear of God' in the Book of Ecclesiastes." *Bulletin of Biblical Research* 25, no. 1 (2015): 13–21.

———. *The Fear of the Lord Is Wisdom: A Theological Introduction to Wisdom in Israel*. Grand Rapids: Baker Academic, 2017.

———. "Wisdom's Response to the Divine Initiative." *Ex Auditu* 30 (2014): 26–41.

Loy, David W. "Luther, Vocation, and the Search for Significance." *Lutheran Quarterly* 35 (2021): 50–72.

Luther, Martin. *Against the Robbing and Murdering Hordes of Peasants*. In *Luther's Works* Volume 46, edited by Robert C. Schultz, 49–55. Philadelphia: Fortress, 1967.

———. *The Babylonian Captivity of the Church*. In *Luther's Works* Volume 36, edited by Abdel Ross Wentz, 5–126. Philadelphia: Fortress, 1959.

———. *The Blessed Sacrament of the Holy and True Body of Christ, and the Brotherhoods*. In *Luther's Works* Volume 35, edited by E. Theodore Bachmann, 45–73. Philadelphia: Fortress, 1960.

———. *Disputation against Scholastic Theology*. In *Luther's Works* Volume 31, edited by Harold J. Grimm, 9–16. Philadelphia: Muhlenberg Press, 1957.

———. *Explanations of the Ninety-Five Theses. In Luther's Works* Volume 31, edited by Harold J. Grimm, 79–252. Philadelphia: Fortress, 1957.

———. *The Freedom of a Christian*. In *Luther's Works* Volume 31, edited by Harold J. Grimm, 79–252. Philadelphia: Fortress, 1957.

———. *The Judgment of Martin Luther on Monastic Vows*. In *Luther's Works* Volume 44, ed. James Atkinson, 251–400. Philadelphia: Fortress, 1966.

———. *The Large Catechism*. In *The Book of Concord*, edited and translated by Theodore G. Tappert, 357–461. Philadelphia: Fortress, 1959.

———. *Lectures on Deuteronomy*. In *Luther's Works* Volume 9, edited by Jaroslav Pelikan, 148. St. Louis: Concordia, 1960.

———. *Lectures on Genesis, Chapters 6–14*. In *Luther's Works* Volume 2, edited by Jaroslav Pelikan. St. Louis: Concordia, 1960.

———. *Lectures on Genesis, Chapters 15–20. Luther's Works* Volume 3, edited by Jaroslav Pelikan. St. Louis: Concordia, 1961.

———. *Lectures on Genesis, Chapters 21–25. Luther's Works* Volume 4, edited by Jaroslav Pelikan. St. Louis: Concordia, 1964.

———. *Lectures on Genesis, Chapters 31–37. Luther's Works* Volume 6, edited by Jaroslav Pelikan. St. Louis: Concordia, 1970.

———. *Lectures on Romans*. In *Luther's Works* Volume 25, edited by Hilton C. Oswald. St. Louis: Concordia, 1972.

———. *Ninety-Five Theses*. In *Luther's Works* Volume 31, edited by Harold J. Grimm, 25–33. Philadelphia: Muhlenberg Press, 1957.

———. *Notes on Ecclesiastes; Lectures on the Song of Solomon; Treatise on the Last Words of David*. In *Luther's Works* Volume 15, edited by Jaroslav Pelikan, 3–187. St. Louis: Concordia, 1972.

———. *Ordinance of a Common Chest*. In *Luther's Works* Volume 45, edited by Walther I. Brandt, 169–94. Philadelphia: Fortress, 1962.

———. "Preface to the Epistles of St. James and St. Jude." In *Luther's Works* Volume 35, edited by E. Theodore Bachmann, 395–98. Philadelphia: Muhlenberg Press, 1960.

———. *Prefaces to the New Testament.* In *Luther's Works* Volume 35, edited by E. Theodore Bachmann, 357–411. Philadelphia: Fortress, 1960.

———. *Psalm 147,* in *Luther's Works* Volume 14, ed. Jaroslav Pelikan, 109–35. St. Louis: Concordia, 1958.

———. *A Sermon on Keeping Children in School.* In *Luther's Works* Volume 46, edited by Robert C. Schultz, 213–58. Philadelphia: Fortress, 1967.

———. *The Sermon on the Mount and the Magnificat.* In *Luther's Works* Volume 21, edited by Jaroslav Pelikan. St. Louis: Concordia, 1956.

———. "Table Talk" (1542). In *Luther's Works* Volume 54, edited by Theodore G. Tappert, 424–25 and 434. Philadelphia: Fortress, 1967.

———. *Temporal Authority: To What Extent It Should Be Obeyed.* In *Luther's Works* Volume 45, edited by Walther I. Brandt, 81–129. Philadelphia: Fortress, 1962.

———. "To George Spalatin." In *Luther's Works* Volume 48, edited by Gottfried G. Krodel, 76–80. Philadelphia: Fortress, 1963.

———. "To Hans Luther." In *Luther's Works* Volume 48, edited by Gottfried G. Krodel, 329–36. Philadelphia: Fortress, 1963.

———. "To John Brenz." In *Luther's Works* Volume 49, edited by Gottfried G. Krodel, 177–80. Philadelphia: Fortress, 1972.

———. "To Philip Melanchthon." In *Luther's Works* Volume 48, edited by Gottfried G. Krodel, 277–82. Philadelphia: Fortress, 1963.

———. *To the Christian Nobility of the German Nation Concerning the Reform of the Christian Estate.* In *Luther's Works* Volume 44, edited by James Atkinson, 115–217. Philadelphia: Fortress, 1966.

———. *Trade and Usury.* In *Luther's Works* Volume 45, edited by Walther I. Brandt, 245–310. Philadelphia: Fortress, 1962.

———. *Treatise on Good Works.* In *Luther's Works* Volume 44, edited by James Atkinson, 21–114. Philadelphia: Fortress, 1955.

———. "Whether One May Flee from a Deadly Plague." In *Luther's Works*. Vol. 43. Edited by Gustav K. Wiencke, 119–38. Philadelphia: Fortress, 1968.

———. *Whether Soldiers, Too, Can Be Saved*. In *Luther's Works* Volume 46, edited by Robert C. Schultz, 93–137. Philadelphia: Fortress, 1967.

Lys, Daniel. *L'Ecclésiaste ou Que vaut la vie? Traduction; Introduction générale*. Commentaire de 1/1 à 4/3. Paris: Letouzey et Ané, 1977.

Lysova, Evgenia I., et al. "Calling and Careers: New Insights and Future Directions." *Journal of Vocational Behavior* 114 (2019): 1-6.

Magarik, Larry. "Darshnut: Bread on Water." *Jewish Bible Quarterly* 28, no. 4 (2000): 268–70.

Manschreck, Clyde L. *Melanchthon: The Quiet Reformer*. New York: Abingdon, 1958.

Marshall, Paul and Lela Gilbert. *Heaven Is Not My Home: Living in the Now of God's Creation*. Nashville: Word, 1998.

Massing, Michael. *Fatal Discord: Erasmus, Luther, and the Fight for the Western Mind*. New York: Harper, 2018.

Mazzinghi, Luca. "The Divine Violence in the Book of Qoheleth." *Biblical* 90, no. 4 (2009): 545–58.

McGrath, Alister. "Calvin and the Christian Calling." *First Things* 94 (June 1999): 31–35.

McIntosh, Mark A. "Trying to Follow a Call: Vocation and Discernment in Bunyan's *Pilgrim's Progress*." In *Revisiting the Idea of Vocation: Theological Explorations*, edited by John C. Haughey, 119–40. Washington, DC: The Catholic University of America Press, 2012.

McKenna, Robert B., et al. "Calling, the Caller, and Being Called: A Qualitative Study of Transcendent Calling." *Journal of Psychology and Christianity* 34, no. 4 (2015): 294–303.

Meilaender, Gilbert. *The Freedom of a Christian: Grace, Vocation, and the Meaning of Our Humanity*. Grand Rapids: Brazos, 2006.

———. "Friendship and Vocation." In *Leading Lives That Matter: What We Should Do and Who We Should Be*, edited by Mark R. Schwehn and Dorothy C. Bass, 204–7. Grand Rapids: Eerdmans, 2006.

———, ed. *Working: Its Meaning and Its Limits*. Notre Dame: University of Notre Dame Press, 2000.

Melanchthon, Philip. *Loci Communes* (1543). Translated by J.A.O. Preus. St. Louis: Concordia, 1992.

Miller, David W. *God at Work: The History and Promise of the Faith at Work Movement*. Oxford University Press, 2007.

Miller, Douglas B. *Symbol and Rhetoric in Ecclesiastes: The Place of Hebel in Qohelet's Work*. Atlanta: Society of Biblical Literature, 2002.

Mitchell, H. G. T. "'Work' in Ecclesiastes." *Journal of Biblical Literature* 32, no. 2 (1913): 123–38.

Moltmann, Jürgen. "Reformation and Revolution." In *Martin Luther and the Modern Mind: Freedom, Conscience, Toleration, Rights*, edited by Manfred Hoffman, 163–90. Toronto Studies in Theology 22. Lewiston: Edwin Mellen, 1985.

Mullet, Charles F. "Toleration and Persecution in England, 1660–89." *Church History* 18, no. 1 (1949): 18–43.

Murphy, Roland E. *Ecclesiastes*. WBC 23A. Dallas: Word, 1992.

———. *The Tree of Life: An Exploration of Biblical Wisdom Literature*. 3rd ed. Grand Rapids: Eerdmans, 2002.

Murray, John Courtney. *We Hold These Truths: Catholic Reflections on the American Proposition*. New York: Sheed and Ward, 1960.

Nash, Laura, and Scotty McLennan. *Church on Sunday, Work on Monday: The Challenge of Fusing Christian Values with Business Life*. San Francisco: Jossey-Bass, 2001.

Neafsey, John P. "Psychological Dimensions of the Discernment of Vocation." In *Revisiting the Idea of Vocation: Theological Exploration*, edited by John C. Haughey, 163–95. Washington, DC: The Catholic University of America Press, 2012.

Nelson, Tom. *Work Matters: Connecting Sunday Worship to Monday Work.* Wheaton: Crossway, 2011.

Neriya-Cohen, Nava. "Rashbam's Understanding of the Carpe Diem Passages in Qoheleth." *Revue des études juives* 175, nos. 1–2 (2016): 30–37.

Newbigin, Lesslie. *Trinitarian Doctrine for Today's Mission.* Repr. Carlisle, UK: Paternoster, 1998.

Niebuhr, Reinhold. "The Ethic of Jesus and the Social Problem." In *Love and Justice: Selections from the Shorter Writings of Reinhold Niebuhr*, edited by D. B. Robertson, 29–39. Louisville: WJK, 1957.

Noll, Mark. "What Lutherans Have to Offer Public Theology." *Lutheran Quarterly* 22 (2008): 125–36.

Noth, Martin, and David Winton Thomas, eds. *Wisdom in Israel and the Ancient Near East.* VTSup 3. Leiden: Brill, 1969.

Novak, Michael. *Business as a Calling: Work and the Examined Life.* New York: The Free Press, 1996.

———. "The Lay Task of Co-Creation." In *On Moral Business: Classical and Contemporary Resources for Ethics in Economic Life*, edited by Max L. Stackhouse et al., 903–8. Grand Rapids: Eerdmans, 1995.

O'Donnell, Douglas Sean. *The Beginning and End of Wisdom: Preaching Christ from the First and Last Chapters of Proverbs, Ecclesiastes, and Job.* Wheaton: Crossway, 2011.

O'Donovan, Oliver. *Resurrection and the Moral Order: An Outline for Evangelical Ethics.* Grand Rapids: Eerdmans, 1986.

O'Dowd, Ryan P. "Epistemology in Ecclesiastes: Remembering What It Means to Be Human." In *The Words of the Wise Are like Goads: Engaging Qohelet in the 21st Century*, edited by M. J. Boda et al., 195–218. Winona Lake, IN: Eisenbrauns, 2013.

Ogden, Graham S. *Ecclesiastes.* Sheffield: JSOT Press, 1987.

———. "Qoheleth XI.7–XII.8: Qoheleth's Summons to Enjoyment and Reflection." *JSOT* 34, no. 1 (1984): 27–38.

———. "Qoheleth's Use of the 'Nothing Is Better' Form." *Journal of Biblical Literature* 98, no. 3 (1979): 339–50.

———. "'Vanity' It Certainly Is Not." *The Bible Translator* 38, no. 3 (1987): 301–6.

Ogden, Graham S., and Lynell Zogbo. *A Handbook on Ecclesiastes*. New York: United Bible Society, 1997.

Packer, J. I. *Knowing God*. Rev. ed. Downers Grove, IL: InterVarsity, 1993.

Palmer, Parker J. *Let Your Life Speak: Listening to the Voice of Vocation*. San Francisco: Jossey-Bass, 2000.

Paterson, John. *The Book That Is Alive*. New York: Charles Scribner's Sons, 1954.

Paulson, Steven D. "Luther on the Hidden God." *Word & World* 19, no. 4 (1999): 363–71.

Pelikan, Jaroslav. "After the Monks—What?" *The Springfielder* 31, no. 3 (1967): 3–21.

Perdue, Leo G. *Wisdom and Creation: The Theology of Wisdom Literature*. Nashville: Abingdon, 1994.

Perry, T. A. *Dialogues with Kohelet: The Book of Ecclesiastes*. University Park: The Pennsylvania State University Press, 1993.

Peterson, Brian Neil. *Qoheleth's Hope: The Message of Ecclesiastes in a Broken World*. Lanham: Lexington Books/Fortress Academic, 2020.

Pippert, Rebecca Manley and Mark Mittelberg. *Out of the Saltshaker and into the World: Evangelism as a Way of Life*. 2nd ed. Downers Grove, IL: InterVarsity, 1999.

Placher, William C., ed. *Callings: Twenty Centuries of Christian Wisdom on Vocation*. Grand Rapids: Eerdmans, 2005.

Plantinga, Cornelius, Jr. *Not the Way It's Supposed to Be: A Breviary of Sin*. Grand Rapids: Eerdmans, 1995.

Preece, Gordon. "A Job and a Life: Reintegrating Faith, Home, and Work." *St. Mark's Review* (Spring 1998): 24–32.

Prince, Gerald. *Narratology: The Form and Functioning of Narrative*. Berlin: Mouton, 1982.

Pritchard, James B., ed. *The Ancient Near East Volume I: An Anthology of Texts and Pictures*. Princeton: Princeton University Press, 1958.

———, ed. *The Ancient Near East Volume II: A New Anthology of Texts and Pictures*. Princeton: Princeton University Press, 1975.

———, ed. *Ancient Near Eastern Texts Relating to the Old Testament*. 3rd ed. Princeton: Princeton University Press, 1969.

Provan, Iain. *Ecclesiastes, Song of Songs*. NIVAC. Grand Rapids: Zondervan, 2001.

———. "Fresh Perspectives on Ecclesiastes: 'Qohelet for Today.'" In *The Words of the Wise Are like Goads: Engaging Ecclesiastes in the 21st Century*, edited by M. J. Boda et al., 401–16. Winona Lake, IN: Eisenbrauns, 2013.

Rainey, A. F. "A Study of Ecclesiastes." *Concordia Theological Monthly* 35, no. 3 (1965): 148–57.

Reed, Esther D. *Good Works: Christian Ethics in the Workplace*. Waco: Baylor University Press, 2010.

Reines, C. W. "Koheleth on Wisdom and Wealth." *Journal of Jewish Studies* 5, no. 2 (1954): 80–84.

Richard, James William. *Philip Melanchthon: The Protestant Preceptor of Germany 1497–1560*. New York: Putnam, 1898.

Richards, Jay Wesley. "Be Fruitful and Multiply: Work and Anthropology." In *Work: Theological Foundations and Practical Implications*, edited by R. Keith Loftin and Trey Dimsdale, 110–26. London: SCM, 2018.

Rindge, Matthew S. "Mortality and Enjoyment: The Interplay of Death and Possessions in Qoheleth." *Catholic Biblical Quarterly* 73, no. 2 (2011): 265–80.

Roper, Leon A., and Alphonso Groenewald. "Job and Ecclesiastes as (Postmodern) Wisdom in Revolt." *HTS Teologiese Studies* 9, no. 1 (2012): 1–8.

Roper, Lindal. *Martin Luther: Renegade and Prophet*. New York: Random House, 2016.

Rössner, Philipp R. "Burying Money? Monetary Origins and Afterlives of Luther's Reformation." *History of Political Economy* 48, no. 2 (2016): 225–63.

———. *Deflation—Devaluation—Rebellion: Geld im Zeitalter der Reformation.* VSWB 219. Stuttgart: Franz Steiner Verlag, 2012.

———. "Martin Luther and the Making of the Modern Economic Mind." *International Review of Economics* 66 (2019): 233–48.

———. *Martin Luther: On Commerce and Usury (1524).* New York: Anthem, 2016.

Rotman, Marco. "Vocation in Theology and Psychology: Conflicting Approaches?" *Christian Higher Education* 16, nos. 1–2 (2017): 23–32.

Rudman, Dominic. *Determinism in the Book of Ecclesiastes.* JSOTSS 316; Sheffield: Sheffield Academic, 1999.

Runham, Nathan. "Why Did Luther *Not* Flee from the Deadly Plague?" *The Presbyterian Banner* (May 2020).

Ryan, J. J. "Humanistic Work: Its Philosophy and Cultural Implications." In *A Matter of Dignity: Inquiries into the Humanization of Work*, edited by William J. Heister and J. W. Houck, 11–22. Notre Dame: University of Notre Dame Press, 1977.

Ryken, Leland. "Ecclesiastes." In *A Complete Literary Guide to the Bible*, edited by Leland Ryken and Tremper Longman III, 268–80. Grand Rapids: Zondervan, 1993.

———. *Words of Delight: A Literary Introduction to the Bible.* Grand Rapids: Baker, 1992.

Rylaarsdam, J. Coert. *Revelation in Jewish Wisdom Literature.* Chicago: University of Chicago Press, 1946.

Sayers, Dorothy L. "The Dogma Is the Drama." In *Creed or Chaos? Why Christians Must Choose Either Dogma or Disaster; or, Why It Really Does Matter What You Believe*, 29–36. Repr. Manchester: Sophia Institute Press, 1974.

———. "The Greatest Drama Ever Staged." In *Creed or Chaos? Why Christians Must Choose Either Dogma or Disaster; or, Why It Really Does Matter What You Believe*, 5–13. Repr. Manchester: Sophia Institute Press, 1974.

———. *Lord Peter: The Complete Lord Peter Wimsey Stories.* New York: Harper & Row, 1972.

———. *The Mind of the Maker.* New York: Harcourt Brace, 1941.

———. "Why Work?" In *Creed or Chaos? Why Christians Must Choose Either Dogma or Disaster; or, Why It Really Does Matter What You Believe*, 89–116. Repr. Manchester: Sophia Institute Press, 1974.

Schaff, Philip, ed. *The Nicene and Post-Nicene Fathers.* Series I, Volume VI. Buffalo: Christian Literature, 1888.

Schilling, Heinz. *Martin Luther: Rebel in an Age of Upheaval.* Translated by Rona Johnston Gordon. Oxford: Oxford University Press, 2017.

Scholes, Jeffery. "Vocation." *Religion Compass* 4, no. 4 (2010): 211–20.

Schultze, Quentin J. *Here I Am: Now What on Earth Should I Be Doing?* Grand Rapids: Baker Books, 2005.

Schuurman, Douglas J. "Creation, Eschaton, and Social Ethics: A Response to Volf." *Calvin Theological Journal* 30, no. 1 (1995): 144–58.

———. *Vocation: Discerning Our Callings in Life.* Grand Rapids: Eerdmans, 2004.

Schwiebert, E. G. *Luther and His Times: The Reformation from a New Perspective.* St. Louis: Concordia, 1950.

Scott, R. B. Y. *Proverbs, Ecclesiastes.* AB. Garden City: Doubleday, 1965.

———. "Wisdom in Revolt: Agur and Qoheleth." In *The Way of Wisdom in the Old Testament*, 165–89. New York: Macmillan, 1971.

Segni, Losarío dei (Pope Innocent III). *De miseria condicionis humane*, edited and translated by Robert E. Lewis. Athens: University of Georgia Press, 1978.

Shead, Andrew G. "Reading Ecclesiastes Epilogically." *Tyndale Bulletin* 48, no. 1 (1997): 67–91.

Shelly, Judith Allen. *Not Just a Job: Serving Christ in Your Work.* Downers Grove, IL: InterVarsity, 1985.

Sherman, Amy L. *Kingdom Calling: Vocational Stewardship for the Common Good.* Downers Grove, IL: InterVarsity, 2011.

Sherman, Doug, and William Hendricks. *Your Work Matters to God.* Colorado Springs: NavPress, 1987.

Shields, Martin A. "Ecclesiastes and the End of Wisdom." *Tyndale Bulletin* 50, no. 1 (1999): 117–39.

———. *The End of Wisdom: A Reappraisal of the Historical and Canonical Function of Ecclesiastes.* Winona Lake, IN: Eisenbrauns, 2006.

Smalley, Beryl. "Some Thirteenth-Century Commentaries on the Sapiential Books." *Dominican Studies* 2–3 (1949/1950): 41–77, 236–74.

Smith, Gordon T. *Courage and Calling: Embracing Your God-Given Potential.* Downers Grove, IL: InterVarsity, 1999.

———. *Listening to God in Times of Choice: The Art of Discerning God's Will.* Downers Grove, IL: InterVarsity, 1997.

Smith, L. Lowell. "A Critical Evaluation of the Book of Ecclesiastes." *Journal of Bible and Religion* 21, no. 2 (1953): 100–105.

Sneed, Mark R. "A Note on Qoh 8,12b-13." *Biblica* 84, no. 3 (2003): 412–16.

———. *The Politics of Pessimism in Ecclesiastes: A Social-Scientific Perspective.* Atlanta: Society of Biblical Literature, 2012.

———, ed. *Was There a Wisdom Tradition? New Prospects in Israelite Studies.* Atlanta: Society of Biblical Literature, 2015.

Spangenberg, I. J. J. "Irony in the Book of Qohelet." *JSOT* 72 (1996): 57–69.

Spitz, Lewis W. "Luther's Social Concern for Students." In *The Social History of the Reformation*, ed. Lawrence P. Buck and Jonathan W. Zophy, 249–70. Columbus: Ohio State University Press, 1972.

Stackhouse, Max. "Vocation." In *The Oxford Handbook of Theological Ethics*, edited by Gilbert Meilaender and William Werpehowski, 189–204. Oxford: Oxford University Press, 2005.

Steenbarger, Brett. "Why Your Career Is Not Your Calling." *Forbes*, December 6, 2015. https://www.forbes.com/sites/brettsteenbarger/2015/12/06/why-your-career-is-not-your-calling/?sh=111c108c62cf.

Steenkamp-Nel, Annalie E. "Transformative Joy in Qohelet: A Thread That Faintly Glistens." *HTS Teologiese Studies* 75, no. 3 (2019). https://hts.org.za/index.php/hts/article/view/5126.

Steger, Michael F., et al. "Calling in Work: Secular or Sacred?" *Journal of Career Assessment* 18, no. 1 (2010): 82–96.

Steinwachs, Albrecht. "The Common Chest as a Social Achievement of the Reformation." *Lutheran Quarterly* 22, no. 2 (2008): 192–95.

Stevens, R. Paul. *Doing God's Business: Meaning and Motivation for the Workplace*. Grand Rapids: Eerdmans, 2006.

———. *The Other Six Days: Vocation, Work, and Ministry in Biblical Perspective*. Grand Rapids: Eerdmans, 2000.

Stupperich, Robert. *Melanchthon: The Enigma of the Reformation*. Translated by Robert H. Fischer. Philadelphia: Westminster, 1965.

Taylor, John W. "Labor of Love: The Theology of Work in First and Second Thessalonians." *Southwestern Journal of Theology* 59, no. 2 (Spring 2017): 201–18.

Tertullian. *The Prescription against Heretics*. In *The Ante-Nicene Fathers*, edited by Alexander Roberts and James Donaldson, 243–65. Repr. Grand Rapids: Eerdmans, 1968.

Thomas à Kempis, *The Imitation of Christ*. Translated by L. Sherley-Price. London: Penguin, 1976.

Torvend, Samuel. *Luther and the Hungry Poor: Gathered Fragments*. Minneapolis: Fortress, 2008.

Treu, Martin. "Katherina von Bora: The Woman at Luther's Side." *Lutheran Quarterly* 13 (1999): 157–78.

Trueblood, Elton. *Your Other Vocation*. New York: Harper & Bros., 1952.

Ukpong, Justin. "The Parable of the Talents (Matt 25:14–30): Commendation or Critique of Exploitation? A Social-Historical and Theological Reading." *Neotestamentica* 46, no. 1 (2012) 190–207.

Ullendorff, Edward. "The Meaning of *qhlt*." *Vetus Testamentum* 12, no. 2 (1962): 215.

Van Leeuwen, Raymond. "In Praise of Proverbs." In *Pledges of Jubilee: Essays on the Arts and Culture*, edited by Lambert Zuidervaart and Henry Luttikhuizen, 308–27. Grand Rapids: Eedmans, 1995.

Veith, Gene Edward, Jr. *God at Work: Your Christian Vocation in All of Life*. Wheaton: Crossway, 2002.

———. "Martin Luther on Vocation and Serving Our Neighbors." https://www.acton.org/pub/commentary/2016/03/30/martin-luther-vocation-and-serving-our-neighbors.

———. "Vocation: The Theology of the Christian Life." *Journal of Markets and Morality* 14, no. 1 (Spring 2011): 119–31.

Volf, Miroslav. *Work in the Spirit: Toward a Theology of Work*. Oxford: Oxford University Press, 2001.

Von Hoogstraten, Hans Dirk. "Reclaiming the Concept of Calling." In *Finding Meaning in Business: Theology, Ethics, and Vocation*, edited by Bartholomew C. Okonkwo, 13–20. New York: Palgrave Macmillan, 2012.

Von Rad, Gerhard. *Old Testament Theology Volume I*. Translated by D. M. G. Walker. New York: Harper & Row, 1962.

———. *Wisdom in Israel*. Translated by James D. Martin. New York: Abingdon, 1972.

Waalkes, Scott. "Rethinking Work as Vocation: From Protestant Advice to Gospel Corrective." *Christian Scholar's Review* 44, no. 2 (Winter 2015): 135–54.

Walsh, Brian J., and J. Richard Middleton. *The Transforming Vision: Shaping a Christian World View*. Downers Grove, IL: InterVarsity, 1984.

Walsh, Jerome T. "Despair as a Theological Virtue in the Spirituality of Ecclesiastes." *Biblical Theology Bulletin* 12 (1982): 46–49.

Watson, Francis. *Text, Church and World: Biblical Interpretation in Theological Perspective*. Edinburgh: T&T Clark, 1994.

Webb, Barry G. *Christian Reflections on the Song of Songs, Ruth, Lamentations, Ecclesiastes, and Esther*. Nottingham, UK: InterVarsity, 2000.

Weber, Lauren. "Forget Going Back to the Office—People Are Just Quitting Instead." *Wall Street Journal*, June 13, 2021. https://www.wsj.com/articles/forget-going-back-to-the-officepeople-are-just-quitting-instead-11623576602.

Welchel, Hugh. *How Then Should We Work?: Rediscovering the Biblical Doctrine of Work*. Bloomington: Westbow, 2012.

Wells, Cynthia A. "Finding the Center as Things Fly Apart: Vocation and the Common Good." In *At This Time and in This Place: Vocation and Higher Education*, edited by David S. Cunningham, 47–71. Oxford: Oxford University Press, 2016.

Westermann, Claus. *Roots of Wisdom: The Oldest Proverbs of Israel and Other Peoples*. Translated by J. Daryl Charles. Louisville: WJK, 1995.

Whybray, R. Norman. *Ecclesiastes*. OTG. Repr. Sheffield: Sheffield Academic, 1997.

———. *The Good Life in the Old Testament*. London: T&T Clark, 2002.

———. "Qoheleth, Preacher of Joy." *JSOT* 23 (1982): 87–98.

Williams, D. H. "Protestantism and the Vocation of Higher Education." In *Revisiting the Idea of Vocation: Theological Explorations*, edited by John C. Haughey, 141–62. Washington, DC: The Catholic University of America Press, 2012.

Williams, James G. "What Does It Profit a Man? The Wisdom of Koheleth." In *Studies in Ancient Israelite Wisdom*, edited by James L. Crenshaw, 375–89. New York: KTAV, 1976.

Wilson, Gerald H. "'The Words of the Wise': The Intent and Significance of Qohelet 12:9–14." *Journal of Biblical Literature* 103, no. 2 (1984): 175–92.

Wingren, Gustaf. *Luther on Vocation*. Translated by Carl C. Rasmussen. Philadelphia: Muhlenberg, 1957.

Wolters, Albert M. *Creation Regained: Biblical Basics for a Reformational Worldview*, 2nd ed. Grand Rapids: Eerdmans, 2005 (1985).

———. "Ecclesiastes and the Reformers." In *The Words of the Wise Are like Goads: Engaging Qohelet in the 21st Century*, edited by Mark J. Boda et al., 55–68. Winona Lake, IN: Eisenbrauns, 2013.

Wright, J. Robert, ed. *Ancient Christian Commentary on Scripture Volume IX: Proverbs, Ecclesiastes, Song of Songs*. Downers Grove, IL: InterVarsity, 2005.

SUBJECT INDEX

A

active life, 5, 68, 107, 160
Acts 6, 10
agriculture, 267, 269
Albrecht of Brandenburg, 144
alienation, 59, 73–74, 136
allegory, 93, 165
almsgiving, 109, 149–50, 155
Alsdorf, Katherine Leary, 61, 93
Anabaptists, 20–21, 138, 161
ancient Near East and wisdom, 164–66
Anderson, William H. U., 192
animals, 61, 166
anxiety, 64, 83, 131–34, 184, 195, 201, 221, 250, 277
Aristotle, 41, 67–68, 107, 224, 263
attentiveness, 250, 252, 259
Augustine, 26, 51, 107, 113, 124

B

Babylonian Captivity of the Church, The (Luther), 43–44, 112, 122
begging, 150, 153–55, 161
Bellah, Robert, 54–55

Benne, Robert, 274–76
Bible, 9, 22, 28, 37–38, 70, 170–71, 174, 198, 246. *See* Scripture
Blickle, Renate, 154
body, 31, 38, 62, 106, 124, 200, 224, 263
body of Christ, 37, 52, 99, 110, 239, 242, 253, 255, 258, 263–64, 272, 277
brotherhoods, 153–55
Brunner, Emil, 162
bubonic plague, 140–42
Bunyan, John, 231, 246
Bushnell, Horace, 262

C

calling
    Calvin on, 159–62
    chooses us, 233
    to Christ, 229–30
    everyday life, 127–28
    general and specific, 229–32
    and human need, 243
    individuality, 137–38
    jobs, 100

Luther on, 49, 68, 73, 109–10, 126–27, 135–37, 158–62, 224, 241
and marketplace, 22, 27, 53, 217, 241
and missions, 227–28
New Testament, 242
Novak, 217
and providence, 211–12, 221, 224, 231, 242
and religion, 213–14
secularization, 213, 225
and theological education, 11–14
and work, 2–3, 6–7, 29, 52, 55, 186, 210–12, 216, 226
and workplace, 9–11, 15, 60, 84–85
as worship, 16
Calvin, John, 42, 45, 68, 111, 127, 135, 159–62, 237, 241, 263
Catechism of the Catholic Church, 88, 239, 273
Catholic social teaching, 238
Centesimus annus, 239
Cherney, Kenneth, 10, 156, 215
Christian community, 9, 12, 22, 51–52, 55, 82, 84, 89, 91, 111, 234, 253, 262–63, 271–72
Christianity
  and culture, 25
  and Ecclesiastes, 206–8
  and marketplace, 10
  ordinary life, 161
  private, 7
  social witness, 81
  stewardship, 25–26
  vocation, 52–53
  and Wisdom literature, 167–68
  work, 31–33
  and world, 38
church
  commission, 37
  and culture, 5
  and FAW, 102
  and marketplace, 1–5
  mother, 263
  and public opinion, 4–5
  redemption, 26
  reformation, 33
  secular vocation, 4
  social ethic, 23
  and society, 21
  and spiritual life, 6–7
  vocation, 27
  and work, 1–4
  and world, 7–8
church-centeredness, 15
church fathers, 117, 124
Church on Sunday, Work on Monday (Nash and McLennan), 12
clergy, 1, 3, 5, 51, 106, 110, 225, 238–39
clergy-laity distinction, 105, 238
common good, 10, 21, 54, 62, 76, 86, 99, 133, 135–36, 139, 143, 149, 156, 158, 160–61, 219, 233–34, 239, 243, 264, 269, 272–75, 277
common grace, 25, 39, 66, 74, 79, 91, 129, 167, 196
communism, 31–32, 103
community, 9–13, 22, 28, 51–52, 55, 82, 84, 89, 91, 110–11, 143, 151, 154, 225, 234, 253, 261–64, 268, 271–73
Conquest, Robert, 32
contemplative life, 5, 68, 107, 160
Courtois, Stéphane, 32
creation
  ancient Near Eastern accounts, 62
  and Christ, 24–26
  co-creation, 72–73
  dignity, 78
  and God, 34–35
  goodness, 39
  humanity, 33–34

and labor, 9
Luther, 122
mandate, 16
misuse, 123
narrative, 7–8
new, 91
priests of, 36
and social ethic, 22
stewardship, 7–8
theology of, 8
and vocation, 236
and work, 33–34
creativity, 61, 86, 91, 98, 160, 200
Creator, 5–6, 9, 34, 63, 81, 88, 90–91, 124, 131, 166, 173, 176–78, 181–82, 184, 186, 191, 200, 202, 205, 209, 219–20, 240–41, 250, 268
Cultural Commission, 36
culture
    accommodation, 92–93
    ancient Near Eastern, 63
    and Christianity, 25
    cultural mandate, 25, 88, 91
    and church, 5
    and faith, 24
    and humanity, 89
    and incarnation, 91
    and Marxism, 31
    and stewardship, 17
    and work, 27
curse, 9, 16, 33–35, 58, 68–69, 89, 173, 179, 208

D

de Kruijf, Gerrit G., 71, 77–79
desires, 115, 200, 218–19, 221, 249, 255–56, 260–61
development, 2–3, 11, 72, 74, 86, 89, 100, 102, 105, 109, 139, 143, 147, 150, 228, 234, 239, 273–74
discernment, 29, 49–50, 62, 166–68, 173, 218, 230–32, 246–47, 250–52, 255, 257, 261–63, 266–67, 269
discipleship, 11, 21, 48, 138, 222, 244–46
doctrine, 15–16, 22–24, 26–27, 29, 34, 36, 38, 44, 48–50, 52, 64, 66, 74–75, 89–91, 96, 109–10, 118, 125, 127, 133, 156, 158, 164, 196, 207–8, 212, 214–16, 220, 226–27, 235, 238, 241–42. *See* theology
dualism, 3, 14, 22, 106–7, 215, 224, 237–38

E

eating and drinking, 124–25, 191, 193
Ecclesiastes
    author, 114, 121, 171–72
    carpe diem, 184, 198–99
    catchwords, 174–75
    Christianized reading, 206–8
    contentment, 173, 177–78, 181, 183, 185–86, 190, 193, 195, 197, 199, 201, 204–5, 210
    death, 174, 183–84, 187, 193, 196, 198, 200, 268–69
    discernment, 173
    double theme, 179
    enjoyment, 98, 125, 130–31, 175, 179, 181, 183, 185, 187–91, 194, 197, 202–3, 210
    and *Epic of Gilgamesh*, 199
    fearing God, 130, 183, 188, 204–6, 208, 235, 237, 268
    God, 180–86
    hebel, 173–75, 183, 188, 193, 198, 200–201, 208
    and humanity, 177–78
    interpretation, 115–16
    juxtaposition, 171–72, 176
    life, 168–70, 172–73, 176, 178–79, 181–88, 190–95, 197–200, 202–7, 209, 219
    Luther, 114–45
    meaninglessness, 85, 169, 172–79, 183, 186–88, 190, 193,

198–204, 210–11, 235, 240, 260, 268
nothing better, 190–92
portion/allotment, 125–26, 175, 183, 186, 189, 193, 195, 198, 211–12
providence, 131–32, 173, 211–12
purpose, 176–77, 192, 195–96, 202–3, 205–6, 208, 211–12, 219–20, 222, 235, 246, 268
relevance, 209
scholarship, 169–71
shifts, 178
two approaches to reality, 168–69
vanity, 29, 70, 115–16, 119–20, 124, 134, 164, 174, 177, 188, 190
and Wisdom literature, 164
work, 28, 123–24, 130, 132, 134, 175, 177–79, 182–86, 189–91, 193, 197–98, 202–5, 208, 210–11
education, 1, 11, 13, 53, 137, 140, 147, 150–51, 157, 215, 221, 225, 249, 259–60, 265, 273
Ellul, Jacques, 66–67, 69–71, 189, 214
employment, 1, 87, 243, 265. *See* workplace
eschatology, 19, 73–74, 77, 82
ethic, 8, 22–24, 51, 60, 66, 76, 144
evangelicalism, 6, 140
evangelistic reductionism, 10
evangelization, 10
exploitation, 33, 97

F

faith
and culture, 24
and justification, 40
Old Testament saints, 46
and works, 40–41
faithfulness, 19, 22, 39, 92, 94–95, 97, 203
FAW, 100–102
foreign culture living, 266
Frankl, Viktor, 83–85
Frederick the Wise, 147–48
freedom, 46, 48–49, 61, 84, 91, 99, 103, 109, 112, 123, 132, 137, 142, 159, 184, 199, 219–20, 229, 235, 264
fulfillment, 64, 80, 87, 226, 239–40, 243–44, 272

G

Genesis, 7, 18, 33, 35–36, 61–62, 64, 69, 77, 118, 155, 179–80, 193, 269
genre, Wisdom literature, 164–69, 208–9
Gideon's fleece, 222, 253–54
gift(s), 21, 27, 45, 48, 52, 64, 66, 70, 80, 86, 88–89, 95–96, 98–99, 110, 115, 122, 124, 126, 129, 131, 134, 151, 162, 169, 174–75, 178–79, 181–82, 185–86, 190–92, 194–95, 200, 202–5, 208–13, 232, 236, 240, 243, 255, 258–60
God
character, 236
and creation, 34–35
and discernment, 255
Ecclesiastes, 180–86
and evil, 195–96
fear of, 130, 166, 183, 188, 204–6, 208, 235, 237, 268
goodness, 195–96
hiddenness, 128–29, 131, 208
and humanity, 35
initiative, 250
inscrutability, 29, 128, 131, 173, 182, 193, 197, 206–8, 211, 246
and joy, 132, 194
likeness, 69
Luther, 111, 130
mystery, 182–83, 196–97, 206, 223, 246, 250, 277
Old Testament, 61
providence, 25, 78, 132, 192, 246

sovereignty, 163, 197, 208, 211, 219, 221
speaks, 249–51
and suffering, 244
vocation, 111
will, 133
Wisdom literature, 63–64
work, 62–63, 69, 186
grace, 25, 35, 39, 41, 45, 49, 66, 74, 79, 91, 99, 109, 112, 120, 129, 131–34, 142, 153, 159, 167, 195–96, 208, 223, 242, 259. *See also* common grace
graduation, 27, 57, 85, 231, 242–43
Great Commission, 35
Greek culture, 67
ground, creation and, 33
guidance, 29, 220, 222–23, 247, 249–50, 252–53, 255, 258, 262–63, 267

H

Hahnenberg, Edward, 49, 106, 108
Hardy, Lee, 53 54, 67
Hauerwas, Stanley, 22, 71–73, 214
holiness, 105–6, 108, 111, 125, 131, 153, 223, 229
Holmes, Sherlock, 59
holy secularity, 275, 277
How to Read the Bible for All Its Worth (Fee and Stuart), 170–71
humanity
  and creation, 33–34
  and culture, 89
  and divine sovereignty, 219
  Ecclesiastes, 177–79
  and God, 35
  likeness of God, 69
  limitations, 177–78, 183–84, 186, 197, 203, 205–8, 218–19, 221
  and providence, 235–36
  redemption of work, 39
  sociality, 263–64
  stewardship, 33

vocation, 49–55
work, divine mandate, 61–62
humility, 25, 259
Hummel, Charles, 237

I

identity, 19–20, 49, 63, 113, 234, 239–41
image of God, 9, 35, 54, 68–69, 89, 168, 193, 233, 239, 256, 261, 263, 269, 272–73. *See next entry*
imago Dei, 16, 33–35, 53, 68–69, 72, 74, 88, 90, 193, 227, 235
incarnation, 81, 89–92, 129, 227, 235–36
individualism, 21, 54, 239–40
indulgences, 143–45, 153
inner person, 251, 256–57
inner voice, 256–57
Innocent III (pope), 119–20
Institutes of the Christian Religion (Calvin), 159
interpretation, biblical, 123
Israel, 18, 65, 94, 128, 164–66, 203, 253–54

J

James, book of, 40–47, 52, 140, 208
Jensen, David, 64
Jerome, 114–19, 121, 124–25, 172
Jerusalem and Athens, 81
Jesus Christ
  calling to, 229–31
  and creation, 24–26
  and human need, 244
  and James, 45–46
  lordship, 25–26, 36, 227–28
  resurrection, 8, 91, 227
  and stewardship, 47–48
  timing, 267
  work, 65
  and works, 45–46
  and world, 8

Job, 165, 205, 209, 245
John Paul II (pope), 7, 27, 72, 157, 226, 239, 245–46
John XXIII (pope), 239
Judeo-Christian tradition, 60, 64, 204, 219
judgment, 26, 46–47, 49, 173–74, 181–82, 193, 200, 208
justification, 43, 45, 51, 109, 123, 133, 140, 153, 156–57, 215, 229, 238

K

Keller, Timothy, 61, 93
Kolden, Marc, 76
Kuyper, Abraham, 27, 51, 78–79, 101

L

labor, 5, 9, 31, 33–34, 39, 52, 60–62, 64, 66–67, 69–70, 72, 76–77, 88, 114, 116, 118–19, 121, 125, 130, 169, 172, 174–75, 178–84, 186, 190–95, 197, 199, 201, 203–5, 210–11, 213, 226–27, 230, 238, 276. *See* work
Laborem Exercens, 72, 226, 239
laity, 3, 5, 7, 51, 102, 105–6, 228, 238. *See also* clergy-laity distinction
language study, 265
Lectures on Genesis (Luther), 43, 137, 155
Lee, Eunny P., 185, 188
Leider, Richard J., 80, 220, 256
Leo XIII (pope), 72, 101
Lewis, C. S., 65
lifeboat theology, 39
Lindberg, Carter, 152
listening, 209, 245, 250–52, 255–57, 262–63
love, 8, 45, 75, 83, 111, 113, 120, 130, 135, 137–39, 142–43, 149–50, 154, 157–58, 161–62, 183, 198, 202, 218, 224, 233, 241, 246, 261, 274–76
Luther, Martin, 29, 40–46, 51, 68, 72–73, 108–15, 119–62, 164, 214–16, 223–25, 238, 275
  calling, 109–10
  and Catholic Church, 157
  and change, 108, 139, 148, 159
  common chest, 149–51
  common good, 135–36, 139, 143, 149, 156, 158, 161
  creation, 122
  Ecclesiastes, 114–16, 121–34
  and economics, 145–47
  freedom, 112
  James, book of, 40–46
  justification, 40
  natural law, 158
  political authority, 135
  providence, 131–32, 136, 161
  relevance, 157–59
  social concern, 43
  social mobility, 139
  and status quo, 139
  vocation, 110–12
  and wealth, 145
  work, 108–14
  works, 40–43

M

marketplace
  calling, 53
  and Christianity, 10
  and church, 1–5
  literature, 16–18
  mission, 37
  stewardship, 21–22
Marshall, Paul, 39
Marxism, 31–32, 54, 67, 73–74, 77, 88, 136
Mary and Martha, 107–8, 160
mask of God, 127–29

Mater et Magistra, 239
McGrath, Alister, 127, 160
meaning, 27, 46, 48, 54–55, 58, 60, 62, 64, 69–70, 79–80, 83–88, 100, 105, 159, 163, 172–73, 176–77, 181, 188, 190, 199, 202, 204, 208–9, 220, 225, 230, 235, 238–41, 244, 266, 275
medieval era, 54, 67, 93, 105, 108, 115–16, 121
Meilaender, Gilbert, 224
Melanchthon, Philip, 42–45, 115, 126, 140, 148, 151, 155
mendicant orders, 154–55
Miller, David W., 14, 100–102
ministry, 3, 5–6, 10–12, 14, 21, 27, 58, 65, 92, 102, 110
missions, 33, 35, 37, 52, 215, 228
Moltmann, Jürgen, 156, 215
monasticism, 51, 108, 113–14, 121, 161, 223

N

natural law, 46, 97, 158
needs, human, 62, 233, 240, 243
neighbor, 45–46, 68, 88, 99, 110–13, 127, 130, 133, 135, 137, 141, 143, 149, 154, 158, 161–62, 224–25, 228, 233, 238, 243, 275
Network for Vocation in Undergraduate Education (NetVUE), 11–12
Newbigin, Lesslie, 227–28
New Testament
 calling, 242
 canon, 40, 43, 46
 futility, 208
 and hierarchy, 5
 and Old Testament, 36
 rewards, 47–48
 wisdom, 208
 work, 66

and works, 47–49
and world, 8–9
Niebuhr, Reinhold, 75
Ninety-Five Theses (Luther), 143–44
Noll, Mark, 139–40
Notes on Ecclesiastes (Luther), 114–15, 123, 131, 159, 164
Novak, Michael, 73, 217–18

O

Oikonomia Network, 11
Old Testament
 God, 61–63
 and New Testament, 36
 reward, 194
 Wisdom literature, 165
 work, 184
"On Monastic Vows" (Luther), 112–13
On Trading and Usury (Luther), 144–45
open doors, 268
ordered liberty, 272
Ordinance of a Common Chest, An (Luther), 144, 149
Origen, 124

P

Palmer, Parker, 256
parables, 47–48, 93–99, 130, 165
 parable of the dishonest manager, 97–98
 parable of the talents, 93–99
parenting, 218–19
pastors, 3, 10, 12, 14–15, 25, 163, 245. *See* clergy
Paul, apostle, 8–9, 36, 40–48, 52, 62, 73, 88, 90, 92, 99, 123, 135, 145, 158, 180, 186, 201, 204, 207–8, 241–42, 257–58, 262, 268–69
Pilgrim's Progress, 93, 222, 231, 234, 246

Placher, William, 67
plan, 34, 133, 220–21, 254, 262
Plantinga, Cornelius, 35
Platonism, 106, 224
poverty, 10, 107–8, 111, 113, 142, 145, 150, 152–55
priesthood of all believers, 6, 13, 51, 109–10, 126–27, 150–51, 158, 164, 216, 223, 238, 275
Programs for the Theological Exploration of Vocation (PTEV), 11, 215
Protestantism
   mainline, 20
   teachings, 50
   and vocation, 105
   and work, 6
psychology, 19, 50, 214–15, 218, 239–41, 255–57
purpose, 2, 8–9, 11, 13, 25, 28, 34–35, 39, 43, 45, 48, 50, 60, 62, 64, 68, 77, 79–80, 82, 84–86, 89, 93, 123, 128–30, 132, 160–61, 172, 174, 176, 181, 188, 192, 196–97, 202, 206–8, 211, 219–20, 222–25, 228–30, 232, 235, 238, 240, 261, 263, 265, 277

Q

questions, vocational, 231
quiet, 123, 134, 251–52, 262–64

R

redemption, 16, 22, 24, 26, 36, 38, 46, 66, 73–74, 88–91, 105, 117–18, 158, 196, 220, 226–27, 235–36
redemptive suffering, 245–46
Reed, Esther D., 8
Reformation, 33, 40, 42, 46, 50–51, 54, 67, 111, 127, 135, 138, 144–45, 148–49, 152, 156, 206, 215–16
Reformed tradition, 75

repentance, 121, 153
Rerum novarum, 72, 101–2
respect for the person, 273
resurrection, 38–39, 71, 74, 90–91, 227
retirement, 27, 85–87, 217, 230, 243, 249
rewards, 46–49, 88, 95–96
righteousness, 43, 112, 155, 157
Roman Catholicism, 6–7, 20–22, 49, 54, 88, 101, 106, 108, 151, 156–57, 214, 236, 238–39, 245, 263–64, 273
Rössner, Philipp, 144–46
Rotman, Marco, 138–39
Russia, 32

S

sacred versus secular, 5–6, 9, 13, 15, 25, 50, 59, 62, 161, 223, 238
Salvifici Doloris, 245
Sayers, Dorothy, 4, 6, 22–24, 27–28, 53, 58, 65, 85, 97, 277
Schuurman, Douglas, 15, 35, 213–15, 228
science, 117, 167–68, 178, 228
Scripture, 6–8, 10, 13, 28, 62, 65–66, 68–69, 71, 73, 76, 86, 88–90, 125, 128, 170–71, 197, 212, 256, 258
secularization, 50, 213, 225, 234
self-help, 18–19, 50, 80, 220, 225
self-interest, 213, 225, 239–40, 244
Sermon on the Mount, 152
service, 3–4, 9–11, 13, 15, 20–21, 26, 28, 37, 48, 62, 68, 70, 81, 86–89, 95, 98–99, 126, 135, 178, 208, 217, 220, 228–30, 234, 236, 238, 240–44, 253, 263, 265, 274–77
sin, 9, 16, 33, 35, 39, 47, 65, 68–69, 91, 121, 123, 128, 133, 153, 167, 173, 245, 252, 269
Smith, Gordon, 264

social ethic, 22–24, 39
social justice, 12–13, 21, 158
social question, 101–2
social reform, 136, 139
social witness, 22, 37, 81–82, 271
solitude, 122, 262–64
Solomon, King, 114, 121, 172
sphere sovereignty, 78
spiritualization, 88, 124–25, 154, 207. *See* allegory
spiritual life, 6–7, 167
sports, 259
stability, 136, 231, 273
stations, 126, 128, 134–36, 213, 216, 224, 229, 241
stewardship
    and Christ, 47–48, 93–99
    Christianity, 25–26
    collective, 99–100
    creation, 7–8
    and culture, 17
    faithful, 21
    humanity, 33
    and incarnation, 92
    marketplace, 21–22
    sowing and reaping, 96–97
suffering, 53, 83–84, 129, 138, 168, 196–97, 207, 241, 244–46, 269–70. *See also* redemptive suffering
suicide, 64, 83–84, 173, 212
Sukkot, 203

T

talent (coinage), 94
talent (gift/skill), 47–48, 83, 88–89, 93–96, 98–99, 213, 218, 229–30, 234, 236, 242, 258–59
Ten Commandments, 34, 42–43, 158, 262
Tertullian, 81–82, 89, 117–18
theocracy, 77–79
theological education, 11, 13

theology. *See also individual doctrines by name (e.g., incarnation)*
    of creation, 8
    dogma, 23, 44
    of the marketplace, 16–18
    rediscovery, 27
    social ethic, 22–24, 39
    of vocation, 15, 27, 49–53, 133, 226, 235, 238
    of work, 7, 10, 58, 69–73, 76, 80, 136, 206, 216
this-worldliness, 238
Thomas à Kempis, 120
Thomas Aquinas, 67–68, 107
timing, 160, 257, 264–68
To the Councilmen of All Cities in Germany (Luther), 137, 144, 151
tradition, 19–21, 40, 50, 54, 60, 64, 75, 91, 93, 118, 121, 157, 172, 204–5, 214, 219, 241
Treatise on Good Works (Luther), 42
two cities, 26, 125

U

University of Wittenberg, 41, 114, 126, 140, 147–48, 151

V

vita activa, 5, 67. *See* active life
vita contemplativa, 5, 67. *See* contemplative life
vocation (definitions), 28, 233–35. *See* calling
Volf, Miroslav, 71, 73–77, 82, 136–37, 214
von Bora, Katherina, 142
vows, monastic, 112–13, 121, 131

W

Waalkes, Scott, 138
weeping, 242, 269
Welchel, Hugh, 227

West Germany, 232, 264–65
Whether One May Flee from a Deadly Plague (Luther), 141
Wisdom literature, 28–29, 63, 98, 164–69, 171, 177, 180, 183, 186, 202–9
witness, 7–9, 14, 18, 22–24, 27, 29, 37, 51, 58, 81–82, 141, 157–58, 161, 165, 176, 198, 206, 219, 239, 245–46, 252, 262, 265, 271–72
Wittenberg, 41, 44, 140–44, 147–53, 155
work
    and calling, 6
    Calvin, 159–62
    and Christianity, 31
    and church, 1–4
    and contemplation, 67–68
    and creation, 33–36
    and culture, 27
    dignity, 15, 27, 39, 53, 55, 58, 62–64, 69, 78, 85, 93, 108, 130, 160, 163, 216, 224, 227, 234, 274, 277
    in Ecclesiastes, 28, 187–202
    Ellul, 66–67, 69–71, 214
    engagement, 212
    and enjoyment, 189–94
    God, 62–63, 69, 186
    hours, 59
    humanity, 61–62
    image of God, 68–69
    lifetime, 59
    Luther, 108–13
    meaning of, 27–28
    and missions, 37, 228
    moral law, 62
    New Testament, 66
    Old Testament, 184
    pneumatological theory, 73–75
    redemption of, 39
    sanctifies, 226
    Scripture, 64
    and Ten Commandments, 34
    theology of, 7
    and vocation, 54–55
    and works, 40–41
workaholism, 234, 240
workplace
    and calling, 9–11
    and Protestantism, 6
    and religion, 1–5
    spirituality, 79–80
works
    and Christ, 45–46
    and faith, 41–46
    James, 40–47
    and judgment, 46–49
    and justification, 45
    Luther, 40–43
    Melanchthon, 44–45
    and New Testament, 47
    Paul, 47–48
    reevaluation, 205
    and work, 40
works-righteousness, 112–13, 155
world
    and Christ, 8
    and Christianity, 38
    and church, 7–8
    contempt for, 114–19, 121–22, 124, 207
    Luther, 110
    and New Testament, 8–9
worship, 12, 16, 62, 66, 69, 88, 97, 155, 161, 176, 203, 233, 273, 277

NAME INDEX

A

Ahn, Jina, 3
Albrecht of Brandenburg, 144
Alsdorf, Katherine Leary, 17–18, 55, 61, 63, 93
Ambrose, 124
Anderson, William H. U., 179, 192
Aristotle, 41, 67–68, 107, 224, 263
Armstrong, Chris R., 59, 225
Atkinson, James, 42, 68, 108, 110, 116, 224
Atkinson, Tyler, 179
Augustine, 26, 51, 107, 124

B

Bachmann, E. Theodore, 43, 154
Badcock, Gary D., 214
Ballor, Jordan J., 78–79, 101
Banich, Marie T., 167
Barth, Karl, 71
Bartholomew, Craig, 169
Bass, Dorothy C., 224
Battles, Ford Lewis, 159, 237
Bayer, Oswald, 109
Bayly, Joseph, 254
Beckett, John D., 17

Bellah, Robert, 54–55
Benne, Robert, 20, 240, 274–76
Benson, David, 6
Bergsma, John, 16
Bilalić, Merim, 167
Blamires, Harry, 90, 220, 222
Blickle, Renate, 154
Boda, Mark J., 120, 122, 209
Börsch-Supan, Axel, 87
Braaten, Carl E., 25
Braaten, Conrad, 142
Brandt, Walther I., 137
Brecht, Martin, 112, 142, 147–48, 153
Brennfleck, Kay Marie, 238
Brennfleck, Kevin, 238
Brenz, Johannes, 115
Bromiley, G. W., 71
Brown, Melissa, 87
Brown, William P., 192, 202, 206
Brunner, Emil, 162
Buck, Lawrence P., 140
Budetti, Peter P., 86
Bunderson, J. Stuart, 213
Bunyan, John, 93, 222, 230–31, 234, 246
Burtless, Gary, 86

Bushnell, Horace, 262
Buttrick, George A., 94, 96

C

Caddell, David P., 2
Cahalan, Kathleen A., 2
Calhoun, Robert Lowry, 277
Calvin, John, 42, 45, 68, 111, 159–62, 237, 241, 263
Caneday, A. B., 207
Carroll, John, 226
Cavanaugh, William T., 218
Chamberlain, Gary L., 230
Chandler, Dawn E., 2
Chanoff, David, 80
Chanoff, Sasha, 80
Charles, J. Daryl, 17, 19, 29, 42, 51, 79, 82, 148, 151, 158, 162, 165, 174, 180, 187, 202, 210, 247, 266
Cherney, Kenneth A., Jr., 10, 156, 159, 215
Chesterton, G. K., 22
Christianson, Eric S., 120
Christie, Agatha, 22
Cilliers, J., 128
Clifton, Jim, 212
Clydesdale, Tim, 215
Cole, G. D. H., 22
Cole, Margaret, 22
Compton, Rebecca J., 167
Conquest, Robert, 32
Conyers, A. J., 252
Cosden, Darrell, 17, 45, 216
Courtois, Stéphane, 32
Covey, Stephen R., 19, 225
Crenshaw, James L., 176, 196
Crosby, John F., 81
Cunningham, David S., 218

D

Damasio, Antonio, 168
Davidson, James C., 2
dei Segni, Losarío, 119

de Jong, Stephan, 179
DeKoster, Lester, 16
de Kruijf, Gerrit G., 71, 77–79
DeLoach, Albertus L., 179
Deratany, Edward, 238
Diehl, William E., 3
Dik, Bryan J., 2, 241
Dimsdale, Trey, 5, 16–18, 106
Dirk von Hoogstraten, Hans, 213
Doberstein, John W., 138
Dobrow, Shoshana R., 241, 256
Donaldson, James, 81, 117
Doriani, Daniel M., 17
Doyle, Arthur Conan, 59
Dreyer, Wim A., 127
Duffy, Ryan D., 2, 241

E

Eaton, Michael A., 165, 177, 200, 205
Edgar, William, 25
Eliason, Eric J., 116, 121
Ellul, Jacques, 66–67, 69–71, 189, 214
Estes, Daniel J., 189, 192–93, 199
Eswine, Zack, 209

F

Farnham, Suzanne G., 255
Fee, Gordon, 170–71
Filbey, Francesca Mapua, 168
Firth, Katharine R., 142
Fischer, Robert H., 148
Forsyth, T., 71
Fox, Michael V., 169
Frankl, Viktor E., 83–85
Fredericks, Daniel C., 192, 199, 209
Freeman, R. Austin, 22
Freud, Sigmund, 83
Fyfe, Douglas R., 189

G

Galles, Jacob A., 2
Gianto, Agustinus, 175, 194
Gilbert, Lela, 8, 38, 82

Glasson, T. F., 201
Glimcher, Paul W., 167
Goodrich, Richard J., 114
Gordon, Rona Johnston, 110
Grabill, Stephen J., 79
Greene, Mark, 6, 10
Grimm, Harold J., 41, 123, 143
Guthrie, Donald, 173
Gutridge, Coralie Ann, 196

H

Hahnenberg, Edward P., 49, 106, 108
Haier, Richard J., 167
Hall, Douglas T., 2
Hall, Stephen S., 167–68
Hanks, Joyce M., 70
Hardy, Lee, 16, 18, 53–54, 67, 74, 77, 121, 162
Hauerwas, Stanley, 22, 71–72, 214
Haughey, John C., 51, 213, 222, 230, 257
Heiges, Donald R., 238
Heister, William J., 60
Heller-Sahlgren, Gabriel, 88
Hendricks, William, 16
Hendry, G. S., 173, 177
Henry, Matthew, 172, 201
Hildebrandt, Franz, 148
Hill, R. Charles, 166
Hillman, Os, 17
Hoffman, Manfred, 156
Holl, Karl, 108
Houck, J. W., 60
Houck, John, 71
Hummel, Charles E., 237
Hunter, Archibald M., 96

J

Jensen, David H., 17–18, 64
Jenson, Robert W., 25
Jerome, 114–19, 121, 124–25, 172
John Paul II, 7, 16, 27, 71–72, 157, 226, 239, 245–46

K

Kallas, Endel, 115–16, 119
Kandel, Eric R., 168
Keller, Timothy, 17–18, 55, 61, 63, 93
Kidner, Derek, 173, 181
Kleinhans, Kathryn, 28, 133, 135
Kloostermann, Nelson D., 79
Knapp, John C., 1, 9, 12
Knox, Ronald, 22
Kohl, Margaret, 157
Kolden, Marc, 76
Kramer, M., 32
Krodel, Gottfried G., 113, 148
Kuyper, Abraham, 27, 51, 78–79, 101–2

L

Lane, Jason D., 41
Lee, Eunny P., 185, 188–89, 200
Lehmann, Helmut T., 112
Lehmann, Karl, 157
Leider, Richard J., 80, 220, 256
Lenz, Janet G., 2
Leo X, 42
Lewis, C. S., 65
Lewis, Robert E., 119
Lim, Steve, 228
Lindberg, Carter, 111, 139, 142, 144, 146, 150, 152–54
Loader, J. A., 172, 176
Loewe, Andreas, 142
Loftin, R. Keith, 5, 16–18, 106
Lohfink, Norbert, 194
Lohse, Bernhard, 114
Longman III, Tremper, 187
Lovekin, David, 71
Loy, David W., 240
Luther, Martin, 27, 40–46, 51, 68, 72–73, 108–16, 119–62, 214–16, 223–25, 229, 238, 275
Lys, Daniel, 180
Lysova, Evgenia I., 3

M

Machiavelli, Niccolò, 147
Mackay, A. T., 71
Magarik, Larry, 200
Marshall, Paul, 8, 38–39, 49, 82, 90
Martin, James D., 166
Marx, Karl, 137
Massing, Michael, 41, 120, 141, 148
McGrath, Alister, 118, 127, 160
McIntosh, Mark A., 230–31
McKenna, Robert B., 2
McLennan, Scotty, 12, 17
McNeill, John T., 159, 237
Meilaender, Gilbert C., 17, 59–60, 224, 227
Melanchthon, Philip, 42–45, 115, 126, 140, 148, 151, 155
Middleton, J. Richard, 82
Miller, David J. D., 114
Miller, David W., 17, 100
Miller, Douglas B., 175
Miller-McLemore, Bonnie J., 2
Mitchell, H. G. T, 179
Mittelberg, Mark, 9
Moltmann, Jürgen, 156
Morrison, A. W., 45, 160
Motyer, J. A., 173
Murphy, J., 32
Murphy, Roland E., 176, 180, 206
Murray, John Courtney, 90

N

Nash, Laura, 12, 17
Neafsey, John N., 257
Neafsey, John P., 221
Nelson, Tom, 17
Neriya-Cohen, Nava, 125
Newbigin, Lesslie, 227–28
Niebuhr, Reinhold, 75
Noll, Mark, 140
Noth, Martin, 165
Novak, Michael, 16, 73, 217–18, 230, 240

O

O'Donnell, Douglas Sean, 207
O'Donovan, Oliver, 74, 76, 227
Ogden, Graham S., 185, 187–88, 191–92, 200
Okonkwo, Bartholomew C., 213, 230
Orczy, Emma, 22
Origen, 124
Osteen, Joel, 19, 225
Oswald, Hilton C., 145

P

Palmer, Parker J., 17, 256
Pannenberg, Wolfhart, 157
Parker, T. H. L., 45, 160
Paulson, Steven D., 129
Pelikan, Jaroslav, 43, 111, 114, 129, 139, 145, 150, 152–53, 164
Perry, T. A., 189
Peterson, Brian Neil, 188
Pippert, Rebecca Manley, 9
Placher, William C., 17, 67, 262
Plantinga, Cornelius, Jr., 35
Preece, Gordon, 10, 106
Preus, J.A.O., 44
Pritchard, James B., 63, 199
Provan, Iain W., 115, 209
Putin, Vladimir, 32

Q

Quinn, Joseph F., 86

R

Rasmussen, Carl C., 111
Reed, Esther D., 8
Richards, Jay Wesley, 5, 106
Roberts, Alexander, 81, 117
Robertson, D. B., 75
Root, Michael, 157
Roper, Lindal, 146
Rössner, Philipp R., 144, 146–47
Rotman, Marco, 138
Runham, Nathan, 142

Rusch, William G., 157
Ryan, J. J., 60
Ryken, Leland, 187

S

Sailhamer, John H., 66
Sayers, Dorothy L., 4, 6, 11, 22–24, 27–28, 53, 58, 65, 97, 277
Schaaf, James L., 147
Schaff, Philip, 107
Schilling, Heinz, 109, 145–49, 155
Scholes, Jeffrey, 50
Schultz, Robert C., 127
Schultze, Quentin J., 230
Schuth, Morten, 87
Schuurman, Douglas J., 15, 17–18, 35, 74–75, 213–15, 222, 228, 231, 240
Schwehn, Mark R., 224
Schwiebert, E. G., 147, 151
Scott, R. B. Y., 173
Sedlacek, William E., 2
Shapiro, David A., 80
Shead, Andrew G., 204
Shelly, Judith Allen, 16, 100
Sherley-Price, L., 120
Sherman, Amy L., 17
Sherman, Doug, 16
Shields, Martin A., 196
Sirach, Ben, 165
Smalley, Beryl, 114
Smith, Gordon T., 17–18, 234, 237, 244, 254, 264
Sneed, Mark R., 165
Spitz, Lewis W., 140
Stackhouse, Max L., 73, 227
Staglen, Garen, 64
Steele, Walter R., 189
Steenbarger, Brett, 60
Steenkamp-Nel, Annalie E., 171
Steger, Michael F., 2
Steinwachs, Albrecht, 151
Stevens, R. Paul, 16–17, 36, 106

Stuart, Douglas, 170–71
Stupperich, Robert, 148

T

Tappert, Theodore G., 44, 129, 136, 141, 155
Taylor, John W., 75
Templeton, John, 217
Tertullian, 81–82, 117–18
Thomas à Kempis, 120
Thomas Aquinas, 68, 107
Thomas, David Winton, 165
Thompson, David, 184
Thompson, Jeffery A., 213
Torrance, David W., 45, 160
Torrance, Thomas F., 45, 71, 160
Torvend, Samuel, 139
Tosti-Kharas, Jennifer, 241, 256
Trapp, Thomas H., 109
Treu, Martin, 149
Trueblood, Elton, 31, 231

U

Ukpong, Justin, 97
Ullendorff, Edward, 171

V

van der Maas, Ed, 79
VanGemeren, Willem, 184
van Heeringen, Kees, 168
Veith, Gene Edward, Jr., 17, 51, 130
Volf, Miroslav, 17, 71, 73–77, 82, 136–37, 214
von Rad, Gerhard, 166
Vos, Pieter, 78
Vriend, J., 176

W

Waalkes, Scott, 138
Wade, Henry, 22
Walpole, Hugh, 22
Walsh, Brian J., 82
Watson, Francis, 176

Weber, Lauren, 212
Wee, Paul, 139, 142, 150
Welchel, Hugh, 227
Wentz, Abdel Ross, 44, 112
Werpehowski, William, 227
Westermann, Claus, 165, 168, 266
Whybray, R. Norman, 188–89
Williams, D. H., 51, 213
Williams, Oliver, 71
Wilson, Gerald H., 176
Wingren, Gustaf, 111, 136
Wise, David A., 87

Wolters, Albert M., 82, 122, 227
Wright, J. Robert, 124
Wyon, Olive, 162

Y

Yoder, John Howard, 22

Z

Zogbo, Lynell, 188
Zophy, Jonathan W., 140
Zwingli, 111